International Migration and Economic Development

For Hayley, Kylie and Sarah

International Migration and Economic Development

Lessons from Low-Income Countries

Robert E.B. Lucas

Professor of Economics, Boston University, USA

IN ASSOCIATION WITH EGDI.

Edward Elgar
Cheltenham, UK • Northampton, MA, USA

Published by
Edward Elgar Publishing Limited
The Lypiatts
15 Lansdown Road
Cheltenham
Glos GL50 2JA
UK

Edward Elgar Publishing, Inc.
William Pratt House
9 Dewey Court
Northampton
Massachusetts 01060
USA

This book has been printed on demand to keep the title in print.

A catalogue record for this book
is available from the British Library

Library of Congress Cataloguing in Publication Data
Lucas, Robert E. B.
  International migration and economic development / Robert E. B. Lucas.
    p. cm.
  "In association with EGDI."
  Includes bibliographical references and index.
    1. Emigration and immigration–Economic aspects–Case studies. 2. Economic development–Case studies. I. Sweden. Expert Group on Development Issues. II. Title.

JV6118.L83 2005
337–dc22   2005046188

ISBN 978 1 84844 033 3

The Expert Group on Development Issues (EGDI)

EGDI consists of a number of international experts in development-related academic fields along with Swedish policy makers. The main task of EGDI is to contribute to an increased understanding of global development and an improved effectiveness of development policies. The group initiates and produces studies of importance to the development debate.

EGDI is funded by the Swedish Ministry for Foreign Affairs. The research interests of the group, as well as approaches taken in EGDI studies, provide important perspectives on the Swedish policy for global development.

More information on EGDI may be found on the website: www.egdi.gov.se

Contents

Figures

Tables

Boxes

Acronyms

APEC	Asia-Pacific Economic Co-operation Group
ARTEP	Asian Regional Team for Employment Promotion
ASEAN	Association of Southeast Asian Nations
EBRD	European Bank for Reconstruction and Development
ECRE	European Council on Refugees and Exiles
EU	European Union
GCC	Gulf Cooperation Council
GDP	Gross Domestic Product
GNI	Gross National Income
HIV-AIDS	Human immunodeficiency virus-acquired immune deficiency syndrome
IADB	Inter-American Development Bank
IDP	Internally Displaced Persons
ILO	International Labor Office
IMF	International Monetary Fund
INS	United States Immigration and Naturalization Service
IOM	International Organization for Migration
MENA	Middle East and North Africa region
NAFTA	North American Free Trade Area
NIC	Newly Industrialized Countries
NYC	National Youth Commission of Taiwan
ODA	Official Development Assistance
OECD	Organization for Economic Cooperation and Development
PPP	Purchasing Power Parity
PRC	People's Republic of China
UAE	United Arab Emirates
UK	United Kingdom
UN	United Nations
UNDP	United Nations Development Program
UNESCO	United Nations Educational, Scientific and Cultural Organization
UNHCR	United Nations High Commissioner for Refugees
US	United States of America
USSR	Union of Soviet Socialist Republics

Acknowledgments

This study has been funded by the Expert Group on Development Issues (EGDI) in the Swedish Ministry for Foreign Affairs. I am most grateful for the opportunity that this afforded.

Ingrid Widlund, at EGDI, has been a constant support throughout; Ingrid's comments have always been insightful and her encouragement indispensable during the long period of preparing this study. Torgny Holmgren, also at EGDI, sat through more presentations of this material than anyone and always provided timely wisdom and reassurance.

Per Ronnås from the Swedish International Development Cooperation Agency (SIDA), Kristof Tamas, from the Swedish Ministry for Foreign Affairs and Manolo Abella from the International Labor Office in Geneva played an instrumental role in initiating and designing the study. I hope it lived up to expectations.

The study benefited considerably from a series of presentations to:
The Global Development Network, *Fifth Annual Conference: Understanding Reform*, New Delhi, January 2004.
The Delhi School of Economics, Delhi, January 2004.
The Inter-University Committee on International Migration, Massachusetts Institute of Technology, Cambridge MA, February 2004.
Institute of Economic Development, Boston University, Boston MA, March 2004.
The World Bank's *Annual Bank Conference on Development Economics*, Brussels, May 2004.
An EGDI Seminar, *International Migration Regimes and Economic Development*, Stockholm, May 2004.

I am particularly grateful to those individuals who agreed to act as discussants at these seminars:

In New Delhi:
Lant Pritchett, Harvard University
Djavad Salehi-Isfahani, Virginia Tech University
Siow Yue Chia, East Asian Development Network, Singapore

In Brussels
Aderanti Adepoju, Human Resources Development Centre, Nigeria
Riccardo Faini, University of Rome Tor Vergata
Louka Katseli, Development Centre, OECD

And in Stockholm
Jean-Pierre Garson, OECD
Anatol Gudim, Center for Strategic Studies and Reforms, Moldova
Devesh Kapur, Harvard University
Susan Martin, Georgetown University
Ernesto Pernia, University of the Philippines School of Economics
Dilip Ratha, World Bank
Ninna Nyberg Sörensen, Danish Institute of International Studies

John Harris, Aki Kangasharju, Sari Pekkala and Sharon Russell read substantial portions of earlier drafts. My thanks to these friends. I trust the final draft is improved.

Along the way, too many people provided unpublished or inaccessible data and papers, advice and clarifications, such that is impossible to thank them all individually. The study benefited enormously from these inputs, some of which are acknowledged at specific points in the text.

Finally, a very special thanks to Ms Abernethy and her sixth grade girls at the Winsor School for the opportunity to share ideas on international migration and for their very pertinent questions and illuminating thoughts.

PART A

Introduction

1. The Context

International migration is attracting increasing attention, both among governments in the industrialized countries and within various international agencies. Each new presidency in the European Union emphasizes the need to harmonize admission procedures, the Bush administration has contemplated a major amnesty for irregular migrants and establishment of a guest worker program on an unprecedented scale, the East Asia crisis forced the newly industrialized economies to face the growing realities of immigration, the United Nations has established a Global Commission on International Migration, and the 2006 issue of the World Bank's *Global Economic Prospects* will focus on international migration.

Amidst this mounting interest, this volume is concerned with the links between international migration and economic development in the lower income countries. This interplay is two-way: development affects migration and migration affects development. The former link has attracted increasing attention in some of the OECD countries where 'the growth of inflows has resulted in unprecedented immigration levels in the past 20 years' (OECD, 2003: 23), and inability to control migration has focused attention on migration management, including the role of economic development at origin as a device for reducing migration pressures.[1] However, it is the second element of interplay, the effects of migration upon development that is the main focus of the present study.

In contrast with interest in co-development as a component of migration management, concern for the development consequences of international migration remains muted among most of the industrialized countries. Yet migration from the lower income countries to the developed regions can have quite profound effects upon economic development in the countries of origin. When Williamson (1990) first introduced the term 'Washington Consensus', summarizing the policy priorities among the Washington-based institutions concerned with the developing regions, international migration received no mention. At that stage, trade liberalization and 'getting prices right' occupied most of the attention. Trade continues to dominate the agenda, though migration is receiving increasing attention for good reason. Recent simulations indicate that small increments to global migration could have far more profound effects in enhancing world production than would complete removal of all policy barriers to trade.[2] Moreover, for many developing countries, remittances have become a critical form of financing their balance of payments, with reported remittances to the developing regions now exceeding official development assistance and total remittances perhaps capping direct foreign investment flows.[3]

In the process of migration, despite the high rents that are extracted by many middlemen in accessing documents, in paying to be smuggled across borders, and in transferring money home, voluntary migrants presumably believe they will gain by moving, though some may be disappointed by their actual experience. Even refugees are probably better off than facing the violence from which they are fleeing. However, the economic consequences of departure upon those left at home is far more ambiguous and is the subject of this book.

In particular, this is an investigation into the effects of international migration to the high income countries upon the economic development of the lower income countries from which many of the migrants originate. The focus is on labor migration, but not exclusively: the margins between migration for work and seeking asylum are blurred, study abroad offers an important route to entry for subsequent employment, and accompanying family members often take up jobs.

These migration outcomes are not unilaterally dictated by immigration controls or lack thereof. Both applications to enter legally and willingness to circumvent controls are affected by the state of economic development in the countries of origin, the other arm of the migration–development nexus, which has led to the recent explorations in co-development as a strategy for reducing migration pressures.[4] Thus social and economic development is one of the essential instruments with which the High Level Group on Asylum and Migration, set up in 1998 by the European General Affairs Council, is charged in drawing up action plans for the countries of concern. Similarly, the US interest in NAFTA and the justification for the bailout of Mexico in 1995 hinged on fears of continued and escalating migration pressures. Yet much of the recent literature questions the efficacy of such strategies, expressing a belief that economic development at origin fails to reduce migration outflows and may indeed exacerbate migration pressures.

The effects of development on migration and of migration upon development are intimately linked and both influences are controversial. Although this book focuses upon the effect of migration upon economic development, the reverse effect cannot be neglected and the contentious nature of both influences is drawn out and re-examined. The prevailing lack of resolution may not be inappropriate: the links between migration and development differ from context to context, varying with the extent and nature of migration streams, the migrants' experiences, and the economic, political and social setting in the home country. Alternative migration regimes, with variegated patterns of skilled and unskilled workers, of temporary and permanent movers, of men and women, of solitary sojourners and families shifting domicile, should not be expected to have uniform consequences for development. It is precisely these divergent experiences that this study seeks to examine.

THE APPROACH: FOUR CASE STUDY AREAS

To explore the diversity of experiences in the linkages between migration and development, four migration regimes were selected for specific attention within this study, each exhibiting distinct characteristics, though all represent major migration streams from lower to higher income countries.

Migration to the European Union

The member countries of the EU have never really intended to encourage permanent immigration, though some has resulted. Over the last half century, three fairly distinct phases of immigration have occurred: the guest worker phase which effectively ended in 1974; a period of migration for family reunification and of clandestine migration; then, especially after 1990, a large influx of asylum seekers. Full harmonization of migration policies remains to be achieved among the EU members, though substantial steps have been taken: the Schengen Agreement in 1985, under which some of the member countries agreed to permit free movement of persons; the Dublin Convention in 1990, which provided for mutual recognition of each state's asylum regulations and hence prevents multiple asylum applications; the Treaty of Amsterdam in 1997, which established the legal basis for a common European migration policy. More recently the European Councils of Tampere, Laeken and Sevilla have continued to deliberate reconciliation between migrants' 'aspiration for a better life and reception capacity of the Union',[5] combined with action plans to address illegal entry. Meanwhile, there has been some revival of the contract labor system and growth in the use of seasonal workers. Migrants to the EU fall into four main regional groups: from Eastern Europe and the former Soviet states, from the Maghreb, from Turkey, and from various former colonies and refugee countries in Sub-Saharan Africa and Asia. In the course of the study, particular attention is directed to the first two groups, the transition economies and the High Maghreb. For some of these countries' economies, the process of migration and remittances has truly major implications: the Moroccan government estimates more than two million Moroccans are living legally in Europe, or nearly 8 percent of Morocco's population, and remittances to Morocco reached almost 10 percent of gross domestic product in 2001; in Moldova remittances amounted to 15 percent of GDP in 2001, and more than a quarter of Albania's labor force has emigrated, almost entirely to the EU, since 1990.

Contract Workers in the Persian Gulf from South and Southeast Asia

There are six member states of the Gulf Cooperation Council: Bahrain, Kuwait, Oman, Qatar, Saudi Arabia and the United Arab Emirates. After 1974 and the first shock to world oil prices, these six states embarked on a regime of labor recruiting operated by government and private agencies abroad. Initial contracts are typically for two years, but contracts can be renewed and visas are actively traded (both legally and otherwise). In the early stages, much of the recruitment was from other Arab countries, but partly out of concern for security and to avoid longer-term settlement problems, recruiting increasingly turned to the countries of South and Southeast Asia. Seven countries have come to dominate this migration stream: Bangladesh, India, Pakistan and Sri Lanka, plus Indonesia, the Philippines and Thailand. Family accompaniment is permitted only for very high income migrants; other migrants come alone and the average duration of stay is some four to five years. Acquisition of citizenship in the GCC states is effectively impossible. Migration to the Gulf is thus utterly temporary and the remittance streams to folks at home are accordingly quite enormous: from 1990 to 2001, recorded remittances from the GCC states amounted to more than a third of all the remittances received by the remaining developing countries. Most of the male workers are drawn from low skill occupations, especially as general laborers and construction workers. From Indonesia, the Philippines and Sri Lanka large numbers of women are recruited, mostly as domestic servants. In the opening sentences of *To the Gulf and Back*, Amjad (1989: 1) wrote:

> From the mid-seventies to the early eighties, for a number of Asian countries no factor more dramatically affected domestic employment and the balance of payments situation than the outflow of contract workers to and inflows of workers remittances from the Middle East ... However ... there is a consensus that the peak of the 'migration boom' is over.

That consensus proved incorrect: despite the interruption of the first Gulf conflict and attempts to expel workers with expired visas and localize jobs in the mid-1990s, recruitment has continued to grow.

The Brain Drain to North America

In contrast to Europe and the Gulf, both Canada and the US belong to the small club of countries that have a long tradition of encouraging permanent settlement. However, the days when the US welcomed the 'huddled masses' are long gone. North America is now very clearly the dominant outlet of the brain drain. Whereas two-thirds of foreign national adults in France have less than an upper secondary education, in Canada the portion is one-fifth. Not only do some 42 percent of all foreign-born adults in the US possess at least a college level of education, according to the US Census Bureau, but some 23 percent of these have post-graduate qualifications. Moreover, three-quarters of these foreign born adults in the US with a tertiary education were born in low income regions or transition economies. Indeed, the incidence of the brain drain to the US is shown in this study to fall disproportionately on the lower income countries: the proportion of all college educated nationals who are in the US, and not at home, is highest among the lower income countries. In the last decade, the US has significantly increased issues of temporary visas. The expansion in H1 visas largely accommodated an influx of information technology engineers from India and visas issued to Chinese students have increased. Few of these skilled migrants from the low income countries go home. Some observers have begun to describe a process of brain gain from this process, whereby the country of origin is supposed to gain from their professional diaspora overseas, an idea which is explored as part of this study.

Migration Transition in East Asia

A migration transition has occurred among the higher income economies in East Asia. Brunei, Hong Kong, Japan, Korea, Malaysia, Singapore and Taiwan have all become hosts to significant numbers of foreign workers in recent years. Some of these are contract workers, many are irregular migrants. The principal labor sources are the lower income countries within the region: Indonesia, the Philippines and more recently Vietnam. Thailand is both a source of such labor and host to about a million Burmese workers. For Indonesia, the Philippines and especially Thailand, entry into the East Asian labor market has offered an important diversification out of reliance on the recruitment in the Persian Gulf. However, the increasing integration of the East Asian labor markets has brought its own risks, as revealed during the East Asia crisis which 'brought home to the labour-receiving countries in Pacific Asia that although their labour migration policies are built on the concept of "temporariness", in reality it might be difficult if not impossible to avoid the use of migrant workers'.[6]

Four Regimes: A Summary

The four selected regimes by no means exhaust the streams of migration from low to high income countries and I am quite cognizant of the omissions.[7] Nonetheless these four regimes do encompass a substantial portion of global migration from low to high income countries and represent a diversity of migration experiences, with contrasting features:

• Migration from South and Southeast Asia to the Persian Gulf area: a case dominated by migration on fixed period contracts, without family accompaniment, exhibiting a rising role for female labor migration.

- Migration within East and Southeast Asia: a case of increasingly integrated labor markets as the higher income countries experience migration transitions, legal migration being almost exclusively short term though combined with widespread employment of trainees, students and irregular over-stayers, all being impacted by the East Asia financial crisis.
- Migration to the US and Canada: a case of selective legal migration in these countries of traditional settlement, resulting in a bimodal distribution of migrant skills; highly skilled migrants are admitted on a more permanent basis with family accompaniment, and unskilled workers enter both with and without legal documentation.
- Migration into the European Union: a case in which coordination of migration policies among member countries, control of irregular migration, widespread use of short-term migrant workers, and strategies toward refugees and asylum seekers come to the fore.

A FRAMEWORK AND OUTLINE

The book is organized in three parts, each of which incorporates materials from the four main case study areas. Chapter 2, the remaining chapter in Part A, sets the stage, sketching the state of migration outcomes, national controls imposed on movement, and the determinants of the decisions to migrate. The six chapters of Part B each address a major component of the potential consequences for economic development in the low income countries from which migrants originate. Part C comprises two concluding chapters: on who gains and who loses in the process of international migration, and on some of the principal policy options that emerge.

Part B is the heart of the book. Within this part, in addressing economic development in countries from which migrants originate, an important distinction must be borne in mind. Out of sight does not necessarily mean out of mind; many governments retain an active concern for their citizens abroad. In judging economic performance and the consequences of international migration, there is then considerable ambivalence as to whether a 'national' or 'domestic' view is more appropriate. The domestic perspective focuses exclusively on incomes of people present at home; on a national basis, the incomes generated by nationals overseas would be included in the metrics of development. One could imagine going further still; why exclude emigrants merely because they have become nationals of their adopted country? In Part B a fairly simple view is adopted: given a presumption that most migrants gain by relocating, the more difficult issues arise with respect to domestic incomes, generated within the home country, and will be the focus of attention.

In particular, the effects of out-migration upon domestic incomes may be conveniently grouped under three headings: departure, diaspora and return. In brief, 'departure' refers to the impact effect on the labor markets for those who stay at home and the related consequences of a brain drain. The section on 'diaspora' refers to economic consequences that migrants may have on the home country from their locations overseas, to financial remittances from absentees abroad and the recent discourse on the potential for brain gain through transnational networks. Lastly, 'return' or circular migration is not only thought to be increasingly common but frequently advocated as a cornerstone of economic gain for the home country. The various chapters of Part B deal with these sequentially, yet there are many simultaneous links among these components, which need to be drawn out in the process. Certainly return migration and the propensity to remit are linked, while the brain drain and brain gain are increasingly viewed as two aspects of a common process. As we shall see, on each of the aspects covered in these chapters, on departure, diaspora and return, the state of debate is far from resolved.

Departure

The focus of Chapter 3 is on the links between the composition of emigration flows, the state of the domestic labor market, and the implications of migration for increased tightening or additional slack in the home country labor markets. It is easy to imagine a scenario in which the departure of working age people might well result in either lower unemployment levels or higher wages for workers left at home. Yet matters are not quite that simple. A number of factors remain to be investigated. Among the more important of these factors is that much may depend on the mix of persons emigrating. For instance, it is not obvious whether the emigration of highly skilled workers results in tighter domestic labor markets for their less skilled compatriots, nor whether departure of males is likely to enhance or worsen the labor market position of women. The answers may well vary with the structure and organization of production, since skilled and unskilled workers may complement each other in some settings while serving as substitutes elsewhere. The significance of emigration, both for domestic employers and employees, also depends not only on whether particular labor markets become tighter, but whether any reduction in slack results in rising wages or simply diminishes unemployment. Whether most emigrants quit jobs upon leaving or were previously unemployed may matter, depending upon how the domestic labor markets respond to withdrawals under both circumstances. Moreover, an issue that is of some importance to the poverty impacts of emigration is the link between international and internal migration: given that international migration typically draws from highly concentrated local populations within a given country, any trickle down effects through labor market changes can depend critically upon the regional integration of domestic labor markets. Far from being obvious, the domestic labor market responses to emigration warrant careful attention, and have important implications for both overall domestic income levels and their distribution.

Although the phenomenon of the brain drain is fairly universally decried, the negative connotations of the departure of the highly skilled are far from well documented. Beyond the labor market impacts of departure of the highly skilled already touched upon, two major categories of cost are commonly invoked in criticizing the brain drain. The first group of costs are the lost benefits that are frequently supposed to derive from the presence of highly educated compatriots: the benefits of higher productivity and more rapid growth, as well as the influences of a more highly educated population on such factors as the performance of civil society and governance, on educational and environmental choices, on fertility and health outcomes. The second category of cost is the tax revenue that would have been derived from the incomes of the educated elite if only they had stayed at home. Against this background, Chapter 4 takes up consideration of the brain drain, with five objectives in mind: first to lay out some of the issues; second to document, in so far as possible, the extent and nature of the brain drain from the developing regions; third to consider such evidence as exists on the two components of presumed cost from the foregone external benefits and fiscal resources of the emigrating educated elite; fourth to explore some of the implications for educational policy, with particular attention to financing of tertiary education; and fifth to evaluate the notion that emigration of the highly skilled induces educational expansion both at home and for study abroad. In the process of this consideration, as noted in the previous section, the case of the brain drain to the US receives particular attention, and a close look is also taken at the contexts of India and the Philippines, which have been among the major contributors of college educated migrants to the US. Certainly, most of the industrialized countries seem to presume that they will gain from admission of the highly skilled: virtually every OECD nation now has in place mechanisms to facilitate entry of professional workers, and the competition to attract the highly skilled to the industrialized countries is intensifying. It seems unlikely that this pattern will change in the foreseeable future, so the policy options open to the lower income countries must be weighed in the face of this reality.

Diaspora

Departure, both of the highly skilled and less skilled, must be weighed against their potential contributions to the home country from afar, both in the form of remittances and possibly through other influences of an active diaspora. The global system for transmitting financial remittances is bifurcated: a formal system operating through transfers between institutionalized financial intermediaries; and an informal system operating through use of 'underground banking networks' of money dealers, such as the *hundi* system in India or *hawala* system in the Middle East. The merits of both formal and informal remittances not only remain the subjects of debate but both have come to attract a good deal of attention very recently. Although reported remittances passing through formal channels have risen in recent years to become a major, counter-cyclical source of funding for many developing countries, a number of explicit doubts linger about the economic benefits derived from these remittances. Among these reservations are widespread claims that remittances fail to fund investment and growth, that transfers to families at home induce withdrawal from the labor force, that remittances prop up the exchange rate which discourages evolution of export activities, and that remittances benefit the relatively wealthy. The book sets out to review these claims with particular reference to the case study regimes. Meanwhile, it may be noted that the governments of many of the migrant-supplying countries do not seem to share the doubts exhibited by a wide range of observers, but rather set out to obtain as much as possible in remittances from their diaspora. On the other hand, the entire underground banking network has recently been under attack for possible links with terrorists and organized crime, while the practice of remitting through these informal channels is subjected to criticism for diverting funding from the formal system and hence from government coffers. Chapter 5 takes up these several debates and reviews the evidence, drawing upon the experiences of several countries within each of the four case study areas, looking at the determinants and consequences of international remittances, as well as policy efforts to shape both.

The term 'brain gain' has increased rapidly in usage. The notion is that a country can actually gain by exporting highly skilled people. Two routes through which this may happen have already been touched upon: financial remittances from overseas professionals and the potential for highly skilled emigration to induce educational expansion. Chapter 6 takes up several other channels, each of which has been hypothesized to operate through various kinds of transnational networks and the information and leverage that they can provide. The diaspora becomes a source of information to the foreign business community, easing the potential for dealing with a home country whose institutions, culture and rules of business conduct are unfamiliar. Through continued contacts with home, the diaspora is also a channel for fresh, credible information about new opportunities emerging in their home country. Emigrants may be well placed to enforce contracts, applying social leverage through friends and family at home, especially in contexts where litigation is relatively ineffective. Knowledge networks, on the other hand, largely provide flows of information and technical expertise from the diaspora to colleagues at home. Through these many channels, international trade, capital flows both from the diaspora and from other investors, and technology transfers may each be enhanced. The potential for such 'brain gain' effects is clear, yet the realities are not. This is a sphere of burgeoning, but very limited evidence, and the study attempts to put this in perspective.

Return

A final element of 'brain gain', not yet mentioned, is any advantage derived from returning migrants with newly acquired skills, or at least with enriching experiences from their period abroad. More generally, Chapter 7 enquires into the patterns of return migration, both of highly skilled and less skilled workers, the evidence on duration of stay, tendency to settle, and policies to induce return. In addition, however, some of the experience with re-entry or assimilation for returning migrants is examined, again with specific reference to the case study contexts. Although return, or at least intent to return, may be an important factor in harnessing the development potential of the diaspora, the realities of return are frequently a source of concern and the supposed gains from freshly acquired skills from overseas often illusive.

Closure

The final chapter in Part B takes a brief journey beyond the overall development implications of migration to look at the possibility that migrant departure may sharpen inequalities and even deepen poverty for some individuals or communities. In the midst of on-going development, pockets of poverty normally persist. Whether the incidence of such pockets is exacerbated by international migration, not alleviated by remittances or imminent return, possibly worsened by some of the social consequences of absence, is the subject of Chapter 8.

The three elements of departure, diaspora and return are intimately connected. Indeed, for many migrants the stages are probably envisaged from the outset, part of a dynamic strategy. In the end, however, each of these components is shaped by the extent of migration and who moves. The departure effects on the labor market depend on mix of skill and gender, remittances and links with the diaspora depend upon the temporary nature of migration and on family accompaniment, the realities of return depend upon the experiences while overseas and the restrictions on repeat migration. This brings us back full circle to where we begin in the following chapter, which deals with the migration outcomes resulting from the intersection of attempts to control migration and of decisions to migrate, before returning to the development consequences of these outcomes in Part B, then the political economy and policy options with respect to international migration and development in Part C.

NOTES

1. For a critique of such a strategy, see the UK report on Migration and Development (UK, 2004).
2. See, for example, Walmsley and Winters (2003).
3. Ratha (2003).
4. 'France's Inter-ministerial Mission on Co-development and International Migration (MICOMI) defines co-development as combining immigration control efforts in Europe with aid efforts to bolster stay-at-home development in migrants' countries of origin.' (*Migration News*, 1 April, 2001).
5. *EU Developments in Migration and Asylum Policies* at www.solidar.org.
6. Debrah (2002: 1).
7. At times, in the course of the study, examples from other migration regimes are drawn upon, such as movements to Australia and New Zealand, and intra-regional migrations to the higher income economies in South America and in Sub-Saharan Africa, for instance, but the four regimes noted here are the main focus. A conscious decision was also taken not to focus on the massive migration from Mexico to the US, in part because it has attracted by far the most prior attention among global movements. For similar reasons, migration from Turkey to Europe does not receive a great deal of attention here either.

2. The Determinants of Migration: Controls, Pressures and Outcomes

Whether international migration today should be seen as part of a rapidly globalizing world, with freer cross-border movements of goods, capital and people, depends very much on one's perspective. The UN Population Division estimates that the stock of international migrants in the world doubled in the quarter century to the year 2000 and notes that, 'Almost 1 of every 10 persons living in the more developed regions is a migrant'.[1] On the other hand, foreign-born individuals amounted to less than 3 percent of the world's population in 2000, and from a longer run perspective 'what used to be "free" world migration has become tightly constrained by tough immigration policies that undoubtedly suppress a vast amount of potential migration that might otherwise have taken place'.[2]

Among the developed regions, North America and Australasia have a long tradition of attracting the world's migrants, and have been joined more recently by Western Europe, the oil rich countries of the Persian Gulf, and some of the wealthier parts of East Asia, as poles for migrants. Across, and even within, these regions, state controls on the migration process differ quite substantially. However, the extent, nature and patterns of migration are not shaped unilaterally by these immigration controls. Migrants' choices, amongst applying for legal entry, attempting to by-pass the legal controls, or staying at home, matter too. These desires are, in turn, shaped by many factors and constrained both by the opportunities presented at home and abroad and by the resources available to take advantage of those opportunities. For refugees any choices may be extremely circumscribed, while footloose professionals may join the set of 'astronaut' international commuters almost at will. The outcomes with respect to international migration reflect the intersection of these migrants' choices and controls imposed, though the two forces are far from independent; choices are influenced by the likelihood of legal entry and policies toward admission are in turn affected by migration pressures.

Section 2.1 of this chapter starts by looking at the outcomes, presenting a snapshot, at around the turn of the millennium, of the size of the foreign-born populations in the four major higher income regions within our case study areas, these migrants' regions and countries of origin, and how these patterns have changed in the last decade or so. Section 2.2 then turns to the mechanisms of legal international migration and their part in these outcomes. Here the particular focus is on principal differences across the migration regimes of the EU, the GCC states, Canada and the US, and within East Asia: the key aspects of recent policy development; the relative roles of major components in legal migration, such as employment-based migration, family reunification, and movements of refugees and asylum seekers; the extent of permanent versus temporary movements; and the degree of irregular migration that is induced. Lastly, Section 2.3 takes up migration pressures and some of the principal determinants of the decision to migrate. A particular concern in this context is the role of economic development at origin in influencing migration pressures. As we have observed, the links between migration and economic development at origin are two-way; economic development affects migration and migration affects development. Section 2.3 addresses the former route, in which the level of development may influence migration pressures, whereas much of the remainder of the book is concerned with the latter, the development consequences of migration. Both are controversial.

2.1 THE INS AND OUTS OF MIGRATION: A SNAPSHOT AT THE MILLENNIUM

Of the stock of 175 million international migrants in the world, estimated by the UN in 2000, nearly one-third was in Europe, another 29 percent in Asia and 23 percent in North America. This section takes a closer look at these stocks, their profiles and recent changes, looking first at our four case study areas, starting with Europe (and the European Union in particular), followed by the Gulf Cooperation Council states in the Persian Gulf, East and Southeast Asia, then Canada and the USA, before turning to a brief synopsis of the role of women in international migration.

Europe

Europe may contain a third of the world's stock of migrants but this figure is deceptive. Many of the foreign nationals within the EU represent internal movements among the current EU members; still more are from the newly admitted members. Nor has the net inflow of migrants been exceptionally high during the 1990s, despite the dramatic changes and events in Eastern Europe and the former USSR.

To illustrate, as of 1 January 2000, the official estimates of non-national populations of the EU-15 members amounted to 18.8 million, or 5 percent of the population (see Table 2.1).[3] However, nearly 31 percent of these migrants were nationals of other EU states, leaving the non-EU national population at only 3.5 percent of the total population. This last fraction is not particularly high as compared to an average migrant stock of 8.7 percent of population among the more developed regions globally, as reported by the UN (2002a).[4] Meanwhile, net migration into the EU is estimated at approximately 8.3 million during the 1990s, which amounts to an average annual net migration rate of some 2.3 per thousand as compared to 2.0 for the developed regions in general, 4.6 for Northern America and 3.0 for Oceania.[5]

It is apparent from Table 2.1 that these EU averages mask considerable variations across the various member countries. Sweden, Austria and the Netherlands each report more than 10 percent of their populations as foreign-born in 2000, and nearly a third of tiny Luxembourg's population are non-nationals, while on the basis of nationality Austria and Germany host the largest stocks of non-EU populations relative to their own national populations.

Table 2.1   *Non-national populations: EU countries, 1990–2000*

	By country of birth or nationality	Non-national population 2000 (1000)	Percent of 2000 population		Net migration (1000) 1990–2000
			Non-nationals	Non-EU nationals	
Austria	Birth	843.0	10.39		
	Nationality	749.1	9.23	8.03	285
Belgium	Nationality	897.1	8.75	3.25	145
Denmark	Birth	308.7	5.78		
	Nationality	259.4	4.86	3.85	130
Finland	Birth	136.2	2.63		
	Nationality	87.7	1.69	1.38	65
France	Nationality	3 263.2	5.54	3.51	555
Germany	Nationality	7 343.6	8.93	6.67	3 590
Greece	Nationality	165.7	1.57	1.15	440
Ireland	Nationality	126.5	3.33	0.90	90
Italy	Nationality	1 270.6	2.20	1.94	1165
Luxembourg	Nationality	152.9	34.87	4.52	40
Netherlands	Birth	1 615.4	10.14		
	Nationality	651.5	4.09	2.86	350
Portugal	Nationality	191.1	1.86	1.35	30
Spain	Nationality	895.7	2.24	1.46	370
Sweden	Birth	1 003.8	11.31	3.49	195
	Nationality	487.2	5.49		
UK	Nationality	2 297.9	3.85	2.41	865
EU Total	Nationality	18 839.2	4.99	3.46	8 315

Sources: Eurostat (2002), OECD (2002) and UN (2002a).

Table 2.2 Non-EU population in EU countries in 2000 by major region and nationality of origin, 2000

	Austria	Belgium	Denmark	Finland	France	Germany	Greece	Ireland	Italy	Luxembourg	Netherlands	Portugal	Spain	Sweden	UK	EU
Europe																
Except EU-15	476.1	103.5	105.1	43.8	360.2	4,071.6	58.5		349.7		137.5	4.3	40.8	153.3	198.1	6128.9
Albania									130.2							
Bosnia				1.6	159.1									23.2		
Croatia						219.4								7.7		
Other former Yugoslavia	337.6	10.3	35.2	1.1	669.2				37.0					17.0		
Poland		7.3	5.6		301.7				29.2							
Romania									62.8							
Russia				19.8	115.2											
Turkey	132.9	58.4	35.4	1.7	208.8	2013.0					98.4			16.1	51.8	
Africa		161.1	25.4	7.8	1419.8	300.6	13.0		411.5		149.8	89.8	213.0	27.7	291.4	3 120.4
Algeria		8.0			477.6								12.2			
Morocco		111.1			504.5				145.9		108.9		178.5			
Tunisia					155.1				41.5		1.4					
Asia		27.0	56.1	13.8	203.4	823.1	27.4	26.3	236.4		62.4	7.9	66.9	84.1	559.0	2 175.6
Latin America		8.2	3.6	1.0	46.7	81.8	3.5	8.0	99.9		19.5	25.8	149.6	20.6	105.9	571.9
Unknown	175.6	18.6	7.7	1.8		74.2	1.5			19.8	66.4	0.3	0.7	10.6	23.8	435.1
Other		15.2	7.7	3.2	37.6	133.6	17.6		24.2		20.2	10.7	18.1	13.5	242.4	
Total	784.6	230.9	215.6	65.3	856.7	7197.3	108.4	34.3	710.2	19.8	404.4	49.0	276.1	298.2	1 181.0	12 431.7

Sources: Eurostat (2002) and OECD (2002).

From where do the non-EU nationals move to the EU? Four major streams may be distinguished (see Table 2.2).[6] The first group are nationals of the countries of Eastern Europe: people from the newly independent states of former Yugoslavia residing largely in Austria and Germany, but also in Denmark, Italy and Sweden; from Albania and Romania in Italy, and from Poland in Germany and Sweden. Second are the two million Turkish nationals in Germany, plus smaller Turkish communities scattered throughout much of the Union.[7] Together, these two groups, combined with nationals of other non-EU European countries, amount to almost half of the entire non-EU national population according to official estimates. A third group are the nationals of the three countries of the Central Maghreb (Algeria, Morocco and Tunisia), who are concentrated in France where they numbered more than 1.1 million in 2000, but also in Belgium and some of the Mediterranean countries. The fourth group is nationals of other developing regions: Africans besides those from the Maghreb region, numbering around 1.25 million; Asian nationals (predominantly in Germany, Britain, Italy and France) represent some 17.5 percent of non-EU nationals; with an additional 4.6 percent from Latin America (mostly in Spain and Italy, and from the Caribbean in the UK).

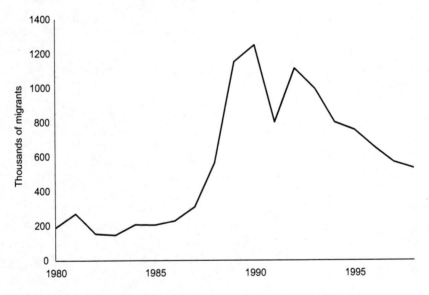

Figure 2.1   Gross migration from transition economies to Western Europe, 1980–98

At the time of the disintegration of the Soviet bloc, fears of apocalyptic flows of migrants to the west were rampant. The reality is depicted in Figure 2.1, which shows the gross annual flow of migrants from the transition economies to the main receiving countries of Western Europe during 1980–98.[8] This gross migration exceeded a million people per year on average from 1989 through 1993, with more than 90 percent arriving in Germany. On the other hand, return migration was substantial also. Nonetheless, from some of the transition economies there was indeed a large net exodus of people, especially from Albania where net out-migration accumulated to more than 21 percent of the 1990 population by the end of the decade (see Table 2.3). Bosnia and Herzegovina, Estonia, Latvia and Moldova also lost very substantial portions of their populations and the absolute net numbers who left Bulgaria and Romania were large too.

Table 2.3   *'European' countries in transition: total net migration, 1990–2000*

	Total net in-migrants (1000)	Percent of 1990 population
Albania	−700	−21.3
Belarus	85	0.8
Bosnia and Herzegovina	−500	−11.6
Bulgaria	−250	−2.9
Croatia	125	2.8
Czech Republic	90	0.9
Estonia	−115	−7.3
Hungary	−5	0.0
Latvia	−170	−6.4
Lithuania	−75	−2.0
Macedonia, FYR	−35	−1.8
Poland	−145	−0.4
Republic of Moldova	−195	−4.5
Romania	−590	−2.5
Russian Federation	3295	2.2
Serbia and Montenegro	100	1.0
Slovakia	20	0.4
Slovenia	75	3.9
Ukraine	−40	−0.1

Source: UN (2002a, 2003)

However a part of these outflows from the transition economies were to other countries in transition within the region.[9] Most particularly, the disintegration of the USSR, Czechoslovakia and Yugoslavia has been accompanied by large movements, often along ethnic or language lines, between the new member states. There has been substantial return migration from the Baltic States, Moldova and the Ukraine to Russia, including many military personnel. Slovakia has been the principal migration partner of the Czech Republic, with migration in both directions though at a declining rate through the 1990s.[10] Similarly, of the 576 000 people who fled from Bosnia-Herzegovina during the 1992–95 conflict, nearly a quarter moved to Croatia.[11] On the other hand, during the same period from 1992–95 nearly 100 000 Croats moved to Germany, though this was almost exactly offset by return migration.[12]

In the later 1990s Moldovans have increasingly migrated to Germany and to the UK and the dominant destinations of emigrants from Albania have been Italy and Greece.[13] Jews, particularly from the former USSR, moved in large numbers to Israel after 1990 but also to the US. Some of the migration streams out of Eastern Europe are also of longer standing; migration of ethnic Turks from Bulgaria to Turkey was already well established in the 1980s, as was emigration from Poland to Germany and from Romania to Austria and Germany. The net result is that by 2000 the official estimates of nationals from the transition economies of Eastern Europe residing in the EU-15 probably amounted to less than 3.5 million people, or 1 percent of the EU population, of whom perhaps close to half a million were Poles who are now members of the newly expanded EU.

The Persian Gulf

The rapid growth in the stock of migrants in the six member countries of the Gulf Cooperation Council during the 1980s is apparent in Table 2.4. The foreign population of Kuwait rose by more than 60 percent and that in the United Arab Emirates doubled during this decade. Even more spectacularly, the foreign population of Saudi Arabia increased more than five-fold from 1974 to 1990. By 1990, non-nationals formed more than a quarter of the population in Saudi Arabia and Oman, 35 percent in Bahrain and well over 70 percent in each of the remaining three member countries. Overall, the number of migrants had risen further still by the end of the century; though both Kuwait and Saudi Arabia experienced substantial net out-migration in the first half of this decade, following the Gulf conflict and various financial difficulties in Saudi Arabia, these patterns were again reversed in the later 1990s.

Recent data on the stocks of Asian migrants in the Gulf are not available. However, Figure 2.2 presents a breakdown of the non-Arab populations of

Table 2.4   Migrant stock in the GCC states: 1970 through 2000 (1000 migrants)

	1970–71	1974–75	1980–81	1990	2000
Bahrain	38	–	112	173	254
Kuwait	391	687	971	1560	1108
Oman	–	–	–	450	682
Qatar	66	–	–	345	409
Saudi Arabia	–	791	–	4220	5255
UAE	–	356	752	1556	1922
Total	–	–	–	8304	9630

Sources: UN (2002a, 2003).

the GCC states on average in 1990 and 1992, at which stage Arabs from other GCC states and elsewhere represented just over 40 percent of the non-national migrant stocks.[14] More than 70 percent of the non-Arab migrant stock

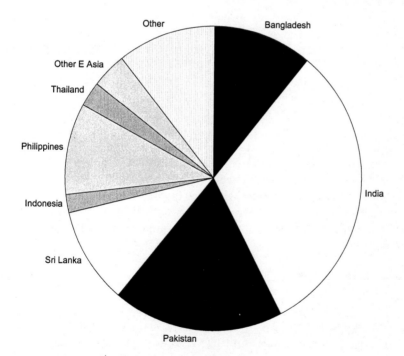

Figure 2.2   Non-Arab migrant population in GCC states by country or region of origin, 1990–92

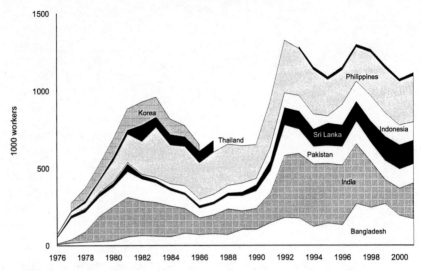

Figure 2.3   Estimated annual flow of Asian workers to the Middle East by country of origin, 1976–2001

were from South Asia, with 44 percent of these from India. An additional 18 percent were from South-East Asia, with more than half of this contingent from the Philippines.

Before 1980, among the non-Arab countries, Pakistan was the main source of contract workers present in the Gulf. However, by the mid-1980s recruitment from Pakistan had actually declined and has recovered only slowly since (see Figure 2.3).[15] In the 1980s, the gross flow from the Philippines was the largest, followed by India, though turnover amongst Filipinos must have been higher than from India, given the relative stock estimates shown in Figure 2.2. After the Gulf crisis in 1991 there was a huge surge in recruitment from India. However, the 1990s have also witnessed more diversity in recruitment, as a large relative expansion in the movement of women from Sri Lanka, Indonesia and the Philippines occurred, and the numbers from Bangladesh grew rapidly also.

East and Southeast Asia

A number of regions serve as migration poles within East and Southeast Asia, though the degree of openness to foreign arrivals still varies considerably within the region. In Japan, which for long was largely closed to immigration, the foreign population began to grow more rapidly after the mid-1980s, when 86 percent of foreigners were Koreans and their descendants. By 2000, the foreign population of Japan had expanded to more than 1.6 million, though foreigners remained at only 1.3 percent of the population, which is far below the average for higher income countries (see Table 2.5). By 1999, the Korean population of Japan had fallen to 41 percent of all legally resident foreigners. Meanwhile, the portion of Chinese had risen to 19 percent and of Filipinos to over 7 percent, with much smaller numbers from Thailand (25 000), Indonesia (16 000) and Vietnam (15 000).[16] Korea, like Japan, has remained relatively closed to immigration though there was some increase in the use of foreign labor during the 1990s, rising to 268 000 documented and undocumented foreign workers by 2000.[17] At this stage, the total foreign population amounted to nearly 600 000 (largely Chinese of Korean descent) though this represented only 1.3 percent of the population.

Table 2.5   Migrant stocks in countries of East Asia, 1990 and 2000

	Migrant stock (1000)		Migrant stock/ population (%)
	1990	2000	2000
China, Hong Kong SAR	2218	2701	39.4
Singapore	727	1352	33.6
Brunei Darussalam	73	104	31.7
Taiwan	1508	–	(1990) 7.9
Malaysia	1014	1392	6.3
Cambodia	38	211	1.6
Japan	877	1620	1.3
Korea, Republic	572	597	1.3
Thailand	386	353	0.6
Papua New Guinea	33	23	0.5
Lao PDR	14	16	0.3
Mongolia	7	8	0.3
Indonesia	466	397	0.2
Myanmar	100	113	0.2
Philippines	163	160	0.2
China	380	513	0
Vietnam	28	22	0

Source: UN (2002a). Taiwan at http://migration.ucdavis.edu/.

In contrast, Taiwan has begun to join the group of East Asian economies that are more open to migration. Immigration has apparently been very substantial since the estimate of 1.5 million foreigners (7.9 percent of the population) in 1990. For example, the number of legally recognized foreign workers in Taiwan grew from 3000 in 1991 to 295 000 by 1999, comprising 47 percent Thais, 39 percent Filipinos and smaller numbers from Indonesia, Malaysia and Vietnam.[18]

The wealthy nations of Singapore and Brunei Darussalam have been even more important magnets for migrants, relative to their size. Both had a stock of foreign population in excess of 30 percent of their total populations in 2000, having established controlled labor importation by the 1970s. In Singapore, the dominant source of foreign labor is from neighboring Malaysia, though the number of contract workers from other parts of Asia increased during the 1990s, with more than 20 000 workers entering Singapore on contract during 1999 from both the Philippines and from Thailand.[19] Meanwhile, Brunei Darussalam has attracted workers from the same three countries.

According to the estimates for Hong Kong by the UN (2002a), reproduced in Table 2.5, Hong Kong has both the largest migrant stock and the highest percentage of foreign-born population in the region. However, this ratio includes persons born in mainland China. Yet, even excluding those born elsewhere in China, the foreign population of Hong Kong is quite large, rising from 140 000 in 1981 to 250 000 in 1991 and 509 000 by 1998.[20] Of these, workers from the Philippines represent the largest group, with much smaller numbers from Indonesia and Thailand.

A broad range of estimates of the foreign population of Malaysia exists, though there is widespread agreement that the number is large. The UN estimate reproduced in Table 2.5 indicates a total foreign population of about 1.4 million, though Hugo (1998) cites an estimate from the Malaysia Department of Immigration of a stock of 1.9 million contract workers from Indonesia alone in 1997. For Thailand, the numbers are also quite uncertain. The UN recognizes about 350 000 foreign nationals in Thailand in 2000, down by some 10 percent from 1990. However, in 1996 the Thai Ministry of Labor estimated a stock of nearly 734 000 illegal labor migrants in Thailand, principally from Myanmar but also from Laos and Cambodia, and IOM (2000) suggests the stock of irregular migrants in Thailand may have reached close to a million workers by the end of the 1990s.

Turning from the migrant poles of East Asia to outward migrations, the Philippines, Thailand and Indonesia have been important sources of emigration, not only within the East Asia region but beyond. A large part of this has involved deployment of contract workers. The overall growth in these systems and the changing pattern of destinations is depicted in Figure 2.4.[21] Large-scale recruitment began earlier in the Philippines than in Indonesia and Thailand, and from each country recruitment for work in the Middle East dominated until the late 1980s. However, for each of the three countries, recruitment to other countries of East Asia increased substantially in importance in the 1990s, as recruitment to the Middle East leveled off from the Philippines and declined markedly from Thailand.

The specific destination countries for contract workers, on average during 1995 through 1999 from these three countries, are depicted in Figure 2.5.[22] From Indonesia and the Philippines, recruitment to the Middle East amounted to just over 40 percent of the total and was dominated in both cases by movement to Saudi Arabia. On the other hand, recruitment from Thailand to the Middle East was less important, amounting to below 10 percent of Thailand's total recruitment, and was largely to Israel and Libya rather than the GCC states. In part, this reflects the outcome of a diplomatic dispute with Saudi Arabia in the early 1990s. Instead, Taiwan has become by far the largest destination of workers from Thailand, followed distantly by Singapore and Brunei Darussalam. The importance of migration from Indonesia to Malaysia is evident in Figure 2.5 though these official numbers are probably a substantial underestimate. But, in addition, Indonesia has diversified its flow of workers to each of the other major labor importers of East Asia.

From the Philippines, important flows occurred to Hong Kong (actually increasing substantially after Hong Kong's reversion to China's sovereignty in July 1997) and to Taiwan. In fact, the Philippines even sends significant numbers of contract workers to Europe (notably to Italy) and to the US. In addition to the land-based workers, displayed in Figure 2.5, the Philippines provides many sea-based workers and a significant flow of more permanent emigrants: thus the total outflow of migrants from the Philippines during

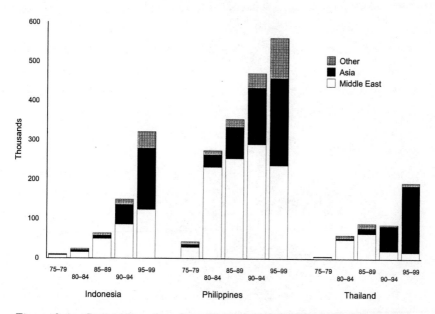

Figure 2.4   Contract workers by major region from Indonesia, Philippines and Thailand, 1970–99

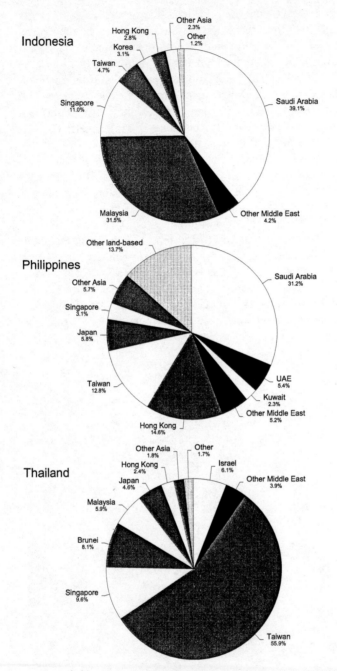

Figure 2.5   Country destinations of contract workers from Indonesia, Philippines and Thailand, 1995–99

1995–99 comprised 58 percent land based workers, 33 percent sea-based workers, and 9 percent emigrants (two-thirds of whom moved to the US).

North America

The foreign-born population in the US in 2000 was 28.4 million, or 10 percent of the total, which was a greater fraction than at any stage since 1930, having doubled since 1970.[23] Estimates of the origins of the foreign-born adults, ages 16 and over, are reported in Table 2.6. Nearly 30 percent of the US foreign-born population is from the North American neighbor countries, almost entirely from Mexico, representing the world's largest sustained international migration stream. Migration from Europe remains important, though far less so than at earlier stages in US history, with nearly 17 percent of foreign-born adults reporting being born in Europe (Germans representing the single largest group).

Perhaps most importantly, the US Census Bureau (2002b) notes that the Asian born population in the US expanded from 800 000 in 1970 to five million in 1990 then 7.2 million by 2000 when 22 percent of the adult foreign-born population of the US had been born in South and East Asia.[24] Filipinos are the largest single group, with about 1.2 million adults in the US. Indians (973 000 adults) are the next largest community, though China is largest of all if one includes the People's Republic (877 000), Hong Kong (189 000) and Taiwan (330 000). There are also very substantial communities from Korea (687 000) and from Vietnam (719 000). On the whole, as we shall see in Chapter 4, these migrants from Asia are highly educated and most have come to stay; thus the US Census Bureau (2002b) reports that 47 percent of the population from Asia in 2000 had acquired US citizenship.

As of 2000, the stock of migrants in Canada was close to 17 percent of that in the US, implying a much greater fraction of immigrants relative to population in Canada (18.9 percent) than in the US (12.4 percent). As in the US, Canadian immigration has become much more Asian orientated as may be seen in Figure 2.6.[25] Arrivals of immigrants from Europe had declined by the end of the 1970s, after which permanent settlers from Asia began to increase substantially, though leveling off during the 1990s. A more detailed composition of the regional origins of these immigrants to Canada during the decade from 1991 to 1999 is shown in the lower panel of Figure 2.6. During this period, slightly over half of immigrants, just over 1.1 million people, were drawn from the Asia-Pacific region. Of these, arrivals from Hong Kong, the People's Republic of China and Taiwan formed over 40 percent. The number of immigrants from Bangladesh is not reported separately, but more than 300 000 permanent settlers came from India, Sri Lanka and Pakistan during the 1990s, and a further 130 000 from the Philippines.

Table 2.6   US adult foreign-born population by country and region of birth, 2000

	Percent of adults	Percent female
Total number of adults (millions)	28.0	
Total foreign-born (millions)	28.4	
North America	28.97	46.6
Canada	2.88	54.8
Mexico	25.94	45.7
Central America & Caribbean	16.41	53.9
Cuba	3.18	51.5
Dominican Republic	2.19	58.7
El Salvador	2.74	51.6
South America	6.14	52.8
Colombia	1.59	54.3
Africa	2.28	39.4
Egypt	0.37	35.8
Morocco	0.11	31.4
Nigeria	0.33	36.7
South Asia	4.65	44.3
Bangladesh	0.27	38.1
India	3.48	45.3
Pakistan	0.69	40.2
East Asia	17.38	56.3
China	3.14	53.4
Hong Kong	0.68	48.7
Indonesia	0.32	45.5
Japan	1.35	62.5
Korea	2.46	57.9
Philippines	4.38	61.2
Taiwan	1.18	57.1
Vietnam	2.57	51.0
Middle East	2.72	43.0
Iran	0.99	43.1
Turkey	0.33	44.8
Western Europe	11.26	53.2
Germany	3.39	60.1
Eastern Europe	5.66	51.2
Poland	1.59	50.5
Russia	1.28	52.3
Other or unknown region	4.53	48.6
Total	100.00	50.6

Source: Derived from US Current Population Survey 2000.

(a) By major region of last permanent residence, 1967–96

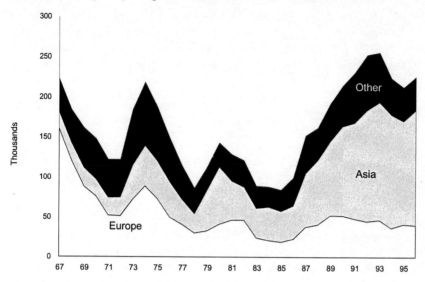

(b) By country of birth, 1991–99

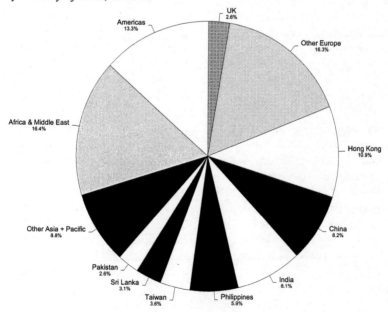

Figure 2.6   *Immigrants to Canada*

Women in Migration

Before leaving this synopsis of migration patterns, and turning to some of the factors that have shaped them, a brief note is in order on the increasing role of women in some of the migration streams discussed in this section.

> [W]omen and girls have accounted for a very high proportion of all international migrants for a long time. Already in 1960, female migrants accounted for nearly 47 out of every 100 migrants living outside of their countries of birth . . . Since then, the share of female migrants among all international migrants has been rising steadily, to reach 48 percent in 1990 and nearly 49 percent in 2000. Although this trend is consistent with an increasing 'feminization' of international migration, the increase recorded is small compared to the high level of feminization that already existed in 1960.[26]

Among international migrants in the less developed regions, the proportion of women did not change from 1960 to 2000, remaining at 45.7 percent. Rather, the slight rise in the relative role of women in migration reflects their increasing share in migration to the more developed regions.

The overall proportion of women among recent immigrants to Canada and among foreign-born adults in the US is almost exactly a half, but this masks very considerable variations by country of birth. From the Middle East and from South Asia (especially from Bangladesh) the proportion of women in the US is below 45 percent and from Africa it is lower still, with only 31 percent of Moroccans being female (see Table 2.6). At the opposite extreme it is from some of the East Asian countries that women dominate (though not from Hong Kong or Indonesia), with more than 60 percent of Japanese and Filipino migrants in the US being female.

In Europe in 1960, according to UN estimates, 48.5 percent of migrants were females and this portion had risen to 52.4 percent by 2000. In the European Union in 2000 (excluding Spain for which data are not available) females are estimated to represent 47 percent of the non-national populations.[27] This ranges from Greece and the UK where women make up more than 53 percent of non-nationals, to Portugal where only 42 percent are female, while women are less than 47 percent of non-nationals also in Germany, Italy, Austria and France. In the earlier stages of migration from Turkey and the Maghreb to Europe, most of those arriving were men, but after 1974 this balance reversed quickly as family reunification came to dominate and females formed more than three-quarters of the new arrivals.[28]

Less systematic information is available on the role of women in migration in Asia and to the Gulf. Nonetheless some partial insights may be gleaned, revealing a very mixed picture. As of 1990, it is estimated that about a fifth of the South Asian non-national populations in the GCC states were women.[29] Thus, Zachariah *et al.* (1999: 28) note with respect to Kerala in India, which provides more than half of India's overseas workers, 'Among the males, migration propensity is 10.3 times higher than among females in the case of emigration.' Similarly, data on overseas employment of Thai workers, for 1995 and 1996, indicate that only 7 percent of those traveling to the Middle East were women.[30] Yet recruitment from some countries to the Middle East has involved a far more substantial role for women. In fact, more than 90 percent of Indonesians recruited in the Middle East from 1997 to 2001 were women.[31] Moreover, Gunatilleke (1998b: 120) notes on Sri Lanka that, 'For the two years (1979 and 1980) for which data on gender distribution are available, a little over 50 percent of migrants were female.' However, during the 1990s, more than two-thirds of workers contracted for overseas employment from Sri Lanka were women.[32] The regime of migration to the Gulf has generally involved far more men than women yet it has also generated a system where women are drawn overwhelmingly from specific countries of origin.

In fact, the relative roles of women may be more a reflection of the countries of origin than of the GCC for they tend to carry over into migration within East Asia; between 1997 and 2001 two-thirds of Indonesians recruited to work on contract elsewhere in East Asia were women; of Thai workers contracted for overseas employment in general in 1995 and 1996 only about 15 percent were female.[33] On the other hand, from the Philippines, the number of female migrant workers to East Asia is known for 1992, 1994 and 1995, when women averaged 49 percent of the total deployment to the region.[34]

Certainly, overall both the relative and absolute role of women in labor migration from the Philippines has risen substantially in recent years, which

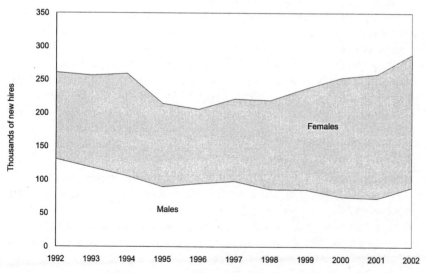

Figure 2.7   Deployed new hires from the Philippines by gender, 1992–2002

is brought out in Figure 2.7.[35] This illustrates the more general point, brought out in the report of the UN Division for the Advancement of Women (UN, 2004: 6), that: 'While many women accompany or join family members, increasing numbers of female migrants migrate on their own. They are the principal wage earners for themselves and their families.'

Summing Up

This synopsis of the migration outcomes across four regimes reveals both important contrasts and some similarities. On the one hand, North America (both Canada and the US) and the GCC states in the Persian Gulf have very large migrant stocks relative to their populations. On the other hand, within East Asia and the EU (after deducting non-nationals from other EU member countries) the migrant stocks relative to populations are much smaller. However, considerable inter-country differences underlie both of the latter averages.

Despite fears of massive migration from the countries in transition after 1990, the net migration rate into the EU, relative to population, has actually been about half of that into North America in the last decade. Indeed, migration to North America exhibits a fairly strong upward trend over recent decades, and migration from Asia to the Gulf was greater during the 1990s than in the previous decade, despite pessimism over the demise of this regime with declining oil prices in the 1980s. Within East Asia, migration has also increased in the last two decades, though again there are considerable inter-country differences in these trends.

Females already represented 47 percent of international migrants by 1960 and this proportion has increased only slightly since then. However, the participation of women differs very much across the four regimes. In North America and Europe women are about half of the migrant stocks, but their proportions vary considerably by country of origin. In the Gulf, male migrants are clearly the overwhelming majority, though women from Indonesia, the Philippines and Sri Lanka play important roles too.

The four regimes also draw on different sets of source countries within the developing regions of the world, though there is some overlap and, in general, the sources of migration in all four contexts have tended to become more diversified recently. Given these differences in the numbers of migrants, the participation of women, and the countries of origin, one can expect quite contrasting development implications in the home countries of migration streams within these four regimes. Indeed, there will prove to be other reasons to anticipate different development implications, driven by the composition and permanence of migration. To begin to understand these differences, and what shapes the patterns observed thus far, Section 2.2 turns first to consideration of the migration policies and mechanisms in place.

2.2   MIGRATION CONTROLS, MECHANISMS AND IRREGULAR MIGRATION

The legal requirements associated with migration, and their enforcement, not only constrain migrants' choices but also shape them. The probability of individuals applying for legal migration is affected by their likelihood of success. Where this likelihood is low, attempts at undocumented entry are encouraged instead, though the risks and costs imposed by such attempts also become high where strict controls are enforced. Either way, these controls are important in defining the nature of migration regimes and this section therefore offers a very brief review of some of the key features and differences in these regimes across our four case study areas.

European Union

Movement between the member countries of the EU has been considerably facilitated since 1995 when the Schengen agreement came into force, albeit without Ireland and the UK, and by subsequent inclusion of the Nordic countries in 2000. In principle, the Amsterdam Summit in 1997 also paved the way for agreement on common treatment of third-country immigrants and of asylum seekers. With further agreements reached at Tampere in 1999, some progress toward coordination in asylum policies has been achieved. On the other hand, specific national interests continue to play a defining role, even with respect to asylum, and there has been little real progress toward coordination of other forms of legal entry for non-EU nationals.[36]

The surge in asylum seekers entering the EU has attracted a great deal of attention. However, the recognition rate of asylum seekers has become fairly low, falling from 20.9 percent during 1982–91 to 14.1 percent in the next decade among the EU-15 (see Section 2.3). In consequence, the total number of asylum seekers recognized has been small relative to gross immigration of non-EU nationals, as may be seen in Table 2.7.[37] Combined with the extent of voluntary repatriation (more than 345 000 persons from Germany alone in the decade to 2001), the result is that the stock of people defined by the UNHCR as refugees amounted to only 12.4 percent of the non-EU population in the EU by 2000. However, this average masks considerable inter-country variation, the ratio of refugees to total non-EU population being far higher for Sweden, Denmark and the Netherlands.

The EU member states severally maintain a system of residence and work permits, which in some cases are subject to quota limits (such as those in Austria, Italy and Spain). Prior to 1974, a series of bilateral treaties set the stage for active recruitment of guest workers, predominantly from Yugoslavia and Turkey. Much of this recruitment came to an end with the oil crisis and its associated recession in Europe. Yet substantial migration continued. A common source was of family members of now established guest workers. In addition, the migrations of *Aussiedler* (persons of German origin) to Germany were encouraged during the 1980s (though later modulated after reunification), as was the movement of Dutch nationals from Aruba and the Dutch Antilles, and of returning Portuguese with decolonization. Meanwhile, some of the Mediterranean countries, including Italy, Spain and Portugal underwent a rapid migration transition from net emigration to net immigration by the end of the 1980s.

The rise of ultra-right-wing parties was fed by xenophobia during the 1990s: Jörg Haider and the Freedom Party in Austria, Jean-Marie le Pen and the National Front in France, the Lijst Pim Fortuyn Party in the Netherlands and the Northern League in Italy each exhibited considerable support. Partly as a result, immigration legislation has been tightened in several countries, with stricter asylum laws in Germany in 1993, the new aliens acts in 1992 and 1997 in Austria, the 2000 Plan Greco in Spain, and the Bossi-Fini Law in Italy in 2002 under which employers must guarantee return travel expenses of migrant workers.

For the most part, labor import to the EU remains temporary, as under the earlier *gastarbeiter* system. Indeed, between 1988 and 1990 Germany re-entered agreements to recruit labor, though now from Hungary, Poland and Yugoslavia with residence and work permits ranging from a maximum of two years for contract workers to three months for seasonal workers. In the same vein, a 2002 amendment to Austria's Aliens Act further restricted labor immigration yet simultaneously eased entry of seasonal workers.

A distinct new tone to labor immigration has begun to emerge, however, namely a conscious effort to attract highly skilled migrants. In France, the RESEDA law of 1998 eased admission of graduates and the highly skilled more generally, since which time the inflow of foreign students has expanded. In August 2000 Germany introduced a 'green card' system for highly qualified people, though again this limits residency to a maximum of five years. Similarly, in January 2002 the UK introduced a Highly Skilled Migrant Program, though only permitting initial entry for one year with an opportunity to renew. In the highly competitive world of attracting the best and the brightest, the traditional focus on admission only on a temporary basis may well prove a drawback to these schemes.

Although most of the labor migration is nominally temporary, migration of accompanying family members remains very large (being more than three-quarters of migrants entering France at the end of the 1990s, for example).[38] Yet the rate at which migrants become naturalized citizens remains fairly low on average in the EU. Thus Table 2.8 reports that the acquisition of citizenship in the EU-15 from 1990–99 was far lower, relative to the migrant stock in 2000, than in Australia, Canada and the US, and only slightly ahead of the rate in Japan. Yet this EU average again masks considerable differences

Table 2.7 European Union: gross non-EU immigration and asylum applications, 1985–99; non-EU population and stock of refugees in 2000

| | Annual average flow (1000s) | | | | | Stock (1000s) 2000 | |
| | Immigration of non-EU nationals | | | Asylum applications recognized | | Non-EU population | Stock of refugees |
	1985–89	1990–94	1995–99	1982–91	1992–2001		
Austria	–	–	–	3.45	1.26	651.7	15.5
Belgium	20.0	27.6	24.9	0.95	1.26	333.5	18.8
Denmark	15.3	15.6	23.6	1.05	1.37	205.6	71.0
Finland	2.6	9.1	6.4	0.01	0.01	71.4	13.3
France	52.1	76.9	57.5	12.20	6.19	2067.7	132.5
Germany	448.0	821.0	525.2	7.68	16.52	5484.9	906.0
Greece	19.5	13.4	–	0.43	0.14	121.6	6.7
Ireland	–	4.5	7.2	–	0.12	34.3	2.5
Italy	22.3	59.2	–	0.43	0.72	1122.1	6.8
Luxembourg	1.3	2.1	2.5	0.00	0.02	19.8	0.8
Netherlands	41.9	61.3	57.7	0.40	3.93	455.6	146.3
Portugal	–	7.8	3.8	0.08	0.01	138.7	0.4
Spain	3.2	10.7	29.8	0.40	0.42	489.1	7.0
Sweden	35.9	48.5	25.8	4.20	0.59	309.8	157.2
UK	101.2	108.8	134.6	1.20	9.27	1438.8	121.3

Sources: Eurostat (2002), UNHCR (2001).

among the member states, with both Sweden and the Netherlands exhibiting very high rates of converting foreign nationals into citizens.

The EU has attempted, for the most part, to limit labor migration to temporary workers. Even the burgeoning attempts to attract highly skilled international professionals are founded on the basis of temporary admission, at least initially. The reality has often proved more permanent even though conversion to EU citizenship is relatively arduous. The number of asylum applications has been extraordinarily large, especially during the first half of the 1990s, but the recognition of asylum seekers has been low and, together with voluntary repatriation, this means that refugees now play far less of a role in the EU countries than might have been expected.

Meanwhile, the continued and increased focus on temporary entry, an increasing focus on more highly skilled migrants, and a high rejection of asylum seekers, have combined to increase pressures for undocumented entry into the EU. The eastern land borders and the southern sea boundary are difficult to patrol and smuggling is rife. Reliable estimates of the number of undocumented people who have managed to enter the EU predictably do not exist, but the International Organization for Migration suggests the presence of at least three million irregular migrants within the EU in 2000, or upwards of 25 percent of the officially recognized population of non-EU nationals residing in the EU. This represents at least a 50 percent expansion on the IOM estimate of irregular migrants in the EU just a decade earlier.[39]

Migration to the Persian Gulf

Prior to 1974, migrants to the six countries of the Gulf Cooperation Council came primarily from nearby Arab states, including Egypt, Jordan, Palestine and Yemen. With rising oil prices in the 1970s, a construction boom and growing demands for services increased labor demands for both unskilled and skilled workers, and both political and cost considerations led to diversification of labor sources toward South and Southeast Asia.[39]

Labor migration to the GCC states is controlled through the issue of temporary work visas. Table 2.9 reproduces part of the results from a survey of 800 South Asian males conducted in the Jaleeb Al-Shayookh district of Kuwait in 1995, as reported in Shah (1998b).[40] Only among Indian nationals are visas that are obtained directly through sponsoring employers reported to be important, and in no instance do government bureaus any longer play a key role in accessing visas. Rather, most visas are obtained, both for skilled and unskilled migrants, either through recruiting agencies or through friends and relatives already in the GCC region. As Shah (1998b: 42) notes, 'Procurement of a visa requires money and connections' and the price of clearance paid by those already employed in the Gulf, to facilitate visas for friends and relatives to follow, is lower than the price to others.[41]

Table 2.8 Rates of acquisition of citizenship: EU-15, Australia, Canada, Japan and US, 1990–99

	Annual average rate of acquisition of citizenship		
	Number (1000)	Percent of migrant stock	Per thousand population
EU-15	336.3	1.40	0.89
Austria [d]	15.2	2.47	1.88
Belgium [d]	24.6	2.77	2.41
Denmark	6.5	2.48	1.22
Finland	1.6	1.69	0.32
France	70.0	1.15	1.18
Germany [d]	68.2	1.08	0.83
Greece [a,d]	1.0	0.21	0.09
Ireland	1.0	0.39	0.28
Italy	7.9	0.53	0.14
Luxembourg [d]	0.6	0.43	1.37
Netherlands	50.6	3.65	3.19
Portugal	0.4	0.22	0.04
Spain	8.6	0.85	0.22
Sweden	32.2	3.63	3.64
UK	47.8	1.23	0.80
Japan [b,d]	12.9	1.03	0.10
Australia [c]	102.6	2.36	5.36
Canada [b]	164.9	3.25	5.36
US [b]	562.0	1.93	1.98

Notes:
Acquisition of citizenship 1990–99, migrant stock on basis of birth, except:
a. Acquisition of citizenship 1990–98
b. Acquisition of citizenship 1991–2000
c. Acquisition of citizenship 1992–2001
d. Migrant stock on basis of citizenship

Sources: Eurostat (2002), OECD (2002), UN (2002).

The growth of a system of recruiting agencies throughout South Asia and in parts of Southeast Asia has been an important factor in accelerating the flow of contract labor to the GCC states over the last three decades. The recruiting agents can be an important source of information, especially for those lacking contacts overseas. Moreover, at least some of these private

Table 2.9   Sources of visas among South Asian males in Kuwait, 1995 survey results (percent)

	Nationals of			
	Bangladesh	India	Pakistan	Sri Lanka
Skilled occupations				
Recruiting agent	37	19	45	75
Government bureau	3	1	1	4
Sponsor	12	46	6	8
Friends & relatives	48	34	48	13
Total	100	100	100	100
Unskilled occupations				
Recruiting agent	69	33	36	82
Government bureau	0	3	0	1
Sponsor	2	37	1	4
Friends & relatives	29	27	63	13
Total	100	100	100	100

Source: Shah (1998b: Table 2.3).

recruiting agents are licensed and regulated by home country government bureaus, with the intention of protecting workers from fraud.[42] However, the agents also charge substantial commissions, adding to the costs of obtaining visas and of any local clearance required (such as the emigration clearance required of Indians).[43]

Shah (1998b) maintains that the difficulties of entering Kuwait, except by air, combine with the threat of a jail sentence to result in negligible numbers of undocumented migrants in Kuwait. However, even documented migration may remain irregular to the extent that visas are bought by employers from initial sponsors, often through visa traders. Such trades can be legalized through mutual consent, but often are not.[44] On the other hand, Sasikumar (1995: 56) describes how, in India, 'Apart from the persons who manage to get valid travel and employment documents, there are others who get to know about employment chances in the Gulf countries from various sources and are prodded on by recruiting agents (both licensed and unlicensed) to go under the guise of tourists, pilgrims and dependants.'[45] Certainly, in some fashion, the number of irregular migrants in the Gulf has been very substantial, as indicated by response to amnesties in all six GCC countries, initiated by the UAE, between 1996 and 1998. During these periods of amnesty each state 'allowed unauthorized workers to leave or regularize their status without facing jail or fines'.[46] More than a million people were repatriated as amnesty returnees during this two-year period, three-quarters of whom were returned from Saudi Arabia and another 200 000 from the UAE.

Family accompaniment of labor migrants to the GCC states is confined to those earning higher salaries and the minimum cut off salary to satisfy this criterion has been steadily raised.[47] To become a citizen of a GCC state is all but impossible (even for other GCC nationals).[48] On the other hand, it is possible for workers to renew a visa and hence lengthen a temporary stay. For example, from the survey of migrants in Jaleeb Al-Shayookh district of Kuwait in 1995, the mean duration of stay of men from Pakistan was found to be 6.2 years, 5.2 years among those from India, and 3.7 and 3.1 years from Bangladesh and Sri Lanka respectively.[49] However, Nair (1998) reports that the average duration of stay in the Gulf, among workers from Kerala, has declined over time and that the proportion staying for more than five years declined from a half to one-third during the 1980s. Moreover, it seems that repeat migration to the Gulf after returning home is rare, even amongst those reporting a desire to do so.[50]

East and Southeast Asia

The four principal migration poles in East Asia (Hong Kong, Japan, the Republic of Korea and Taiwan) and the four in Southeast Asia (Brunei Darussalam, Malaysia, Singapore and Thailand) have already been noted in Section 2.1.

Prior to 1979 Hong Kong essentially admitted all Chinese from the People's Republic who were able to visit and wished to remain. However, in 1979 the draconian restrictions placed on those attempting to leave the People's Republic were substantially relaxed and a mass exodus to Hong Kong began. In response, in 1980, the authorities in Hong Kong revised immigration policy to subject all unauthorized migrants to repatriation and the exodus was quickly stopped. On the other hand, by the late 1980s, Hong Kong began to admit significant numbers of people on temporary employment visas, ranging from highly skilled professionals to domestic servants and construction workers for the massive port and airport project. The result, during the earlier part of the 1990s, was a two-way flow of workers arriving (largely from the Philippines) even as residents left in anticipation of the reversion of Hong Kong to Chinese sovereignty in July 1997.

In the other three major migrant poles in East Asia, immigration has remained tightly controlled throughout recent decades, though with some relaxation for temporary entry of workers more recently. In Japan, the 1989 Immigration Control Law reorganized visa categories, granting more recognition of the need to permit entry of highly skilled professionals, while reaffirming the need to discourage unskilled worker entry.[51] Similarly in

Korea, most of the registered foreign workers are professional and technical people who enter with employment visas E1 through E5, amounting to three-quarters of the documented employees in 1999.[52] However in both Japan and Korea entry of unskilled workers has increased in thinly disguised forms (see Table 2.10). In both countries, nominal industrial training programs for foreigners are de facto mechanisms for employing unskilled workers. In Korea this was formalized under the 1991 Industrial and Technical Training Program which was subsequently extended to allow three years of training, while in Japan the Technical Internship Trainee Program was launched in 1993.[53] Both countries have also become relatively open to admission of people with similar ethnic background – Chinese with Korean ancestry being admitted to Korea and ethnic Japanese (principally from Brazil) settling in Japan. To these groups must be added students in Japan who fill part-time, often fairly unskilled, jobs. However the largest group of unskilled foreign workers in Japan are those designated to be over-stayers, while in Korea the use of undocumented workers increased also, despite increments to fines on employers.[54] By 2000, undocumented workers amounted to almost a third of the foreign workers in Japan, and in Korea the fraction was close to two-thirds. Yet, even including these undocumented workers, the fraction of the total workforce that is foreign remained at just over 1 percent in both countries by 2000.

In Taiwan too, the number of foreign workers remained quite tiny as late as the mid-1980s. By 1989 a limited number of foreign construction workers were permitted to enter, after pressure on government from entrepreneurs dissatisfied with progress on public infrastructure projects.[55] Subsequently, the 1992 Employment Services Act allowed entry of workers for up to two years, but only for employment in a closely designated range of activities. Nonetheless, since the passing of this Act, there has been substantial growth in migration into Taiwan, both legally (halted temporarily by a freeze in 1996) and in clandestine form.

Malaysia has a longer history of using foreign workers, particularly in the plantation sector and in forestry clearing. In 1984 this process was formalized, initially with Indonesia with the signing of the bilateral Supply of Workers (Medan) Agreement, followed by similar agreements with the Philippines, Thailand, Bangladesh and Pakistan. Nonetheless, irregular migration has been rampant, especially from Indonesia.[56] A series of amnesties has been invoked in 1989, 1992 and again in 1998, though more recently the government of Malaysia has focused on repatriation of detained irregular workers. Meanwhile, the admission of highly skilled workers is officially encouraged and unskilled workers are permitted only in sectors with labor shortages. Nonetheless, foreign workers have now penetrated beyond their traditional strongholds on the plantations and in forestry. For example, Kassim (2002) reports that 32 percent of temporary work permits issued in

Table 2.10 Foreign labor force in Japan and Korea by status (1000s)

	1986	1990	1992	1995	2000
Japan					
Work permit holders	4.0	68.6	136.8	193.7	233.2
Of Japanese descent	29.0	68.0	85.5	88.0	154.7
Others					
Designated activities (trainees)	5.2	16.5	23.8	6.6	29.7
Students working part-time	17.8	42.2	61.8	32.4	59.4
Over-stayers	63.1	124.8	292.8	284.7	232.1
Total	119.1	320.1	600.7	605.4	709.1
Korea					
Documented employees	–	–	3.4	8.2	16.0
Trainees	–	–	4.9	38.8	79.0
Undocumented	–	–	65.5	81.9	173.0
Total	–	–	73.9	128.9	268.0

Sources: Athukorala and Manning (1999), Iguchi (2002), OECD (2002), Yoo and Uh (2002).

Peninsular Malaysia in the first nine months of 2000 were in manufacturing (fairly evenly divided between Indonesians and Bangladeshis) and only 21 percent were on plantations. Even on Sarawak more than 60 percent of foreign workers are reported employed in manufacturing, though on Sabah more than 70 percent remain in agriculture. Only Indonesians and Filipinos are permitted to work on the East Malaysian islands of Sabah and Sarawak.

Neighboring Singapore permits only highly skilled workers (defined by salary level) to settle permanently and to be accompanied by family members, and even for this group acquisition of citizenship is virtually impossible. Singapore actively discourages the employment of unskilled foreign workers in part by imposing a levy on employers for their use. Moreover, the penalties on both employers and workers caught without documentation are among the harshest in the world. Nonetheless, the estimated inflow of undocumented aliens has increased.[57] By 2000, just over a quarter of Singapore's population were foreign nationals, and just over a third of the non-nationals were permanent residents (the highly skilled and their families). The number of Malaysian workers in Singapore has declined as the Malaysian economy has grown, and their place has been taken largely by Filipinos and Thais, with clandestine workers also from China, India and Myanmar. In contrast to the city-state of Singapore, Stern (1998) notes the difficulties of enforcing Thailand's visa requirements along its border. For example, in 1998 the Ministry of Labor and Social Welfare estimated that illegal foreign workers amounted to more than 80 percent of the total foreign workforce.[58]

Throughout East Asia most of the movement of labor is thus either on a temporary basis or irregular. Against this background, the financial crisis hit first in Thailand in 1997 and spread rapidly to Indonesia, Korea, Malaysia, the Philippines and Thailand. Several governments ceased official admission of workers and many sought to extricate their irregular foreign labor forces. In Korea an amnesty was announced for undocumented workers and some 53 000 workers took advantage of this and left the country. In Malaysia an additional levy was imposed on the use of foreign labor and many workers left, while in Thailand, some 600 000 people were reported repatriated to Myanmar during 1998–99. Yet most of these adjustments appear to have been short lived (see Chapter 8).

North America

The number of immigrants admitted permanently to both the US and Canada has been on an upward trend since the Second World War, returning to the peak levels of the early 1900s by the 1990s (see Figure 2.8).[59] The US Immigration and Nationality Amendment Act of 1965 ended the national origins quota system and ushered in a set of preference categories for immigrants from the eastern hemisphere. A 1976 amendment extended a

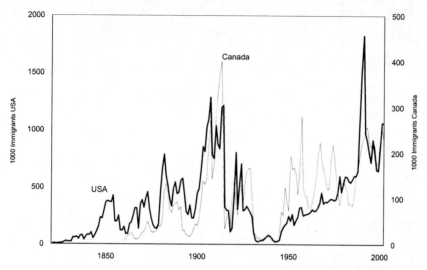

Figure 2.8   Immigrants admitted to the USA and Canada, 1821–2002

version of the preference categories to the western hemisphere too and a 1978 Amendment combined the two hemisphere quotas, leaving only a worldwide ceiling on immigration. Thereafter, the 1986 Immigration Reform and Control Act offered an amnesty to irregular migrants, introduced employer sanctions and attempted to tighten border controls, while the Immigration Act of 1990 substantially expanded the number of visas available and redefined employment categories with the intent of increasing the skill content of US immigration. In Canada, the Immigration Act of 1976 introduced a point system for the independent class of economic immigrants, based on language skills, education, occupation and experience. Again, this point scale remains largely intact, though the Immigration and Refugee Protection Act of 2001 reshaped the system by shifting away from occupation as a basis.

In both the US and Canada, admission of family members, either of those already in the country or accompanying new entrants, represents the dominant mechanism of entry, amounting to more than 60 percent of immigrants each year (see Table 2.11). On average during the decade to 2001 the US admitted 110 000 immigrants each year on employment basis, which is only slightly over 13 percent of the total. From 1996–2002, Canada admitted 51 000 immigrants a year as principal applicants for Skilled Worker Visas or Business Class Visas, representing 21.8 percent and 2 percent of all immigrants respectively. In both countries, a further 12 percent were refugees and asylum seekers granted immigrant status.

Despite these similarities, there are also some contrasts between Canada and the US, such as indications of a greater degree of permanence in migration

Table 2.11 *Immigrants and non-immigrants admitted to the US and Canada by select major class, 1992–2002*

	Annual average flow (1000)	Percent of total	Annual average flow (1000)	Percent of total
	Immigrants and refugees			
	USA 1992–2001		Canada 1996–2002	
Employment based	110	13.2	51	23.8
Refugees	99	11.9	26	12.1
Family	519	62.3	133	61.6
Other	105	12.6	5	2.5
Total	833	100.0	216	100.0
	Non-immigrant workers, students and their families			
	USA 1992–96, 1998–2002		Canada 1992–2002	
Foreign workers	586	–	79	–
Workers' families	187	–	–	–
Students	758	–	45	–
Students' families	79	–	–	–

Sources: US data from the US INS website at http://www.immigration.gov/; Canadian data from the Citizenship and Immigration Canada website at http://www.cic.gc.ca/; DeVoretz (2001) and Citizenship and Immigration Canada (2003a).

to Canada. For instance, during the 1990s more than half a million persons became US citizens on average each year. Relative to both the migrant stock and relative to total population, this rate of acquiring US citizenship is well above the EU average, yet it is considerably below the rate for Canada (see Table 2.8).

The US also relies more on temporary visas to admit foreign labor than does Canada. In fact the number of immigrants admitted to the US from 1992–2001 on an employment-based preference was only about one-fifth of the number of non-immigrants granted temporary work visas.[60] For Canada this ratio has been far larger. In fact, in Canada, while the inflow of immigrants as skilled workers has increased in the last decade the number of foreign workers entering as temporary residents has not. In contrast there has been a substantial increase in the admission of temporary workers to the US since 1990, especially in the number of 'skilled' temporary workers as the annual quota on H-1 visas has been raised, though unlike employment-based immigrants these temporary workers are largely unaccompanied by family.[61]

The US attempts to restrict undocumented entry both through very active border controls and through the use of employer sanctions.[62] Nonetheless, large numbers of people manage to enter or remain in the US illegally and to work there. As of January 2000, the US INS (2002) estimated there were about seven million unauthorized people in the US, as compared to 3.5 million in 1990. The INS also reported that nearly 70 percent of these unauthorized persons were nationals of Mexico in 2000; most of the remainder were from other parts of the Americas, with much smaller numbers from China, India, Korea and the Philippines. Of the 3.5 million unauthorized persons in the US in 1990, the INS believes that about 43 percent remained in the US a decade later, still unauthorized. This implies a gross rate of entry of nearly half a million people per year, or about 96 percent of those entering the US with temporary work visas and their families during the same period. In essence, the US system of entry attempts to admit workers on the basis of skills, increasingly on a temporary basis, but the net result is probably admission of about equal proportions of skilled and unskilled workers with the latter entering largely illegally.

2.3 THE DECISION TO MIGRATE AND FORCED MIGRATION: OPTIONS AND LIMITS

Although immigration controls are imposed everywhere on legal migration, attempting to restrain numbers, to limit duration of stay, and to select among classes of persons, these controls do not unilaterally shape realized migration streams. The desire to migrate plays a central role also, both in determining the pool of applicants for legal entry and the willingness to attempt evasion.

The decision to relocate abroad and the subsequent choice of destination are forged from weighing many components. Moreover, the differing circumstances of individuals and their families can lead to quite different emphases being placed upon these components. Concerns about lifestyle in an alien context may deter some, while the thrill of change may attract others; the presence of kith and kin abroad can allay concerns and ease a transition for those possessing such network connections; the threat of violence in the current setting is more pressing for some than for others; and while perceptions of economic gain may be one component in forming these choices, family commitments and familiarity with the home surroundings matter too.

In the aggregate, across an entire population of potential migrants, no one element represents the single contributing force in promoting migration pressures. Moreover, discourses on whether push (origin) or pull (destination) factors matter, are largely misplaced. For the most part it is the difference in circumstances that matter: the perceived gap in potential incomes, the prospect of greater personal security than is offered by the violence at home, and comparisons of the benefits of having a network of friends at home versus those overseas. The available analysis that duly recognizes these complexities is limited in extent, especially outside of the context of migration to North America. Nonetheless, the remainder of this section takes up some of the issues, evidence and findings with respect to some of the major contributing factors within the four case study areas, first noting briefly the roles of both geography and social networks, then looking in greater depth at the role of economic development in the sending countries, and finally turning to forced migration.

Geography and Social Networks: Limits to Migration

Ninety-seven percent of the world's population remain in the country where they were born. 'Why have more people not emigrated? Prevailing migration theories would have us assume that migration from poorer to richer countries had taken much larger proportions ...'[63] One plausible answer is that state controls on migration limit legal movements and even restrict undocumented flows by imposing a cost on irregular entry. More generally, the financial costs of international relocation can be prohibitive for many. Yet financial and legal barriers alone may not suffice to explain the limitations observed on international migration. In reality, many people simply prefer to stay at home in familiar surroundings, with friends and family. This last concern may offer important insights into two well-observed patterns in international migration, namely the tendency not to move far and the propensity to move where others have gone before.

On the influence of geography

Geography has a profound effect both upon the extent of migration and upon who moves where. A moment's reflection on the patterns discussed in Section 2.1 will affirm this. The dominant sources of migrants to the EU are the remaining portions of Europe, the Maghreb and Turkey, all of which are neighboring regions. For the US, the overwhelming source of migrants is Mexico. The wealthier nations of East Asia have turned to other countries within the region to supply their unskilled labor needs, with the largest flow in the region from Indonesia to neighboring Malaysia.

There are, of course, exceptions. Japan has shown a preference for ethnic Japanese migrants from further afield. The GCC states recruit largely from outside of their immediate region, though at an earlier stage Arabs formed the dominant group. Perhaps, more importantly, the migration of the highly skilled to North America is widely dispersed; a part of a more general known pattern in which distance is less of a deterrent among highly educated populations. Nonetheless, systematic, statistical analyses of cross-country migration patterns reveal that distance significantly and substantially discourages movement.[64]

It is clear that distance matters: it is far less clear why. A number of possibilities have been hypothesized.[65] Transport costs obviously assume greater importance the further the move contemplated. Yet transport costs (even two-way) tend to be small in relation to potential income gaps between home and abroad.[66] Instead, it seems more likely that it is the lack of information about opportunities available and an increasing sense of alienation in more distant lands that are the root causes underlying the deterrent effects of distance. Both of these latter effects may be ameliorated by various forces: a common language between home and destination, colonial connections, or familiar religious or ethnic structures. Certainly, in Europe the influence of both language and previous colonial history is apparent, in migration from the Maghreb to France and to Belgium, from the Portuguese-speaking countries to Portugal and from the former bits of the British Empire to the UK, for instance.

Whatever the causes, some of the implications are straightforward.[67] Other things being equal, countries that are proximate to potential sending countries can expect the greatest migration pressures. Second, this effect is not confined to country patterns; geographical regions on either side of a border tend to be the source of and host to most migrants. Third, small countries tend to experience higher gross emigration rates, simply by virtue of the fact that a greater portion of their populations on the move will happen to encounter an international border in moving a given distance.

But what is the link between distance, as a deterrent, on the one hand, and perhaps the most important ameliorating factor, namely access to social networks in the receiving countries, on the other hand?

On social networks

Having access to a community of familiar persons upon arrival makes transition much easier for migrants in a number of ways. Such a community may act as a more complete, or more credible, source of information, prior to moving, about opportunities and conditions in the destination area, though improved information may either encourage or deter movement. By staying with friends or relatives migrants can lower their initial housing costs, and contacts can help circumnavigate the legal barriers to entry. In addition, such contacts frequently speed the process of finding a job, either identifying a job vacancy to which the migrant is called or aiding job search after moving. More generally, entering a community that is familiar to the migrant lowers their sense of alienation, easing social as well as economic assimilation.

These many facets render ambiguous the relevant concept of a social network. The roles played by immediate family members, by kin, friends, fellow villagers, a common ethnic group or fellow nationals may be quite distinct or overlapping across these facets. In any event, prior migrants delimit such groups, though in some instances even returned migrants may prove useful. The commonly observed effect is therefore a rise in the likelihood of the next wave of potential migrants electing to move, the more substantial is the pool of prior movers. As a result, migrants' origins become highly concentrated, from specific countries or from specific communities or locations within a country. Conversely, people from communities with little or no prior migration are quite unlikely to move and cumulative inertia increasingly isolates such groups from the world community.[68]

Although such a scenario makes eminent sense, detecting just how important such effects really are in shaping international migration remains difficult for at least two reasons. The first resides in the ambiguity of defining a relevant community pool to measure. The second is in discerning causality when both prior and current migrations may be driven by some common, but unobserved, effect, resulting in a spurious correlation between the two streams.[69]

A very extensive literature exists describing migrants' social networks, their roles and influences. In the context of migration to the Gulf, for example, Shah (1998b) notes the role that relatives play in obtaining Azad (illegal) visas; Azam (1998), from his study of two districts of Pakistan, tabulates that some 40–50 percent of overseas migrants report obtaining their placement through friends and relatives abroad; Nair (1998) notes the positive influence of being part of the Muslim community on the likelihood of migrating to the Gulf from Kerala; and Gunatilleke (1998a) describes the influence of returning female migrants from Sri Lanka in diminishing fears of abuse among the next round of female migrants. This last example not withstanding, Curran et al. (2003) emphasize that much of the discussion has ignored the likelihood that social networks operate in quite different ways for females than for males, and address these differences in the context of migration in

Thailand. It should also be noted that the influence of social networks is by no means confined to unskilled migrants; Saxenian (1999) offers an excellent account of the influence that networks play among the information technology communities from Asia living in California's Silicon Valley for instance. In addition, a wide range of statistical analyses of migration flows demonstrate a positive effect of the existing stock of prior migrants in furthering continued migration though, as noted already, imposing causal interpretations on such statistical patterns is problematic.

In the end, the underlying causality behind both geography and social networks as determinants of migration remains inadequately understood. Nonetheless, together they suggest important implications. Initial migrations tend to become self-perpetuating and cumulative. They are also geographically concentrated, often over shorter distances. Countries, regions and communities left out of the initial process, partly as a result of their relative location, are left behind in this globalization dynamic, lacking an impetus to initiate the first substantial movements.

However, although these cumulative forces have interesting and important dynamic consequences for the migration process, the policy implications from these observed patterns are not obvious. For the governments of either sending or receiving countries to attempt to alter migration experiences by promoting or demobilizing social networks is unlikely to be effective, and geography is immutable. In contrast, other factors that may potentially shape migration are subject to far more policy influence, at least within the sending countries, and to these the following two sections turn.

Aspects of Economic Development: Controversy and Evidence

The summary of proceedings at a recent conference on migration and development lists among the 'Old and discredited ideas ... The wishful thinking that economic development can reduce migration pressures in the short term ... '[70] The US Commission for the Study of International Migration and Cooperative Economic Development went further in their afterword: 'The major paradox the Commission found, however, is that the development process itself tends to stimulate migration in the short to medium term ... the development solution to unauthorized migration is measured in decades – even generations.'[71] As the Chairman of the US Commission notes, 'In the course of their deliberations, the commissioners became convinced that ... there is likely to be a J-curve effect.'[72] This effect is known as the 'migration hump' and is now widely accepted.

> What the migration hump shows is that there is little migration at low levels of development ... but that as development takes place and income levels rise, so too does migration ... Migration continues to rise with income levels until an income

threshold is reached. Once this threshold is reached, and the domestic economy begins to offer people opportunities at home, migration starts to taper off.[73]

The issue is of central importance, raising serious doubts about the efficacy of a strategy to accelerate economic development in the sending countries as a means of diminishing migration pressures. The position of the US Commission would suggest that development is actually counter-productive in this regard, at least among the poorer nations. An '... implication which poses a dilemma for those who would like migration management to reduce migration, is that developed countries cannot expect to solve their immigration problems by reducing poverty in developing countries. Indeed the migration hump suggests that if we are successful in reducing poverty, we should expect increased out-migration from developing countries.'[74]

The force of the popular contentions with respect to the role of economic development in affecting migration is both surprising and controversial. Targeting aid and other policies to promote development in order to manage migration pressures may well be criticized. Such efforts could divert resources away from some of the most indigent and prove clumsy instruments in the process (see Chapter 10). This would be particularly true if the migration hump is real, for then restraining development of the lowest income nations would postpone rising migration pressures. Accordingly, the notion of a migration hump is re-examined here first. The balance of this section then turns to evidence on the role of economic development and gaps in economic opportunities as factors in promoting migration between countries, drawing upon our case study areas.

A migration hump?

At least five distinct explanations have been put forward as to why a migration hump might occur:

1. A migration hump may reflect an underlying demographic hump, to the extent that population growth rates initially rise with income levels prior to passing through a demographic transition. In turn, more rapid population growth may affect emigration with a lag, both directly by expanding the base of potential migrants and indirectly through downward pressure on earnings potential at home.
2. The second hypothesis stems from a standard line of argument in the international trade literature. Reforms that liberalize a highly protectionist trade regime result in temporary dislocation, as workers and other resources move from contracting to newly expanding sectors. In the interim, some workers may be hurt, either by spells of unemployment, or by lower real wages where workers primarily consume the increasingly expensive export items.[75]

3. This possibility is essentially a variant on the second, though emphasizing any potential disruptions that might be associated with longer-run, structural shifts accompanying economic development.
4. The fourth idea emphasizes the difficulties inherent in financing the initial costs involved in international migration. As incomes rise, financing these costs becomes easier and hence out-migration may grow. However, at higher incomes the economic and other attractions of staying at home come to dominate and departures again decline.
5. The last line of argument is that the returns on migrants' savings are particularly poor when remitted to a low income home area. As incomes rise these returns are improved and migration for target saving and remittance are encouraged.

It is worth emphasizing that in each of the first three versions the concept that tighter domestic labor markets discourage migrant departures is retained. However, the process of development may temporarily result in slack in the local labor market and hence accelerate migration. Certainly each of these lines of argument is more or less feasible.[76] What does the evidence show?

The first type of evidence frequently cited refers to the mass migrations from Europe in the nineteenth and early twentieth centuries, which clearly did rise with income levels in Europe, as industrialization proceeded. However, in this context Hatton and Williamson (1994, 1998, 2002) find that the gap in earnings between origin and destination areas added significantly to emigration pressures and offer no support for the notion of a hump in this relationship. Instead, Hatton and Williamson attribute the rising migration largely to accelerated population growth twenty years earlier, reinforced by the cumulative effect of prior migration and, more weakly, to the structural shift of the labor force out of agriculture. The combined effects of rising wages with higher incomes, and a population growth rate which first rises then declines with incomes, can clearly generate a migration hump, though a hump which would occur at a lower income level than the turning point with respect to population growth. In the 2000 *World Population Prospects*, the UN (2002c: 22) notes 'that the fertility transition ... has become a virtually universal process'. Although population growth rates remain high in the least developed countries, the UN estimates that they are no longer rising and are projected to decline from here. Any potential for economic development to accelerate outward migration through rising population growth, as historically in Europe, may thus largely have passed, though a lag effect may continue for some years in the lowest income contexts.

A second type of evidence tests for migration humps in relation to incomes within more recent migration streams. Stark and Taylor (1991) indeed find that the probability of adults from the Patzcuaro region of Mexico moving to the US initially rises with household income level then declines at higher incomes.

Similarly, Faini and Venturini (1993) estimate that migration from Greece, Portugal, Spain and Turkey, between 1962 and 1988, exhibited a positive association between GDP per capita in the home country and rate of emigration at low income levels, but a negative association at higher income levels. However, in both of these studies the levels of income at which the hump is estimated to occur are so low as to be practically irrelevant to these countries.[77] Vogler and Rotte (2000) analyze the inflow of migrants into Germany from 86 Asian and African countries during 1981 to 1995; their estimates suggest a turning point in the migration hump at an income per capita of about 92 percent of the 1987 income levels, which presumably refers to a stage relatively close to the beginning of their sample.[78] Among asylum seekers to Germany, the comparable estimate by Vogler and Rotte occurs at 55 percent of the 1987 income levels. Clark *et al.* (2002) examine immigration to the US from 81 countries during 1971–98, finding that higher income levels at home diminish emigration among countries with more equal income distributions but this pattern is reversed among more unequal societies.[79] The overall effect is that growth in incomes is estimated to diminish emigration to the US among upper and moderate income countries but that pattern is reversed at income levels typical of Africa. On the other hand, when Hatton and Willamson (2002) look at net migration from twenty countries of Sub-Saharan Africa, predominantly during the 1980s, this latter pattern is not supported, which they attribute to lower costs of moving from one African country to another and hence a diminished role for development in easing financing costs.

The last type of evidence is more global, based on observations such as that in Massey (2003: 25–6) who lists as the first of 'several basic truths about international migration … international migration does not stem from a lack of economic growth and development, but from development itself … the poorest and least developed nations do not send the most international migrants today'. Yet the most recent cross-country evidence on migrant flows does not support this. Figure 2.9 depicts net migration during 1995–2000 per thousand population according to GDP per capita for 164 countries.[80] In this figure, negative net migration refers to outward migration dominating arrivals and vice versa. A significant pattern is observed and is represented by the downward sloping, solid, straight line: on average, net out-migration declines significantly as levels of income per capita rise across countries. Also superimposed on this graph is a closer look at this pattern at different income levels, represented by the dotted lines.[81] Among the lowest income countries, the emigration propensity actually declines as income per capita rises, and does so in a statistically significant fashion, denying the hypothesized lower arm of a migration hump. Moreover, this pattern reveals that net out-migration is never statistically significantly higher than at the lowest income point. This latter fitted curve allows for the possibility of a hump in the migration pattern, but no hump is observed.[82]

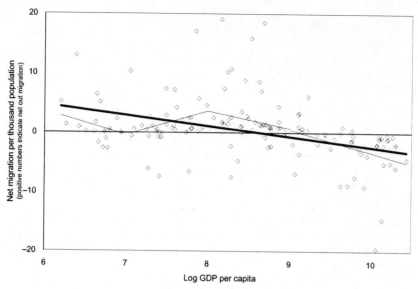

Figure 2.9   Net migration rates 164 countries, 1995–2000

Although the notion of a migration hump is now often depicted as conventional wisdom, empirical support for the existence of such a pattern may readily be questioned. As the UN (2002a) reports, the rate of net out-migration is no lower for the least developed regions than for the less developed, and is actually higher for Africa than for South America or for the less developed regions as a whole.

Gaps in economic opportunities: the issues

There seems widespread agreement that differences in economic opportunities across countries do play a part in shaping migration patterns. There is less agreement about which components of these opportunities matter and about just how responsive are migration streams to changes in these relative opportunities. What are the issues?

A number of dimensions of the gap in economic opportunities between sending and receiving countries may be noted:

- The relevant gap is the potential gain that a migrant can realistically aspire to, given the skill level, language proficiency and other factors determining employability of the individual migrant. The fact that the average agricultural laborer in the developing regions would face very circumscribed employment opportunities in the OECD countries does much to explain limited observed migration in the face of large wage gaps. Conversely, as education levels and language skills rise in the developing world, employability overseas is enhanced and migration pressures are likely to rise.

- The financial costs of international migrations can be very substantial.[83] One implication is that difficulties in financing these initial costs may present an effective barrier to movement. In consequence, the extent of mobility may remain limited even in the face of significant potential gains in incomes. A second implication is that extended periods at higher incomes may be necessary to recoup these costs and hence reap the returns to relocation. This feature is often suggested as an explanation for the fact that most migrants are comparatively young, but in practice the decline in most migrations in the middle years of life is too steep to stem from such a simple explanation alone.[84]

- For risk-averse individuals, the economic uncertainties inherent in staying or moving matter and not merely the potential to gain on average. The specter of spells of unemployment at home or abroad then influences the likelihood of migrating, as does income instability more generally. In addition, the concern for economic security drives families to seek some mechanism to insure their livelihoods against times of adversity. Lacking more formal insurance alternatives, the family and perhaps a wider community may assume importance in offering effective insurance when some members suffer losses while others fare better. If such mutual support is more readily accessible at home than abroad, as seems likely, then departure may remain quite limited despite significant expected income gains.

- The decision whether to migrate is not always the domain of the individual migrant. The decision may be taken by a family head, a spouse, a parent, or by mutual consent. Moreover, even where effective decisions can be made by individual migrants they may act with some degree of altruism toward the interests of others. The individual migrant may then fail to gain from an observed move, yet the overall decision is to the betterment of the family. This may be true in the sense that having a family member well placed abroad can offer greater economic security to the family should times become worse at home.[85] Alternatively, parents may elect to emigrate to enhance the future prospects of their children even though the parents are harmed economically or otherwise by such a move.[86] A related issue arises with respect to joint employment amongst couples, which on the one hand can require a partner to move despite personal losses and on the other hand may retard migration despite potential gain for a spouse.[87]

- More generally, long-term economic prospects are likely to dominate decisions to relocate permanently, whereas the current economic situation may play a more important role in temporary migration decisions. Large disparities in today's incomes may then not induce huge movements that involve substantial costs of relocation if the expectation is that these disparities will narrow later.

- To the extent that income differentials and vagaries indeed shape migration decisions, all sources of incomes tied to specific locations matter and not merely labor incomes alone. If migrants would lose all or some part of their incomes from assets upon leaving the old country, mobility would be deterred. Underlying causes of loss in asset returns might range from legal restrictions on capital flight to poor monitoring among absentee landlords. Conversely, the right to various state transfers in the new country may prove tempting both in terms of income enhancement and also diminished risk.
- Lastly, the gaps in cost of living between nations need to be accounted for in comparing real opportunities. These gaps offer considerable real advantages where it is possible to work in one country and spend in another. Target saving by temporary international migrants is thus encouraged and return migration may in part be motivated by these gaps in cost of living. Similarly, it may be cost effective to leave non-working family members at home to take advantage of cheaper living conditions, despite the limitations of conjugal separation and parental absence.

Economic development and opportunities: the evidence

Together these elements suggest a series of economic measures that might be anticipated to affect the propensity to migrate: the costs of moving, differences in the uncertainty of incomes and in access to unearned incomes. Nonetheless, given these measures and other factors discussed later in this section, the greater is the difference in tightness in labor market opportunities, that is in real wages and the incidence of unemployment between home and abroad, the more people are likely to move.

How quickly, and indeed whether, labor markets become more attractive at home as development proceeds is partly a question of the development strategy chosen. Emphasizing investments in heavy industries that generate few jobs, or even pursuing more labor-intensive strategies in the context of rigid labor markets, may do little to improve average work opportunities at home. The evidence in support of a migration hump may be questioned, but what of the other contentions as to the irrelevance of economic development as a determinant of international migration, such as those quoted at the outset of this section? Do differences in economic opportunity matter and does economic development appear to reduce migration pressures more generally?

Europe The low rates of migration from Spain, Portugal and Greece upon entering the European Union, despite a large disparity in wages with Northern Europe, have led some observers to conclude 'that wage differentials are not the driving force behind European migration'.[88] However, a few researchers have looked at the responsiveness of additional migration to changes in earnings opportunities, finding that migration indeed responds positively to the gaps in incomes between home and abroad, though most of the evidence refers to a period prior to 1990.[89]

For example, Straubhaar (1986a) looks at annual migration between 1962 and 1983 from Greece, Italy, Portugal, Spain and Turkey into Western Europe (defined by Belgium, France, Germany and the Netherlands). Straubhaar's results indicate that the migration streams indeed increased significantly both with expected incomes in Western Europe (per capita income multiplied by the employment rate) relative to incomes at origin, and also with the relative expansion in employment rates in Western Europe during the previous year. Zimmermann (1995) adds Yugoslavia to Straubhaar's list of countries of origin and extends the period of analysis to 1960 through 1991 but focuses on net migration into Germany alone. Zimmermann detects a significant break in behavior; before 1974 net migration increased with growth in the German economy and presumed growing labor demands, but after this point in time the positive association became weaker. Zimmermann maintains that the earlier period can be characterized by demand-pull migration whereas the later period reflects supply-push particularly from Yugoslavia and Turkey. However, Sala-i-Martin (1995) comments on the lack of controls for sending-country conditions in this analysis and the general difficulties of discerning both causality and push from pull factors within this framework. Nonetheless, as already noted in Section 2.2, the migration milieu did shift significantly in 1974 in Germany, as elsewhere in Western Europe, with effective cessation of the system of guest worker recruitment.

Faini and Venturini (1993) are able to exploit more complete explanatory data to look at gross migration from Greece, Portugal, Spain and Turkey between 1962 and 1988. In particular, Faini and Venturini control for the level of GDP per capita in the sending countries while examining the effects of relative labor market opportunities at home and abroad. The estimated effects on unemployment rates at both origin and destination are generally mixed and add little to the outcomes. However, growth in employment at destination indeed adds significantly to the flow of migrants (with the exception of migrants from Portugal). More importantly, from each country, the rate of departure is shown to rise with the ratio of average wages at home to those at destination.[90]

With the exception of the inclusion of Turkey in these studies, the foregoing results refer to source countries which are now EU members. Far less analysis is available on migration to the EU-15 member states from non-EU source countries. In Section 2.1, four such major flows were identified: from the Maghreb, from Turkey, from the transition economies of Eastern Europe, and from other developing regions. During the 1960s, migration flows from Algeria, Morocco and Tunisia to France, but also to Belgium, Germany and the Netherlands, were high under various bilateral state agreements.[91] However, these agreements, as many others, were suspended by the Europeans (and also by Algeria) in 1974, following the oil crisis.[92] Rising oil prices enabled the Algerian economy to grow relatively quickly during the 1970s, but by the 1990s growth was much slower despite reduced reliance on central state planning during the 1980s and 1990s (see Table 2.12). Moreover, job creation in Algeria has been sluggish and outstripped population growth by less than 1 percent during the 1990s culminating in a peak in the reported unemployment rate at an astonishing 41.8 percent in 2000 up from 22.1 percent in 1989. Not surprisingly against this background, net migration out of Algeria has been fairly high. During 1995–2000 about 52 000 net migrants left Algeria per year, a rate of migration relative to population surpassed only by Sudan within Northern Africa. In contrast, the Tunisian economy continued to grow quite quickly during the 1990s and Tunisia has the highest GDP per capita of the three central Maghreb countries. Partly as a result, the net migration rate out of Tunisia, relative to population, was lower than from either Algeria or Morocco in the last decade, averaging only 8500 persons per year.[93]

Morocco is not only the poorest of the three central Maghreb countries but economic growth has slowed over the last three decades and has been highly erratic from year to year. This lack of development has no doubt contributed to the fact that Morocco has the largest foreign population in the EU of any of the Maghreb countries. Giubilaro (1997) records more than a million Moroccan nationals in the EU in 1993, for example, compared to about 650 000 Algerians, although the home country populations are roughly comparable.[94] Moreover, the flow of Moroccans to the EU-15 averaged more than 330 000 per year from 1970 to 1990. Faini and de Melo (1994) examine this annual pattern of gross migration from Morocco to Belgium, France, Germany and the Netherlands during 1977–88. They find that migration from Morocco diminished significantly with expansion in modern sector employment per capita in Morocco, and rose with both GDP per capita in the destination countries of Europe relative to that in Morocco, as well as with employment growth in Europe. Although Morocco's development strategy has resulted in a faster pace of job creation than in Algeria, unemployment nonetheless rose sharply during the 1990s, from 13.9 percent in 1988 to 21.5 percent in 2000. In light of Faini and de Melo's findings, it is not then surprising to see a high continued rate of net outward migration, given the comparatively slow growth and mounting unemployment of the 1990s, with Spain emerging as a relatively new major destination during this decade.

Table 2.12 also shows comparable data for Turkey, where growth has been both fairly high and consistent on average over the last three decades, though year-to-year growth again has been highly erratic. Indeed, within the last ten years, the Turkish economy has suffered two major crises accompanied by massive outflows on financial account, in 1994 and in 2001, in both of which GDP fell by more than 5 percent within a single year. The additional crisis

Table 2.12 *Economic growth, unemployment and net migration: the Maghreb countries and Turkey*

	Average annual percent growth GDP per capita			Employment growth per capita % 1989–99	Unemployment rate % 2000	GDP per capita US$ PPP 2000	Net annual migration			
							1990–95		1995–2000	
	1970–80	1980–90	1990–2000				Rate	1000s	Rate	1000s
Algeria	–		-0.3	0.98	41.8	5308	-1.1	-30	-1.8	-52
Morocco	2.5	1.7	0.7	1.38	21.5	3546	-1.6	-41	-1.5	-44
Tunisia	4.9	0.7	3.2	–	–	6363	-1.0	-9	-0.8	-8
Turkey	1.7	2.5	2.5	-0.03	6.6	6974	-0.8	-46	-0.8	-54

Sources: Migration data from UN Population Division, Department of Economic and Social Affairs website: http://www.un.org/esa/population/unpop. htm; Economic data from World Bank (2002), UNDP (2002), and IMF statistics at http://www.imfstatistics.org/.

in 1999 was only slightly milder. In fact, despite moderate overall growth, formal sector employment failed to keep pace with population growth in Turkey during the 1990s, though unemployment remains low in comparison to the Maghreb countries. Nonetheless, some 54 000 people are estimated to have left Turkey net, on average, each year between 1995 and 2000. Within the EU, the principal destination remains Germany, where the stock of Turkish nationals rose by just over 300 000 from 1990 to 2000,[95] although migration from Turkey did diversify during the 1990s with increasing movement to Russia.[96] Yet by 2000 Turkey had reached a GDP per capita, measured in purchasing power parity exchange rates, of US$6974 and out-migration flows are now much diminished compared to the 1960s.

In addition to the migrations from the Maghreb region and from Turkey, the transitions in Eastern Europe and the former Soviet Union around 1990 generated a massive surge in migration to Western Europe. Although Figure 2.1 may have the appearance of a migration hump, such an interpretation would be far too simplistic. Rather, the UN (2002b 1, 2) concludes that 'The disintegration of Czechoslovakia, of the USSR and of Yugoslavia contributed to this increase ... In addition, the transformation of the communist federations coincided with rising ethnic tensions, sometimes violent, and resulted in numerous displacements ... Most migration flows have been politically or ethnically motivated.'

As Table 2.13 shows, during 1990–94 average GDP growth was negative in every single country in transition in Eastern Europe and the 'European' states of the former USSR. On the other hand, by the second half of the 1990s this negative performance had been turned around in each country except Bulgaria, Moldova and Ukraine. Nonetheless, estimates of unemployment remained high by 2000 in most of the region. Eleven of the countries listed in Table 2.13 underwent net out-migration during the first half of the 1990s, and massively so in the case of Albania and Bosnia-Herzegovina. For each of these eleven countries, the rate of net out-migration either declined or was reversed during the second half of the 1990s. Seven countries listed in Table 2.13 experienced net inward migration even during the first half of the 1990s, and of these seven only the Ukraine reversed that pattern in the later 1990s. More generally, 'Long-term migration leveled off in the second half of the 1990s, as the main armed conflicts subsided and receiving countries hardened their migration and asylum policies.'[97] Nonetheless it may be noted that the rate of net out-migration across countries, over these two time periods, is also negatively and significantly correlated with growth in GDP per capita at home.

By way of example of the interplay between political and economic crises, King and Mai (2002: 1–2) note that 'Emigration from Albania since 1990 has been the most dramatic instance of post-Cold War East-West migration ... March 1991 saw post-Cold War Europe's nightmare immigration scenario: a flotilla of assorted craft, crammed with some 26 000 desperate migrants

*Table 2.13   Economic growth and net migration: countries of Eastern
Europe, 1990–2000*

	GDP annual growth		2000 GDP/ capita US$ PPP	Net annual migration		
				Rate per thousand		migrants (1000)
	1990– 94	1995– 2000		1990– 95	1995– 2000	1995– 2000
Albania	−5.2	6.4	3 506	−24.7	−19.1	−60
Belarus	−6.8	3.6	7 544	1.3	0.3	3
Bosnia-Herzegovina	−14.5	29.1	–	−52.0	27.0	100
Bulgaria	−5.7	−0.1	5 710	−4.7	−1.2	−10
Croatia	−7.6	4.0	8 091	5.5	0.0	0
Czech Republic	−2.5	2.0	13 991	0.7	1.0	10
Estonia	−8.1	4.8	10 066	−8.9	−6.1	−9
Hungary	−3.2	3.6	12 416	−0.3	0.2	2
Latvia	−11.3	4.3	7 045	−8.8	−4.4	−11
Lithuania	−15.9	4.1	7 106	−2.1	−1.9	−7
FYR Macedonia	−11.1	2.3	5 086	−3.2	−0.5	−1
Rep. of Moldova	−16.2	−2.2	2 109	−5.9	−3.2	−14
Poland	−1.4	5.4	9 051	−0.4	−0.4	−14
Romania	−4.4	0.1	6 423	−4.6	−0.5	−12
Russian Federation	−10.2	0.5	8 377	2.5	2.0	287
Serbia-Montenegro	–	2.2	–	–	−1.9	−20
Slovakia	−4.5	4.6	11 243	0.4	0.3	2
Slovenia	−2.2	4.3	17 367	6.9	0.5	1
Ukraine	−13.2	−3.6	3 816	1.3	−1.5	−76

Sources: UN (2002a) and update at http://www.un.org/esa/population/unpop.htm; EBRD
(1997, 2003), UNDP (2002).

fleeing political and economic chaos in Albania ... Five months later ... a
further 20 000 arrived ... A third exodus of Albanian "boat people" occurred
in March 1997, consequent upon renewed political and economic chaos that
hinged on the collapse of a set of huge pyramid investment schemes which
bankrupted more than half the Albanian population.'

Along similar lines, Pyshkina (2002) argues that the undermining of real
wages (by price realignment under trade liberalization) combined with two
crises (with Transdnistria in 1992 and with Russia in 1998) to exacerbate
migration pressures in Moldova.

Prior to 1990, the three Baltic States were each significant net recipients of migrants, largely comprising ethnic Russians from Russia, Belarus and the Ukraine. The impact of the departure of these ethnic Russians after 1990 in reversing net migration has already been noted in Section 2.1. In addition, however, since 1990 there has also been migration from Estonia, largely to Finland and Germany, and from Latvia and Lithuania to Israel, the US and Germany. Kielyte (2002) examines a part of these flows, analyzing movements to the EU in total from each of the three Baltic countries in the post-Soviet period in relation to the gap in incomes and differences in unemployment, controlling for the stocks of prior migrants and distance. Pyshkina's results indicate that a larger gap in incomes between the Baltic States and the EU significantly increased emigration to the EU in the following year, although any association with differences in unemployment rates is statistically much weaker.

In each of these three illustrative cases, migration has been affected by economic development, or lack thereof, though certainly overlain with major effects from ethnic conflicts. The level of economic development is certainly not the only factor shaping migrations from and between the transition economies, yet economic development probably has been a contributing factor, particularly when one recognizes how inextricably economic performance, political turmoil and violence have been interlinked in the region.

The Gulf The labor market in the GCC states is highly segmented, with a large gap in incomes between citizens and migrant workers. Nonetheless, the gap in wages between what migrants would receive in South or Southeast Asia and their earnings in the Gulf is also large.[98] For example, Gunatilleke (1998b) reports an average foreign wage of contract workers from Sri Lanka 8.4 times that of the local wage and Shah (1998b) notes that the corresponding gap for unskilled workers from Bangladesh is 13 times. Yet almost no direct evidence exists on how responsive are the streams of migrants to the Gulf with respect to fluctuations in these wage differentials.[99]

On the demand side, oil prices have clearly played a role, both in the sharp rise in migration during the 1970s and in the slowing of migration with declining oil prices after 1980. Moreover, the switch from a preponderance of migrant workers from other Arab states to increased reliance on workers from South and Southeast Asia during the 1980s and 1990s, apparently reflected not only the higher cost of labor from nearby countries in the Middle East, but also the greater ease of denying family accompaniment to the contract workers from Asia as well as concerns for internal security.[100] Thereafter, the dynamics of the migration process have led to growth in migration from South and Southeast Asia, though with interruptions during the two wars in the Gulf and in Iraq. Social networks evolved and aided legal and undocumented job placements and the number and size of recruitment agencies have grown. Within these growing numbers, it seems the proportions from the various sending countries has also been shaped, to some extent, by the nature of work available within the GCC states. In particular, as the demands of construction activities have varied, the number of unskilled workers from Bangladesh, India and Pakistan have adjusted accordingly. Meanwhile there has been significant growth in female migration to the Gulf, from Indonesia, the Philippines and Sri Lanka, as the demand for household servants has expanded.

Yet there are indications that developments in the principal sending countries have played a role also. The rapid take off of the Korean economy witnessed a cessation of any recruiting from that source by the mid-1980s. Moreover, the financial crisis in East Asia in 1997–98 resulted in renewed levels of labor recruitment from the three principal sending countries of South East Asia.[101]

The crisis reversed a strong, on-going growth performance in Indonesia and Thailand, though the Philippine economy has continued with serious difficulties for more than two decades (see Table 2.14). In contrast, the growth records of the South Asian economies continued to be successful through the 1990s, especially that of Sri Lanka. Even India has broken out of its long-term sluggish growth pattern, with steady reforms starting in the 1980s, followed by more trade liberalization in the 1990s.

Table 2.14   Economic development: principal countries of Asia sending migrants to the Middle East

	GDP growth per capita Average annual percent rate			2000 GDP per capita US$ PPP
	1971–80	1981–90	1991–2000	
Bangladesh	3.33	1.89	2.48	1602
India	0.77	3.65	3.67	2358
Pakistan	1.61	3.07	1.90	1928
Sri Lanka	2.38	2.84	3.91	3530
Indonesia	5.83	3.54	2.46	3043
Philippines	3.17	−0.64	0.69	3971
Thailand	4.30	6.08	3.52	6402

Sources: GDP 2000 from UNDP (2002); GDP and population growth from http://www.imfstatistics.org/.

Against this background of economic growth records, a significant pattern can be detected. Controlling for a trend effect and for migration in the previous year (partly to reflect the cumulative effects of social network build-up), the patterns of migration to the Middle East, depicted in Figure 2.3, respond negatively to GDP levels in the home countries in the prior year.[102] A 1 percent increase in GDP per capita at home is estimated to result in nearly a 2 percent decline in migration per capita; excluding the Philippines (which appears to be somewhat of an exception to this pattern), the response rises to more than a 3 percent decline in migration, an effect which is statistically very significant. Over time, allowing for the cumulative effects through networks, this amounts to almost a 7 percent decline in recruitment to the Middle East with each 1 percent growth in home GDP per capita. It seems that economic development in the sending countries does deter migration to the Gulf.

East Asia Upon reviewing the available evidence for Asia and the Pacific, Massey *et al.* (1998: 175) conclude that 'the accumulated weight of empirical evidence generally supports ... [the] ... proposition that movement into and out of countries is tied to wage differentials ... To date, however, most studies have been descriptive and not analytic. Rather than relating wage rates and migration directly to one another in an empirically convincing fashion, investigators have tended to show only that gaps in income exist and then make the inferential leap that these gaps must have caused the observed movement.' Although inherently risky, such a conclusion is at least consistent with the migration transition experienced in parts of East Asia.

In Hong Kong, Japan, Korea, Malaysia, Singapore and Taiwan, rapid economic growth, initially focusing on labor-intensive manufacturing, combined with slow natural population increase to generate substantial growth in real wages (see Table 2.15).[103] In the process, most of the higher income economies have become important destinations for migrants from the lower income countries within the region. Even in Japan, the stock of foreign labor has now expanded and was estimated at 670 000 in 1999 (including nearly 252 000 over-stayers).[104] The migration transition is, however, perhaps most apparent in Malaysia, which continued to be 'a significant labour exporter during the years of labour surplus, and even after labour markets began to tighten for the first time in the late 1970s',[105] but by 1995–2000 had added 79 000 net foreign migrants per year,[106] largely from Indonesia.

Thailand has a per capita income in the mid-range of development within the region and has significant migration flows in both directions. In 1999, more than 200 000 documented Thai nationals left for work overseas. More than half, primarily unskilled, went to Taiwan. In the same year nearly 320 000 illegal immigrants, almost entirely from Myanmar, were arrested and deported. In 2000 more than 444 000 were arrested.[107] However, Thailand is not alone in generating significant two-way migrations. Hong Kong, Korea and Taiwan each host substantial numbers of relatively unskilled workers, largely from the lower income countries of East and Southeast Asia, but each also sends a substantial flow of more highly skilled workers to North America.

As already noted, GDP growth in the Philippines has generally been poor;

Table 2.15   Economic development in East and Southeast Asia

	2000 GDP per capita US$ PPP	GDP growth per capita Average annual percent rate		
		1971–80	1981–90	1991–2000
Japan	26 755	3.41	3.55	1.13
China, Hong Kong	25 153	6.75	5.33	2.76
Singapore	23 356	7.44	4.82	4.80
Republic of Korea	17 380	5.60	7.38	5.33
Brunei Darussalam	16 779	–	–	–
Malaysia	9 068	5.76	3.31	4.50
Thailand	6 402	4.30	6.08	3.52
China	3 976	–	7.72	9.06
Philippines	3 971	3.17	–0.64	0.69
Indonesia	3 043	5.83	3.54	2.46
Papua New Guinea	2 280	–	–0.90	–7.31
Vietnam	1 996	–	–	5.78
Mongolia	1 783	–	2.35	–
Lao PDR	1 575	–	3.06	3.72
Cambodia	1 446	–	–	–
Myanmar	1 027	–	–0.50	4.73

Sources: GDP 2000 from UNDP (2002); GDP and population growth from http://www.imfstatistics.org/.

from 1985 to 2000 employment growth was even slower. During the 1990s, the outflow of land-based Filipino workers almost doubled, from nearly 335 000 during 1990 to over 640 000 during 2000.[108] The large flows of Filipino workers to the Middle East have already been depicted in Figure 2.3, but during the 1990s the export of workers to the higher income economies within East and Southeast Asia grew rapidly. In addition, the stock of Philippine-born population in the US by 2000 exceeded 1.2 million adults, the majority of whom held college degrees.[109] There can be little doubt that the poor performance of the Philippine economy has contributed to rendering the Philippines one of the world's largest sources of migrants. This is supported by the evidence in Gonzalez (1995), in which the emigration rate (normalized on labor force size) in 1988, from each of thirteen administrative regions in the Philippines to various destination countries, is shown to be significantly positively related to the gap in incomes between the home region and destination country, controlling for transport and job intermediation costs.

In contrast, GDP growth has been more rapid on average in Indonesia.

During the 1970s this performance was helped by rising oil prices, but since then exports and the manufacturing base have become more diversified. The massive capital flight in 1998 led to a drop in Indonesia's GDP by more than 13 percent and the economy has been slow to recover, but employment actually continued to expand even through the crisis of 1998.[110] Nonetheless, the higher income economies of East and Southeast Asia continue to attract Indonesian workers. Hugo (2002a: Table 36) estimates the stock of overseas contract workers throughout the East and Southeast Asia region at a little over 1 543 000 of whom 1.3 million were in Malaysia in 2000.

To this general picture of very substantial migration from low to high income countries within the region, there are, however, some important exceptions. To a large extent, China, Cambodia, Laos and Vietnam are not parties to this pattern. Although overseas contract work began officially in China in the late 1970s it has become significant only much more recently, amounting to a stock of perhaps half a million workers by 2000.[111] In the same year, the stock of adults in the US who were born in China (excluding Hong Kong and Taiwan) was about 877 000. Although these absolute numbers are large, they are nonetheless small relative to China's population. Moreover, apart from movement to Hong Kong, labor flows from China within the East Asia region have not been very large.[112]

The war in Indochina and the turmoil of the Khmer Rouge regime in Cambodia generated a significant outpouring of refugees. By 2000 there were over 700 000 adults in the US who had been born in Vietnam, though the numbers were much smaller from Cambodia (116 000) and Laos (76 000).[113] Yet the export of labor from these three countries to other parts of the region remains small. At least from Vietnam this is partly because a stock of about 200 000 workers were employed in the Soviet bloc before 1990 and alternative destinations for Vietnamese labor export have been slow to evolve since the cessation of this arrangement.[114]

With these exceptions in China and Indochina, where emigration controls and conflict have been the principal shaping factors until recently, it is probably fair to say that most of the rest of the region indeed exhibits clear signs of the role of economic development in influencing migration patterns. The wealthier nations no longer export unskilled labor, as in earlier days, and most now import unskilled workers from the lower income countries of the region. However, at least some of the wealthier economies now send more highly skilled workers, some initially as students, beyond the region, to North America, Australia and New Zealand.

North America Most of the systematic evidence on the role of wage differences in shaping international migration refers to the US context, though even this evidence is largely confined to migration streams from Mexico and Puerto Rico, which are dominated by movements of less skilled workers.[115]

Analysts have looked at the rates of legal migration from Mexico to the US over time, the rates of border apprehensions at the Mexico–US border, village survey data in Mexico on whether or not individuals move, long-term historical trends in immigration to the US, and applications for labor certification to enter the US for work. In each case, differences in earnings opportunities, as reflected in wage differentials or employment rates, or both, have significantly contributed to the form of migration examined.[116] As Freeman (1993: 444) notes, wage differences are certainly not the only contributing force, for 'in the 1950s the number of Mexican immigrants barely exceeded the number of Canadian immigrants, and the number coming from South and Central America was one-sixth that from Europe'. Yet Freeman goes on to note that, allowing for the dynamics of cumulative migration effects, the responsiveness of migration to the US in terms of economic gain is roughly similar to estimates of the responsiveness of inter-state migration within the US or inter-provincial migration within Japan.[117]

Summing up

Almost all of the available evidence supports the proposition that migration rises with the gap in earnings opportunities between home and abroad. This certainly does not mean that labor market conditions are the only factor affecting migration streams, nor even that employment opportunities are the most important elements, either in the sense of having the largest normalized effect, or in the sense of explaining most of the variation in migrations.[118] Rather, what matters is the simpler observation that such evidence as we possess indicates that tighter labor markets, with higher wages and more employment creation at origin, do diminish migration and vice versa.[119]

Does economic development in the source countries diminish migration pressures? This does not automatically follow from any assertion that differences in earnings opportunities contribute significantly to migration pressures. Tighter labor markets do not always accompany more rapid economic growth, though they are certainly positively correlated. Some have argued the opposite, that economic development among the poorer nations may actually exacerbate migration pressures. Yet, if there is a lower arm to a migration hump then any such hump seems to turn at very low incomes, and the evidence to support such a turning point seems tenuous in recent migration patterns.

Migration out of Eastern Europe certainly spiked during the period of economic collapse in the first half of the 1990s and slowed with modest economic recovery in the second half of the decade. Economic recovery probably did contribute to this diminution of migration pressures, but it is certainly not the only factor underlying this reduction. Among the Maghreb countries, the evidence suggests that economic development at origin indeed tends to slow migration. For Morocco there is direct evidence of this. Recruitment of workers for the Gulf, from the seven principal sending countries of Asia, has been shown to have responded negatively to development achievements at home. Moreover, the newly industrialized countries of East and Southeast Asia have experienced a migration transition as development proceeded, a transition from export of unskilled labor, to unskilled labor importation from some of the lower income countries of the region combined with export of highly skilled workers to North America and Australia.

On the other hand, the North American regime, which concentrates upon attracting the highly skilled, exhibits quite different links with development at origin. Some fairly low income countries are among the largest absolute suppliers of highly skilled people to the US, and the US draws most of its highly skilled migrants from the developing regions. As a proportion of their population the poor countries send no more highly educated people than do the richer nations, though this does imply that the poorer nations send a far higher portion of their highly educated population, an observation to which Chapter 4 returns.

Forced Migration

For many asylum seekers, any choice whether or not to migrate is very circumscribed at best and some international migration is simply coerced by traffickers. Both forms of forced migration have been on a broad upward trend. The estimated number of refugees in the world rose fairly steadily through the 1980s, peaked at the beginning of 1993 but again rose slightly after the turn of the century.

The vast majority of refugees remain within their region of origin. Preliminary estimates by the UNHCR for the end of 2002 indicate that more than a third of recognized refugees originate from the countries of Africa and it is African countries that provide asylum for almost the same number (see Table 2.16). In understanding the causes of migration, the role of refugees and asylum seekers plays a significant role in a number of ways within our four case study areas. At the close of 2000, Canada and the US together were the countries of asylum for just over a million refugees and asylum seekers. The sources in both Canada and the US are quite diversified, and the number of refugees originating from within the Americas is comparatively small. The three largest groups of refugees in Canada, at the end of 2002, were from Sri Lanka, Afghanistan and Bosnia-Herzegovina and in the US from Bosnia-Herzegovina, Vietnam and Somalia. Geography is clearly not the dominating factor in dictating admission as a refugee to North America. In contrast, the GCC states are neither major sources of, nor hosts to, large numbers of refugees. However, among the principal countries sending workers to the Gulf, Pakistan plays the country of asylum to well over two million refugees from Afghanistan, which has had a major economic, political and security

Table 2.16   Refugees and asylum seekers by country of asylum and origin, 2002

	By country of asylum		Refugees by country of origin		By country of asylum		Refugees by country of origin
	Refugees	Asylum seekers			Refugees	Asylum seekers	
EU-15	1 592 833	298 998	1 165	Middle East	1 785 030	10 918	1 033 594
Austria	14 130	29 494	–	Turkey	3 301	2 591	86 694
Belgium	12 578	19 847	–	Kuwait	1 521	185	421
Denmark	73 597	6 068	–	Oman	0	25	–
Finland	12 373	3 443	–	Qatar	46	23	–
France	102 182	34 588	–	Saudi Arabia	245 290	124	–
Germany	903 000	50 000	1 165	UAE	163	277	–
Greece	2 788	1 738	–	South Asia	1 550 780	2 173	2 901 094
Ireland	5 380	6 967	–	Bangladesh	22 025	22	5 232
Italy	8 571	7 281	–	India	168 855	501	11 912
Luxembourg	1 201	1 043	–	Pakistan	1 227 433	1 608	15 133
Netherlands	148 362	58 159	–	Sri Lanka	28	13	126 466
Portugal	462	245	–	East Asia	514 472	3 889	623 146
Spain	6 780	6 309	–	Cambodia	200	81	33 436
Sweden	142 193	33 016	–	China	297 277	7	147 031
United Kingdom	159 236	40 800	–	Hong Kong	1 496	190	–
Other W. Eur.	115 548	47 749	–	Indonesia	28 596	237	9 819

E. Europe	408 984	20 411	827 804
Albania	17	52	8 757
Bosnia-Herzeg.	28 022	457	371 570
Bulgaria	3 658	1 140	1 889
Croatia	8 392	52	269 733
Czech Rep.	1 297	7 656	1 010
Estonia	10	7	411
FYR Macedonia	2 816	62	4 909
Hungary	6 088	1 055	986
Poland	1 591	5 153	1 501
Romania	1 857	39	4 772
Slovakia	444	4 508	266
Slovenia	390	193	723
Yugoslavia	354 402	37	161 277
Former USSR	361 685	11 886	440 210
Japan	2 657	316	–
Lao PDR	0	0	10 989
Malaysia	50 612	1 571	–
PNG	4 941	312	–
Philippines	114	47	45 473
Rep. of Korea	17	72	–
Singapore	2	2	–
Thailand	112 614	1 050	–
Timor East	1	4	28 097
Vietnam	15 945	0	348 301
Africa	3 343 663	159 560	3 666 068
Algeria	169 233	5	8 628
Morocco	2 127	115	427
Tunisia	102	11	1 859
N. America	615 121	446 078	–
Canada	129 950	52 761	–
United States	485 171	393 317	–
Other America	41 056	9 095	92 021
Oceania	60 410	3 543	1 071
Other	0	0	803 409
Total	10 389 582	1 014 300	10 389 582

Source: UNHCR at http://www.unhcr.ch/

impact on Pakistan. The flight of Tamils from Sri Lanka has also been significant, while the number of refugees in Thailand from Myanmar is far larger than the officially recognized numbers. More generally, however, the numbers of recognized refugees originating from and currently within East Asia is fairly small relative to population (though refugees from Vietnam in China remain significant).

In Europe the flow of asylum seekers has attracted considerable recent attention. For the period from 1982–2002, the total number of asylum seekers arriving in the EU-15 countries is shown in Figure 2.10.[120] During the decade to 2001, applications for asylum in the EU were more than triple those in Canada and the US combined (see Table 2.17). From 1982 to 1993 the recognition rate of asylum seekers fell as applications rose, though there has been a mild increase in the recognition rate again since 1994 (see Figure 2.10). [121] By the close of 2002, the UNHCR estimated the number of refugees recognized in the EU at nearly 1.6 million persons with an additional 300 000 still seeking asylum.

Once again, these EU-wide average recognition rates mask very considerable differences among the member countries, though the rates in some countries have also varied substantially over time, which is brought out in Table 2.17. Germany has been by far the largest recipient of asylum applications within the EU, both during the 1980s and the 1990s and has maintained a low recognition rate throughout, as have Finland and Italy. Only the Netherlands had a higher recognition rate in the 1990s than in the previous decade, though the UK has had the highest recognition rate in the

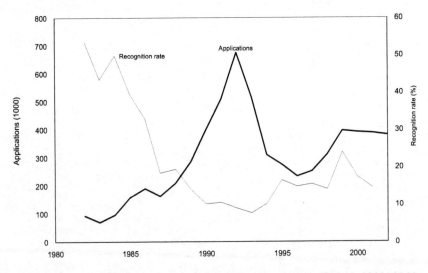

Figure 2.10   Asylum applications and recognition rates in EU-15, 1982–2002

Table 2.17   Asylum applications and recognition rates: EU-15, Australia, Canada and US

	Total applications		Recognition rate	
	1982–91	1992–2001	1982–91	1992–2001
Austria	134.0	128.0	36.3	13.4
Belgium	69.7	219.5	46.2	30.3
Denmark	45.3	97.4	36.0	19.5
Finland	5.3	18.2	2.2	0.8
France	347.4	281.0	33.2	20.8
Germany	996.9	1597.3	11.9	10.6
Greece	35.2	24.4	30.9	7.3
Ireland	–	39.7	–	8.0
Italy	55.1	83.4	9.2	12.3
Luxembourg	–	7.0	–	3.9
Netherlands	95.0	358.6	5.7	18.1
Portugal	3.7	5.7	22.2	3.9
Spain	37.5	84.2	23.2	7.8
Sweden	183.2	228.6	26.6	2.5
UK	164.5	576.6	26.1	18.5
Australia	30.1	89.3	15.3	16.8
Canada	239.4	286.3	56.0	59.3
US	437.7	869.0	25.0	27.7

Source: UNHCR (2001).

latter decade and has also experienced a sharp increase in the volume of applications.

Although the disintegration of Yugoslavia resulted in a huge number of asylum applicants, the origins of asylum seekers in the EU are widely dispersed (see Table 2.18). While refugees from the countries of Eastern Europe number about 800 000, this same group of countries is host to about half this number of refugees; the newly formed countries of the former USSR host more than 80 percent of the number of refugees originating internally from that group.

In fact, of the refugees in the EU in 2002, almost a third originate from the developing regions of Africa, the Middle East and Asia.[122] Critics question the motivation, which underlies these refugee flows in general. However, Castles *et al.* (2003) note that repression of minorities or ethnic conflict exists in all of the top ten countries of origin listed in Table 2.18 and is one of the few factors that they share in common. Moreover the spike in asylum seekers from Yugoslavia and Bosnia-Herzegovina in the early 1990s, which accounts

Table 2.18   Applications to EU countries for asylum by major countries of origin, 1990–2000

	Total applicants (1000)
Yugoslavia, Fed. Rep.	835.5
Romania	399.7
Turkey	355.5
Iraq	211.1
Afghanistan	155.2
Bosnia and Herzegovina	145.7
Sri Lanka	130.4
Iran	128.2
Somalia	115.7
Congo, Democratic Rep.	109.5
Bulgaria	107.4
Pakistan	88.3
India	85.2
Nigeria	79.3
Russian Federation	75.7
Vietnam	75.5
Algeria	74.2

Source: Castles *et al.* (2003: Table 2.1).

for much of the spike clearly visible in Figure 2.10, and a later, smaller spike again from Yugoslavia in 1998–99 clearly correspond to the two main phases of conflict in that region.

The link between the flows of refugees and the incidence of conflicts seems clear. On the other hand, this same report also notes that these top ten countries exhibit a wide range of income levels, though emphasizing that this 'should not be interpreted as indicating the absence of a link between the economic situation and forced migration. Rather the link appears to be more complex'.[123] At least two possible links may be mentioned.

The first emphasizes the state of economic development at destination. As Castles *et al.* (2003: 29) note, 'there is evidence that some, although not all, asylum seekers have a degree of control over where they go'. For most refugees this choice is extremely circumscribed. Most are compelled to remain in overwhelmingly poor, neighboring nations or to return home. A tiny portion is resettled in the OECD countries (approximately 90 000 during 2001).[124] As Castles *et al.* note, geographic proximity shapes the flow from southeastern Europe into Austria and Germany, and from North Africa into Southern Europe, while language and colonial links help to explain the presence of francophone asylum seekers in Belgium and Nigerians in the UK.

However, some analysts have also suggested that economic conditions at destination play a significant part in affecting any choice of destination. For example, Zimmermann (1995) looks at asylum applications in ten EU countries, from four regions (Eastern Europe, North Africa and the Middle East, Sub-Saharan Africa and Asia) in each year from 1983 through 1992. Zimmerman reports that, controlling for the 1991 stock of residents within each host country from the same region as the asylum seekers to proxy for social network support, as well as controlling for geographic distance, economic differences between home and destination significantly contribute to the rate of asylum applications. The number of applications rises with the gap in real wage between origin and destination, and falls with the difference in the unemployment rate.[125] From this, Zimmermann (1995: 338) concludes, 'that asylum seekers and refugees are highly sensitive to differences in the economic conditions of potential host countries in the European Union. This does not, however, make them (illegal) economic migrants. It merely suggests that economic considerations play an important role in their choices.' A different approach would be necessary to distinguish whether the differences in employment opportunities, examined by Zimmermann, affect the total flow of asylum seekers to the EU, or merely their allocation among the EU member states. It would also seem plausible that, to the extent asylum seekers have any choice, they may also be swayed by the likelihood of recognition. As noted, this rate has varied considerably across countries and over time. In turn, the rate of recognition may be partly shaped by macroeconomic conditions in the receiving country, as well as political pressures.

The second link emphasizes economic development at origin, noting the potential for simultaneity between the likelihood of conflict and the state of economic development. For example, Collier and Hoeffler (1998: 72) examine the global incidence of civil wars from 1960 until 1992 and conclude that, 'The higher is per capita income on an internationally comparable measure, the lower is the risk of civil war', controlling for differences in natural resource endowments, ethno-linguistic fractionalization, and population size. The authors interpret this as a reflection of the higher opportunity cost of rebellion at higher income levels.[126] In a sequel paper, Collier (1999: 182) then looks at the economic consequences of civil wars and concludes that 'During civil wars GDP per capita declines at an annual rate of 2.2 percent relative to its counterfactual'. Moreover Collier finds that whether there is a peace dividend or a war overhang effect after the cessation of hostilities is mixed. On average his data indicate that shorter wars result in a continued decline in GDP at almost as rapid a rate as during the war, whereas longer wars which have resulted in deeper destruction of the capital stock are typically followed by periods of relative recovery. Taken together, these suggest that successful promotion of economic development may lower the incidence of civil wars which, in turn, aids long-term growth. Conversely, where conflicts can be prevented from erupting, economic prospects also appear brighter. Both economic development and avoidance of internal violence, which are intimately entwined, seem to lower migration pressures.[127]

2.4   CLOSING REMARKS

In each context of migration to the high income countries, irregular migration is prevalent. The US attempts to promote skilled migration, though increasingly on a temporary basis, yet unskilled irregular migration runs on a par with documented temporary admissions. The oil-rich countries of the Persian Gulf issue temporary visas to overseas contract workers, but there is active trading in these visas and abuse of the visa system, organized partially by recruiting agencies. Within East Asia, Japan and Korea both recognize the relatively large-scale presence of overstaying, unskilled workers and training schemes are thinly disguised mechanisms for circumventing controls. Even estimates for Singapore indicate escalating clandestine migration. Europe has passed through three phases of migration in the last three decades, from guest workers, to family reunification, to asylum seekers. The focus on temporary admission throughout, even for the recent programs intended to attract the highly skilled, has combined with low recognition rates among asylum seekers to encourage irregular migration. Controls do not prevent significant, irregular migration anywhere.

The extent and patterns of migration are not shaped by immigration controls alone. Migration pressures at source clearly influence the outcomes too. The current conventional wisdom has, at best, prematurely dismissed the effects of economic development at origin on the desire to move; at worst, these effects may have been misrepresented. Where a migration regime permits movement of relatively unskilled workers, economic development at origin apparently does serve to diminish migration pressures. This is particularly, and possibly only, true when the development strategy chosen in the sending nations serves to tighten labor markets at home.

The evidence indicates that lack of economic development in the sending countries indeed contributes to migration pressures, yet this by no means denies a role for other key explanatory factors. Despite the skepticism of critics, the evidence does indicate that asylum seekers and refugees are fleeing situations of conflict; violence which is both influenced by economic development and in turn prejudices development prospects.

The outcomes of these forces of controls and pressures vary substantively from regime to regime, with differing prospects for inducing or deterring economic development in the sending nations. The extent to which migrants are drawn from the developing regions, the skills of those migrants, the permanence of their movements, the accompaniment of families and participation of women in the migration process prove quite different. It is precisely these differences that are of central interest in the remainder of this book.

NOTES

1. UN (2002a), Wall Chart. Migrant stock here refers to mid-year estimates of people residing in countries other than where they were born, or of foreign citizens for those countries in which data on foreign-born population are not available. Refugees are included in the estimates of migrant stocks.

2. Hatton and Williamson, (2002: 2).

3. The stocks of non-nationals for France and the UK refer to 1999 and for Greece to 1998.

4. Note that the EU non-national populations exclude the foreign-born who have acquired local citizenship, whereas the global aggregate is raised by mixing measures of foreign-born as well as foreign national populations. During the 1990s approximately 3.4 million people acquired citizenship in an EU-15 member country. For comparison, in 2000 the US foreign-born population amounted to 11.1 percent of total population, whereas non-nationals comprised 6.3 percent of the total.

5. On the other hand, natural population growth in the EU is low with the result that net migration contributed almost two-thirds of total population expansion.

6. It should be recognized that the data reproduced in Table 2.2, and the summary comments in the text, are derived from sources that are not strictly comparable across the EU member states. In particular duration of residence necessary to be defined as part of the resident foreign population varies as does the ability to estimate the undocumented foreign population.

7. Acma (2002) estimates 3.9 million Turkish nationals living overseas, of whom more than 3.3 million are in the EU-15.

8. The source of the data is UN (2002b: Tables 3 and 5). 'The group of countries with economies in transition includes: Albania, Armenia, Azerbaijan, Belarus, Bosnia and Herzegovina, Bulgaria, Croatia, the Czech Republic, Estonia, Georgia, Hungary, Kazakhstan, Kyrgyzstan, Latvia, Lithuania, Poland, the Republic of Moldova, Romania, the Russian Federation, Slovakia, Slovenia, Tajikistan, the Former Yugoslavian Republic of Macedonia, Turkmenistan, Ukraine, Uzbekistan and Yugoslavia' (UN, 2002b: viii). The total for Western Europe in Figure 2.1 comprises Austria, Belgium, Denmark, Finland, France, Germany, Greece, Italy, Luxembourg, the Netherlands, Norway, Sweden, Switzerland and the UK.

9. See IOM (2002).

10. However, a part of this apparent migration simply reflects registration of de facto residents and, in addition, economic success has attracted a return home of former Czechoslovakian nationals.

11. UN (2002b). These estimates are according to foreign statistics, rather than national sources at origin. The two sets of reports often differ quite substantially though the foreign statistics appear more reliable.

12. See final subsection of Section 2.3 on forced migration and the recognition rates of asylum seekers.

13. 'Precise figures on Albanian immigrants are difficult to gather due to the potentially high number of non-declared (illegal) individuals either settled or working short time periods in the host countries. For example, officially 4300 Albanians were issued a residence permit in 1997 in Greece. But when the country adopted a regularisation programme (between November 1997 and May 1998) for undocumented immigrants, 239 000 Albanian immigrants applied' (De Coulon and Piracha, 2002: 3).

14. The data are extracted from Evans and Papps (1999) who report estimates from a study by Birks and Sinclair.

15. The gross migration data are derived principally from Wickramasekera (2002) and IOM (2000) but also from Chalamwong (2002), Go (2002), Hugo (1998), IOM (2003b) and Siddiqui (2003). Note, however, that although these official estimates, provided largely by home country government sources, are often considered indicative of the evolving patterns, the numbers are probably underestimates given the extent of undocumented movement (see Saith, 1989: 31; and UN, 2003). Data on recruitment from Pakistan after 1998 are rough approximations.

16. UN (2003: Table 35).

17. Yoo and Uh (2002).

18. UN, 2003.

19. UN (2003: Table 38).

20. IOM (2000: 63).

21. UN (2003: Table 28).

22. Indonesia (IOM, 2000; Hugo 2003a); Philippines (Go, 2002); Thailand (Scalabrini Migration Center, Asian Migration Atlas 2000 at http://www.scalabrini.asn.au/atlas/amatlas.htm).

23. US Census Bureau (2002a).

24. The US Census Bureau estimates that slightly over 25 percent of the total foreign-born population was born in Asia.

25. Data source for the upper panel is DeVoretz (2001). Canadian Immigration changed the major regional composition of data during the 1990s, so comparable data after 1996 are not readily available. Data for the lower panel are from OECD (2002) and refer to region of birth as opposed to region of last permanent residence in the upper panel.

26. Zlotnik (2003: 1).

27. Eurostat (2002) which does not provide a breakdown of the non-EU national population by gender.

28. Giubilaro (19979.

29. Estimate by Birks Sinclair, reproduced in Evans and Papps (1999).

30. UN (2003: Table 31).

31. Hugo (2002a: Table 37).

32. Sri Lanka Bureau of Foreign Employment at http://www.slbfe.lk/statisticsnew.html.

33. UN (2003: Table 31).

34. UN (2003: Table 30).

35. Data are from the Philippines Overseas Employment Administration at http://www.poea.gov.ph/html/statistics.html. See also Figure 3.2 on the increasing role of female overseas workers from Sri Lanka.

36. See ECRE (2001).

37. Immigration in Table 2.7 refers to persons entering 'with the intention of residing in the country for a certain period. This period varies from one month for a Dutch person returning to the Netherlands to twelve months for any person entering the United Kingdom' (Eurostat, 2002: 62). Asylum applications exclude people granted Temporary

Protection Status (numbering some 95 000 who arrived in Austria primarily from Bosnia-Herzegovina between 1992 and 1995, for example).

38. See Stalker (2002) for a recent review.

39. For more complete accounts, see (Shah 1998b), Evans and Papps (1999), IOM (2000) and UN (2003).

40. The sample is structured such that each cell (country of nationality by skill level) comprises 100 observations.

41. See Nair (1998: 272).

42. On the defraud and abuses of migrants from Asia, see Wickramasekera (2002), and ILO (1997) for a broader perspective.

43. See Nair (1998), Zacharia *et al.* (1999) and Chapter 9.

44. For an analysis of the economic efficiency implications of such trading, see Bivins and Krishna (2001).

45. Quoted in Nair (1998).

46. IOM (2000: 113).

47. See Evans and Papps (1999: 223).

48. Migrant workers also receive only very limited legal protection from abuse, deception and cheating. Wickramasekera (2002: 29), notes that 'neither major labour sending countries nor receiving countries in Asia have ratified ...the ILO Migration for Employment Convention ... [or] ... the ILO Migrant Workers Convention'.

49. These are weighted means of the figures reported by Shah (1998b: Table 2.1) for those arriving before the Iraqi invasion of Kuwait and those arriving after liberation. See also the information on duration of stay in Chapter 7.

50. See Nair (1998), who cites the results of a 1985 survey in Kerala.

51. Even so, almost the only permanent residents recognized in Japan are the result of a special category introduced in 1992 granting permanent residence to a group of Korean and Taiwanese nationals who had lost their Japanese nationality following the 1952 peace treaty but had continued to reside in Japan. Moreover the low rate of acquisition of Japanese citizenship is apparent in Table 2.8.

52. Yoo and Uh (2002).

53. See Yoo and Uh (2002), and UN (2003).

54. The efficacy of the new guest-worker program in Korea, initiated in March 2004, in limiting use of irregular migrant workers remains to be seen.

55. UN (2003).

56. See Hugo (1998), on irregular migration processes from East Indonesia and Lucas and Verry (1999).

57. See Hui (2001).

58. See Chalamwong (2002: Table 12.6).

59. US data from the US INS website at http://www.immigration.gov/. The apparent spike from 1989 through 1991 reflects a large surge in admittance of Mexican nationals under a normalization program. Canadian data from the Citizenship and Immigration Canada website at http://www.cic.gc.ca/ and Citizenship and Immigration Canada (2003a).

60. Temporary workers here refers to Temporary Workers and Trainees, Intracompany Transferees, and Professional Workers under the NAFTA and the Canada–US Free Trade Agreement. The INS does not report a data breakdown for 1997. On the other hand, only slightly over half of all immigrants were new arrivals; the remainder were those adjusting status, frequently having already been employed in the country on a temporary work visa or illegally. See Martin *et al.* (2000), on the vagaries of the US labor certification process in this context.

61. Admissions of highly skilled persons on H-1B visas dropped significantly in 2002, following the downturn in the information technology industry in the US.

62. Far more people have died attempting to cross the Mexico–US border than died on the Berlin Wall. On the use of employer sanctions in the US, see Martin and Miller (2000).

63. Hammar and Tamas (1997: 1). Freeman (1993: 444), poses the same question with respect to migration to the US from Mexico.

64. See for example, Lucas (1975), Long *et al.* (1988) and Hatton and Williamson (2002).

65. For a review, see Lucas (2001b).

66. This may be less true of some of the other costs involved in relocating, such as the fees typically paid for permits and to recruiters, but these costs are less clearly tied to distance. See Chapter 9.

67. For an elaboration, see Malmberg (1997).

68. These ideas are well expressed in the context of internal migration in Molho (1995).

69. See Munshi (2003), on distinguishing these two processes in the context of Mexican migration to the US.

70. O'Neil (2003a: 2). See also the conclusions of a study commissioned by the Danish Ministry of Foreign Affairs in Nyberg-Sørensen *et al.* (2002).

71. Commission for the Study of International Migration and Cooperative Economic Development (1991: 241).

72. Asencio (1991: viii).

73. UK Government (2004: 20– 21).

74. UK Government (2004: 83).

75. For a clear exposition in the context of international migration, see Venables (1999).

76. For a more complete exposition, see Martin and Taylor (1996) Philip Martin (2001) or Hatton and Williamson (2002).

77. See Lucas (1999), for calculations of the implied turning points.

78. This refers to the fixed effects estimates in Tables 2 and 3 in Vogler and Rotte (2000).

79. This approach assumes that inequality and economic growth may be treated independently. In practice, however, there appears to be a two-way dependence; inequality affects growth and growth affects inequality, with evidence that both patterns may themselves be nonlinear, see Lucas and Salem (2002).

80. The data on net migration are from the UN Population Division, Department of Economic and Social Affairs website: http://www.un.org/esa/population/unpop. htm. This measure of net migration is derived largely as a residual after subtracting estimated natural population increase from overall population growth. The data on GDP per capita are expressed in purchasing power parity equivalent US dollars and taken from UNDP (2002). Figure 2.9 omits two extreme outliers, Rwanda and Luxembourg, to improve legibility of the remaining data. See also Fischer *et al.* (1997b) who present a similar view in their Figure 4.1 though based on net stock of migrant data and encompassing only the major immigration and emigration countries.

81. This is a fairly parsimonious regression, estimated in piecewise linear form by ordinary least squares. Splines are included at log GDP values of 6, 7, 8, 9 and 10.5. Statistical tests are based on heteroskedasticity robust standard error estimates.

82. Hatton and Williamson (2002) explore a much more detailed, multivariate model based on net migration data for a smaller sample of 80 countries but covering 1970 through 2000 to conclude (p. 23), 'Africa is the only region where the overall effect of a rise in home income is negative for net immigration.' Adams and Page (2003a) estimate a statistically significant migration hump in the stock of migrants from some seventy developing and transition economies, relative to home country population, present in the US and OECD European countries. However, in this case the lower arm of the hump appears to result from

inclusion of a large number of zero migration cases which may either reflect limitations of the OECD data deployed or that migration is to non-OECD higher income countries. See the discussion in Lucas (forthcoming).

83. See Chapter 9.

84. See the discussion in Lucas (1997).

85. See Lucas and Stark (1985).

86. Berman and Rzakhanov (2000) consider the selectivity of emigration of Soviet Jews and of immigration to the US in terms of planned fertility, in light of such inter-generational altruism

87. See Faini *et al.* (1997) on the role of joint decisions in affecting south–north migration in Italy.

88. Massey *et al.* (1998: 125).

89. It is important to distinguish between the level of migration occurring at any given wage differential versus the effect of a widening gap in inducing additional migration. The two issues are quite distinct. In opening to legal migration, where none has existed before, the extent of migration likely to be induced at the prevailing wage differential is indeed of interest. However, thereafter, it is the responsiveness of additional migration to changes in earnings opportunities that is more relevant to policies that may affect labor market performance.

90. On the other hand, although this effect is not small, it is statistically quite weak for Portugal and Turkey.

91. See Safir (1999) for a summary including earlier migrations.

92. Giubilaro (1996: graph 7.1) brings out how dramatic was the decline in worker migration from the Maghreb region after 1974, but also records a sharp rise in migration of family members after this date.

93. The IMF does not report unemployment rates for Tunisia. However, Giubilaro (1997) notes that even in Tunisia unemployment was a growing concern by the early 1990s.

94. More broadly throughout the whole of Europe, Bourchachen (2001) reports 1.31 million Moroccans as of 1995; slightly more than half of whom are in France, and another 44 percent scattered throughout the Netherlands, Belgium, Spain, Italy and Germany.

95. Note that the stock of foreign nationals excludes those who have become citizens of the host country. In Germany the rate of acquisition of German citizenship among former Turkish nationals accelerated dramatically during the 1990s, from 3529 in 1991 to 82 861 in 2000. (OECD, 2002).

96. IOM (2000).

97. UN (2002b: 1).

98. The South African Chamber of Mines has deployed a system of temporary international labor recruitment not dissimilar to that in the Gulf. In the South African context, centralization of recruiting played an important role in keeping down labor costs by not bidding up wages through over-recruitment, precisely because migration streams proved responsive to wage differentials see Lucas (1987).

99. An exception is provided by Kandil and Metwally (1992) who demonstrate that migration from Egypt to the Gulf indeed proved sensitive to income differentials from 1966 to 1986.

100. See UN (2003) and Seccombe (1988).

101. See the discussion in UN (2003: 63).

102. The brief period of observation on recruitment from Korea is omitted from this analysis. More precisely, this regression analysis uses fixed effects with different intercepts and time trends permitted in each of the seven sending countries. Observations after 1998 are omitted for lack of reliable data on Pakistan.

103. For a theoretical exposition see Fields (1994). For empirical evidence see Abella (1995) or Athukorala and Manning (1999).

104. Iguchi (2002).

105. Athukorala and Manning (1999: 175).

106. http://www.un.org/esa/population/unpop. htm.

107. Chalamwong (2002).

108. Go (2002). See also Saith (1997).

109. Lucas (2001a).

110. Fallon and Lucas (2002).

111. Feng (2002).

112. For example, the Korean Ministry of Justice estimates that there were some 43 000 registered workers from China in Korea in 2000 and about 69 000 Chinese who had overstayed their visas in 1999. The majority of both groups are Chinese of Korean ancestry.

113. Lucas (2001a).

114. Loi (2002).

115. See the review of evidence in Massey *et al.* (1998).

116. See, respectively, Blejer *et al.* (1978) on the flow of legal and illegal migrants from Mexico; Bean *et al.* (1990) on border apprehensions; Taylor (1987) on discrete migration decisions by Mexican villagers, Hatton and Willamson (1992) on historical immigration; and Lucas (1975) on applications for labor certification from 103 countries. Massey *et al.* (1998) provide an excellent survey.

117. Freeman's observations are based on estimates for international migration by Borjas, 1987, and on internal migration by Barro and Sala-i-Martin (1992).

118. Similarly, whether the wage gap or difference in employment rates has the larger effect is largely moot in this context, as is the issue of whether migration disappears only in the absence of (expected) wage differences. See, however, the discussion in Massey *et al.* (1998).

119. Notice, however, the danger in interpreting tighter labor markets in terms of wages (or employment) alone. For example, attempts to raise wages through minimum wage legislation do not signify tighter labor markets; indeed the additional unemployment which typically results may nullify or even exacerbate out-migration despite higher wages. See the discussion of the effect of raising the minimum wage in Puerto Rico in Castillo-Freeman and Freeman (1992).

120. UNHCR (2001) and ECRE (2003).

121. The recognition rate is the number of applications recognized under the 1951 Convention as a percent of recognitions, plus rejections, plus those allowed to remain by default.

122. This estimate is very approximate, being derived from UNHCR data cross-classifying refugees by country of asylum and origin, in which Greece, Ireland, Luxembourg, Portugal and Spain are omitted from the former.

123. Castles *et al.* (2003: 22).

124. UNHCR (2002).

125. Zimmermann (1995) also notes that applications rise with the relative size of the host country labor market, though it is less clear how to interpret the role of this controlling factor.

126. In the context of Yugoslavia, Schierup (1993) argues that economic disintegration helped to precipitate the conflict.

127. Violent conflict can disrupt migration inflows as well as adding to outflows. For example,

Evans and Papps (1999) note an initial slight slowing of recruitment to the Gulf at the time of the Gulf War, followed by an acceleration because of an increased concern to reduce dependence on Arab workers and thereby to reduce settlement rates. However, any such dip in recruitment is not statistically observable in the annual data in Figure 2.3, controlling for incomes at home and trend effects.

PART B

Consequences for Economic Development in the Countries of Origin

3. Labor Market Responses to Emigration

Virtually all of the evidence indicates that tighter labor markets at home discourage departure. Does departure of international migrants also result in tighter labor markets for people who are left behind? Are wages raised or unemployment diminished in the home country and, if so, for whom?

There are a number of reasons why these are important questions. First, if departure tightens domestic labor markets this is likely to reduce further migration pressures, perhaps ultimately generating a self-limiting process. Second, the political economy of home country support for strategies to encourage or discourage migrant departures is very much influenced by the impact on labor costs for domestic employers. Third, and perhaps most importantly, for the majority of families who depend largely upon labor incomes for their livelihoods, who gains and who loses in the ensuing labor market adjustments is obviously a critical question.

Given the potential importance of these factors it is rather surprising that investigation of labor market responses to emigration remains almost entirely neglected in the empirical literature. This omission is particularly curious in view of the vast amount of attention that has been devoted to examining the counterpart issue, the effects of immigration on host country labor markets.[1] The omission is all the more remarkable, given that labor market responses to emigration can be far from straightforward. Neither a vision of removing surplus labor, reducing under-employment by the extent of emigration, nor a presumption that wages are driven up by increased competition for all who remain at home, is generally tenable. The first section of this chapter consequently takes time to sketch some of the more important factors in potential labor market adjustments to emigration, before turning to the experiences in some of the case study areas in Section 3.2.

3.1 A SKETCH OF THE ISSUES

The nature of labor markets and how they respond to change and shock are far from uniform. No one would expect identical labor market responses to emigration in China and the Philippines, in Pakistan and South Africa, in

Sri Lanka and Albania. For one thing, the composition of emigration is very different across these settings. In addition, however, there are substantive contrasts in the nature of the labor markets. For example, the extent to which wages adjust quickly to shocks or prove more rigid under collective bargaining and state intervention matters, as do the state of unemployment or under-employment and the degree of segmentation between skilled and less skilled workers, between ethnic groups, or between urban and rural workers. In sketching how some of these differences shape labor market responses to emigration, an obvious place to begin is with emigrant withdrawal and the effects on the labor supply.

Labor Supply Responses

Emigration, even of working age adults, does not necessarily mean a commensurate decline in the size of the domestic labor force. First, by no means all working age adults who emigrate are in the labor force prior to departure. In some contexts, as we shall see, housewives emigrate to take up work abroad; similarly students often emigrate directly upon leaving the educational system. Second, emigration may induce new people to enter the labor force: an encouraged worker effect. For instance, if emigrants vacate jobs upon leaving, those empty posts may tempt new people to seek work. Even if the emigrants were unemployed prior to departure, the reduction in the length of the queue for jobs may induce new labor market entry. On the other hand, a potentially important counter-force to this may arise from remittances sent home by migrants; by supporting the family at home these transfers can obviate the need to work.[2] Thus, although labor supply is usually reduced by emigration the effect is unlikely to be a one-for-one reduction in the aggregate workforce; the overall labor supply reductions may either overshoot or fall short of the number of people leaving

In the short run, the changes in composition of labor supply resulting from emigration may be even more important than the change in the aggregate workforce level. However, as time goes by, some substitution often proves possible to replace departing workers, both in terms of occupational categories and in given locations. Replacing carpenters recruited for construction in the Middle East may require training and time, depending upon the reserve pool of carpenters at home. On the other hand, replacing a general laborer is easier, while replacing a surgeon is far more difficult. Instances of emigration of highly skilled persons inducing replacement immigration from a third country are not uncommon and, over time, the departure of the highly skilled may induce more extended schooling among the nest generation remaining at home.[3] Thus some adjustments to supply of specific categories of labor are possible, and more so as time goes by.

The issue of spatial substitution arises because emigrants are normally drawn from highly concentrated geographic settings, from specific regions and even from some villages and not others within a region. Whereas the majority of emigrants come from urban settings in some countries, elsewhere most migrants leave directly from rural areas. This raises an important question of how highly localized are the labor market responses to emigration, which in turn depends very much on the degree of integration of spatially separated labor markets and hence on the links between internal and international migration. Mass departure of agricultural laborers from one region may induce movement from neighboring areas; departure from metropolitan areas may induce further rural–urban migration. Indeed other links between international and internal migration are common too, such as the use of remittances to finance a family move into town and the tendency of some returning emigrants to prefer an urban location rather than resettling in the home village. All of these factors contribute to shifting labor supplies between locations.

Wage and Unemployment Responses

Where labor supply is reduced through emigration, in the aggregate or within occupational categories and specific locations, one might reasonably expect tighter labor markets to ensue. If there is significant unemployment prevailing in the specific job market for that occupation and location, departure of emigrants (or departure to replace emigrants from elsewhere) will generally serve to shorten the queue for work. When labor shortages emerge, wages will normally begin to rise for that category of worker.

Unfortunately, economic theory teaches us that things may not be quite so simple. Many other adjustments may accompany the reduced labor supplies, offering a truly bewildering array of possibilities. One of the key components is the nature of substitution or complementarity among productive inputs. If skilled workers emigrate does this raise or lower the domestic demand for less skilled workers? There is no unique answer, because much depends upon the technology involved and possibly the institutional setting. If doctors emigrate are the duties and demands on nurses increased or do nurses become redundant without doctors? If tractor drivers are hired overseas to drive on construction sites, will the demand for general agricultural laborers rise to replace tractor operations with manual work, or fall because general laborers are ineffective without tractors to plough? In either event the effect on agricultural prices and hence production may dominate, lowering the demand for agricultural laborers.

Another key assumption in the plethora of hypothesized effects is the degree of openness of the economy to international trade. Indeed, some early models of international trade even suggest that no changes in wages need accompany emigration: the patterns of trade do the adjusting instead.[4] According to this view, reduction in supply of a particular type of labor will simply lead to diminished production of items that use this type of labor intensively, fully off-setting the departure without resort to wage adjustments. However, while some adjustment in production patterns may be induced by emigration, to have labor markets clearing without any adjustment to wages proves very sensitive to the precise assumptions of these models. Most particularly, the story with respect to absence of any wage adjustment is a long-run proposition, in which investments can be transferred from declining to newly expanding sectors; in the shorter run, the impact of emigration on local labor markets remains a very viable force.

Davies and Wooton (1992) explore the theoretical impact of international migration on wages and income distribution within a long-run framework in an economy which is open to international trade. Three productive inputs are recognized: capital, skilled labor and unskilled labor. Following a terminology introduced by Ruffin (1981), any pair of these inputs are called 'friends' if an increase in the cost of one input increases demand for the other; otherwise they are termed 'enemies'. Davies and Wooton consider a context in which trade patterns do not adjust sufficiently to re-establish the initial wage patterns after emigration, even in the long run.[5] If skilled and unskilled labor are 'enemies' then emigration of skilled workers harms unskilled workers. On the other hand, if skilled and unskilled labor are 'friends' then departure of either category will enhance the pay of both. Thus, the nature of substitution or complementarity among productive inputs again becomes a controlling feature despite the context of an open economy in the long run.[6]

Most of this trade-related literature presumes that domestic labor markets are well integrated, leaving fairly uniform levels of pay for any class of worker no matter where they live. Thus, if urban workers emigrate then the wages of rural laborers also rise as a result of induced rural urban migration. Yet in reality wages in more remote locations may well prove far less than fully responsive to wage increments in the capital region, raising important issues with respect to any trickle-down effect from emigration.

Lastly, before leaving this brief diversion into the realm of economic theory, two additional, potentially important components may be mentioned. In the context of internal migration a puzzle sometimes emerges when average wages are actually observed falling as out-migration proceeds. At least two types of explanation may be offered for this apparent contradiction. First, reduced spending levels in the area of out-migration may depress labor markets through demand deficiencies; thus wages may fall in an area (or even country) from which emigrants are drawn if a significant cut in local spending occurs. Second, scale economies may actually raise the productivity of workers in more concentrated settings; in particular, the reduction in colleagues with whom to interact locally may lower the contribution of various professionals and hence their pay.

Capital Intensity and Output Responses

Where labor costs are driven up by emigration, businesses and farmers are likely to respond by adopting more capital-intensive techniques of production. In itself, this is certainly not a problem, but the issue has arisen in some contexts as to whether this shift toward capital intensity proves reversible in the face of return migration.[7] A second area of concern is the overall output effect of labor withdrawal through emigration. Some strong assertions have been common in this regard, presuming that emigration of surplus labor leaves domestic production unaffected in the presence of unemployed labor. Given the potential for induced shifts of labor when confronted with shorter queues for jobs, neither the mere presence of unemployment nor even emigration of unemployed workers is sufficient to guarantee such an absence of domestic output loss. On the other hand:

> This question has all too frequently been analysed at the level of the migrant's household where, not surprisingly, it is often found that domestically generated earnings drop. In agricultural households less land is found to be cultivated with a parallel drop in household-level output and income. Others have frequently made the assumption that the migrant's wages, prior to his/her exit, provide the measure of the loss of output. Such deductions are, of course, untenable. The land given up by the family of the migrant farmer might now be cultivated by some other rural household ... Similarly, where there is substantial unemployment, and/or labour substitution, the migrant's wages would be earned now by some previously unemployed worker. (Saith, 1989: 39)

Summing Up

In the end, economic theory offers few unambiguous hypothesized effects of emigration upon local labor markets. Emigration probably does reduce labor supply overall, and more specifically reduces the availability of the departing labor categories, even in the longer run. Whether this results in increased wages or diminished unemployment in the market for workers, similar to those who are leaving depends upon institutional barriers to wage flexibility in that particular market, upon the prevalence of surplus labor of this type, the role of international trade in the relevant product markets, ability of others to rapidly acquire skills or relocate residence to take up vacated positions, and the passage of time. The cross-market effects are even more ambiguous: little can be said a priori about the effects of skilled labor departure on wages or employment of the less skilled, or about the consequences of emigration from one region for trickle-down gains elsewhere. Suffice to say that in the end the responses across the many differentiated domestic labor markets impacted by substantial emigration are almost impossible to characterize a priori. Evidence is clearly required.

3.2   EVIDENCE IN THE CASE STUDY AREAS

Unfortunately, as noted in the introduction to this chapter, the available evidence on home country labor market responses to emigration is remarkably scant. Moreover, careful analysis is ultimately required to disentangle the effects, for it is likely that migration affects wages and unemployment while labor market tightness simultaneously affects migration. Identifying these two effects can be difficult. Nonetheless, some insights can be gleaned from studies and data on some of the principal countries of emigration, even in the absence of such systematic analyses, because the two effects act in opposite directions. Any effect of migrant departure on local wages is likely to result in a positive association, while the effects of local labor market tightness on migration suggest a negative association. In the following review of evidence from some of the case study countries, the extent and composition of migrant labor departure is therefore briefly characterized and any association between relevant wage movements and migration sought.[8]

Pakistan

According to government estimates, there are about 3.2 million Pakistani nationals abroad, about half of these being in the Middle East, a million in Europe (mostly in the UK) and 600 000 in North America.[9] 'Emigration to the developed countries has, by and large, involved young men from better off and upwardly mobile families and communities . . . some of them are highly skilled and sought after professionals . . . while others are unskilled labourers. What they do share, however, is at least 12 years of schooling and, in this regard, they are from among the top one-seventh of Pakistan's population.'[10] However, it has been the migration to the Gulf that has attracted most of the attention.

Between 1978 and 1983 almost a quarter of the net addition to the labor force found employment abroad, principally in the Gulf. Over the next few years, partly as a reflection of declining oil prices, recruitment to the Gulf from Pakistan fell and return migration dominated the outflow, though more recently migration has again returned to a net outflow (part of which is now undocumented migration to East Asia).[11]

Most estimates indicate that no more than seven percent of Pakistan's labour force ever worked overseas at any one time. Even when migration was at its height, many more workers entered the domestic labour force each year than were able to find employment abroad. At best, migration would seem to have made only a modest contribution toward reducing domestic unemployment. In fact, Pakistan's labour markets underwent a more complex series of changes. (Addleton, 1992: 168)

Among the *Pakistani workers registered going abroad* from 1971 to 1996, most of whom went to the Gulf, about 95 percent were ages 25 to 40, and 99.06 percent were male. An estimate for migrants leaving during the 1970s indicated that 59 percent were married prior to leaving.[12] In terms of location of origin, 'The 1981 population census indicated that 83 percent of all migrants were from rural areas'[13] and, in particular, 'Migrant workers have always come disproportionately from *barani* [rain-fed cultivation] areas of the NWFP [North West Frontier Province] and Punjab, regions with relatively sparse populations and limited economic opportunity.'[14]

During the period from 1977–85 less than 2 percent of migrants went to work in professional or managerial positions in the Gulf, nearly a half were general laborers and the remainder entered a variety of skilled jobs.[15] In particular, nearly 18 percent of emigrating workers during this period were masons, carpenters and electricians heading for construction projects in the Middle East. Two studies from the early 1980s estimate that 3–5 percent of the migrants were unemployed before leaving. However, Azam (1986) notes that the average duration of unemployment before migration was only three months which, as he points out in a later contribution, suggests that it did not reflect the actual unemployment, but rather the time required in some cases for transition from the domestic job to the overseas employment.[16]

The withdrawal of these workers began to put upward pressure on wages, and especially on the wages of skilled construction workers. From Figure 3.1 it is clear that the real wages of masons have tracked overseas departures remarkably closely.[17] This association reflects not only the initial surge of migration in the 1970s and the subsequent decline through the early 1980s, but also the revival of emigration thereafter, and the association has continued to be significant even during the 1990s. Mahmood (1990) explores the roles of various productive inputs to the construction sector in Pakistan and concludes that in the short run, unskilled workers would be displaced from the construction sector by the departure of their skilled counterparts. However, in the longer run, as more capital-intensive methods are adopted, the demands for unskilled workers in the construction sector would actually be enhanced. In the balance, as Addleton (1992: 177) notes, 'Remarkably, unskilled wage labour also benefited.' Although the index of the real wage for unskilled construction workers in Figure 3.1 overall shows a much weaker association with the rate of labor departure, at least after 1980 the wages of unskilled workers in construction began to track those of their skilled counterparts quite closely. Despite the fact that 'Unskilled emigrants … went mostly from the construction sector',[18] the very partial data do suggest a substantial increase in real wages of unskilled workers both in agriculture and

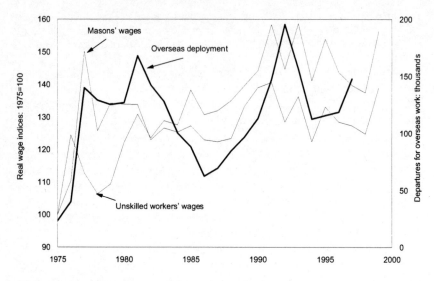

Figure 3.1   Real wages of construction workers in Lahore and deployment of Pakistani workers overseas, 1975–99

in manufacturing from 1970 through 1983, although the real value of skilled workers' earnings remained unaltered during this same interval.[19] Moreover, at least from 1985 through 1996, the correlation coefficient between the growth in real wages of agricultural casual workers and those of unskilled workers in construction remained at over 0.6.[20] There is, thus, evidence consistent with considerable pass through of wage increments beyond the construction sector alone resulting from the mass migration to the Gulf.

Indeed, although most of the migrants were from rural areas and virtually all were male, 'The impact of labour migration on employment was not confined simply to the departure of male workers to the Middle East. On the contrary, women and children also withdrew from the formal labour force – in the case of women to the home, where they were not engaged in wage employment; and in the case of children to school.'[21] Moreover, 'emigration to the Middle East appears to be the most potent factor that seems to have lowered rural–urban migration in 1972–1981'.[22]

Thus, migration to the Gulf has affected the construction sector in Pakistan, apparently serving to raise real wages of skilled construction artisans and possibly helping to enhance wages of unskilled construction workers too. More general impacts are difficult to discern, though some wider shifts in the labor force appear to have been induced, especially reductions in the rate of urbanization, and there is some evidence consistent with a positive impact on unskilled workers beyond the construction sector.

Sri Lanka

From Sri Lanka the trickle of permanent settlers moving to the OECD countries and of Tamils seeking asylum are dwarfed by the movements of contract workers in recent years. By 2002, the stock of Sri Lankan contract workers overseas amounted to 970 000, more than 14 percent of the labor force.[23] Of the stock of overseas workers in 2002, three-quarters were in the six GCC states, another 12 percent in Jordan and Lebanon, and 60 000 in Italy. This stock estimate for 2002 represents an increase of 94 percent over the stock in 1995 and more than a three-fold increase over the stock in 1990.

Figure 3.2 presents estimates of the total outflow of migrant workers from 1976 to 2002 and the gender mix after 1986.[24] The number of migrants, and of women in particular, has clearly risen during the 1990s. By 2002 70 percent of the stock of workers overseas were females.[25] The occupational composition of foreign employment taken up by those going overseas from 1996 to 2002 is illustrated in Figure 3.3.[26] Nearly 90 percent of the women went as housemaids or as unskilled workers, whereas 44 percent of the men went as unskilled workers and an additional 42 percent were skilled. Among professionals, middle level and clerical workers, 84 percent were male.

Papanek (2003: 16, 18) maintains that 'Migration to the Gulf States and elsewhere reduced the labor supply and the pressure on wages of a large number of unemployed ... Migration contributed to rising wages for women during the period when it increased most rapidly.' On the other hand,

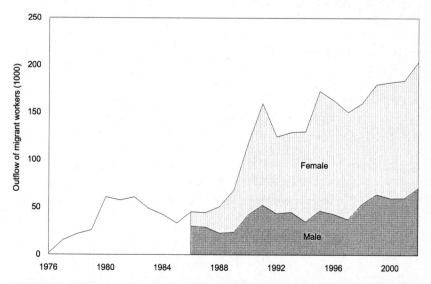

Figure 3.2   Estimated outflow of migrant workers from Sri Lanka by gender, 1976–2002

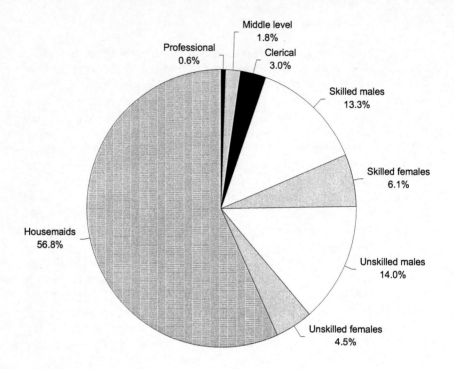

Figure 3.3   Departures from Sri Lanka for foreign employment by manpower level and gender, 1996–2002

Gunatilleke argues that 'As the majority of these [housemaid] migrants have not been in the labour market, and are unlikely to enter the labour market on their return, their migration may have no significant impact on the labour market and the labour force. According to surveys, only about 15 percent had been employed or were seeking employment prior to migration.'[27] Real wage developments in Sri Lanka from 1976 through 2001 are illustrated in Figure 3.4.[28] During the 1980s, the real wages of females on the tea plantations and of men in construction indeed rose at the same time that migration was growing. However, since the early 1990s both sets of wages have declined in real terms and migration has grown rapidly. Similarly, although not shown in the figure, real wages of both genders in manufacturing stagnated in the first half of the 1990s then fell after 1995, despite moderate overall growth, and wages of men on tea plantations have moved in parallel with those of women throughout. Forces other than migration have been the main factors in shaping wage developments in Sri Lanka. Indeed, it is quite probable that the declining wages at home, albeit offset by a small reduction in the unemployment rate, have contributed to the escalation in overseas migration.

Figure 3.4   Real wages in Sri Lanka, 1976–2001 (1995 rupees per day)

The Philippines

The Philippines has one of the highest rates of out-migration in the world. According to estimates by the Commission on Filipinos Overseas as of the end of 2001 there were 7.4 million Filipinos overseas, or nearly 10 percent of the population. Of these 2.5 million were reported by the Commission to be in the US, 1.4 million in the Middle East, 1.3 million in East and South Asia, and three-quarters of a million in Europe. Estimates from the US Census Bureau suggest a substantially smaller number of Filipinos in the US but, whatever the figure, most of the adults are college educated and the majority is female. To the implications of the departure of this highly skilled group, Chapter 4 on the brain drain returns. Meanwhile, in the present context, the focus is on the Filipino overseas workers.

Saith (1997) estimates that most families in the Philippines that reported income from abroad as their main source of support in the 1988 Family Income and Expenditure Survey were urban-based. As a result, 8.35 percent of urban families reported such dependence whereas the comparable rural figure was 4.18 percent. From similar 1991 data, Saith also estimates that the incidence of migration was highest from four regions, the National Capital Region, Ilocos, Southern Tagalog and Central Luzon all of which are on the main Luzon island and relatively prosperous, though substantially higher portions of women migrants came from lower income regions.

Figure 3.5 shows that from 1992 to 1999, 57 percent of the newly hired, land-based overseas workers leaving the Philippines were women.[29] The largest group of women went as domestic helpers, followed by entertainers and various service workers while 70 percent of the men went as production workers. In addition, sea-based workers (predominantly male) represented 23 percent of the total workers deployed overseas during the same period. At least from an early study in 1983, Tan and Canlas (1989) show that the majority of workers reported the same broad occupational category for their employment prior to departure as overseas.

The massive migration of overseas workers from 1980–2000 took place from a domestic labor market characterized by a high rate of unemployment, estimated by the National Statistics Office to have averaged nearly 10 percent from 1980 to 2000 with no discernible trend. Given this extent of slack in the domestic labor market and the ease with which the skills of most of the departing workers could be replaced through on-the-job training, Tan and Canlas (1989: 245) argue that labor markets are likely to prove very flexible in replacing departing workers overseas, nonetheless 'the effect of an increase in demand for labour abroad is to raise current wage relative to normal or permanent wage rate. This will then induce an increase in the labour supply.'

In fact, as Figure 3.6 illustrates, real wages in manufacturing indeed tracked deployment overseas remarkably closely, particularly in view of the

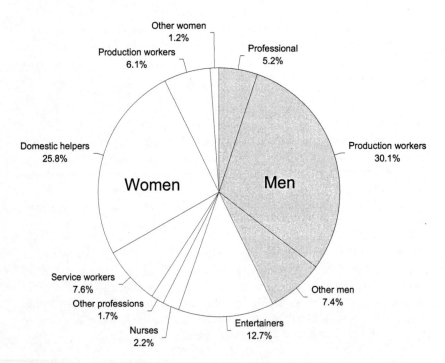

Figure 3.5   Deployed new hires from the Philippines by major occupation, 1992–99

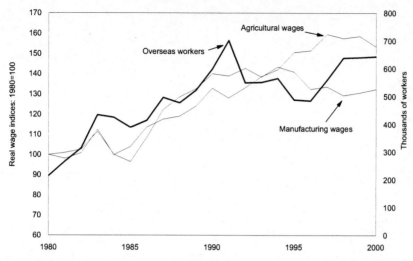

Figure 3.6   Real wages and land-based workers deployed overseas: the Philippines, 1980–2000

persistent unemployment, at least from 1980 until the mid-1990s, though the East Asia crisis clearly hurt manufacturing wages thereafter.[30] Saith (1997) notes the link that has also occurred between international and internal migration within the Philippines. While most overseas workers, at least amongst the men, have been drawn from the higher income regions on Luzon island, internal migration has occurred simultaneously from the lower income into the higher income regions. Saith points out that there is little evidence to indicate that this is a process of step migration: the poorer internal migrants do not subsequently emigrate from Luzon. Nonetheless Saith expresses skepticism of any substantial trickle-down effect as a result of the simultaneous migration processes. Thus, whereas real wages in agriculture showed an upward trend from 1980 until the onset of the crisis in 1998, the year-to-year growth in real agricultural wages was not correlated with growth in overseas deployment.

Albania

In Albania, job losses in the state sector spawned rapidly declining employment in the first two years after 1990 (see Figure 3.7).[31] By 1992, the number of people who were registered as unemployed amounted to 26.5 percent of the estimated domestic labor force (excluding emigrants). Employment in the private sector has expanded rapidly, largely as a result of the privatization of agriculture; thus, based on data from the Albanian Institute of Statistics, Çuka *et al.* (2003) estimate that private sector employment rose from a

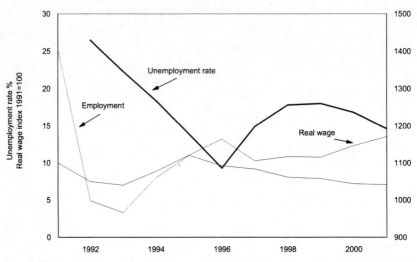

Figure 3.7   Employment, unemployment and real wages: Albania, 1991–2001

quarter of total employment in 1992 to nearly 80 percent in 1997. However, total employment has failed to recover its 1990 levels. Only approximate indications of real wage developments in Albania can be gleaned, but the estimates in Figure 3.7 suggest both a drop in earnings immediately after the transition process started and another drop following the collapse of the pyramid scheme in 1997 when inflation accelerated and undermined nominal wages.

In this process of transition in the Albanian labor markets emigration has played an important part. In the absence of an emigration alternative there can be little doubt that domestic unemployment and downward pressure on the newly emergent private sector wages would have been considerably sharper. In the transition from state to private employment a significant portion of workers emigrated rather than continuing a job search at home and 'working abroad for a period allows an emigrant to build up savings, which can then be used to finance new investment and job opportunities after returning'.[32] More particularly, in the Albanian context, two aspects of the role of emigrant finances in the job market transition emerge: first is the ability to afford a move into the urban areas, both for family members left at home and for the returning migrant; second is the establishment of small businesses financed by remittances or set up by returning migrants though it seems these businesses have not created much employment beyond that of the family operators themselves.[33]

3.3 TOWARDS CONCLUSIONS

Despite the importance of the impact of emigration on the labor market experiences of those left behind, remarkably little systematic evidence has been amassed in prior studies. Although drawing any general conclusions would require a good deal of speculation, perhaps two categories of cases may be discerned from the sketch of issues and evidence presented here.

The first is the set of countries where departing workers are indeed easily replaced with no discernible loss in output or rise in wages at home. This may occur where emigration is very small in relation to the overall labor market, where those departing were previously unemployed, or where departing employed workers are easily replaced through migration or training without significant decline in worker quality. Thus, in summarizing a series of studies on migration to the Persian Gulf during the 1980s, Amjad (1989: 9, 10) notes:

> Given the existing high levels of underemployment and unemployment in almost all of the major Asian labour exporting countries, migration to the Middle East has had no obvious unfavourable impact on output or output growth ... Only in the case of a few industries, especially construction, did some of the major labour exporting countries face skill shortages. But these were quickly overcome given the short gestation period for skill replacement.

For example, within this project Mahmud (1989) cites a study of Bangladesh by Islam *et al.* (1987) which,

> shows that migration has in fact led to a shortage of local agricultural labour, and this gap is being filled up by a process of internal migration from nearby regions. [There are in, in fact, several contributing factors for this labour shortage, namely the departure of migrants, the subsequent withdrawal of the returning migrants and their dependents from agricultural work, and the rapid increase in local non-farm employment in construction and services.] As a result, there has been some localised increase in agricultural wages, but this may only reflect the cost of labour relocation.[34]

Certainly on India, Nayyar (1994: 69) presumes an absence of any impact: 'Given the magnitude of labour outflows and the reservoir of surplus labour, it would be reasonable to infer that the impact of the withdrawal of labour, if any, on output in India would have been negligible', and on Indonesia Nayyar (1997: 15) again surmises precisely the same. Moreover, from the review of the case of Sri Lanka in Section 3 there is no obvious association between the increase in overseas labor recruiting and the evolution of real wages over time either of Sri Lankan women on tea plantations or of men in construction.

A second set of cases is situations where significant upward pressure on wages is indeed discernible. To some extent Pakistan appears to fit into this setting, given the fairly clear connection between wages of skilled construction workers and emigration to the Gulf, a connection which has continued over the last three decades, and there are weaker indications that wages of unskilled construction workers and possibly of agricultural workers may also have been enhanced.[35] Similarly, real wages in the Philippines appear to have responded remarkably closely to out-migration. This is notably true in Philippine manufacturing, though any trickle-down effect on agricultural wages appears weak in this context, in part because less recruiting takes place from lower income agricultural areas than in Pakistan. Indeed, it is tempting to speculate from the closeness with which manufacturing wages in the Philippines track overseas deployment, despite sustained high unemployment, that in essence the overseas and domestic labor markets on Luzon have become very closely integrated. On a more global basis, the tiny selection of empirical studies of emigration impacts on home country labor markets offer additional examples of this second type. For example, Mishra (2003) finds a strong, positive effect of migration of Mexican workers to the US upon wages in Mexico between 1960 and 1990 and Lucas (1987) found a positive effect of mine labor migration to South Africa on wages in both Malawi and Mozambique.

No matter whether emigration thus results in tighter labor markets by replacing emigrants with under-employed or unemployed people without significant wage increments as in the first set of countries, or whether wages are drawn up through emigration as in the second set, both types of examples appear to indicate labor market gains for those who remain at home. The experience of Albania even suggests the possibility that emigration may serve a positive role in job creation, in that case by easing the transition to private sector employment. Yet, as Stahl and Habib (1991: 166, 168) note there is a less positive possibility:

> Basically, the argument is that labor emigration may actually contribute to unemployment as a result of the contraction of productive activities caused by the loss of irreplaceable or difficult to replace emigrant workers ... However, this pessimistic view of the labor market consequences of exporting labor hinges on the assumption that emigrating workers are very difficult to replace. At least in the context of the overpopulated, labor abundant countries of Asia, where highly educated persons often find employment difficult to obtain, it is unlikely that the emigration of skilled manpower is having a decisively detrimental developmental effect.

But that is the subject of the following chapter.

NOTES

1. See, for example, the surveys in Borjas (1994), Friedberg and Hunt (1995), Lalonde and Topel (1997).
2. The issue of labor supply among returning migrants is taken up in Chapter 7.
3. See the evidence and discussion of this issue in Chapter 4.
4. See Rybczynski (1955) and the survey of related issues in Ruffin (1984).
5. Specifically, the number of commodity categories is assumed less than the number of factor inputs distinguished.
6. McCulloch and Yellen (1975, 1977) explore the effects of migration in trading economies where wages are set by emulation of overseas wages rather than through competitive processes.
7. See, for instance, the discussion in Amjad (1989).
8. More systematic analyses are nonetheless clearly needed, though beyond the scope of the present study.
9. Scalabrini Migration Center, Asian Migration Atlas 2000, http://www.scalabrini.asn.au/atlas/amatlas.htm.
10. Gazdar (2003: 9). The initial emigrants to the UK in the 1950s and 1960s came disproportionately from the Kashmir region, though emigration to the OECD countries has apparently been more geographically diversified in origin since then.
11. See Majid (2000), Gazdar (2003).
12. Azam (1991) and IOM (2003b). The latter adds (p. 23) 'Pakistan does not permit the migration of women under 45 as domestic aides'.
13. Azam (1991: 55).
14. Addleton (1992: 172).
15. Kazi (1989: Appendix). By 1990–96, the portion of professional migrants to the Middle East averaged nearly 8 percent. Scalabrini Migration Center, Asian Migration Atlas 2000 at http://www.scalabrini.asn.au/atlas/amatlas.htm.
16. Azam (1991: 56).
17. The correlation between the real wage of masons and overseas deployment is 0.68 over this period, an association which remains strong and statistically significant even if controls for GDP in Pakistan and a time trend are included. The nominal wage data in Figure 3.1 are from the *Pakistan Economic Survey* for various years. These are deflated using the consumer price index from the IMF *International Financial Statistics*. The data on deployment of Pakistani workers overseas are from Figure 2.3.
18. Mahmood (1990: 126).
19. Mahmood (1990: Table 4).
20. See the data in Majid (2000: Table A2).
21. Addleton (1992: 173).
22. Abassi (1987) as quoted in Addleton (1992: 171).
23. Sri Lanka Bureau of Foreign Employment at http://www.slbfe.lk/statisticsnew.html.
24. These data show estimated totals from the Sri Lanka Bureau of Foreign Employment from 1977–85 and from 1995–2002. From 1986–90, data refer to officially reported flows from the Sri Lanka Bureau of Foreign Employment times the average adjustment factor applied by the bureau in the earlier years. The estimate for 1991 is from Gunatilleke (1998b) and for 1992–94 from Wickramasekera (2002). The gender data apply the proportions of female migrants for each year from the Sri Lanka Bureau of Foreign Employment to these totals.
25. Centre for Women's Research at http://www.cenwor.lk/.

26. Data are from the Sri Lanka Bureau of Foreign Employment.

27. Gunatilleke (1998b: 126). See, however, Samarasinghe (1998) on the growing role of women in the wage labor market in Sri Lanka.

28. ILO *Yearbook of Labor Statistics*.

29. Scalabrini Migration Center, Asian Migration Atlas 2000 http://www.scalabrini.asn.au/atlas/amatlas.htm.

30. From 1980–2000 the simple correlation between the annual growth rates in overseas deployment and in real wages in manufacturing was 0.36. Wage data are from the ILO *Yearbook of Labor Statistics* and deflated using the consumer price index from the IMF *International Financial Statistics*. The data on deployed workers overseas are from Figure 2.3.

31. Data derived from EBRD (1997, 2003), Mancellari *et al.* (1996), Çuka *et al.* (2003).

32. Çuka *et al.* (2003: 218).

33. See the evidence cited in Konica and Filer (2003).

34. Mahmud (1989: 89). The portion in brackets appears in a footnote.

35. In Kerala too, real wage growth of urban carpenters and of unskilled, male construction workers appears to have been positively correlated with migration to the Gulf (*Statistics for Planning*, Government of Kerala, various years). However, only partial data could be obtained in this context.

4. Emigration of the Highly Skilled: Regimes, Costs and Responses

The international mobility of highly skilled people takes a wide variety of forms: everywhere, applicants for permanent residence are granted points or preference on the basis of education or occupation; temporary work visas are issued to those with unusual skills. To date, Mode 4 trade provisions have been restricted to professional services; transfers of intra-company employees have expanded in parallel with direct foreign investments; more and more students are attending colleges abroad. Whatever the mode of movement, it is commonly presumed that the departure of highly skilled people, who do not return, imposes a cost on those remaining at home; the specter of a brain drain, particularly from the lower income countries, evokes widespread criticism.

The focus of this chapter is on the nature of these costs. In some contexts, the losses imposed on those left behind may be very real; but in other contexts, departure of the highly skilled may even benefit those remaining at home. Not all migration of highly skilled people from the lower income countries represents a brain drain; much depends upon the nature and context of emigration. Indeed, even the concept of 'highly skilled' is rather nebulous, encompassing highly educated persons, people with particular skills, knowledge or talent, or simply the best and brightest.

Section 4.1 looks at the patterns of international mobility of the highly skilled, their destinations and origins. Section 4.2 then reviews the issues and potential costs, looking at the role of highly skilled people in the process of economic growth, in the provision of basic needs and key services, and in contributing to the fiscal coffers. Section 4.3 takes up two aspects of induced educational responses to the opportunity for international migration among the highly skilled: educational expansion at home and study abroad. Finally, Section 4.4 addresses the limited range of policy options open to countries hurt by the brain drain, as well as the policy dilemmas faced by countries of immigration.

4.1   MIGRATION REGIMES AND MOBILITY PATTERNS OF THE HIGHLY SKILLED

The educational profiles of the adult foreign populations, ages 25–64, for several OECD countries is depicted in Figure 4.1.[1] The data are sorted in increasing order of the proportion of foreign adults with a tertiary education. The UK and Norway top the list with the US third. Comparisons are difficult, given the many differences in definitions. However very rough estimates, based on UN migrant stock data combined with the ratios in Figure 4.1, suggest that there are more than twice as many tertiary-educated, foreign-born adults in the US than in the twelve EU countries in Figure 4.1 combined, and that the US alone has far more foreign graduates than all of the other sixteen countries combined. The dominant destination for highly skilled migrants clearly lies in the US. Yet these stock figures tell us nothing of the origins of these highly educated populations. Many of the highly educated non-nationals within the EU are clearly citizens of other EU countries. Moreover, the OECD data in Figure 4.1 omit the Asian OECD members as destinations, not to mention the Persian Gulf. A closer look at the patterns of mobility among the highly skilled is clearly required.

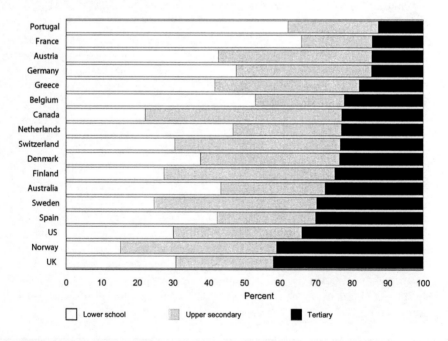

Figure 4.1   Foreign adult population by education level: select OECD countries, 2001–2002

Migration Regimes and Highly Skilled Migrants from Low Income Countries

Following the selection of case study areas, this section starts with a look at North America, the migration of highly skilled persons to the US and Canada, before turning to the case of Europe and then a briefer look at the Persian Gulf and Asia, where less information is available.

North America

By far the largest flow of highly skilled international migrants is to North America, a reflection of both opportunities within and the admission strategies of Canada and the US. Some indications of the extent of these movements are provided for the US in Table 4.1, which shows estimates of the adult, foreign-born population in the US in 2000, by education levels, regions and select countries of birth. US migrants are quite well educated; 42 percent of all foreign-born adults in the US possess at least a college level of education (though for the US-born population the comparable figure is very nearly 50 percent).[2] At the turn of the millennium, there were nearly 10.4 million foreign-born adults in the US with a tertiary education (about 23 percent of whom had post-graduate qualifications) and an additional 8.7

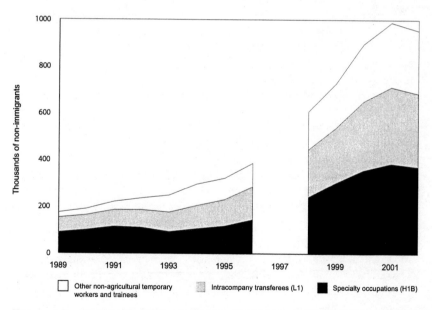

Figure 4.2   Non immigrants admitted to the US by select class of admission, 1989–2001

million with a secondary education. Of the foreign-born in the US with a tertiary education, about three-quarters, some 9.4 million graduates, were born in low income regions or transition economies.[3] Mexico is the largest source of tertiary educated migrants in the US, although nearly half of the Mexican adults in the US are estimated to have only a primary education. After Mexico, the Philippines and India (both within our case study purview) provide the largest groups with a college degree. Nearly three-quarters of the 1.2 million Filipino adults in the US have a college degree, and there are more than 650 000 college educated Indians in the US, half of whom have post-graduate training.

Since 1990, there has been a very substantial expansion in admission to the US of highly skilled non-immigrants on temporary visas, as illustrated in Figure 4.2.[4] In particular, both admissions of persons with Specialty Occupations and the number of Intra-Company Transferees have grown rapidly. No details are available on how many of these admissions were of people from the lower income countries, but in fact almost all of the expansion in H1B visas granted in the late 1990s went to information technology professionals, largely from India.

Among the half million immigrants and refugees admitted to Canada between 2000 and 2002, more than 45 percent possessed at least a college degree (see Table 4.2). The chief vehicle of entry for these college educated persons is under the Skilled Worker and Business Classes; about 80 percent of the principal applicants and nearly 45 percent of their adult dependants in these two classes possessed a college education. Moreover, more than half of the principal applicants for these two high skill classes were from the Asia-Pacific region (especially from the People's Republic of China, but also from India, Pakistan and the Philippines: see Table 4.3). Nearly another fifth were from Africa and the Middle East, especially from the Maghreb countries.

Thus it is clear that, like migrants to the US, Canada's immigrants are also well educated and that a large proportion of the highly skilled is drawn from low income regions. Even of the European Skilled Worker immigrants in the last five years, more than 15 percent were from Romania. In fact, and quite remarkably, almost a quarter of the refugees admitted to Canada in the last three years (a third from Africa and the Middle East, a third from the Asia-Pacific region, and a fifth from Europe) also possessed a college degree.

Europe

In contrast, at least until the very recent attempts in France, Germany and the UK to attract more highly skilled manpower, the tradition in Europe has been one of importing fairly unskilled workers. For example:[5]

• By 1995, 28.1 percent of recognized foreign workers in the Netherlands were in the three major professional occupational groups.[6] However, nearly

Table 4.1   US foreign-born adult population by country of birth and level of education, 2000

	Primary	Secondary	College	Post-Grad.
North America	3 120 795	2 672 468	1 081 552	168 823
Mexico	3 081 310	2 398 000	835 740	59 775
Central America &	939 666	1 691 910	1 130 803	184 718
Caribbean				
Cuba	177 716	350 079	249 378	66 048
Jamaica	36 430	209 710	183 276	20 379
South America	148 485	646 708	570 691	128 482
Colombia	53 485	163 415	160 013	26 022
Africa	15 926	127 304	300 109	109 941
Egypt	3 480	18 010	48 394	26 777
Morocco	1 625	8 900	15 387	3 758
Nigeria	2 630	15 910	62 299	28 321
Sudan	960	3 715	8 055	−
Tunisia	390	1 625	3 540	−
South Asia	61 371	208 612	477 424	389 054
Bangladesh	6 000	20 095	28 606	14 479
India	41 185	127 540	334 183	333 872
Pakistan	11 630	43 365	77 481	32 950
Sri Lanka	495	5 695	15 630	−
East Asia	434 983	1 215 458	2 058 312	572 340
China	173 545	217 185	262 035	194 015
Indonesia	1 460	12 065	26 586	13 059
Japan	6 140	81 426	194 717	45 390
Korea	26 397	186 510	319 151	78 460
Philippines	90 200	228 955	763 939	80 461
Taiwan	5 903	47 700	135 185	93 361
Vietnam	106 153	274 340	224 731	27 265
Middle East	54 345	192 768	275 216	140 520
Iran	8 436	67 899	96 456	76 024
Turkey	8 905	18 090	23 705	14 080
Western Europe	292 048	1 026 211	1 227 121	355 686
Germany	22 635	283 924	418 626	110 867
Eastern Europe	132 805	478 142	532 425	223 561
Albania	3 540	12 400	9 845	−
Croatia	6 725	14 350	14 380	−
Poland	48 764	159 356	141 348	47 016
Russia	22 735	72 544	130 756	73 319
Other or unknown	158 357	432 668	345 828	109 147
region				
Total	5 358 780	8 692 249	7 999 481	2 382 272

Sources: Adams (2003) and derived from US Current Population Survey (2000).

Table 4.2   *Canadian immigrants and refugees, ages 15 and over by level of education, gender and class of admission, 2000–2002*

	Total	Skilled Workers and Business Class Principal applicants		Refugees		Family Class		Skilled Workers and Business Class dependants	
		Male	Female	Male	Female	Male	Female	Male	Female
Primary	81 702	1 827	838	8 386	10 228	15 186	27 392	7 101	9 508
Middle	94 062	3 845	1 608	11 203	8 701	18 058	26 621	6 884	15 648
High school	48 128	5 329	2 284	3 450	2 268	7 607	11 859	3 944	10 422
Trade	26 641	4 717	1 629	1 999	1 479	4 365	4 971	1 497	5 060
Diploma	49 501	10 767	3 695	2 927	2 455	5 076	9 069	2 460	10 730
BA	183 778	73 489	23 170	3 601	2 326	11 000	20 235	9 546	37 323
MA	53 839	27 480	7 479	654	308	2 275	4 442	2 334	8 698
Doctorate	9 903	5 687	1 424	196	93	591	506	505	856
Total	547 554	133 141	42 127	32 416	27 858	64 158	105 095	34 271	98 245

Source: Derived from Citizenship and Immigration Canada (2003a).

Table 4.3   Canadian immigrants and refugees by class, region and select country of origin, 2000–2002

	Total	Skilled Workers	Business Class	Refugees
		Principal applicants		
Africa and Middle East	135 031	32 210	1 800	28 509
Algeria	–	3 239	–	–
Morocco	–	5 017	–	–
Sudan	–	–	–	2 929
Congo	–	–	–	2 662
Somalia	–	–	–	2 542
UAE	–	3 364	254	–
Asia and Pacific	372 243	86 851	7 137	29 326
Afghanistan	–	–	–	8 198
China, PR	110 262	35 450	3 039	2 614
India	82 751	17 510	328	3 464
Pakistan	43 689	10 403	455	5 450
Philippines	34 002	6 904	–	–
Iran	19 087	4 192	605	4 220
Korea, Rep.	24 559	4 808	1 611	–
Sri Lanka	16 316	–	–	7 946
S. and Central America	56 508	9 733	210	7 704
US	17 005	1 906	225	157
Europe	124 954	33 645	1 596	16 973
Bosnia-Herzegovina	–	–	–	1 679
Romania	15 702	5 284	–	–
Yugoslavia	9 131	–	–	5 920
France	–	7 116	–	–
UK	14 717	4 137	358	–
Not stated	1 180	83	5	438
Total	706 921	164 428	10 973	83 107

Source: Derived from Citizenship and Immigration Canada (2003a).

three-quarters of these were from other EU countries. Of documented, non-EU, foreign workers, less than 14 percent were in these professional categories having fallen from nearly 20 percent in 1987.
• According to the French 1990 census, only 12 percent of all foreign workers were professionals, administrators, managers and technicians (though 58

percent of these were non-EU nationals and the proportions of EU and non-EU foreign workers in these professions were almost identical).
• In Belgium in 1989, about two-thirds of non-EU workers were in blue-collar occupations.

Moreover, these official measures clearly undercount the many irregular and short-term migrants in low skill positions. From Turkey and the Maghreb countries, much of the migration certainly has been of unskilled labor though some emigration of highly skilled persons has occurred also.[7] For example, Leichtman (2002: 125) describes:

> three periods of Algerian brain drain. The first was during 1962–75, after Algeria gained independence from French colonial rule, a natural time to leave for those educated by the French system, political exiles, and those who opposed the new political system. Between 1975 and 1986 the brain drain continued in a mass sending of students abroad, funded by the Algerian state. These scholarship recipients were sent mainly to the US and Canada, England and Belgium. This act diversified the receiving countries and increased the number of migrants. Finally from 1986 until the present, Algerians began to emigrate because of socio-political problems.

Even the collapse of the former Soviet bloc has apparently not really resulted in massive migration of professionals from Eastern Europe to the EU, although 'The growing interest in the phenomenon has taken place within a vacuum of systematic data'.[8] Straubhaar and Wolburg (1999) provide some rare evidence, at least for the case of migration from Eastern Europe into Germany, from unpublished Eurostat labor force survey data. These findings are summarized in Table 4.4. Eleven percent of the migrants arriving in Germany from Eastern Europe during 1992 to 1994 are reported to have been 'highly qualified', which essentially refers to possessing a tertiary education. This amounts to 82 000 people, or about a third of the inflow of tertiary educated people migrating permanently to Canada during the three-year period covered in Table 4.2.

From Bulgaria and Hungary, more than a third of new arrivals were designated as highly qualified according to the data from this study by Straubhaar and Wolburg (1999). However, return migration was not uncommon and the fractions of the stocks of populations, present in Germany, that were deemed highly qualified from both of these countries was considerably lower than the proportions in the gross flows. Indeed, in the case of Bulgaria, Gächter (2002) cites a 1996 study which reported that of 6005 scientists who lost their jobs between 1989 and 1996 only 600 emigrated. More generally, Gächter (2002: 18) concludes 'There has been a trickle of highly qualified emigrants, no more, and even cumulatively it is not big enough to make any difference at all'. Similarly:

Table 4.4   Highly skilled migration from Eastern Europe into Germany, 1992–94

Sending country	Gross migration into Germany: 1992–94			Stock of highly qualified as percent of total: average 1992–94
	Total (1000)	Highly qualified (1000)	Highly qualified as percent of total	
Albania	14.72	1.11	7.5	7
Bulgaria	9.65	3.74	38.8	17
Former Czechoslovakia	10.60	1.76	16.6	21
Hungary	10.87	3.78	34.8	22
Poland	48.41	9.02	18.6	19
Romania	63.47	6.11	9.6	21
Former USSR	370.63	37.79	10.2	27
Former Yugoslavia	236.16	18.58	7.9	4
Total	764.51	81.89	10.7	9

Source: Straubhaar and Wolburg (1999: Tables 2-1 and 2-2).

> In Poland between 1980 and 1991, 9.5 percent of scientific personnel left the country ... However the rate of loss decelerated after the collapse in 1989 ... In 1991 the Hungarian Academy of Sciences estimated that 15 percent of all Hungarian researchers were working abroad ... One year later it appeared that the number of Hungarian émigré scientists had also decreased.[9]

Despite prior overstaffing and severe budget cuts, migration of the highly skilled from East Europe has hardly amounted to an exodus, though the rate of emigration of scientific personnel has apparently been greater from the countries of the former Soviet Union. However, from the former Soviet Union '45 percent of the 90 000 scientists or academics who left in 1991 were Jews who arrived in Israel. A further 37 percent were ethnic Germans who went to Germany. It would seem these were ethnic migrations as opposed to brain migrations'.[10]

Asia and the Persian Gulf

With regard to the skill composition of migration to the Persian Gulf, the data are very incomplete, and in particular no clear picture is available of the professional or educational profile of non-nationals in Saudi Arabia, which is the largest host to migrant workers in the region. Nonetheless a partial, though rather dated, image may be derived from Table 4.5.

In none of the three countries reported in Table 4.5 is the proportion of male, non-national workers who are in professional, administrative and managerial posts greater than 14 percent, though in both Oman and Qatar the proportion of the much smaller number of females in professional positions is far higher. In each of the three countries where an educational profile is available, a half or more of each gender of non-nationals has a primary education or less. In Bahrain and Qatar, the fraction of female non-nationals with a higher education exceeds 19 percent, but for the remaining gender-country groups the portion ranges from about 11 to 13 percent. Nonetheless, the stocks of foreign population are sufficiently large that the total number of non-nationals with a higher education in Bahrain, Kuwait and Qatar alone amounted to about 216 000 people in 1990. Clearly, the brain drain to the GCC states is not trivial though the overall picture remains opaque in the absence of data on Saudi Arabia and in the absence of any indication of the nationality of the highly educated populations in the GCC states.[11]

Reports from some of the sending areas in Asia suggest that education is a factor in access to work in the Gulf. Nair (1998) notes that migrants from Kerala, in India, to the Gulf fall into two groups: the vast majority are unskilled or semiskilled, but there is also a smaller group of white-collar workers who emigrate. However, it seems that even among the former group, average education levels are somewhat greater than the norm and Nair (1998: 268) notes that 'On the whole emigrants are an educated group'. Accordingly, a 1987 survey indicated that nearly 16 percent of emigrants from Kerala were college educated and a further 25 percent had matriculated, while only 15 percent were illiterate.[12] On the other hand, Zachariah *et al.* (1999) remark that out-migrants from Kerala are more generally better educated than the population as a whole, but emigrants are less well educated than are internal out-migrants. Nair (1998) argues that while it is suspected that the skill levels of migrants from India to the Gulf have been rising there is no evidence against which to test this. On the other hand, the evidence presented in Gunatilleke (1998b) does suggest a rising skill level of migrants from Sri Lanka. Yet from 1996 through 2002, three-quarters went as unskilled workers and housemaids while less than 1 percent were designated professionals (see Figure 3.3). In contrast, Tan (1993) reports that 22 percent of Filipinos going on contract to the Middle East in 1986–87 went as professional, technical, managerial or administrative personnel. More recent reports of how many of the Filipino overseas workers in the Middle East are professionals do not appear to be available. However, of all deployed new hires from the Philippines from 1992–2000 about 24 percent were professional and technical workers and less than 1 percent managers or administrators; among the professional workers, three-quarters were women of whom nearly 80 percent were designated as dancers, musicians

Table 4.5 Non-nationals in select GCC states by education, professional status and gender

	Bahrain		Kuwait		Oman		Qatar	
	Males	Females	Males	Females	Males	Females	Males	Females
	Number of non-national workers by gender and professional status 1993 (Qatar 1986)							
Total	–	–	421 244	113 223	386 658	44 605	162 923	16 508
Professional	–	–	51 813	14 945	52 972	15 835	14 989	3 335
	Percent of non-national population by gender and level of education 1990							
Illiterate	20.6	34.6	15.7	18.3	–	–	20.7	34.5
Read and write	29.7	10.4	19.4	16.4	–	–	29.7	10.4
Primary	11.9	4.0	18.5	18.7	–	–	11.9	4.0
Intermediate	9.2	9.6	20.8	20.8	–	–	9.2	9.6
Secondary	15.4	22.3	13.6	14.9	–	–	15.4	22.3
Higher	13.2	19.1	12.0	10.9	–	–	13.1	19.2
Total	100.0	100.0	100.0	100.0	–	–	100.0	100.0

Sources: Evans and Papps (1999) and UN (2003).

and singers.[13] How many of the latter went to the Middle East as opposed to East Asia is unknown.

Within East Asia, much of the movement of highly skilled people is associated with multinational investments. There is, for instance, a growing presence in China of managers from some of the newly industrialized countries in the region. Yet overall, any brain drain to the economies of East and Southeast Asia remains quite small.[14] In 2000, the non-dependant 'expatriate' professionals in Peninsular Malaysia numbered less than 23 000, while Singapore reported 74 000 administrative, managerial and professional, foreign, non-resident employees, though employment of information technology personnel on short-term contracts, especially from India, has however become increasingly common in Singapore. In Japan, as of 1999, there were less than 126 000 registered, foreign, professional workers and an additional 47 000 students working part time. In the Republic of Korea in the same year, there were less than 10 000 people working on professional visas. Migration within the East and Southeast Asia region thus remains largely a movement of low skill workers.

Relative Rates of Departure of the Highly Skilled

It seems that the EU, the GCC states and the wealthier economies of East Asia have not attracted huge numbers of highly qualified people; Canada and the US have attracted far more, especially from the developing regions. But how large are these migrations of highly skilled people relative to the stocks of educated people remaining at home? It is clear from the estimates by Carrington and Detragiache (1999) that the migration of secondary educated persons has generally been small compared to their numbers at home.[15] The same is not true of those with a tertiary level of education. A fresh view of this is provided in Table 4.6.[16] The countries included in this table are among those with the highest relative rates of migration of tertiary educated population to the US within a given region.[17] From some of these countries, the rates are very high indeed. This is especially true of some of the countries of Central and South America, in part because of proximity. The estimated number of Mexicans in the US reporting having a college degree or higher is about 28 percent of the number with completed tertiary education reported in Mexico. For Cuba and Haiti the proportions are far higher.

The large absolute numbers of tertiary educated Asians in the US have already been noted. For several Asian nations these withdrawals are also significant relative to the stock of home populations with completed tertiary education. People born in Vietnam, who now live in the US and possess higher education, represent about a third of those with college degrees in Vietnam. For at least five other Asian countries, including the Philippines, this ratio exceeds 10 percent and very poor countries such as Afghanistan

Table 4.6   *Relative emigration rate to the US of tertiary educated population: adults age 25 and over from selected countries in 2000*

	Tertiary education complete		US/home (percent)
	In US (1000)	Home population (1000)	
Haiti	126	26	485.1
Cuba	315	630	50.1
Dominican Rep.	128	399	32.1
Guatemala	56	180	31.0
Mexico	896	3 168	28.3
Vietnam	252	701	36.0
Hong Kong	103	360	28.7
Philippines	844	4 694	18.0
Taiwan	229	1 350	16.9
Iran	172	1 260	13.7
Israel	61	447	13.6
Afghanistan	18	181	9.8
Pakistan	110	1 475	7.5
Korea	398	5 537	7.2
Iraq	22	513	4.4
India	668	16 095	4.2
Myanmar	19	528	3.7
Syria	19	515	3.6
Bangladesh	43	1 292	3.3
China	456	17 516	2.6
Ghana	37	66	55.5
Kenya	18	105	17.0
Sudan	8	178	4.5
South Africa	44	1 667	2.7
Egypt	75	2 911	2.6
Croatia	29	264	10.9
Poland	188	2 333	8.1
Hungary	33	777	4.3
Romania	39	1 143	3.4

Sources: Tertiary educated population in US from US Current Population Survey 2000 and Adams (2003) tertiary educated population in countries of birth from Barro and Lee (1993) and its update at www.ksg.harvard.edu/CID.

are not far behind. Even for a large country like India, the 670 000 college educated adults in the US represent more than 4 percent of those over age 25 with higher education completed at home. Moreover, as Table 4.6 indicates, even from Africa and some of the transition economies of Eastern Europe the rate of emigration to the US in relation to the college educated populations at home has been large. More generally, calculations similar to those reported in Table 4.6 proved possible for sixty countries. Across these countries, the rate of emigration of highly educated adults to the US tends to be greater the lower is GDP per capita in the country of origin, which is brought out in Figure 4.3.

Suffice to say that emigration to the US of highly educated people has indeed been an important feature for a fairly wide range of countries and, relative to their stock of college educated populace, this has been more pronounced for some of the lower income countries. Given that many of the same countries arose in depicting highly skilled migration to Canada (not to mention Australia), it seems clear that the overall withdrawal of college graduates can be very large indeed. Yet numbers alone may not fully reflect the potential importance of the brain drain. If it is the brightest, from among the college educated, who manage to migrate, the relative significance of their withdrawal may well be larger than the already large proportions in the population.

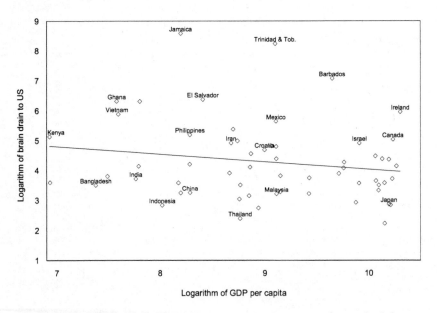

Figure 4.3   Relative rate of emigration to US of tertiary educated adults against GDP per capita

4.2 WHEN DOES MIGRATION OF THE HIGHLY SKILLED REPRESENT A BRAIN DRAIN?

As Lowell (2003: 1) notes, 'Two conditions are necessary for the term "brain-drain" to apply to a given country. First, there must be a significant loss of the highly educated population. Second, adverse economic consequences must follow.' The first has been established in Section 4.1; the second condition, the adverse economic consequences, is the focus here.

The earliest 'brain drain' literature considered the effects of departure of one more skilled person, leading to a simple proposition. If this person would have received pay, at home, commensurate with their incremental contribution to domestic production, then no net cost is imposed on those remaining at home.[18] More generally, though, the finite out-migration of any workers, whether skilled or not, lowers the returns on capital and other complementary inputs to the production process. The overall decline in production thus exceeds the income previously paid to emigrants, even if pay is in line with contributions to production, imposing a cost on stayers. Nonetheless, even in this simple view, some stayers can gain; most particularly any direct competitors with the departing workers may well be left better off. Yet any such gains are outweighed by losses to others. The combined loss becomes greater, the more difficult it is to substitute in production for the departing workers.[19] Moreover, in the longer run, costs may be curtailed by induced tendencies to adjust the mix of industries, adapting to the new realities of remaining productive factors available.[20]

In any case, the extent of aggregate costs imposed on stayers may depend very much on the nature of local labor markets. Thus it is frequently assumed that unemployed or under-employed workers at home negate any concern with respect to emigration; if professionals at home are not effectively deployed, their skills wasted, then little harm may follow from their departure. Yet such a view may be too simple. For example, as Bhagwati and Hamada (1974) argue, even if doctors are observed driving taxi-cabs in the home country, the emigration of doctors then raises the average rewards to qualifying as a doctor and can induce further enrolment in costly medical programs, only to produce more taxi drivers. Moreover, Hamada and Bhagwati (1975) note that the doctor driving a taxi may well be waiting for a visa to enter the US; in the absence of an emigration opportunity, the erstwhile doctor might be induced to migrate internally and begin to practice medicine.

The argument, thus far, is not at all specific to emigration of the highly skilled, as opposed to departure of workers more generally, or to capital flight. So why is there so much concern over a brain drain in particular? At the heart of this concern is a belief that the presence of educated or highly skilled persons generates free benefits among stayers. In particular, at least three categories of such potential benefits may be distinguished: the effects of the highly skilled on productivity of others and on economic growth; the contribution of the highly skilled as key personnel in the delivery of specific services and social goods; and the net transfer of fiscal resources to others from highly skilled people who stay at home.[21]

Productivity, Growth and the Highly Skilled

Possessing a more highly educated labor force may enhance aggregate production in at least three ways. First, educated workers may simply be more productive themselves. To the extent that pay remains commensurate with this productivity, however, this effect offers no free benefit to others; the educated worker reaps the rewards. Rather it is the remaining two effects that are of interest here. The second effect is when the earning levels of individuals are raised not just as a result of their own education but as a result of others' education, reflecting enhanced productivity from neighborhood or agglomeration effects. The remaining effect reflects the contribution of skilled personnel to the rate of technical progress in society, accelerating economic growth and potentially benefiting all.[22]

Both of these latter effects remain extremely controversial. There is certainly evidence that highly educated workers receive greater pay where highly educated personnel are geographically concentrated, which might seem to support the former, productivity argument.[23] There is even US evidence that pay of individuals is correlated with average education in their neighborhood, but as Acemoglu and Angrist (2001) emphasize, the difficulty is in disentangling the directions of causality underlying these correlations. Indeed, Acemoglu and Angrist find no evidence that average, local, secondary-schooling levels affect individuals' earnings in the US, after correcting for reverse causality.[24] Indeed, after reviewing both the macro and micro evidence, Davies (2003) concludes that there is no evidence to support the notion of static, market, external benefits operating on income or earning levels of others. Perhaps results would differ in the developing countries if any evidence were available, but meanwhile most of the attention shifts to the third, or dynamic effect of educated fellow workers.

The so-called 'new economic growth theory' is founded on a presumption of significant external benefits accruing from the presence of a highly educated labor force; the mutual interaction of highly skilled workers, enhancing each other's productivity, denies the forces of diminishing productivity in this scenario. If concentration indeed serves to raise productivity, then any initial concentration of highly skilled personnel serves to attract others, leading to divergent growth experiences.[25] Similarly, in the recent development literature, the critical roles of institutional foundations and governance have come to the fore. A well-educated elite is commonly presumed to play a key role in establishing public institutions, including a legal structure and the ability to enforce contracts, and in setting the norms for governance. In this sense, the departure of the highly skilled postpones establishment of such an institutional infrastructure that may be a precondition for sustained development.[26]

Certainly there is substantial evidence of a correlation between the average years of schooling achieved and the rate of economic growth across countries. Moreover, the emerging indications are that most of this contribution is routed through the effect of a higher stock of human capital on technical progress, partly in the form of technology adoption in the lower income countries, rather than a labor productivity augmenting effect of human capital growth. Nonetheless these growth effects of education are not universally accepted; some serious doubts have been expressed about whether educational expansion causes growth or whether expanding incomes permit educational expansion (Bils and Klenow, 2000). In addition, which level of schooling matters more has proved unclear.[27] Indeed, even if tertiary education does promote growth, this would still not demonstrate that the educated elite does not capture most of the benefits from this process. Establishing an effect by no means establishes the existence of free benefits. To infer that all of the effects of education on growth that act through higher technical progress provide no private reward to the educated person who generates or promotes adoption of the new ideas seems excessive. Whether higher education diffuses benefits throughout society in ways which basic education does not, and hence whether emigration of highly educated workers imposes very special costs, remains largely unproved.

Basic Needs and Social Goods: Key Professions

If the concept of development is broadened beyond mere economic growth, then the presence of a highly educated populace, and of key professional personnel in particular, may take on added significance. In the provision of basic needs, access to healthcare workers matters; for quality education of the next generations, effective teachers are required; political stability and human rights may be furthered by an enlightened elite. None of these is entirely separate from economic growth: good health, better and more education, and political stability may each contribute to continued economic expansion. Yet each takes on additional significance in its own right.

There is substantial evidence of a positive correlation between education levels and a range of indicators with respect to these basic needs and social goods. McMahon (1999) offers an exhaustive exploration of the cross-country data relating education levels to various 'non-monetary benefits': better health and lower net population growth; establishment of democracy, human rights and political stability; reductions in poverty and inequality; a cleaner environment and lower crime rates. McMahon's results point quite uniformly to a positive correlation between education levels and each of these benefits.[28] Davies refers to such benefits as static, non-market outcomes and notes that, 'There have been a large number of studies on the non-market effects of education ... many believe they provide evidence of strong effects.'[29] Yet Davies goes on to raise two specific concerns. First is the problem of discerning whether correlations between average education and these outcomes reflect a causal effect, as opposed either to reverse causality or to a spurious effect, in which both education and the specific outcomes are mutually dependent on some unobserved commonalities. Second, even if causality can be supported from education to non-market outcomes, establishing an effect by no means establishes the existence of external benefits; doctors, teachers or the political elite might internalize most of the rewards that they contribute to society.

Establishing causality is difficult; measuring external benefits is extraordinarily difficult. Yet this does not deny that both may be important. Perhaps our best guess at this juncture is that the contributions of an educated elite to social improvements and to basic needs varies with the context. A brain drain may well be harmful to others in some settings and far less so in others. While the presence of an educated elite may improve the quality of governance in some societies, it may lead to a concentration of power and corruption elsewhere. Do teachers, researchers and business leaders receive pay commensurate with their contributions to society? The answers surely vary.

Healthcare workers are probably a case apart: they not only help their individual patients but prevent the spread of diseases with far wider benefits to the nation. As a result, the emigration of healthcare workers, of both doctors and nurses, has become the subject of very specific recent concern: a concern heightened by the HIV-AIDS epidemic.[30] Nonetheless, even an exodus of healthcare workers may have questionable effects on healthcare delivery if these workers were ineffectively deployed at home.

Fiscal Effects

The third major component of cost imposed by highly educated emigrants on those remaining at home is the potential loss of fiscal resources. Two components arise: the loss of any net contribution that the educated emigrant would have made to the fiscal balance, had they remained at home; and the fact that education is subsidized, and hence the view that emigration also exports the returns on this public investment.

Net fiscal losses

To the extent that taxes are progressive and highly educated individuals receive higher incomes at home, emigration of the highly skilled reduces tax revenues by more than emigration of the less skilled. On the other hand, reductions in discretionary state spending on the migrant, and perhaps the migrant's dependants too, ought then to be weighed in the balance, as should any tax revenues derived directly or indirectly as a result of remittances from the educated diaspora (Johnson, 1967). Computations are rare, but Desai *et al.* (2001) report some estimates for the brain drain from India to the US. The authors predict earnings that non-resident Indians in the US could have expected in India, and hence simulate indirect and income tax revenue losses (assuming no evasion) based on these incomes. With rapidly escalating emigration to the US, these tax losses are estimated to have been about 9 billion rupees, some 0.04 percent of GDP, by 2001. However, on an assumption that public expenditures (other than defense and interest payments) are a constant proportion of incomes, the simulated savings from departure of emigrants to the US dominate tax losses on average from 1990 to 2001, even assuming no tax revenues accruing from remittances. However, these results apparently prove very sensitive to the precise assumptions and, in a subsequent version, Desai *et al.* (2002: Abstract) conclude:

> foregone income tax revenues associated with the Indian-born residents of the U.S. comprise one-third of current Indian individual income tax receipts. Depending on the method for estimating expenditures saved by the absence of these emigrants, the net fiscal loss associated with the U.S. Indian-born resident population ranges from 0.24% to 0.58% of Indian GDP in 2001.

The very sensitivity of these results for India suggests just how sensitive any net fiscal losses or gains from emigration of the highly skilled are likely to prove under varying conditions in other countries. The balance of the outcome is far from obvious in general, and will depend critically upon the direct and indirect tax systems in place as well as patterns of public spending across socioeconomic groups. One should not expect a uniform answer.

The costs, returns and financing of higher education

One of the chief complaints against the brain drain is the loss of investment of public spending in the education of emigrants. Higher education is certainly expensive and 'with developing country systems heavily dominated by public universities that tend to have low tuition fees, the costs fall predominantly on the state'.[31] The World Bank (2000a) estimates that in 1995 the costs of tertiary education per student amounted to 77 percent of GNP per capita, on average, worldwide. However, for many of the poorer countries this ratio has been a great deal higher, as may be seen from Table 4.7.[32] Indeed for the countries of Sub-Saharan Africa included in the World Bank calculations, the average ratio was more than five times the global average. Not surprisingly, the higher income countries spend more public funds on educating each

Table 4.7 Public spending per tertiary level student relative to income per capita, 1995 and 2000

	Tertiary spending per student as % of			Tertiary spending per student as % of			Tertiary spending per student as % of	
	GNP/Cap	GDP/Cap		GNP/Cap	GDP/Cap		GNP/Cap	GDP/Cap
	1995	2000		1995	2000		1995	2000
Malawi	979	–	Mongolia	74	–	Germany	35	–
Burundi	941	924	Hungary	73	32	Ecuador	34	–
Lesotho	399	690	Hong Kong	52	73	Czech Rep.	–	33
Ethiopia	592	–	Bolivia	67	–	Guatemala	33	–
Kenya	540	–	Cyprus	–	64	Thailand	25	33
Mali	522	–	Sri Lanka	64	–	Singapore	32	–
Togo	521	–	Saudi Arabia	63	–	Myanmar	–	32
Guinea	498	–	Mexico	61	44	Israel	31	30
Benin	240	–	Honduras	59	–	Estonia	–	30
Gambia	235	–	South Africa	59	56	Australia	30	26
Chad	234	–	Costa Rica	44	55	France	24	30
Zimbabwe	234	–	Denmark	55	–	Colombia	29	–
Congo	224	–	Switzerland	–	54	Greece	29	20
Jamaica	193	81	Paraguay	52	–	Slovakia	–	29
Zambia	160	–	Turkey	51	45	Uruguay	28	20
Mauritania	157	–	Norway	50	41	US	23	28
Nepal	156	98	Brazil	–	49	Portugal	25	27

Country	1995	2000	Country	1995	2000	Country	1995	2000
Sierra Leone	–	141	Canada	36	49	Italy	23	26
Jordan	111	–	Cambodia	–	48	Indonesia	–	24
Egypt	108	–	Panama	47	–	Latvia	–	23
Trin & Tob	77	98	Finland	46	–	Chile	21	20
Tunisia	89	–	Belgium	35	45	Bulgaria	21	16
Namibia	86	–	Austria	32	44	Spain	18	20
Iran	62	82	UK	44	26	Japan	16	17
China	81	55	Netherlands	44	42	Argentina	17	–
Malaysia	77	81	Poland	42	17	Philippines	–	15
Lao	55	78	Romania	40	–	Oman	–	8
India	78	–	Bangladesh	30	40	El Salvador	8	–
Sweden	76	52	New Zealand	39	26	Korea, Rep.	6	8
Morocco	74	–	Ireland	38	30	Dom. Rep.	5	–

Sources: For 1995, World Bank data available at www.ksg.harvard.edu/CID; for 2000, calculated from UNESCO data at www.unesco.org.

student enrolled in higher education. However, this rise is less than in proportion to incomes, so spending per student in higher education is greater, relative to incomes, in the poorer countries. This is illustrated from data for some 90 countries in Figure 4.4, in which the upper panel shows an index of the real cost of education per student and the lower panel displays this cost as a fraction of income per capita.

The labor markets in most of the lower income developing regions offer relatively large salary gains for those who complete a college education, even if they do not emigrate. Thus the private rate of return, in terms of subsequent, enhanced pay relative to earnings forgone during the years of education, is quite high in lower income countries, though no higher than the private returns to primary education (see Table 4.8). On the other hand, given the very high public costs of tertiary education, the overall return on higher education for lower income countries does not appear very attractive, as compared to expanding primary and secondary education (see the last three columns in Table 4.8). If one adds to this the fact that it is the children from relatively wealthy families who typically continue onto college and hence benefit from public subsidies to higher education, and that this education often serves as a vehicle to leave the country, then the merits of the considerable subsidization of tertiary education may well be doubted.

Table 4.8　Rates of return to education by level of education and income level

Country group	Private rate of return			Rate of return including public costs		
	Primary	Secondary	Higher	Primary	Secondary	Higher
Low income	25.8	19.9	26.0	21.3	15.7	11.2
Middle income	27.4	18.0	19.3	18.8	12.9	11.3
High income	25.6	12.2	12.4	13.4	10.3	9.5
Overall	26.6	17.0	19.0	18.9	13.1	10.8

Source: Psacharopoulos and Patrinos (2002) Table 2.

The World Bank's Task Force on Higher Education, 2000, makes the counter argument:

The Task Force … believes that traditional economic arguments are based on a limited understanding of what higher education institutions contribute. Rate-of-return studies treat educated people as valuable only through their higher earnings and the greater tax revenues extracted by society. But educated people clearly have many other effects on society: educated people are well positioned to be economic and social entrepreneurs, having a far-reaching impact on the economic and social

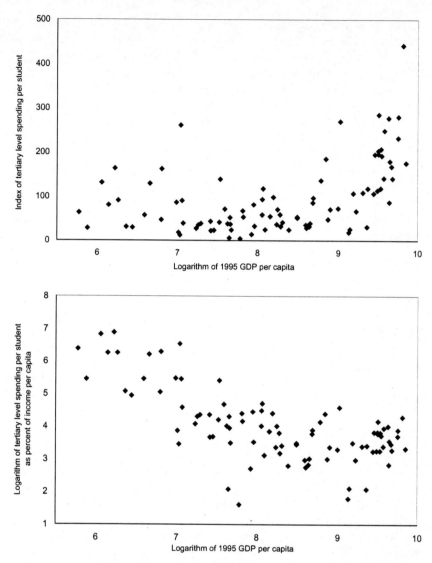

Figure 4.4   Tertiary level spending per student against 1995 GDP per capita

well-being of their communities. They are also vital to creating an environment in which economic development is possible. Good governance, strong institutions, and a developed infrastructure are all needed if business is to thrive – and none of these is possible without highly educated people. Finally, rate-of-return analysis entirely misses the impact of university-based research on the economy – a far-reaching social benefit that is at the heart of any argument for developing strong higher education systems. (World Bank, 2000a: 39)

Important as these counter-arguments may be, measuring the magnitude of indirect benefits conferred has, as we have seen, proved elusive. Subsidizing the costs of education may well be justified, either in terms of equating opportunities to further education among poorer families, or even in terms of enhancing inefficiently low rates of continuing education. For example, too little training is typically realized when financing is limited or excessively costly, as well as when education at any level confers benefits on society beyond those reaped by the educated individual. Taxpayers who bear the costs of subsidizing education, only to be denied any indirect benefits of this education once graduates emigrate, are understandably frustrated. Indeed, this frustration may be particularly justified to the extent that it is the children of the wealthy who benefit from low cost college educations, especially if these elites would hardly have abated their education even if charged fuller costs of tuition.

4.3   ASPECTS OF INDUCED EDUCATION

Two aspects of education induced by emigration of the highly skilled are considered in this section. The first addresses additional education undertaken at home, while the second explores the link between overseas education and the brain drain.[33]

Education in the Home Country

The simple notion here is that emigration of the highly skilled can raise the financial attractions of continued education at home. This may act through at least two principal mechanisms. First, the demand for a higher education may be stimulated either because a college education provides a vehicle for exit, raising the odds of being able to relocate abroad, or because the gap in salaries between home and abroad rises at higher education levels.[34] Second, the departure of people with a tertiary education may raise the relative pay of graduates who remain at home, offering a stimulus to further education even among those not contemplating departure. As Mountford (1997) notes, if this induced expansion is sufficiently large, and if only some portion of those induced to continue their education actually emigrate, then the average level of education of those at home may be raised as a result of the potential for emigration.

There are certainly contexts in which education at home appears geared to the emigration market. This seems true in the case of the Philippines, for instance (see Box 4.1).[35] By 2000, 18 percent of all Filipino college graduates were living in the US. Given the income level of the Philippines, the tertiary enrolment rate is amongst the highest in the world. As of 2001, 72 percent of all students enrolled in higher education were in private institutions, and public spending on tertiary education is low per student, though the private rate of return to higher education for those who remain in the Philippines is comparatively low. It is thus difficult to believe that these high, privately-financed enrolment rates are not induced by the possibility of emigration upon graduation. There are even signs that the choice of major field of study among Filipino students responds to shifts in international demands.[36] Higher education in the Philippines is almost certainly induced to a significant extent by the potential for emigration. Whether the Philippines is left with more educated people at home in the balance, as hypothesized by Mountford is less obvious.

BOX 4.1 HIGHER EDUCATION AND THE BRAIN DRAIN: THE CASE OF THE PHILIPPINES

More than 7 million persons born in the Philippines are living abroad; close to 10 percent of the population. Nearly three-quarters of a million people left the Philippines, either as emigrants or for temporary work abroad, each year during the 1990s, and nearly 40 percent of those leaving were college graduates. This massive stream of highly educated people has headed largely to North America. More than 40 percent of Filipino migrants are in the US and Canada, and by 2000 some 18 percent of all Filipino college graduates were living in the US.

The economy of the Philippines has performed very poorly; the virtual absence of any growth over the last two decades left the Philippines with a real income level below that of China at the turn of the millennium. The unemployment rate has risen and the unemployment rate of those college graduates who remained in the Philippines fluctuated between 12 and 16 percent during the 1990s.

Most of the Filipino graduates living in the US obtained their education in the Philippines; only 16 percent of these graduates in the US received their highest degree in the US, and even amongst those with a post-graduate qualification from a US university, nearly 60 percent had obtained their BA qualification outside of the US.

Given the level of economic development in the Philippines, the gross enrollment rate at the tertiary level is amongst the top ten countries globally. This ratio rose from less than 20 percent in 1975 to 38 percent in 1985 and by 2000 stood at 31 percent. The gross enrollment rate of women is more than 25 percent greater than that of men and 60 percent of the Filipino graduates in the US are female. On the other hand, the Philippines have one of the lowest rates in the world of public spending on tertiary education per student, relative to GDP. In part this reflects the proliferation of private universities and colleges; in 2001, 72 percent of all students enrolled in higher education were in private institutions. The quality of tertiary education is reported to have declined since the 1970s, when the Philippines was one of the leading education centers in Asia. The University of the Philippines is now ranked forty-fourth out of 80 top ranking universities in Asia. Declining quality of education and poor labor market prospects combine to offer a private rate of return to higher education, for those who remain in the Philippines, that is far below the norm for other countries with similar income levels.

A college education is an important vehicle of exit from the Philippines and its lagging economy. The expansion in college enrollments, despite declining quality of education and prospects of high unemployment amongst those who stay at home, may well reflect this opportunity to emigrate. Even the selection of fields of study tracks developments in the global labor markets, rather than those at home.

The Philippines has one of the highest rates of brain drain in the world. Yet the economic losses from this may not be large, given the state of the labor markets and the low rate of public subsidies per student trained. Would reduction in the rate of withdrawal of the educated elite suffice to reverse the economic woes of the Philippines?

In a more global analysis, however, Faini (2002) finds little to support the notion that a greater rate of emigration of the highly skilled induces higher enrollments at home.[37] Faini reaches this conclusion by relating gross enrollment rates across 51 countries to measures of the extent of high skilled emigration to the OECD from these countries, controlling for GDP per capita at home.[38] The measure of emigration to the OECD area, adopted in Faini's study, is that presented by Carrington and Detragiache (1999), some of the limitations of which have already been discussed in the first section. Nonetheless, Faini's results prove revealing.[39] A higher probability of migration among workers with a secondary education is estimated to have no significant impact on secondary school enrollments across countries with similar GDP levels; a greater propensity for migration of tertiary educated workers is found to be associated with a higher secondary school enrollment rate, but a lower rate of tertiary enrollment. 'We interpret this result as suggesting that prospective migrants may want to strengthen their chances for admission to the host country by pursuing graduate studies there. The most talented individuals would then have an incentive to migrate at a relatively early stage of their school curriculum, thereby definitely reducing the average enrolment ratio in the home country's educational system.'[40] In other words, Faini's results offer no support for the notion that a brain drain may induce expanded higher education at home. Rather the reverse, that the inducement is to seek an overseas education.

Study Abroad

Study abroad is not only a form of migration of the highly skilled in its own right but presents important opportunities to turn overseas education into more permanent forms of migration: opportunities both for the student and the host country. Being a student abroad not only permits easier job search after graduation, but signals seriousness of purpose and reveals qualities of the person in terms understood by foreign employers. From 1980 to 2000, the number of tertiary level foreign students in the 19 OECD countries shown in Table 4.9 more than doubled.[41] As Salt (1997: 23) notes, 'the provision of tertiary education internationally is now a major business ... the volume of international student migration is enormous.'

The US universities have traditionally been the most common destination for foreign students and the US continues to be the single largest host to tertiary level students. However, by 2001, foreign students represented only 3.5 percent of all tertiary level students in the US and almost a third of these were from other OECD countries. Meanwhile, study in Europe, Australia and Japan has also become increasingly common among foreign students and, during the 1990s, the countries of the EU overtook the US and Canada combined in attracting foreign students. In Europe, a part of the expansion was increasing mobility of students within the EU. By the mid-1990s almost a third of the foreign students in the EU were from the countries of Western Europe (see Table 4.10).[42] Nonetheless, among the thirteen EU countries listed in Table 4.9, enrollment of non-OECD students increased by 55 percent from 1990 to 2001, the largest additional intakes being in the UK and Germany.[43] By 2001 the number of non-OECD tertiary level students in EU universities exceeded those in the US (see Figure 4.5).

As of the mid-1990s, almost two-thirds of the foreign students in the US and half of those in Canada were drawn from Asia. Europe was, however, the major destination for students from Africa, with the countries of the EU educating about two-thirds of all African tertiary students who were overseas. Similarly, the EU hosted nearly 40 percent of the East European students who were abroad though, at least by the mid-1990s, the numbers remained

Table 4.9   Tertiary level foreign students in selected OECD countries, 1980–2001

	Number of foreign students (1000)			Foreign students (2001)	Non-OECD students (2001)		% Increase non-OECD students 1990–2001
	1980	1990	2001	% of tertiary enroll-ment	% of foreign students	% of tertiary enroll-ment	
Canada	28.4	35.2	129.8	10.7	49.6	5.3	145.1
US	311.9	407.5	475.2	3.5	63.4	2.2	6.3
Austria	11.8	18.4	31.7	12.0	30.6	3.7	87.0
Belgium	12.9	33.3	38.2	10.6	40.2	4.3	−6.8
Denmark	3.0	6.7	12.5	6.5	57.4	3.7	85.2
Finland	0.6	1.6	6.3	2.3	64.6	1.5	396.3
France	110.8	136.0	147.4	7.3	71.9	5.2	4.3
Germany	68.9	107.0	199.2	9.5	48.0	4.6	91.8
Ireland	2.8	3.3	8.2	4.9	24.2	1.2	85.3
Italy	29.4	21.8	29.2	1.6	55.8	0.9	67.9
Netherlands	4.1	8.9	16.6	3.3	40.7	1.3	89.4
Portugal	1.3	3.8	6.1	1.6	80.9	1.3	58.2
Spain	11.0	11.1	39.9	2.2	35.4	0.8	81.0
Sweden	10.4	10.7	26.3	7.3	39.9	2.9	179.3
UK	56.0	80.2	225.7	10.9	41.1	4.5	126.9
Norway	1.1	6.9	8.8	4.6	52.0	2.4	6.5
Switzerland	14.7	22.6	27.8	17.0	27.9	4.7	26.1
Australia	8.8	29.0	121.0	14.3	77.6	11.1	249.1
New Zealand	2.5	3.2	11.1	6.5	76.1	4.9	141.6
Japan	6.5	34.5	63.6	1.6	66.6	1.1	144.3

Sources: OECD (2003), UNESCO (1992), Salt (1997), UNESCO statistics at http://www.unesco.org/and Canadian immigration statistics at http://www.cic.gc.ca/.

comparatively small and East European students formed only 7 percent of the foreign students in the EU. In contrast, the Asian universities have not really been major attractions for foreign students within their own region though the Japanese government has targeted an increase in foreign student enrollment, and by 2001 about half of the 64 000 tertiary level foreign students in Japan were from China.

Foreign training is something which the richer countries are better

Table 4.10   Tertiary level students abroad by region of origin and region of study, c. 1995

Region of study	Total	Region of origin					
		Asia	Africa	S. America	E. Europe	W. Europe	Other
US	453.8	290.9	20.8	22.3	17.1	49.3	53.3
Canada	35.5	17.0	5.8	0.9	0.7	5.5	5.5
EU	680.4	170.6	124.0	18.9	47.5	243.4	76.0
Other Western Europe	51.4	7.3	3.5	2.4	3.9	28.1	6.3
E. Europe & former USSR	147.7	66.5	11.1	1.2	53.2	14.4	1.3
Australia & New Zealand	48.0	35.4	0.9	0.1	0.2	1.5	9.9
East Asia	83.3	71.0	0.9	0.8	0.7	3.2	6.7
Middle East	64.9	48.3	7.6	0.0	1.8	1.6	5.6
Africa	28.4	7.4	14.8	0.1	0.1	3.7	2.2
Latin America	16.9	0.2	3.2	9.9	0.0	0.6	3.0
Total	1610.1	714.5	192.6	56.7	125.1	351.2	170.0

Source: UNESCO (1998).

able to afford. This is brought out in Figure 4.6, which shows the number of tertiary students abroad in relation to home country population against GDP per capita for 164 countries in (approximately) 1995.[44] Each 1 percent rise in GDP per capita is associated, on average, with about a 0.7 percent increase in the number of tertiary students abroad per capita. Clearly there are significant variations in this pattern, for various reasons; interestingly, the three countries with the lowest rates of overseas college students, given their level of GDP, are the People's Democratic Republic of Korea, the US and Myanmar.

Countries with smaller populations send significantly more students for foreign training, given their income levels. This is particularly true of countries with populations below 3 million, though even countries with populations in the range of 10 to 25 million send more students per capita than their larger counterparts. To some extent, this presumably reflects the various economies of scale that are possible in organizing college level education for larger student populations (the evolution of distance learning notwithstanding). On the other hand, there is little sign of any effect of higher gross domestic enrollment rates either encouraging or discouraging the

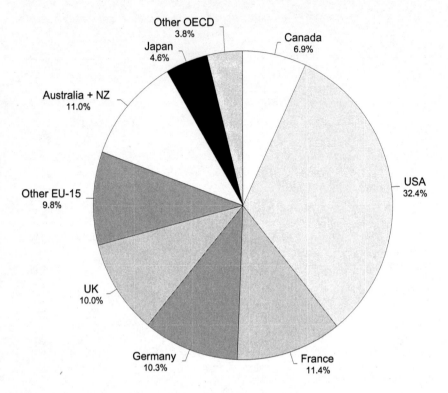

Figure 4.5   Non-OECD tertiary level students in OECD countries, 2001

extent of foreign training, given income levels.[45] In other words, there is little evidence to indicate that going abroad for training reflects difficulties with limited tertiary educational capacity at home. Finally, given income levels, the regional variations in the prevalence of foreign training are not very pronounced; the incidence of foreign training per capita is somewhat lower in East and South Asia, given their income levels, and lower in Latin America too, but Africa and the transition economies of East Europe and the former USSR hardly differ from the average for their income levels.

Among the scientists and engineers receiving doctoral degrees from US universities, only about half leave the US within five years of completing their degree and the stay rate is highest among scientists and engineers from the lower income countries. These findings emerge from an on-going exercise, the latest results of which are reported in Finn (2001) and summarized in Table 4.11.[46] On average 51 percent of people receiving doctorates in science and engineering from US universities between 1994 and 1995 were working in the US in 1999. Inter-country variation in this stay rate is, however, very wide; whereas only 15 percent of Koreans in the sample remained in the US, 91

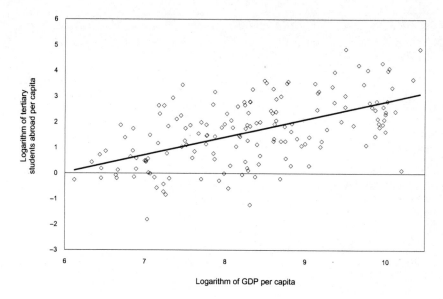

Figure 4.6   Tertiary level students abroad per capita in relation to GDP per capita

percent of Chinese stayed and 87 percent of Indians. Indeed for both China and India the numbers of scientists and engineers is very large, as reported in Table 4.11, and for both the stay rate has risen since Finn's first report, which covered stay rates through 1995 of comparable persons who graduated in 1990–91.

Figure 4.7 graphs the stay rates for the various countries in Table 4.11 against their 1995 GDP per capita. Some of the high income countries clearly have fairly high stay rates, but among the developing countries (through South Korea) a significant negative association exists between rate of stay and income level (as shown in Figure 4.7), and the lowest income countries clearly have the highest stay rates of all. In France, foreign science and engineering doctorate recipients also have a high stay rate, though no data are available by country of origin. Johnson (2001: 11) reports that 'In 1998, the overall return rate of foreign doctoral recipients from France to their countries of origin was 28 percent in natural sciences and 20 percent in engineering fields.' In contrast, 'in 1998, most foreign S&E doctoral degree recipients at U.K. universities returned home after earning their degree. In fact, among the ten top countries of origin, all doctoral recipients from Malaysia and Turkey returned to their home country.' However, Johnson also reports that only 59 percent of the science and engineering doctorate recipients from China returned home from the UK.

Overseas training, at least in the US, proves a particularly potent mechanism for attracting and retaining some of the very brightest people

Table 4.11   Temporary residents who received science and engineering doctorates from US universities in 1994 and 1995: percent in the US in 1999

	Number of doctorate recipients 1994–95	Percent working in US in 1999
China	1 649	91
Taiwan	2 268	42
Japan	233	27
Korea, Republic	1 943	15
Other East Asia	391	27
India	1 995	87
Iran	198	61
Israel	121	31
Turkey	252	44
Other West Asia	981	44
Australia	85	34
Indonesia	119	16
New Zealand	29	63
Other Pacific	103	66
Egypt	157	37
Nigeria	50	85
South Africa	50	40
Other Africa	542	42
Greece	276	49
UK	140	60
Germany	262	53
Italy	106	37
France	142	47
Spain	87	34
Other Europe, East	283	69
Other Europe, West	338	39
Canada	430	55
Mexico	223	31
Argentina	67	45
Brazil	255	21
Chile	57	26
Colombia	66	29
Peru	37	66
Other Central & S America	254	49
Total	14 189	51

Source: Finn (2001: Table 5).

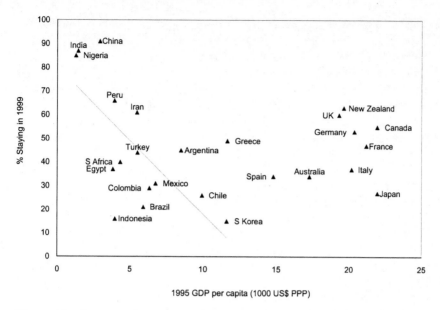

Figure 4.7   Stay rate of scientists and engineers in US against home country GDP

from the lower income countries, and for the US there are other indications that foreign students tend to stay. As of 1993, it is estimated that 60 percent of all foreign-born people in the US with a college degree obtained their highest degree from an American university (see Table 4.12). Moreover, more than 60 percent of those with higher degrees from US universities also obtained their BA from a US university. Obtaining a US degree is indeed a major vehicle of entry to the US.

However, these averages hide some important variations across regions and countries of origin and Table 4.12 includes some examples to illustrate. For example, for nearly three-quarters of the Filipino college graduates in the US in 1993 the highest degree was a BA from a non-US university, and even amongst those who possessed a higher degree from a US university nearly 60 percent had obtained their BA from outside of the US. Similarly, although many Indians in the US have higher degrees, as already noted, about 80 percent of those with US higher degrees had completed their BA elsewhere. In other words, about 83 percent of Indian-born college graduates in the US either possessed their highest degree or their BA from a university outside of the US, though one cannot be sure how many were educated in India. In sharp contrast, 81 percent of degree holders born in Vietnam had their highest degree from a US university (and 91 percent from Nigeria). This suggests a potentially high tax burden on the Philippines or India in educating people for migration to the US, whereas the presence of highly educated Vietnamese in the US apparently does not indicate a similar burden (given that scholarships would rarely have been provided from Vietnam). Even where college training is received in the US, the public costs of lower education levels are typically borne by the home country. Moreover, in some instances, a US college education represents a second undergraduate training; the first having been received at home.[47] Nonetheless, the high incidence of US-based training of their foreign, college educated population indicates that by no means all migration of the highly educated implies a commensurate 'brain drain' in the form of sunk public costs on behalf of the home country.

Table 4.12   Highest degree held and whether US or non-US degree: US foreign-born college graduates by region of origin, 1993

	Degree type and source (percent)									US post-grad, non-US BA (percent)
	Non-US degree				US degree				Total	
	BA	MA	Doc	Prof	BA	MA	Doc	Prof		
N. America	15.2	3.9	1.4	3.0	43.4	19.7	6.1	7.4	100.0	24.8
C. America	16.2	3.7	2.5	5.7	45.0	19.2	3.3	4.4	100.0	11.3
S America	19.4	5.2	2.1	6.3	38.3	19.7	4.4	4.6	100.0	27.1
W. Europe	14.3	5.4	3.9	2.6	42.0	20.8	5.7	5.2	100.0	16.0
E. Europe	18.6	16.7	5.5	6.1	27.1	15.5	6.6	3.9	100.0	17.7
Hungary	12.8	12.0	7.1	3.3	34.1	18.9	5.9	5.9	100.0	14.8
Romania	22.5	27.4	4.5	4.8	17.4	17.1	4.2	2.0	100.0	35.5
Former USSR	32.5	20.9	6.6	4.0	19.5	10.4	3.4	2.9	100.0	7.4
E. Asia	42.9	3.7	1.0	4.3	22.3	18.4	5.2	2.2	100.0	58.5
China	25.8	5.9	1.9	2.7	18.2	29.3	14.0	2.2	100.0	65.4
Philippines	73.5	2.4	0.8	6.9	10.2	5.0	0.5	0.7	100.0	58.8
Vietnam	13.0	1.8	1.0	3.3	60.4	13.4	2.8	4.5	100.0	29.4
S. Asia	29.2	12.0	3.6	9.6	9.7	24.8	7.9	3.2	100.0	77.4
India	29.3	11.9	3.7	9.2	8.6	25.5	8.2	3.6	100.0	78.4
W. Asia & ME	16.0	4.8	2.2	5.8	34.9	23.9	8.0	4.4	100.0	34.8
Africa	21.6	4.3	2.3	5.7	30.6	23.0	8.2	4.2	100.0	38.7
Egypt	41.8	5.9	1.8	6.9	15.4	14.8	8.4	5.1	100.0	50.0
Nigeria	2.8	0.3	0.6	5.6	43.3	35.6	9.2	2.6	100.0	26.6
Oceania	28.6	4.1	5.3	4.0	26.5	13.3	16.1	2.3	100.0	50.9
Total	26.7	6.0	2.5	4.9	30.4	19.9	5.7	3.8	100.0	39.1

Source: Derived from US National Survey of College Graduates 1993 at http://srsstats.sbe.nsf.gov/.

4.4 POLICY OPTIONS

Not all movements of highly skilled migrants, from low to high income countries, necessarily represent a 'brain drain' in the sense of imposing a net loss. In the end there is a dearth of evidence establishing clear costs. Yet one should not infer from the lack of systematic evidence that costs are never incurred. No doubt the truth is mixed. It is doubtful that the departure of information technology experts from India since 1990 has imposed very real losses on the average Indian at home; the same can be said of most professionals leaving the Philippines; the loss of medical personnel from South Africa may be quite another story. In the balance, the number of governments that seem actively concerned with the process of brain drain is less than one might think. Indeed, a number of governments have become sufficiently concerned with the lack of opportunities at home for their college graduates, and the political threat that this poses, that they are quietly encouraging and aiding emigration. With respect to the Asia-Pacific region, Hugo (1996: 218) reports:

> Some researchers are referring to there being a 'brain overflow' rather than a brain drain ... and argue that the brain drain reflects the basic inability of the origin country's *'economy to absorb the going supply of certain high level skills'* ... Support for such a view can be gathered in several countries in Asia where there appears to be some mismatch between the skills of the graduates of the educational and training system and those required by the local economy ... it could be argued that it may be to the country's net benefit to export their 'excess' skilled workers.[48]

Although distinguishing cases where costs from emigration of the highly skilled are, and are not, incurred is quite difficult, we may nonetheless ask what are the policy options where a problem is considered to arise? An early proposal to compensate the countries of origin by collecting an income surtax on nationals overseas offered interesting potential but met with legal objections to imposing different taxes on the basis of national origin.[49] More recently, the notion of refunding the country of origin, at least for educational costs incurred, has resurfaced in another guise, with proposals to compensate for state recruitment of healthcare workers from the developing countries.

> [S]ince less-developed countries bear the cost of educating the doctors that subsequently emigrate, should they not be reimbursed for the loss of that investment, when the graduate leaves to work in another country? The gaining country should be prepared to reimburse the cost of medical education. This cost should be chargeable for a number of years after graduation, and could be administered by the World Health Organization. (Bundred and Levitt, 2000: 246)

> Compensating the donor country for the cost of educating the migrating health professional may be more likely to preserve individual freedom than policies to

restrict exit or entrance of individuals, though evidence and further analysis are needed to support such a policy recommendation. If costs are to be used as a basis for compensation, then those other than education costs have to be accounted for. (Stilwell *et al.*, 2003)

Compensation schemes might serve to limit demands for migrant healthcare workers while simultaneously offering some relief, but at present such suggestions lack specificity, particularly with regard to mechanisms for collecting and setting compensation. Moreover, the political realities offer little likelihood that any significant compensation will ever occur.

In synthesizing a recent ILO study of migration of highly skilled persons from developing countries, Lowell and Findlay (2001) emphasize the potential for bilateral and multilateral agreements to limit the extent of a brain drain. Amongst other components this report suggests encouraging temporary rather than more permanent movements of the highly skilled, restricting duration of stay or immigration of people from at-risk occupations in specific countries, and facilitating return migration. A few agreements have been struck in specific spheres, notably in recruitment of healthcare workers. For example, 'Since 1995, South Africa has banned the recruitment of doctors from other Organisation of African Unity (OAU) countries in an attempt to reduce inflow from poorer countries.'[50] Moreover, in 2001 Britain's National Health Service promised to cease actively recruiting nurses from developing countries, though this promise appears not to have been terribly effective (see Chapter 10). On the other hand, some governments have shown little intent of restraint:

A committee of the Alberta Health Ministry has hired a professional recruiter to find doctors to fill the many vacancies for physicians in rural communities. The committee chair and the recruiter traveled to South Africa in March, 1997, and interviewed doctors who had been recruited through the press. They arranged for these doctors and their families to visit rural communities in Alberta and as a result they were able to recruit more than 40 South African doctors.[51]

More generally the OECD countries appear to be heightening the competition to attract the most able, not only in North America but more recently in Europe and, at least by statement of intent, in East Asia. It seems unlikely that the industrialized countries will show much restraint in their efforts to recruit the highly skilled; the world is exhibiting skill-biased technical progress and the demands on the highly skilled are steadily increasing. Any limits to the flow of highly skilled people from the low to the high income countries must realistically come from the developing countries themselves, though hopefully not in the form of emigration restrictions that can readily violate the basic human right of exit.

Encouraging return of the highly skilled is an option, though such attempts generally prove very expensive and meet with limited success. Moreover, the skills and experiences acquired abroad often prove of limited value in the lower technology settings of the developing countries (see Chapter 7). Curtailing overseas training might help to diminish the extent of ultimate mobility, though such aspirations are not always effective. (See Box 4.2 on restrictions on persons wishing to leave India for medical training.) Moreover, globalization is enhancing the value of foreign training; familiarity with other languages and cultures is increasingly vital in business; and students traveling abroad can exploit the comparative advantages of different host countries for specific training. Expanding domestic universities might attract some talented folks to stay at home, though the evidence suggests that any lack of capacity in home country universities is an insignificant force in driving students to leave (except in the very small countries).

BOX 4.2 RESTRICTING EMIGRATION OF MEDICAL PERSONNEL: THE CASE OF INDIA

Medical education in India is heavily subsidized by government. Nonetheless the number of doctors per capita remains only about two-thirds that of the average for the low income countries, and less than half of the number per capita in China.

For more than three decades, India has imposed various restrictions on medical education abroad. 'It started initially with the objective of controlling foreign exchange outflow and optimum use of facilities in India. Later the rationale was to regulate the out-migration of doctors and derived benefits of highly subsidized medical education provided to them for the country's poor' (Khadria, 2002: 39).

Permission for overseas training is granted under two categories. The Professional Trainee category permits a stay of up to seven years, with no additional time permitted to sit examinations, but requires a two-year stay in India that cannot be waived through issue of a No Obligation to Return to India Certificate. The category permitting visits abroad by teachers, professors, research scholars and specialists in medicine requires a No Objection Certificate which is issued only for designated categories of specialists, clearance by the Educational Commission for Foreign Medical Graduates in India, and posting of a bond. More recently there has been discussion of the possibility of introducing legislation to permit payment of fees, in lieu of education costs, for the issue of No Objection Certificates and for No Obligation to Return to India Certificates. 'The issue of compulsory rural service for a few years by the doctors going abroad also came up before the committee. But it was not agreed upon' (Khadria, 2002: 39).

On average from 1991–92 to 1997–98 only 442 Indian students are reported by the Ministry of Human Resource Development as going abroad to study medicine, pharmacy, dentistry and veterinary sciences, which is quite tiny in relation to the 14 800 students enrolled in medicine in India in 1992. On the other hand, the ministry reports fewer than 5000 students in total leaving the country annually during these seven years, whereas UNESCO reports a stock of more than 40 000 Indian students abroad around 1995. It seems plausible that many Indian students circumvent any exit regulations.

Moreover, the restrictions on study of medicine abroad do not appear to stem the brain drain of doctors. In 1997, the US National Science Foundation estimated there were more than 7500 Indian-born life scientists working just in the US universities, and a 1992 study of the All India Institute of Medical Sciences in Delhi estimated that about 56 percent of their graduates between 1956 and 1980 were now abroad.

A last option is to reconsider the financing of higher education in the lower income countries. As we have seen, the social costs of tertiary education are extraordinarily high, especially relative to incomes in the poorer countries. The social rates of return on this higher education are lower than on additional funding to more basic education. The major beneficiaries of college education are frequently the sons and daughters of the wealthy elite. The outcome of these heavily subsidized educations, at least in some contexts, is a brain overflow and emigration after graduation.

Widespread deliberations to restructure the financing of higher education are ongoing. An important part of this agenda involves shifting some of the burden of costs onto families who are able to pay, while maintaining an 'assurance of access for those of high ability and motivation, from families otherwise unable to pay'.[52] A wide range of scenarios is under discussion in various contexts, ranging from charging more realistic tuition fees (at least to those able to pay), to replacing systems of grants with student loan schemes, to greater selectivity in supporting institutions, and encouraging more private sector initiatives.[53]

Altering the financing of higher education will not answer concerns with shortages of medical professionals, of gifted teachers for the next generation, and of an enlightened elite. However, imposing a larger portion of the costs on those who benefit privately from a higher education may alleviate some of the frustration with those who leave after receiving a heavily subsidized education.

In closing, though, we should remind ourselves that not all movements of highly skilled migrants from low to high income countries represent a brain drain. Where emigration does not irreparably harm basic needs delivery, where higher education is largely paid for by the migrants themselves, where a brain overflow emerges, the costs of departure of the highly skilled may well be minimal. The potential benefits may also be significant. Goldfarb *et al.* (1984) calculate that the remittances from Filipino doctors overseas probably more than compensated for the cost of their training. Thus remittances and other potential contributions from an active diaspora, the subjects of the next two chapters, can turn a brain drain into a brain gain. Investing in education can prove worthwhile for emigration.

NOTES

1. The data on Australia, Canada and US refer to foreign-born adult populations, and in Denmark adults are ages 15–64.

2. According to the OECD estimates in Figure 4.1, 33.9 percent of the US foreign-born population possess a tertiary education. In comparison, the US Census Bureau (2001) reports that 42 percent of the 2000 US foreign-born population, ages 25 and over, have some tertiary education and 25.8 percent possess a bachelor's degree. Note, though, that the content and quality of a 'college' degree clearly varies across countries. Moreover, relying upon self-reported qualifications in any household survey bears its own risks.

3. This refers to all of Africa, South and Central America including Mexico, Asia except Japan, and Eastern Europe.

4. Data are from the US INS website at http://www.immigration.gov/. No data are available for 1997. 'Other nonagricultural temporary workers and trainees' refers to all Temporary Workers and Trainees other than those with H1B and H2A (Agricultural Workers) visas.

5. Salt (1997). On the other hand, Salt also notes that the UK 1995 Labour Force Survey showed that, although 42 percent of the non-EU labor force were employed in manual jobs, 30 percent were professionals, employers and managers. There is also a fairly high rate of non-EU intra-company transfer of employees to the UK, again suggesting a significant entry of high skilled workers, though many of these highly skilled are no doubt from non-European, OECD countries (especially the US).

6. That is, scientists, artists etc., managerial, executives, and administrative.

7. Mghari (2004) laments the loss of information technology personnel from Morocco to the US and Europe and of Moroccan researchers to France, though few data are available.

8. Salt (1997: 20).

9. Salt (1997: 21).

10. Salt (1997: 21). See also Malakha (2002).

11. Before 1974 most non-national professionals in the GCC states were Arab, though the role of the countries of South and South East Asia as a source of highly skilled migrants has almost certainly increased since then.

12. See Nair, 1998, Table 8.7.

13. Scalabrini Migration Center, Asian Migration Atlas 2000 at http://www.scalabrini.asn.au/atlas/amatlas.htm

14. On the other hand, the flow of professionals and of students from East Asia to Australia

has been more substantial. For example, Iredale (2000: table 2) reports the arrival of nearly 10 000 settlers from Asia, in 1996–97 alone, who subsequently became employed as managers, professionals, administrators and para-professionals.

15. See also the update by Adams (2003).

16. The results in Table 4.6 are similar to those for 1990 in Carrington and Detragiache (1999) and for 2000 in Adams (2003) but incorporate a broader set of countries. The measure of tertiary education among the home country population in Table 4.6 includes only those with completed qualifications, which differs from the two earlier studies. Both of the prior studies also present comparable results on migration to the OECD countries as a whole. Although such measures would be of considerable interest they are not reproduced here because of the difficulties of interpreting some of these estimates. Both studies are founded on the assumption that the educational content of migration to non-US OECD countries is identical to migrations to the US. For example, migrants from Morocco to France are assumed to have the same educational profile as migrants from Morocco to the US. Second, the stocks of migrants in the various OECD countries may well be biased downwards by the inclusion only of migration from the largest source countries, and by the omission of many short-term and illegal movers. Third, as an approximation of the total brain drain any estimates for the OECD alone are necessarily biased downwards by omission of movements to the Middle East or within much of East Asia, for example.

17. Calculations proved possible for some 76 countries. Table 4.6 omits all higher income countries and countries with population, ages 25 and over, of less than three million.

18. Grubel and Scott (1966).

19. For a concise summary, see Bhagwati and Rodriguez (1975).

20. For reviews, see Lucas (1981, 1997).

21. For an excellent survey and discussion of these components, see Davies (2003).

22. Davies (2003) refers to these as static and dynamic market externalities respectively.

23. Ciccone and Hall (1996).

24. Specifically, average schooling is instrumented on variations in compulsory schooling and child labor laws.

25. In contrast to the potential for international migration to lead toward convergence in global pay structures, international migration of highly skilled workers may then, instead, become cumulative. For applications of these ideas to international migration see Miyagiwa (1991), Haque and Kim (1995) and Faini (1996).

26. See Kapur (2001).

27. On the effects upon economic growth of the number of years of schooling completed on average in the population, across countries, see Barro (1999). On the roles of primary and secondary school enrollment rates in contributing to growth, see Barro (1991) and the sensitivity analysis in Levine and Renelt (1992), who note that a measure of secondary schooling complete is difficult to distinguish from primary schooling or literacy measures. In a similar vein, Chatterji (1998) inserts tertiary enrollment and again finds little difference from secondary school effects. Straubhaar and Wolburg (1999) undertake related work, demonstrating that average labor productivity in Eastern Europe is positively associated with more highly skilled people in the labor force.

28. See also the study by OECD (2001).

29. Davies (2003: 25).

30. See, for example, Buchan *et al.* (2003) on the international migration of nurses and OECD (2003) on South African health professionals in particular.

31. World Bank (2000a: 54).

32. Figure 4.4 is based on the data in Table 4.7, which incorporates both the World Bank estimates for 1995 and an update by the author for 2000, permitting inclusion of a wider set of countries.

33. A third, though rather different aspect is the induced migration of replacement skilled workers. 'The *South African Medical Journal* describes a "medical carousel", in which doctors seem to be continually moving to countries with a perceived higher standard of living. Pakistani doctors move to the UK, UK doctors move to Canada, and Canadians move to the USA' (Bundred and Levitt, 2000).

34. The latter suggests that estimates of the private returns to higher education, based on domestic salaries alone, can significantly underestimate these personal gains.

35. See also Alburo and Abella (2002) and Tan (1993).

36. 'Supply responses to the overseas market are evident in the increase in the number of private schools specializing in medicine, nursing and maritime training' (Tan, 1993: 321). To some extent the expansion in information technology training in India reflects the same phenomenon.

37. In contrast, Beine *et al.* (2001) report a positive effect of the overall rate of migration to the OECD countries upon the average level of education in the home country population among the 29 lower income countries from a sample of 37 countries. As Faini (2002) notes, however, this could simply reflect the withdrawal of sufficient unskilled workers to raise average education amongst those remaining at home and, in consequence, Faini prefers to turn to data on enrollment rates rather than the stock of educated population.

38. Faini (2002) also explores controls for educational spending relative to GPD and for the export share of natural resources but finds that neither of these additional controls matter after controlling for GDP per capita.

39. A similar pattern to that found by Faini (2002) can also be confirmed, at least with respect to tertiary education, based on our estimates of the rate of emigration to the US from sixty countries (some of which are reported in Table 4.6). An ordinary least squares regression analysis, with the logarithm of gross tertiary enrollment rate in each country in 2000 as dependent variable, provides:

$$-2.51 \quad -0.90 HSE + 0.15\ HSE^2 + 0.66 \log \text{GDP}$$
$$(3.63) \quad (2.03) \qquad (1.71) \qquad (9.23)$$

where *HSE* represents the rate of high skilled emigration as in Table 4.6, divided by 100 (60 observations, $R^2 = 0.67$, t-statistics in parentheses). This pattern is fairly robust to inclusion of major regional dummy variables to proxy for the effects of distance, and indicates a decline in enrollment up to a brain drain rate at 300 percent on the scale in Table 4.6.

40. Faini (2002: 9).

41. The data for 1980 and 1990 refer to the closest year available. The data for Portugal in the 2001 column refer to 1994–95 and in that instance non-OECD refers to non-European.

42. The data in Table 4.10 again include only students in the 50 countries with the largest tertiary foreign student populations. In particular the EU totals omit data for foreign students in Greece and Luxembourg, though in both the total were apparently less than 1500 students.

43. The overall growth rate of non-OECD students in the EU-15 was slower than in all but two of the member countries because of the very slow expansion in France, which already hosted 41 percent of the non-OECD students in the EU by 1990.

44. The data on students abroad are from UNESCO (1998) and include only the numbers reported in the top 50 countries with tertiary level foreign students. Data on population and GDP per capita (measured in US$ at purchasing power parity prices in 1995) are from the United Nations Development Program (1998), *Human Development Report*, New York: Oxford University Press with additional population data from Eurostat (2002) and UN (2002a).

45. The data on gross enrollment rates are downloaded from www.ksg.harvard.edu as originally reported in UNESCO Statistical Yearbooks.

46. Finn's (2001) measures of the stay rates are derived by matching social security numbers of foreign doctorate recipients with those from employment records.

47. I am grateful to Boris Pleskovic for drawing my attention to this possibility.

48. Hugo (1996) attributes the inset quote, in added italics, to 'Pernia, 1976, p. 71'.

49. Bhagwati and Partington (1976).

50. Bundred and Levitt (2000).

51. Bundred and Levitt (2000).

52. Johnstone (1998: conclusions, pages unnumbered).

53. For reviews of some of the issues involved and extensive references, see Ziderman and Albrecht (1995) and Johnstone (1998).

5. Reported and Informal Remittances: How Much? Who Sends? Who Benefits?

Among those developing and transition economies where labor market slack is a chronic problem, exporting labor in return for remittances poses an attractive component of a development strategy. Certainly global remittances have grown steadily and have come to be a major source of international finance for the developing regions. Yet reported remittances received vary substantially across the developing countries, even among the major countries of emigration. Three questions are therefore posed in this chapter:

1. What are the determinants of cross-country variations in remittance flows? Here, the intent is twofold: to learn how much of the variation in remittances received by different countries is attributable to such factors as whether their migrants are skilled or unskilled, permanent or temporary, men or women, refugees or contract workers, and hence provide a link with our more general discussion on migration regimes; and to consider the role of macroeconomic factors that shape remittances to guide policy discussion.

2. To what extent do migrant sending countries really benefit economically from the remittances returned, and what can be told about how any benefits are distributed among the home country population? Perceptions of the economic benefits derived from remittances are very much in the eye of the beholder. The governments of many of the major migrant sending countries see remittances from their overseas nationals as an unsolicited resource, providing much needed foreign exchange and savings. Yet doubts have been raised about the economic benefits of remittances; doubts about whether remittances are translated into investments, about the moral hazard effects on labor supply, the potential for inflation, and whether remittances contribute to income inequality across families.[1]

3. How effective are the various policy options for reshaping both the extent and economic benefit from remittances?

Section 5.1 establishes a general background against which these three questions may be deliberated, describing the broad nature of global remittance patterns and sketching some of the ideas and issues that arise with respect to both causes and consequences of migrant remittances. Section 5.2 then turns to the evidence with special attention to our case study countries. Finally, Section 5.3 returns to a broader perspective, attempting to draw comparisons across our case studies and placing these in the context of wider results.

5.1   THE SETTING: MAGNITUDES AND ISSUES

The global system of remittances comprises both formal and informal transfers. Systematic data exist only on the formal flows, and some key patterns in these data are brought out in the first part of this section. Far less is known about the flows of remittances through informal channels, though it is commonly hypothesized that these flows are correlated with black market premia on foreign exchange. Some of the evidence, including simulated informal flows derived from this presumed correlation, is therefore also summarized here. The next subsection then offers a brief review of some of the hypotheses that have been put forward with respect to both the determinants and economic consequences of remittance flows, by way of providing a framework for reviewing the evidence from our case study areas in Section 5.2.

In Perspective: The Magnitudes of Formal and Informal Remittances

The World Bank's 2003 *Global Development Finance Report* notes that remittances to the developing countries are large, stable and growing:

> In 2001, workers' remittance receipts of developing countries stood at $72.3 billion, much higher than total official flows and private non-FDI flows, and 42 percent of total FDI flows to developing countries ... Remittances are also more stable than private capital flows, which often move pro-cyclically ... By contrast, remittances are less volatile – and may even rise – in response to economic cycles in the recipient country. They are expected to rise significantly in the long term, once sluggish labor markets in G-7 economies recover.[2]

Each of these features is illustrated in Figure 5.1.[3] As the top panel shows, both direct foreign investment and remittances received by the developing countries have grown rapidly during the 1990s. The measure of remittances in this top panel shows inflows minus outflows, which is naturally smaller than the gross inflow of US$72 billion cited by the World Bank. However, the net receipt of remittances of the developing regions (excluding the GCC states) amounted to nearly US$58 billion in 2001, as compared to ODA of US$50 billion and direct investment of US$176 billion. Each of these three items goes toward financing the balance of trade on goods and services. The top panel of Figure 5.1 therefore also shows the deficit on trade in goods and

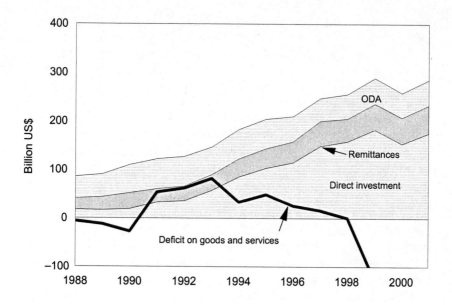

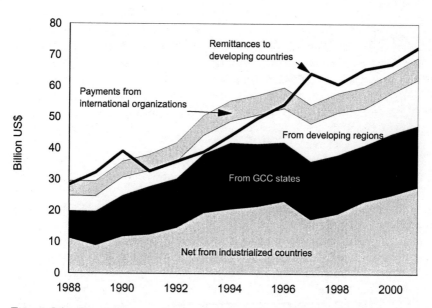

Figure 5.1 *Remittances to the developing countries, 1988–2001*

services for the developing countries (again excluding the GCC states). From 1991 through 1997, this deficit averaged nearly US$41 billion, of which net remittance receipts equaled more than 95 percent. Since 1998, the balance of goods and services has turned to a surplus for the developing countries (even excluding the oil-producing GCC states), as has the balance on current account. Nonetheless, a wide range of developing countries continues to possess a chronic balance of trade problem, and for these countries, remittances may play a key role in the ability to finance the deficit.

The lower panel of Figure 5.1 shows the total gross inflow of remittances to the developing countries, excluding the GCC states, according to IMF estimates. If there were global country coverage and no errors in reporting then clearly total inflows should equal total outflows of remittances. In this event, the inflow of remittances to the developing countries should equal the total of all outflows minus the inflow to the industrialized countries. Accordingly this latter total is also shown in the lower panel of Figure 5.1, represented by the outer edge of the shaded area. Accordingly this latter total is also shown in the lower panel of Figure 5.1, represented by the outer edge of the four shaded areas. The bottom portion of these shaded areas depicts the net remittances from the industrialized countries to the developing countries. The next three portions represent gross remittances sent from the GCC states, from other developing countries, and payments by international organizations. These latter three components include transfers both to industrialized and **to** developing countries. However, most of the transfers from the GCC states are to the developing regions. The total for the GCC states, shown in Figure 5.1 omits Qatar and the UAE for which data are not available. From the four remaining GCC states, remittances between 1990–2001 amounted to 92 percent of the remittances from the entire set of industrialized countries to the developing countries, and more than a third of the total remittances received by developing countries.

The *Global Development Finance Report* also goes on to show that 'Remittances to low-income countries were larger as a share of GDP and imports than were those to middle income countries'.[4] Indeed, the report demonstrates that both shares decline systematically across higher income groups of countries (see Table 5.1).

This property is demonstrated in more detail in Figure 5.2, in which the upper panel shows remittances relative to GDP for 83 developing countries in 2000 on the vertical axis, against GDP per capita.[5] The best-fit line is drawn through these data and exhibits a negative slope. However, the developing countries in this sample are clearly spread widely around the line, and indeed the association with GDP per capita is relatively weak statistically. The lower panel of Figure 5.2 shows the same set of countries, but now places remittances received per capita, rather than relative to GDP, on the vertical axis, revealing a statistically significant positive association with income level.[6] In other words, gross remittance receipts per person are lower in the poorer countries. It is precisely because these are poorer countries that receipts relative to income are somewhat greater in the poorer economies, though there are wide variations to these average patterns too.

Table 5.1   Remittances relative to GDP and relative to imports, 2001

	Remittances relative to	
	GDP (%)	Imports (%)
Low income countries	1.9	6.2
Lower middle income countries	1.4	5.1
Upper middle income countries	0.8	2.7
High income OECD countries	0.2	0.7

Source: Ratha (2003: Figure 7.2).

Do the countries exhibiting large remittances simply reflect the extent of out-migration or is there more to the observed patterns? One way to consider this is to ask how particular countries deviate from typical remittance levels given their migration rates. The only systematic, cross-country data on migration available are the UN estimates of net migration. However, in looking at net migration levels, it is important also to recognize that many developing countries are not only recipients of remittance inflows but are themselves sources of outward remittance flows. For 76 developing countries, data on net remittances (inflows minus outflows) during 2000 can be compared to the reported rate of net outward migration from 1990 to 2000. The association is positive, with larger net migration flows producing larger remittances on average, and the effect is statistically significant. Moreover net out-migration during the last five years of the 1990s had a larger effect on remittances than out-migration in the first five years of the 1990s.[7] The ten countries with the highest rates of reported net remittances, given their rate of net migration, and the ten with the lowest reported remittances, are both listed in Table 5.2.[8]

Several countries from our case study areas appear in these lists. For instance, India, the Philippines, Turkey, Russia and Morocco are amongst the highest recipients of remittances, given their net migration rates, while Thailand, Bangladesh, Sri Lanka and Tunisia are also within the top twenty countries. On the other hand, Pakistan, Indonesia, Bulgaria and Romania record only small remittances despite high net out-migration levels. The last column in Table 5.2 reminds us that a number of countries report no gross remittance receipts at all between 1995 and 2001, according to the IMF *Balance of Payments Statistics*, despite fairly substantial net out-migration during this period.

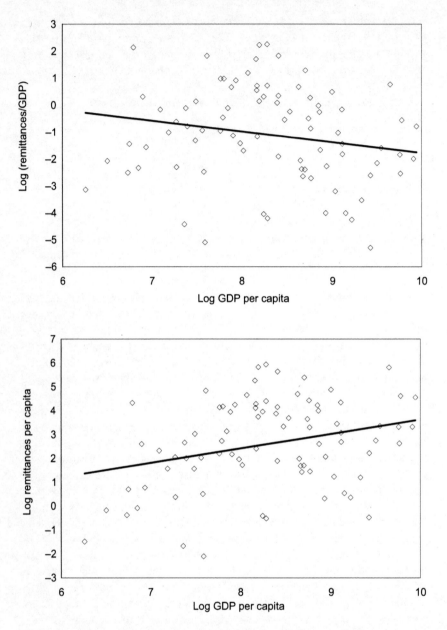

Figure 5.2   Remittances received by per capita income: 83 developing countries, 2000

Table 5.2 Top and bottom ten net remittance recipient countries conditioned on extent of net migration

Highest net remittance receipts relative to net migration	Lowest net remittance receipts relative to net migration	Zero remittances 1995–2001: despite high net out-migration level
India	China	Iran
Mexico	Israel	Burundi
Philippines	Kazakhstan	Burkina Faso
Turkey	Pakistan	Sierra Leone
Russian Federation	Indonesia	Haiti
Egypt	Ukraine	Chile
Jordan	Bulgaria	Malawi
Yemen	Romania	Guyana
Rwanda	Czech Republic	
Morocco	South Africa	

Source: Author's calculations

Many factors may underlie these differences and consideration of some of these is taken up in the next section. Meanwhile, however, one potential factor warrants particular consideration, for some of the differences across countries, such as those noted in Table 5.2, may actually be a reflection of the manner in which data are collected. Thus, the World Bank's figure of $72.3 billion in total remittances to the developing countries during 2001, depicted in Figure 5.1, is both large and an underestimate. Remittances recorded on balance of payments account by the IMF represent only the officially recorded flows of remittances. For the most part, these official figures leave out all transfers occurring through informal channels.[9] These informal networks of money dealers commonly offer speedier and cheaper means of transfer than going through the formal channels. However, a number of concerns have been expressed with respect to the operation of the informal fund transfer system, ranging from potential links with terrorist funding, to macroeconomic consequences with respect to exchange rate determination and tax collection. Not surprisingly, the extent of informal transfers is nowhere recorded. However, it seems plausible that the relative portion of funds passing through informal channels is greater where the black market premium on foreign exchange is higher; in part, such an association would result from the inducement to take advantage of this parallel exchange market. A recent IMF study makes use of this likelihood to simulate unrecorded transfers to fifteen developing countries which have high rates of out-migration and a history of parallel exchange markets. It should be emphasized that the parameters of this model are 'judgmental, based on our current understanding of the factors that bear on hawala remittances in each of these countries'[10] since no data are available for actual estimation. Nonetheless it is interesting to note that the calculations and impressions of the authors of this IMF study indicate that perhaps 40 percent of total remittances were conveyed through informal channels to the fifteen selected countries, on average, during the last two decades of the twentieth century. For Algeria, Bangladesh, Iran, Pakistan, Sudan and Tanzania the authors suggest that more than half of remittances were informally transmitted; for India, the Philippines and Turkey, within our case study areas, the proportions were far less. The implication would also be that for most countries that do not exhibit an active parallel exchange market, informal transfers are likely to be far less than for the fifteen countries purposely selected for analysis by the IMF, and indeed the study suggests that informal remittances may have declined substantially over time as black market premia have generally been eroded.

On the Determinants and Consequences of Remittances: A Synopsis of Issues

What are the main hypotheses and ideas that have been put forward to explain both how much migrants remit and how these flows affect the home country?

Determinants

A number of ideas have been suggested to explain why migrants remit at all and what determines how much they send. These ideas may be divided roughly into two broad categories: those which focus on the circumstances of migration and the migrants' connection with the home setting; and those which focus on the macroeconomic conditions and policies in both the home and host countries.[11]

The first, obvious notion within the former group is that the migrant behaves altruistically toward family or kin left behind.[12] To the extent that this is a principal driving force one might then expect to see more remittances, out of any given level of migrant's income, where migration results in family separation, and especially where the family at home is less well-off economically. At the opposite extreme, a number of reasons for migrants to remit out of pure self-interest may be envisioned. For example, the migrant may intend to return home and wish to acquire a home, land and goodwill, in the home area, in anticipation of this return. Given that the family at home is particularly well placed to ensure the migrants' investments are protected, as well as to enhance his reputation, these investments may well be passed initially to the family as remittance income. Presumably such remittances by target savers are likely to be larger among migrants who are, in some sense, temporarily away. Moreover, no matter whether the motive is target saving by the migrant or altruism toward those at home, remittances are likely to rise with the migrants' income received while overseas. Another possibility is that remittances arise from a mutual agreement between migrant and home to share incomes in times of adversity; the migrant may be supported from home during an initial period of adjustment overseas, and in turn send relief in the event of bad times at home. The combination of altruism, target saving and mutual insurance raises a further set of issues about the interrelationships between remittances and other sources of transfer. For example, where poverty alleviation programs are in place, public pension schemes exist, or disaster relief is available, the possibility that these may displace the need for remittances emerges.[13] Remittances may also reflect effective repayment of an implicit loan;[14] for instance, understandings are reported to be common that a family, or extended family, invests in educating a promising member who is then expected to support the family, while working overseas, in return. Whether skilled migrants are thus likely to remit more is complex; on the one hand they may have an obligation to repay their education costs and they presumably earn more (and hence can afford to be more altruistic), but on the other hand, emigration by skilled migrants is more likely to be permanent and to involve family accompaniment, both tending to diminish remitting. Finally, special mention may be made of the distinction between refugees and other types of migrants. Refugees, asylum seekers and exiles in general might be anticipated to have severed their concerns with the country of origin. Moreover, most refugees lack the resources to contemplate much by way of remittances. However, where refugees are resettled in more affluent settings or manage to gain asylum in higher income countries, the question arises as to how much remitting occurs, either to family and kin remaining at home or to those still in another country of first asylum.[15]

Different groups of migrants are thus likely to behave quite differently with respect to remitting to their home areas, suggesting that alternative migration regimes can have very different implications for the extent of transfers. On top of this, however, the remitting behavior of all migrant groups is likely to be affected by the macroeconomic climate in both the migrant-sending and the host country. In the host country, the better the earnings opportunities for a given group of migrants, the greater are remittances likely to be. In other words, economic growth within a given host country and greater concentration of migration toward the higher income countries are both normally hypothesized to lead to greater remittance flows (other things equal). Most other aspects of the macroeconomic setting are far more ambiguous.

For example, the effects upon remittances of currency depreciation in the home country may, in principle, go in either direction. On the one hand, depreciation makes it more affordable to support those at home and this may tempt the migrant to increase the real level of support provided. On the other hand, each given level of support requires less foreign exchange. The issue then becomes which effect dominates and the balance may go either way.[16] Of course, in either event it is the real buying power of the currency in which the person remitting is really interested. More rapid inflation in the migrant-sending country requires greater remittance of foreign exchange to achieve given purchasing power, and hence requires greater remittance to ensure the well-being of kin at home or to repay debt. Conversely though, rapid and fluctuating inflation rates may signal instability and hence discourage remitting. Even the role of differences in interest rates has been hypothesized to be ambiguous. To the extent that migrants are concerned to invest their savings, the greater is the interest rate at home, relative to returns available abroad, the more is likely to be remitted for investment.[17] Yet Glytsos (2001) notes this could be offset if a rise in the host country interest rate increases migrants' wealth and hence affords greater remittances, though perhaps for most migrants this additional effect is likely to be small.[18] Finally, a rise in the premium exchange rate on any active, parallel market may well encourage switching from recorded to informal remittances, though the effect on (unmeasured) total remittances is far less clear.

There is sufficient ambiguity in the hypothesized effects of some of the macroeconomic determinants of remittances, as well as in some of the attributes of migrants (such as their level of education), that empirical evidence is clearly called for to disentangle the various components. Most studies focus on the macroeconomic determinants, using officially recorded, annual time series data, or cross-country data, or panels incorporating both. A few studies have examined more micro-evidence, decomposing remittances by types of migrants and families, but in a common macroeconomic setting so that differences in exchange rates or interest rate structures are irrelevant. Both are reviewed in Section 5.2. The interests in doing so are rather distinct. The main interest in the macroeconomic determinants of remittances is really with regard to policy potential to enhance transfers from a given set of migrants. On the other hand, the variation in remittance behavior among different types of migrants provides an important link with the composition of population movements and hence the policies that shape these migration outcomes.

Economic consequences

Most remittances are sent to family or extended family members in the home community of the migrant. This does not necessarily imply that the family's income increases by the amount of the remittance, however, for the family may elect to make some adjustments for themselves. One possibility, for example, is that the family at home may reduce their willingness to participate in the labor force, given access to remittance income instead.[19]

Nonetheless, the distribution of incomes across families will be altered by the impact of remittance receipts, depending upon whether it is the wealthier or more indigent families that receive most of the transfers.[20] In turn, the remittances received by a typical family at any point on the income distribution scale may be decomposed into three issues: the likelihood of emigration according to income class of the family; the correlation between family income and earning power of the migrant; and the effect of family income upon the decision of the migrant to remit. At least two of these components are ambiguous. Whether migrants are more likely to be drawn from poor or from rich families represents a mix of effects, ranging from lower income opportunities at home for the poor, to greater ability to finance costly moves, or to possess contacts to enable migration, for the rich. Similarly, whether migrants will remit more to poor or to wealthy families, out of a given level of earnings, is also mixed. Altruism may motivate greater remittance to poor families, whereas concerns about inheriting family assets or the ability of wealthy families to channel investments effectively for the migrant may swell remittances to richer families instead. On the other hand, the higher levels of education typical of the children of wealthier families normally mean greater earning potential overseas, as well as higher chances of gaining entry to the higher income countries, both tending to enhance remittances to the upper income classes, though offset by greater permanence of removal of the better educated migrants.

To deduce who benefits and who loses from such impact effects alone may, however, be quite misleading.[21] The enhanced incomes that result from remittances can, in turn, induce higher incomes even for families that receive no remittances at all. One mechanism through which this may operate, in demand-deficient economies, is through the multiplier effects of expanded spending. As migrants' families increase their consumption of services or goods produced in sectors with excess capacity, the additional demand can create jobs for other families who in turn spend and create further demands. One important aspect of this is the extent to which any such beneficial effects of additional spending out of remittances are concentrated solely within the community or region from which migrants originate. The origins of migrants tend to be concentrated in particular areas or even specific villages, in part driven by the cumulative effects of migrant networks. If the multiplier effects of demands out of remittances are concentrated largely in these specific communities, then the economic benefits derived in other regions may be relatively limited.[22]

The extent to which remittances lead to additional investments has been much discussed, though some of the discussion has been confused. The issue of whether the cash received is actually spent on investments is not the point. First, remittances represent a fungible source of funds to the family; a more appropriate starting point is therefore to examine whether families with incomes enhanced by remittances save more. Second, it should be recognized that spending on education, housing and land are forms of investments. Third, what may be an investment by one family may or may not be an investment for the country. For example, if the family receiving remittances buys additional land, an existing house, or even repays outstanding debts, the question arises as to how the recipient of these payments spends the income. Fourth, at the macroeconomic level, the mere inflow of remittances on balance of payments account does not imply addition national investment any more than do additional inflows on capital account; the inflow may instead be consumed either privately or through government spending.[23] How much is invested depends upon the returns that can be obtained by those whose incomes are increased by the remittances. In turn, this raises some important questions about the role of publicly-provided infrastructure as a complement to induce investments out of remittances, and of the potential for micro-credit organizations to channel resources effectively.

In fact, the mere potential of support through remittances from absent migrants, in the event that things go badly, may suffice to encourage the family at home to adopt riskier strategies and technologies, even if remittances are not the norm in more typical times.[24] Assuming that a trade-off exists between choices that are less risky and those that pay better on average, this insurance aspect of remittances has consequently also been hypothesized to raise incomes at home.

At the macroeconomic level, remittances can also serve as an important source of foreign exchange.[25] Clearly the value of this to any given country depends very much on just how scarce is foreign exchange and the uses to which additional reserves can be put. However, for countries that are encumbered with debt overhang, are experiencing severe and chronic trade imbalances and difficulties attracting foreign direct or financial investors, or that are otherwise constrained in production by inability to import materials, the contribution of remittances to economic expansion is potentially considerable. Whether the foreign exchange inflow is permitted to translate into monetary expansion is largely discretionary. Nonetheless, remittances may increase upward pressure on prices, where key production capacities are limited, through demand expansion. In addition, remittances may allow a real appreciation of the exchange rate, or at least postpone real depreciation, which in turn serves to limit development of import competing and export industries, together with their employment potential. This last effect has led some observers to compare the effects of remittances to those of the Dutch disease problem, engendered by foreign exchange inflows from mineral exports.[26]

In sum, the extent to which remittances are a net benefit to recipient families, whether other families benefit at all, the balance of macroeconomic benefits, and the consequences for income inequality, cannot be resolved from theory alone. Empirical evidence is essential to resolution and may well vary from context to context as the type of migration alters.

5.2 DETERMINANTS, CONSEQUENCES AND POLICIES: SPECIFIC COUNTRY EXPERIENCES

The intent in this section is consequently to look at the experiences with remittances in our case study areas, to consider what has influenced the flows of remittances, what effects remittances have had upon the countries of origin, and the role of policy in both. Section 5.3 then summarizes these observations in the context of more global evidence and tries to draw out some of the differences between the various migration regimes. Before commencing our case-by-case review, Table 5.3 attempts to place these case studies in perspective by first looking at the officially recorded outflows of remittances in each of our four regions.

In 2000, the total global outflow of Workers' Remittances and Compensation of Employees, according to the IMF *Balance of Payments Statistics*, summed to US$101.8 billion. The UN (2002a) estimates that just over 95 percent of the world's stock of migrants in 2000 were residing in the set of countries represented in these IMF estimates. Among the countries where both migrant stock and remittance estimates thus exist, remittances amounted to some $572 per migrant in officially recorded flows alone.

Figure 5.3 shows a breakdown of these remittances by major region of origin. The pie chart displays the totals while the bar chart shows remittances per migrant stock. The two tell quite different stories. Whereas the US is the single largest source of remittances, relative to migrant stock remittances from the US are actually slightly lower than from the EU.[27] From Australia and New Zealand remittances, even per worker, are reported to be quite small and Canada reports no remittances at all in any year (which certainly reflects the vagaries of the reporting system). The four East Asian newly industrialized countries for which data are available (see Table 5.3), combined with Japan, contribute only 3.5 percent of global remittances.[28] In fact, per migrant among the remaining developing countries (for which the IMF reports remittance data), the average is 37 percent of the amount per migrant sent from East Asia. Reported remittances were clearly very small in 2000 from the East Asia economies and this is also true relative to the extent of migration. On the other hand, the massive remittances per migrant from the GCC states are apparent in the bar chart in Figure 5.3. Data are available for only four of the GCC states (see Table 5.3) and from these four Workers' Remittances were reported to total nearly $20 billion, which is $2687 per migrant.

Variations in the systems of reporting even formal remittances, not to

Table 5.3 Recorded remittances by source country of remittance in 2000

	Workers' Remittances (US$m)	Compensation of Employees (US$m)	Remittances per migrant ($)		
			Workers' Remittances	Compensation of Employees	Total
World total	56 626	45 219			
World total where migrant stock known	56 626	38 679	340	232	572
EU-15	9 489	14 994	359	567	926
Austria	280	383	370	507	877
Belgium-Luxemb.	431	2 932	414	2 817	3 231
Denmark	0	662	0	2 178	2 178
Finland	0	100	0	746	746
France	2 693	1 093	429	174	603
Germany	3 191	4 234	434	576	1 010
Greece	295	251	552	470	1 022
Ireland	4	105	13	339	352
Italy	541	1 960	331	1 200	1 531
Netherlands	522	925	331	587	918
Portugal	173	127	742	545	1 288
Spain	1 325	414	1 052	329	1 381
Sweden	34	488	34	491	526
UK	0	1 320	0	328	328
Other W. Europe	1 703	6 346	805	2 999	3 804
Bahrain	1 013	0	3 988	0	3 988
Kuwait	1 734	0	1 565	0	1 565
Oman	1 451	0	2 128	0	2 128
Saudi Arabia	15 411	0	2 933	0	2 933
Hong Kong	0	7	0	3	3
Japan	2 259	272	1 394	168	1 562
Korea	227	51	380	85	466
Malaysia	0	490	0	352	352
Singapore	0	0	0	0	0
Australia	0	592	0	126	126
New Zealand	124	0	146	0	146
Canada	0	0	0	0	0
US	18 610	8 210	532	235	767
Developing countries	4 606	7 717	60	100	160
Africa	1 474	860	107	63	170
Asia	1 093	1 512	65	90	154
Europe	243	1 458	7	45	52
Middle East	501	3 422	60	407	466
Americas	1 295	465	245	88	333

Sources: IMF *Balance of Payments Statistics 2002* and UN (2002a).

(a) Total remittances

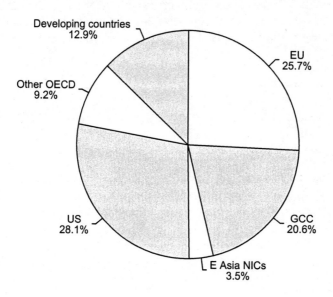

(b) Remittance per migrant

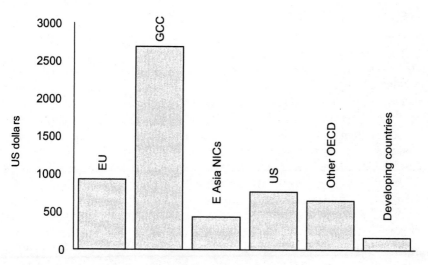

Figure 5.3   Reported remittances by region of origin, 2000

mention issues in measuring the migrant stocks, make comparisons difficult. Nonetheless the broad picture seems clear. The US and the EU are major sources of remittances and appear to provide roughly comparable remittances per migrant on average. Reported remittances are small in the case of the East Asian economies, but quite massive from the GCC states both per worker and in aggregate.

The European Union

Three dominant streams of migration to the EU were distinguished in Chapter 2: from Eastern Europe, especially since 1990; a longer-run migration pattern from Turkey and the Maghreb; and smaller numbers of migrants and asylum seekers from other parts of the developing world. Given the complete absence of data on bilateral remittance flows, it is almost impossible to judge how much of the remittances received by the third group of countries originates from the EU. Indeed, any indications of how much of the remittances that are debited to the EU members also appear as credits, being transfers among the EU-15 members, are very partial at best. However, it seems probable that a large part of the remittances entering the countries bordering Europe to the east, as well as to the Maghreb countries and Turkey, originates from the EU and other countries of Western Europe. The average annual remittances reported by the IMF, between 1995 and 2001, to some of the individual countries in these two regions are summarized in Table 5.4.[29] To understand a little better the importance of these remittances, however, a closer look is taken at three individual countries: Albania, Moldova and Morocco.

Albania

Much of the massive migration from Albania since 1991 has been to Greece and to Italy, with increasing onward movement to countries such as the UK.[30] Although there were perhaps 600–800 000 Albanians living abroad in 2000 (close to a quarter of the population), the UNHCR recognized only 8757 Albanian refugees, residing mostly in Canada and the US at the end of 2002. Indeed, the recent study by King *et al.* (2003) notes that a large portion of the migrants are undocumented, and goes on to note some important characteristics of these migrants. They are predominantly young (ages 15–39), single and overwhelmingly male; Albanian women have migrated largely within the context of family migration rather than alone. Konica and Filer (2003) estimate that the population with secondary schooling is over-represented among emigrants, while university graduates and those with primary schooling are under-represented, a fact that is shown by Konica and Filer not merely to reflect the age structure of the emigrants. Nonetheless, most Albanians work abroad in fairly low skill occupations. Some of the migration to Greece has apparently been on a transient basis with back and

Table 5.4   Average annual reported remittance inflows: select countries of Eastern Europe, the Maghreb and Turkey, 1995–2001

	Million dollars	Dollars per capita	Relative to	
			GDP (%)	Exports (%)
Albania	498	147		211.18
Belarus	45	4	0.42	0.76
Bulgaria	53	6	0.44	1.13
Croatia	606	133	3.07	13.47
Macedonia	71	36	1.87	5.87
Moldova	116	30	7.84	13.18
Romania	57	3	0.15	0.60
Russia	335	2	0.12	0.38
Ukraine	23	0	0.03	0.15
Morocco	2200	79	6.40	30.82
Tunisia	758	81	3.88	13.04
Turkey	4042	63	2.21	13.62

Sources: IMF *Balance of Payments Statistics* and *International Financial Statistics.*

forth movement to Albania. Indeed, Konica and Filer (2003) more generally report a fairly high rate of return migration to Albania perhaps reflecting a relative ease of re-entry to the EU (see Chapter 7). The migrants are drawn from larger than average families, come mostly from rural areas and 'emigration has been particularly intense from the northern and southern extremities of the country'.[31] In other words, migrants are drawn from some of the poorest settings, for 'The incidence of rural poverty was found to be five times higher than urban poverty and is highest in the North of Albania, where a large portion of families own less than 0.5 hectare of land each.'[32]

'Remittances are the key to survival for those who remain – mainly older people, plus some younger women and children.'[33] This reliance on remittances is not surprising. 'Already in 1995, around a quarter of Albanian families had one or more of their members involved in migration; a third of these had two or more members abroad'[34] and the impacts of the pyramid and Kosovo crises of 1997 and 1999 were yet to be felt. Moreover, 'the remittances sent by one Albanian migrant are equivalent to 2.5 times the sum of the average wages of all members of a family'.[35]

Interviews conducted by King *et al.* (2003) indicate that remittances decline after the first few years away, and that migrants who have not yet established a family abroad remit more.[36] Sons send more to their parents than do daughters, but this is partly because many of the women who are overseas are married and expected to support their in-laws rather than their own parents. Indeed, the entire system of remitting is described as patriarchal, with men controlling both the sending and spending. Nonetheless the outcome is a fairly common story emerging from many contexts:

> Remittances ... were first and foremost used for day-to-day survival (food, clothing etc.), then to improve living conditions – indoor toilets, piped water, furniture and domestic appliances – and then for the building of a new house or house extension. Only a few instances were found of remittances being invested in business activities (mostly shops, agricultural improvements etc.). Lack of credit facilities and infrastructures (reliable power, decent roads and other communications, irrigation systems etc.) were barriers to returnees and 'residual' households initiating business ventures.[37]

In Albania, some of the effects of international remittances may also be linked with internal migration. Although many of the overseas migrants are from the poor areas of the north, their families had frequently relocated to the towns of central Albania, prior to the migrant's departure. Moreover, evidence from interviews in Albania suggests that remittances from international migration are often used to finance internal migration to the urban areas, a form of investment that is not often recognized as such, while overseas migrants express an intent to return to the towns of Albania.[38] It seems probable that this urban relocation may concentrate the benefits of migration, whether direct or indirect, upon Tirana and the other main towns rather than upon the poorest areas of the north. Nonetheless, in their poverty reduction strategy paper, the World Bank (2000b: 2) notes that 'Especially in rural areas, the poverty rate is minimal where household heads have migrated and returned home; the poverty rate is slightly higher where household heads abroad are currently sending remittances.' Yet this observation may simply reflect the inability of the heads of the poorest households to return, because of the need to continue remitting, rather than implying that absence of heads causes additional poverty.

Certainly the World Bank (2000b: 2) goes on to note that 'remittances constitute a major informal safety net' in Albania. Remittances have also represented a key source of foreign exchange, which is brought out in Figure 5.4 which shows how Albania's rapidly mounting deficit on trade in goods and services since 1990 has been financed. Both official and private financial inflows on capital account have played a relatively small role, although there has been some increase in direct investment in Albania since the turn of the millennium. It is remittances that have financed more than 70 percent of the deficit since 1995.[39]

There is little sign that these remittances have been a serious source of inflation. In the decade to 2002, consumer prices rose on average by nearly 20 percent per year. However, most of this inflation was concentrated in the earlier years, and from 1999–2002 inflation in consumer prices has averaged

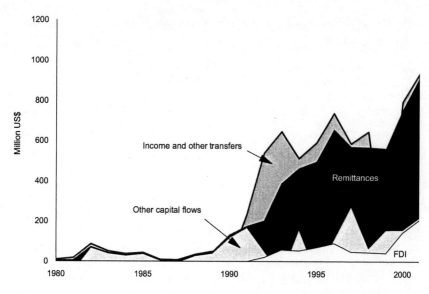

Figure 5.4   Financing Albania's balance of goods and services deficit

below 3 percent, despite a continued upward trend in dollar-denominated remittances.[40] On the other hand, the availability of remittances has permitted a fairly stable exchange rate; from 1992 to 2002 the lek depreciated by some 7.6 percent per year on average against the US dollar. Since this is less than inflation, this means a real appreciation of the lek, and this rate of real appreciation has continued at more than 7 percent on average in the five years to 2002. No doubt exports would have been stronger in the absence of this real appreciation, yet dollar earnings from merchandise exports grew on average by almost 20 percent in the decade to 2002, outstripping import growth, though exports started from a much smaller base.

Albania has come to depend very substantially upon remittances; as a source of income and foreign exchange, and as a safety net. The remittances may have imposed some costs, notably in terms of postponing real currency depreciation and hence potential export growth. Nonetheless, in view of the dismal employment opportunities at home, emigration and remittance have offered a lifeline out of poverty for many families and perhaps especially those from the poorest high emigration areas. Yet this may not remain a sustainable option, given the tendency to curtail remittances after some time away, unless high migrant turnover continues.

Moldova

Moldova is the poorest country in Europe, having suffered a particularly deep recession in the transition since independence in 1991, and Moldova remains deeply indebted. Estimates of the extent of migration out of Moldova since 1991 vary considerably:

> Official statistics say there are no more than 234,000 Moldovans working abroad both on legal or illegal basis ... with men accounting for 68.3 percent and rural residents for 69.6 percent of the total ... Although ... unofficial ... expert estimations seem to be more realistic. These vary between 600 000 and 1 000 000 of people working abroad ... Further calculations show that approximately 20 percent of all inhabitants and about one third ... of those able to work have left the country.[41]

Gudim (2004: 2), reports from a 2003 study that, 'one or more members of every third family are working abroad'. He goes on to note that 70 percent of the migrants are male and about a third are from rural areas. Much of this migration is undocumented, particularly departures to the Mediterranean countries, while trafficking in women has become rampant and a major concern. Within Europe, common destinations for migrants include some of the EU countries (Germany, Italy, Portugal, Spain, Greece), as well as some of the new EU members (Czech Republic, Poland, Cyprus) and others (Turkey and even Albania, but especially Russia). Germany reports more than 30 000 Moldovan workers, mostly employed in construction in East Germany. The Moscow authorities report over a quarter of a million illegally employed Moldovans. Sleptova goes on to argue that most of the migrants are employed as unskilled workers, even those who are qualified in professions at home.

> Main fields of employment are construction, agricultural works, transportation, mining industry, household services and finally sex industry. Seasonal trends are remarkable and migration volume rises by 30–40 percent in the period of planting and harvesting in agriculture. Most of migrants are young or in a fertile age between 20 and 30 years old ... Sending the excessive unused labour away from home in fact eases the burden of domestic unemployment ... But the most important positive effect ... is workers' remittances and transfers.[42]

The remittances, even those officially recorded, have grown dramatically since 1995 (see Figure 5.5). By 2001, Compensation of Employees on Balance of Payment account reached US$221 million, though there is no clear indication how much of this refers to earnings or remittances of seasonal workers as opposed to longer term migrants. Either way, in 2001 remittances represented 15 percent of GDP, 61 percent of the deficit on Goods and Service Balance, and over 100 percent of Gross Fixed Capital Formation.[43] It should, however, be emphasized that the last of these ratios does not mean that all investments were financed by savings out of remittances, nor that any additional remittances were matched 100 percent by additional investments. Remittances are an important source of income for Moldova, though it is less clear how much additional saving and investment result from

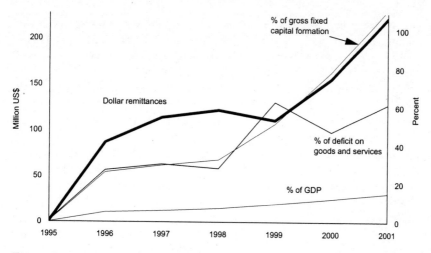

Figure 5.5 Remittances to Moldova

these remittances. In fact, from 1999 to 2001 real consumption spending grew at an annual rate of more than 14 percent, apparently spurred partly by increased availability of remittances.[44] This increase in spending has in turn enabled significant growth for the first time since independence. Moreover, the earlier, extremely rapid inflation in consumer prices has fallen below 10 percent a year in the last two years, despite any increases in spending out of remittances. The trade deficit remains at almost a quarter of GDP and exports have been hurt by the loss of regional markets and by the crisis with Russia in 1998. However, the massive remittances have also meant that the real effective exchange rate in 2002 was almost identical to that in 1995. In other words, while remittances have clearly conferred major economic benefits on Moldova, partly through the multiplier effects of spending, they have also probably contributed to poor export performance.

Morocco

Migration from Morocco, primarily to Europe, has a much longer history. As noted in Chapter 2, during the 1960s and until 1974 much of the migration was of male, unskilled workers on contract, but after 1974 family reunification became much more important, with an increasing role for female migrants, combined with growth in movement for seasonal work and of clandestine movement.[45] The evolution of reported remittances from these migrants is depicted in Figure 5.6 for the period after 1972.[46] Clearly remittances continued to climb throughout, despite the virtual cessation in recruitment of guest workers and the reunification of Moroccan families in Europe after 1974. Moreover, the real consumption potential out of these remittances rose in parallel, which is illustrated by the curve depicting remittances expressed in dirham at constant, 1995, consumer prices. By 2001, remittances amounted to 9.6 percent of GDP, 43 percent of Gross Fixed Capital Formation and nearly three times the deficit on Goods and Services Balance.

On the other hand, the upward trend in remittances has not been entirely smooth. Faini (1994) examines the fluctuations in Morocco's remittances from 1977 to 1989.[47] The results indicate that migrants significantly increased remittances, measured relative to consumer prices in Morocco, as Morocco's real exchange rate depreciated. This supports the idea that the real currency depreciation stimulated additional transfer of real buying power to the family at home because of two underlying effects: first, the devaluation enhances the overall buying power of the migrant; second, real devaluation lowers the relative price of buying consumer goods in Morocco, as compared to overseas, inducing the migrant to substitute family consumption for his or her own consumption. In terms of foreign currency transfers relative to overseas prices the effect proves ambiguous though; the short-run impact effect of a real depreciation reduces foreign currency remittances relative to European prices, but over time this effect is reversed and remittances again expand.

Other factors have no doubt played a role in the evolution of Morocco's remittances. Throughout the Maghreb region, foreign exchange controls have probably discouraged formal remittances and led to swap arrangements as a popular form of informal, unrecorded remittance.[48] Similarly, exchange controls imposed by France in 1982 probably limited the ability to remit. On the other hand, during the 1980s, Morocco, together with the other Maghreb countries, introduced a series of policies intended to stimulate remittances (in

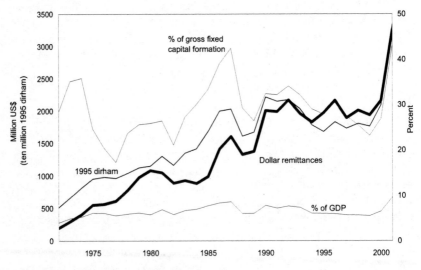

Figure 5.6   Remittances to Morocco

part in reaction to declining export commodity prices).[49] Morocco added to these incentives in 2003, by also exonerating interest payments on migrants' deposits, made in dirhams, from 'taxes on personal revenues'. The 2003 policy followed a slight drop in remittances in 2002, which the World Bank attributes to 'fears stemming from the Euro advent and from greater scrutiny of Arab funds post September 11, 2001'.[50] During the first three months of 2003, remittances again grew by 25 percent, though it is unclear how much of this was due to the depreciation of the dirham rather than the tax incentives on interest rates, given that Faini's (1994) results for the earlier period indicate that remittances to Morocco were unresponsive to home interest rate increases.

In 1974, the portion of remittances that were sent through the French banking system to Morocco amounted to about 45 percent of total remittances reported arriving in Morocco.[51] Over the next two decades, this fraction rose fairly steadily, reaching 63.7 percent of the total in 1992.[52] Leichtman (2002: 124) argues that 'The structure of emigration began to change in the 1980s. Over the past two decades, most Moroccan emigrants left Morocco with their entire families … As a result … the amount of remittances were beginning to decrease.' Yet real remittances from France to Morocco (expressed in constant 1995 French consumer prices) rose fairly steadily, despite a broad decline in the flow of documented migrants to France, and despite a very major increase in the portion of documented arrivals admitted as family members after 1974 (see Figure 5.7).[53] In other words, in this context, it is not apparent that family reunification did much to retard remittances.[54]

Since 1990 remittances to Morocco have diversified significantly in terms of the countries of origin. By 2001, the World Bank (2003b) reports that French remittances had fallen to only 40 percent of the total, with increasing remittances from Italy, Spain, Britain and North America. Although incomes clearly tend to be higher in North America than in Europe, and nearly two-thirds of Moroccans in the US are college educated (see Chapter 4), rough calculations suggest that remittances per Moroccan migrant in North America have been about 20 percent lower than from Europe.[55] It should be noted that this gap is not because more of the Moroccans in North America are studying and therefore remitting less; in 1997, the 1599 Moroccan tertiary level students in Canada and the US represented 1.9 percent of Moroccans in North America, whereas the 31 948 students in Europe were 2 percent of the Moroccan population in Europe.

Whatever the source, for a long period, remittances to Morocco have been massive. From 1975 to 2001, remittances amounted to nearly 29 percent of Gross Capital Formation and exceeded the deficit on Goods and Services Balance by nearly 50 percent. Glytsos (1998, 2002a) demonstrates that both consumption and investment have responded relatively quickly to increased remittances to Morocco, and suggests that this reflects confidence in the

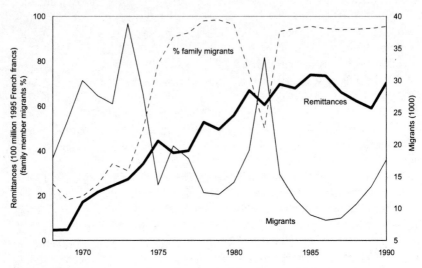

Figure 5.7   Remittances from France to Morocco and Moroccan migration to France

continuation in this source of income. Indeed, the investment response at the macroeconomic level proves fairly strong, yet Glytsos's evidence also indicates only modest growth responses over the last quarter century from additional remittances. As Glytsos notes, this could reflect a high proportion of investments being in housing, which is known to be the case out of remittances in Morocco, resulting in limited recorded expansion in output. In addition, however, 'This evidence also points to a negative impact on agricultural output, because some farmers are able to live from remittances and abandon cultivation.'[56]

Remittances may consequently have accelerated urbanization in Morocco, as in Albania. Moreover, Leichtman (2002: 124) notes that 'Migrants took a triangular route to reach the urban area from the rural region by means of international migration'. Nonetheless, in the interim, the World Bank (2003b: 7) notes 'The importance of workers' remittances ... in improving the living standard of many poor families, mainly from rural areas.'[57]

The Gulf and South Asia

The fact has already been noted that remittance flows out of the GCC region have been massive, both in the aggregate and per migrant. The four principal countries of South Asia have been major recipients of these remittances and their aggregate inflows have indeed been large, as may be seen in Table 5.5. Indeed, despite the large absolute sizes of the recipient economies and their populations, reported remittances do assume a significant role relative to GDP (certainly in Sri Lanka) and, more clearly, relative to export earnings. To portray more carefully the roles which these remittances have played, however, this section takes up the cases of India and of Pakistan for closer inspection.

Table 5.5   Average annual reported remittance inflows: countries of South Asia, 1995–2001

	Million dollars	Dollars per capita	Relative to GDP (%)	Exports (%)
Bangladesh	1651	13	3.86	32.42
India	9181	8	2.19	25.68
Pakistan	1344	10	2.48	16.86
Sri Lanka	993	53	6.57	21.56

Sources: IMF *Balance of Payments Statistics* and *International Financial Statistics.*

India

As may be seen in Table 5.6, India's diaspora has spread across the affluent countries of North America and Europe, as well as the GCC states in the Middle East and a significant range of other developing countries throughout Africa and the Americas, as well as neighboring countries in Asia.[58]

Private transfers from this diaspora grew from about US$80 million in 1970–71 to nearly US$13 billion in 2000–2001. A very approximate regional breakdown of these remittances and the evolution of the total are shown in Figure 5.8.[59] Transfers from the Persian Gulf grew rapidly with rising oil prices in the 1970s, are projected to have slowed during the 1980s, then again increased after 1990 as recruitment from India again grew rapidly (see Chapter 2). Remittances from the dollar area, meaning predominantly from Canada and the US, also increased significantly after 1990, as the Indian-born population in the US more than doubled from 450 000 in 1990 to just over a million in 2000 and Canadian immigrants admitted from India grew also.[60] Comparisons are difficult across the regions. Nonetheless, it is interesting to note that relative to the diaspora sizes reported in Table 5.6 transfers per migrant, by 1995, were roughly the same from the Gulf as from North America. The propensity to remit from the Gulf is thus very strong indeed, given the much higher income levels in North America on average, and especially when 80 percent of Indians in the US have a college degree and half of those have post-graduate qualifications with commensurate salaries.

In addition to private transfers, financial investments can be made by

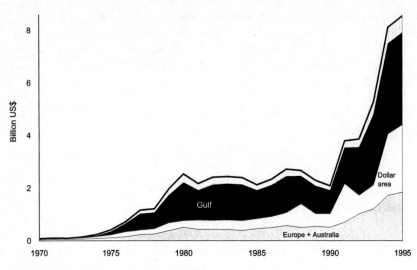

Figure 5.8   Private transfers to India by region

non-resident Indians in various advantageous deposit schemes, offering exoneration from wealth taxes and from income tax on interest, as well as premium interest rates. Nayyar (1994) notes that these schemes became increasingly popular during the 1980s, relative to transfers, and concludes 'that capital inflows into external rupee accounts were sensitive to exchange rate risk and capital inflows into foreign currency denominated accounts were responsive to interest rate differentials, just as capital outflows from both sets of accounts were sensitive to international perceptions of credit worthiness'.[61] He goes on to speculate that, in view of the apparent sophistication in investment strategies indicated, 'the repatriable deposits probably originated from relatively high-skill, high-income, permanent migrants, largely based in the industrialized countries',[62] though there is no hard evidence to support this. By 1990–91, deposits under these schemes were approximately equal to private transfers, but in the decade since the balance of payments crisis, which led to talk of potential default in 1991, non-resident Indian deposits have averaged less than 18 percent of private transfers. This decline may also have been compounded by fraud perpetrated by some of the banks, leading to the disappearance of deposits.[63]

The IMF *Balance of Payments Statistics* remittances to India almost entirely in the form of Workers' Remittances. These refer to 'information furnished by authorized dealers regarding remittances received under this category, supplemented by the data collected in the survey of unclassified receipts regularly conducted by the RBI on a quarterly basis' (IMF, 2000: 222). Clearly, both the IMF estimates and those reported by the Reserve Bank omit any informal transfers through the *hundi* system. As noted in

Table 5.6   Persons of Indian origin and Indian citizens abroad, December 2001

Europe	1 770 682
UK	1 200 000
Netherlands	217 000
Other Europe	353 682
Middle East	3 478 865
Saudi Arabia	1 500 000
UAE	950 000
Oman	312 000
Kuwait	295 000
Qatar	131 000
Bahrain	130 000
Yemen	100 900
Other Middle East	59 965
Asia	5 140 458
Myanmar	2 902 000
Malaysia	1 665 000
Singapore	307 000
Other Asia	266 458
Africa	2 283 313
South Africa	1 000 000
Mauritius	715 756
Réunion	220 055
Kenya	102 500
Other Africa	245 002
Americas	3 688 363
US	1 678 765
Canada	851 000
Trinidad & Tobago	500 600
Guyana	395 350
Suriname	150 456
Other Americas	112 192
Oceania	581 899
Fiji	336 829
Australia	190 000
Other Oceania	55 070

Source: Government of India (2001).

Section 5.1, the recent IMF study by El Qorchi *et al.* (2003) suggests that the proportion of India's remittances that are likely to have passed through *hundi* schemes is relatively low, estimated to be some 16 percent between 1981 and 2000. Moreover, this study suggests that the informal portion may well have declined with the black market premium on the rupee, which stood at 2 percent in 2000 as opposed to 28 percent in 1983.

The total of Workers' Remittances together with the small amounts reported as Compensation of Employees on Balance of Payments are depicted in Figure 5.9, measured at constant consumer prices in 1995 rupees. The growth in these remittances after 1990, in terms of real buying power in India, is apparent. Nonetheless, even at the peak level (over US$11 billion in 1999) this still amounted to only some 2.5 percent of GDP. 'Given such orders of magnitude, it is reasonable to infer that the impact of remittance flows on income, consumption or prices is likely to have been marginal, though not negligible, in the context of the national economy. This is simply because India is a very large country.'[64] On the other hand, 'The macro-economic impact on savings and investment is likely to have been more significant.'[65] Relative to Gross Fixed Capital Formation, remittances reported by the IMF rose throughout the 1970s, declined in the 1980s then rose fairly strongly in the 1990s, reaching 11.5 percent of Gross Fixed Capital Formation in 1999. Gross Fixed Capital Formation and remittances, measured in constant prices, have clearly risen together over time. Perhaps more interestingly, these two measures have also moved strongly together around their respective trend lines; in times when remittances have been exceptionally high, investment

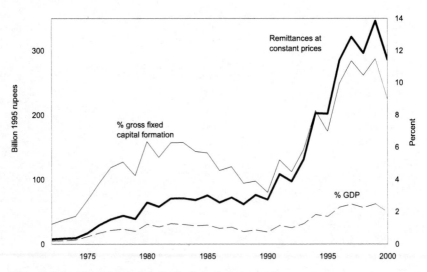

Figure 5.9   Remittances to India in relative terms

has also been exceptionally high.[66] Of course, as Nayyar (1994) notes, such a correlation may simply be spurious. Nonetheless, we cannot reject, out of hand, the notion that remittances to India may indeed have aided domestic investment efforts significantly.

Nonetheless, Nayyar (1994: 79) argues that 'It is clear, indeed obvious, that the most important macro-economic impact of financial flows arising from international labour migration is on the balance of payments (and through that on the economy as a whole).' On average in the last quarter century of the millennium, India's remittances amounted to almost exactly half of the deficit on trade in goods and services, though this ratio has been subject to a significant upward trend over the years and remittances rose to three-quarters of the deficit in the last five years of the century. Despite this major role on balance of payments, Nayyar (1994: 93) argues that 'remittance inflows were not a determinant of the exchange rate'. To the extent that the rupee rate has been managed for much of the last few decades, Nayyar argues that this management has been more concerned with effects on merchandise trade than with consequences for remittances, a significant portion of which have in any case been deposited in foreign exchange accounts. In fact, the rupee has depreciated, both against the US dollar and in real terms, fairly continuously and substantially since 1980, and exports (measured in dollars) more than doubled from 1992 to 2000. Whether the exchange rate would have depreciated even more in the absence of the massive remittances is thus largely moot.

If remittances have been a significant factor for India as a whole, for the state of Kerala they have assumed far greater importance. About half of India's migrants in the Gulf are from Kerala, which has about 3 percent of India's population. Women represent only about 10 percent of the emigrants from Kerala and, at least in the UAE, about a third of the migrants are unskilled, working in construction, production and transport; nearly a fifth are professional and technical workers and the remainder are in clerical, sales and service activities.[67] Remittances from degree-holding emigrants are reported to have been about 22 percent higher than from illiterates, which is surely less than the gap in overseas earnings between these two classes.[68] In any case, annual average remittances to Kerala, during 1998–2000, were US$3.2 billion, with more than 91 percent of this arriving from the Gulf region.[69] This represents about a third of India's total remittances and almost 20 percent of the net domestic product for Kerala in 2000.

Naturally, remittances on this scale have had a major impact on living standards; 'remittance inflows, particularly in the poorer districts of the state, raised levels of per capita income and consumption to an extent that would not have been possible in the absence of migration. There is however, no evidence to suggest that these remittances had an inflationary impact because prices in districts of Kerala which received remittances did not increase any more than other districts, just as prices in Kerala did not increase any faster than in other states of India.'[70] On the other hand, it is not clear that this migration process raised growth in production within Kerala; from 1980–81 to 2000–2001 net domestic product in Kerala (measured in constant prices) grew on average at 4.5 percent compared to 5.6 percent growth in GDP for India as a whole. Moreover, there was no significant correlation between the proportion of population migrating to the Gulf and growth in net domestic product from 1970–71 to 1993–94 across the districts of Kerala.[71] In consequence, the migration process has not exacerbated inequality in either incomes or consumption across districts.[72] On the other hand, although most migrants from Kerala to the Gulf are poor at the time of initial migration, 'the poorest persons ... have not until now participated, to any noticeable extent'.[73] Although overall poverty may thus have been relieved by the direct effects of remittances, any relief for the poorest would only have stemmed from indirect effects induced by overall economic expansion.

In fact, a large portion of remittances is reported spent on housing, which is fairly typical, and there has been a construction boom in Kerala. However, Kerala generally runs a trade deficit vis-à-vis the rest of India and Nair (1998) argues that remittances have simply allowed this deficit to increase, dispersing the benefits elsewhere in India. Yet this is not entirely clear. The Gulf crisis in 1990 resulted in mass return of workers to Kerala and to India more broadly, but by 1992–93 'only nine percent of returned migrants from Kuwait were left back in Kerala'.[74] Nonetheless in the interim, in 1991, the economy of Kerala suffered exceptionally slow growth. In fact, more generally over the period from 1981–82 to 1997–98, the trend in Kerala's net domestic product was significantly correlated with total migration of workers from India to the Gulf in the previous year.[75]

In 1996, Saudi Arabia set out to implement more strictly the 'Saudization' laws intended to replace overseas workers with nationals. Starting in the same year, Saudi Arabia and several other GCC states expelled substantial numbers of undocumented non-nationals, including many Keralites and other Indians. In July 1999, the UAE government stopped accepting applications for visas for unskilled workers from India, Pakistan and Bangladesh. Again there is discussion of 'Emirization' of employment. Moreover, unskilled workers from India are now being undercut by lower wage workers from Bangladesh. Yet there is little indication that this has had any serious impact on remittances to date. Remittances to India have continued to grow since 1996, and provisional estimates suggest they may have crossed US$14 billion in 2002, though in part this reflects the growing, highly skilled diaspora in North America as well as sustained flows from the Gulf.

Pakistan

The Global Council of Pakistan claims some four million Pakistanis abroad. The UK 2001 census shows about three-quarters of a million persons reporting

Pakistani ethnicity and North America has approximately another quarter of a million people born in Pakistan. However, the largest concentration of overseas Pakistanis is in the Gulf, perhaps numbering around a million. Recruitment of contract workers to the GCC states rose sharply in the 1970s, peaked in 1981, fell by almost two-thirds by 1986, but again revived after the 1991 Gulf crisis.

The surge in officially recorded remittances to Pakistan from 1972 through 1983 clearly corresponds to the growth in recruitment to the Gulf, though recuperation in the 1990s is far less apparent in these data (see Figure 5.10).[76] However, it is widely recognized that a major portion of Pakistan's remittances enters through the informal (*hawala*) system. El Qorchi *et al.* (2003) estimate that some 55 percent of Pakistan's actual remittances may have been unrecorded between 1981 and 2000, in part to take advantage of the premium on the foreign currency black market. As Figure 5.10 shows, this premium has fluctuated quite considerably over time and, in particular, has again risen through the 1990s, no doubt explaining the lack of resurgence in recorded remittances during that decade.[77]

The Government of Pakistan has attempted to divert more remittances through formal channels by issuing a series of foreign currency bonds, which not only offered premium rates and tax exemption, but were advertised as convertible either to domestic or foreign currency with no questions asked. The Foreign Exchange Bearer Certificates, introduced in 1985, were initially successful to the extent that approximately US$300 million worth of certificates were issued by the State Bank in the first three years.[78] However, the announcement of the sequel Foreign Currency Bearer Certificates (FCBC), in 1992, was undermined by the concurrent major financial scandal and closing of the Bank of Credit and Commerce International. The Government attempted again with a new issue of FCBC in 1998. However, as Passas (1999: 64) notes:

> Only a few months later, the credibility of the government and the public confidence in the bond programs suffered greatly. One of the most important incentives to invest in such bonds was the assurance that the FCBCs did not have to be encashed in rupees, given that many local and overseas investors would like to hold their accounts in foreign currency ... In the aftermath of Pakistan's nuclear bomb test and the negative international response to it, foreign currency accounts were frozen and withdrawals could be made only in rupees at a government-set rate of exchange. The public showed its distrust to both conventional banks and the government by going back to the time-honored hawala and hundi networks. Overseas remittances through banks dropped from US$150 million per month down to US$50 million.

Given the dominance of informal transfers, together with their fluctuation over time, analysis of recorded remittances is not terribly informative. Perhaps the incompleteness of recorded remittances helps to explain why Burney (1989)

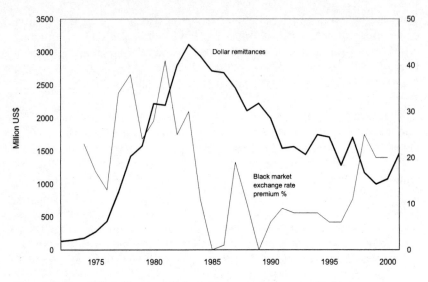

Figure 5.10   Officially recorded workers, remittances to Pakistan

finds an absence of any positive correlation between formal remittance flows and private investment, over time, in Pakistan. The data collected by a survey of returned migrants in 1986 has, however, proved useful in gaining some further insights.[79] This study indicates that about a third of remittances are invested; half is invested in real estate while the migrant is overseas, and the remainder is invested (in real estate and elsewhere) upon the migrant's return.[80] The survey data do, however, confirm a general absence of deposits in formal savings schemes out of migrants' remittances, no doubt in large part because these schemes offered negative real returns at the time.[81] Alderman (1996) considers another source of household panel data to look at consumption smoothing by rural families during shocks to their incomes. In the course of this analysis, Alderman (1996: 343, 363) finds that 'Unlike domestic remittances, international remittances appear to be treated much as transitory income shocks ... households save virtually all of international remittances.' Adams (1998: 170) looks at a version of the same data (adding two more years of observation) and finds that 'external remittances have a positive and significant effect on the accumulation of ... irrigated and rainfed land. By contrast, internal remittances do not.' Whereas Glytsos's (2002a) results for Morocco indicated a rapid increase in consumer spending with additional remittances, Alderman's and Adams's results for Pakistan indicate the opposite, namely that families are apparently quite unsure of the continuation of international remittances and consequently save and accumulate assets. Given that the starting date for collection of the Pakistan data was 1986, it may not have been unreasonable for families to be skeptical of the prospects of continued, reliable remittance streams; at least reported remittances were plummeting (see Figure 5.10).

Since 1992 the Pakistan economy has grown only slowly, but from 1972 to 1992 the economy grew fairly steadily at just over 6 percent per year and poverty rates fell significantly. Migration and its associated remittances probably contributed in a significant way to this process of poverty alleviation. First, many of the migrants were relatively poor, possessing little or no education and coming overwhelmingly from rural areas.[82] Second, 'the direct and multiplier impacts of migration were on the whole so directed, especially on domestic wages and employment, as to have an overall favorable impact on poverty alleviation'.[83] Third, the work of Ilahi and Jafarey (1999) illustrates that the benefits of remittances to Pakistan have been distributed beyond the immediate family in an interesting way. These authors show that the cost of initial emigration is often shared with the extended family. When this occurs, remittances to the immediate family tend to be lower, as are savings retained abroad by the migrant, presumably reflecting additional transfers to the extended family network.

On the other hand, although poverty may well have been reduced by the process of emigration and remittance, the poorest appear to have been bypassed, at least directly. Most of the poorest live in the rural sector and Adams (1998) shows that, among his sample of rural families, the richest 20 percent of households derived nearly 14 percent of their incomes from external remittances, while international remittances were the source of only 1 percent of income for the poorest 20 percent of families.[84]

Southeast Asia

Remittances to several lower income countries of Southeast Asia have also become important, though officially reported remittances do not always reflect this. The IMF total of Workers' Remittances and Compensation of Employees, during 1995–2001, for three of the principal labor exporting countries in the region, is summarized in Table 5.7. Whereas the Philippines reports very large compensation of their overseas employees, the Indonesian figures appear quite tiny in relation to the extent of migration which, as we shall see, is misleading. In most of the other countries in the region, reported remittance inflows have tended to be small too, though again this may reflect under-reporting. For example, for Cambodia and Laos the IMF reports average remittances of US$14 million and less than US$1 million respectively, whereas Hugo (2003a: 10) notes 'While there are little data, it is clear that the diaspora of Indochinese which was predominantly created by the refugee outflows in the 1970s and 1980s has resulted in substantial remittance inflows to Laos, Cambodia and especially Vietnam.' The IMF reports no data on remittances to Vietnam, but the State Bank of Vietnam reports remittances of about US$2 billion in 2002 (more than half from the US with 70 percent directed to South Vietnam).[85] The cases of Indonesia and the Philippines are chosen for a closer look here.

Table 5.7   Average annual reported remittance inflows: principal labor exporting countries of Southeast Asia, 1995–2001

	Million dollars	Dollars per capita	Relative to GDP (%)	Relative to Exports (%)
Indonesia	925	5	0.62	1.71
Philippines	5942	80	7.92	22.27
Thailand	1570	26	1.15	2.72

Sources: IMF *Balance of Payments Statistics* and *International Financial Statistics.*

Indonesia

In 2000, there were some 2.1 million Indonesian contract workers overseas.[86] By far the largest group was in Malaysia (1.3 million), nearly half a million in the GCC states, about 100 000 in the US, and most of the rest scattered throughout East Asia. An estimate by the Ministry of Manpower of the composition of remittances to Indonesia during the Fifth Plan period, 1989–1994, shows 96 percent of all remittances originating from Saudi Arabia alone.[87] This is because virtually all of the remittances from the huge diaspora in Malaysia go unrecorded.

Indonesia's overseas contract workers are overwhelmingly unskilled, with little education; they are also drawn predominantly from some of the poorest rural areas.[88] Whereas the bulk of official overseas contract workers are recruited from West Java, much of the undocumented migration originates from East and Central Java and from parts of Eastern Indonesia (East Nusa Tanggara, West Nusa Tanggara and South Sulewesi).[89] From a survey of villages in East Flores, within Nusa Tangarra, Hugo (2002a) shows that some 80 percent of remittances from migrants who are still away were sent though friends and family, and hence would not be recorded in the official flows. For women this portion was 90 percent. Moreover, both genders bring back with them far more money than they send while away, which again goes unrecorded. In 1997, the modal amount brought back by a returning male migrant in East Flores was estimated to be about US$575 (more than half of national income per person) and returning females brought about 85 percent of this amount.

During the East Asia crisis, starting in 1997–98, the prior growth in recorded remittances to Indonesia slowed, though there was no actual decline in the dollar value of remittances. In fact, in the East Flores study villages, unofficial remittances actually increased, though it is difficult to judge how much of this reflects concerns for the income of family at home versus the inducement of a massively depreciated rupiah.

It does seem clear that remittances have been far more important, as a source of support for rural families in Indonesia, than might have been anticipated looking at the official data. Moreover, it seems likely that much of this relief has come to particularly low income areas and, within rural Java, Ravallion and Dearden (1988) show that the impact effects of transfers in general tend to be income inequality reducing, though the reverse holds for transfers in urban Java.

On the other hand, it is less clear to what extent these remittances were able to stimulate the local economies.

> While there can be little doubt that households and villages with migrant workers in Sabah [in East Malaysia] have benefited, East Flores and indeed NTT [the Nusa Tenggara Timur region] remain among Indonesia's poorest areas. It is a peripheral area with limited agricultural potential with low levels of education which is neglected by the central government ... The reasons for the limited impact of remittances on regional development are as follows:
>
> • The remittances are focused on an isolated peripheral area.
> • The illegality of the migrants sending the remittances.
> • The lack of sufficient physical infrastructure, especially transport infrastructure, which would create a favourable environment for small investors.
> • The lack of integration of the remittance recipients into regional planning efforts.
> • The lack of appropriate training/education programs to assist returning migrants in making effective investment decisions.[90]

Perhaps largely as a result, a considerable portion of funds remitted to East Flores are either transferred elsewhere within Indonesia or spent outside of East Flores on goods or education. In turn, this latter spending on education frequently provides the means for internal migration out of East Flores, in search of better opportunities.

Philippines

The Commission on Filipinos Overseas estimates that, at the end of 2001, there were 7.4 million Filipinos overseas, or about 10 percent of the population.[91] The dispersion of the Filipino diaspora is reported in Table 5.8.[92] The largest group were documented, temporary overseas residents, composed mostly of contract workers, with 1.2 million in the Middle East (primarily in Saudi Arabia), 800 000 in East and South Asia (primarily in Hong Kong, Japan and Taiwan), but with large contingents also in Europe, the Americas and on the seas. During 2000–2001, of those recruited to the Middle East about two-thirds were men, whereas to East Asia two-thirds were women.[93] Some 2.7 million Filipinos are estimated by the Commission on Overseas Filipinos to be permanently settled abroad, with 1.9 million in the US alone.[94] As reported in Chapter 4, Filipinos in the US are highly educated, more than 70 percent of adults possessing a college degree, and 61 percent of Filipino adults in the US are women. In addition, Table 5.8 reports more than 300 000 permanently settled Filipinos in Canada and 200 000 in Australia.[95] However, the Commission on Overseas Filipinos also estimates 1.6 million Filipinos overseas on an irregular basis, with half a million in East Asia (again primarily in Malaysia as from Indonesia), and another half million in the US.

The reported remittances from this diaspora have grown significantly during the 1990s, peaking at US$6.9 billion in 1999 (see Figure 5.11).[96] By 2001, reported remittances amounted to more than half of Gross Fixed Capital Formation in the economy, and nearly 9 percent of GDP. The IMF study by El Qorchi *et al.* (2003) suggests that informal remittances may have been less than 10 percent of the total over the last two decades.[97] Other observers suggest that unrecorded remittances may have been larger. For instance, a 1991 survey indicated only 40 percent of cash remittances coming through the banking system, and that the use of money couriers had increased over time.[98] Rodriguez (1996: S428) notes from the Survey of Overseas Workers from the same year, 1991, 'that regular cash transfers account for about 26 percent of total transfers; most of the rest is cash brought home on return'.

Rodriguez goes on to examine these latter survey data in much greater detail, controlling for various characteristics of the migrants (age, gender, education) their region of destination and occupation abroad, duration of absence, and characteristics of the migrants' families (whether urban or rural, age, gender, marital status and education of the head). This study indicates that, controlling for these other factors:[99]

- men remit more than women, but men remit a smaller fraction of their (estimated) overseas earnings (though neither difference is statistically significant).
- both the amount remitted and the portion of overseas earnings remitted rise with education level of the migrant up through college, but then decline slightly among university educated migrants.
- migrants to the Middle East remit most, both in absolute terms and relative to their earnings (though the data refer only to registered workers and thus omit skilled emigrants to North America).
- both the amount remitted and the portion of overseas earnings remitted initially rise with time away from home then begin to decline, but apparently not until after about twelve years away. Rodriguez and Horton (1995) suggest that this reflects an initial effect of rising earnings with duration away, followed by less commitment to remit.

The Philippines has introduced a series of policies aimed at increasing amounts remitted even more. The mandatory remittance requirements of the

Table 5.8   Stock estimate of overseas Filipinos, December 2001

	Permanent	Temporary	Irregular	Total
World total	2 736 528	3 049 622	1 625 936	7 412 086
Africa	271	46 515	18 114	64 900
Egypt	53	1 018	1 400	2 471
Libya	75	4 350	485	4 910
Nigeria	18	10 500	1 500	12 018
Asia, East & South	70 349	817 144	511 363	1 398 856
Brunei	26	20 240	1 500	21 766
Hong Kong	404	171 485	2 000	173 889
Japan	65 647	138 522	36 379	240 548
Republic of Korea	1 510	13 781	15 235	30 526
Malaysia	310	58 233	363 000	421 543
Singapore	152	56 377	71 917	128 446
Taiwan	1 901	116 480	4 300	122 681
Asia, West	1 546	1 232 962	118 287	1 352 795
Bahrain	61	26 356	5 000	31 417
Israel	41	9 058	21 136	30 235
Kuwait	92	53 067	10 000	63 159
Lebanon	19	19 825	5 500	25 344
Oman	18	18 551	1 500	20 069
Qatar	13	37 626	1 000	38 639
Saudi Arabia	239	897 000	18 000	915 239
UAE	373	128 604	38 000	166 977
Europe	152 851	411 248	174 936	739 035
Austria	3 205	1 191	2 000	6 396
France	925	4 804	26 121	31 850
Germany	41 321	7 005	4 392	52 718
Greece	84	7 514	17 500	25 098
Italy	2 431	69 998	78 000	150 429
Netherlands	7 632	2 351	700	10 683
Spain	33 643	5 687	4 000	43 330
Switzerland	605	5 953	9 300	15 858
United Kingdom	45 889	15 767	8 344	70 000
Americas	2 291 311	236 745	773 537	3 301 323
Canada	338 561	21 146	4 000	363 707
United States	1 910 844	60 373	532 200	2 503 417
Northern Mariana Islands	80	16 205	3 705	19 990
Guam	41 541	434	2 025	44 000
Oceania	220 200	50 009	29 699	299 908
Australia	204 075	687	2 041	206 803
New Zealand	16 045	236	100	16 381
Papua New Guinea	63	1 661	7 339	9 063
Sea-based workers	–	255 269	–	255 269

Source: Table prepared by the Commission on Filipinos Overseas.

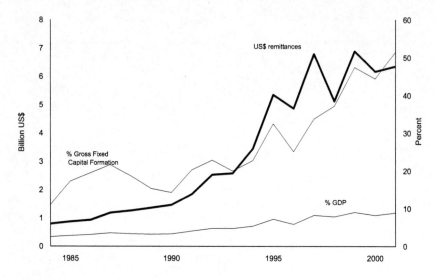

Figure 5.11   Remittances to the Philippines

1980s largely failed to enhance remittances, and have steadily been replaced by financial incentives, such as establishment of government run duty free shops for returning migrants and convergence to a market rate convertibility on currency. In addition, the government has facilitated opening of Filipino banks in major migrant destinations and issued small denomination bonds.[100] As Figure 5.11 demonstrates, the amounts of reported remittances have clearly increased, though, as Rodriguez (1996: S431) notes, 'Reducing transaction costs and offering a market rate for the hard currency increases the amounts transferred under the legal system without necessarily increasing the total remittances.'

The impact effects of foreign remittances on income distribution within the Philippines remain a matter of some dispute. While many of the overseas contract workers are relatively unskilled, and hence perhaps tend to be drawn from lower income families, the emigrants to North America are certainly not. From a 1983 survey Ulack (1986: 353) concludes 'Some argue ... that those who are best off receive remittances, and therefore inequalities increase. The findings here simply do not support this contention, since no relationship was found between income or educational level and cash remittances received in rural areas, and such relationships were weak for the city.'[101] On the other hand, and in contrast to other parts of Asia, most of the overseas workers originate from the urban, relatively affluent communities of the Philippines,[102] in large part reflecting the failure to create urban jobs. This 'positive effect of urban location would indicate that households with higher average incomes and education receive larger remittances, suggesting that international remittances could increase inequality in the Philippines'.[103] Moreover, even within regions there is evidence to indicate that the fraction of income derived from foreign remittances is greater at the upper deciles of family incomes. As a result, 'The bottom five deciles account for a paltry 4.27 percent of the total sum of "income from abroad" received by all Filipino families; the top decile alone accounts for a staggering 55.71 percent; if the top twenty percent of the families are considered, their share rises to 76.71 percent of all receipts from overseas.'[104]

Certainly the Philippines have become increasingly dependent upon the cycle of emigration and remittance. Economic growth has been disappointing, averaging only 3.5 percent each year in the fifteen years after Ferdinand Marcos stepped down in 1986. Yet it is far from clear that such slow growth stems from any Dutch disease effects of remittances. Growth in remittances has been significantly, positively correlated with appreciation of the real effective exchange rate since remittance data became available in 1984. Yet exports have actually grown most rapidly in times when the real exchange rate has been appreciating quickly. Rather, the performance of the Philippine economy seems to have been driven much more by concerns for stability, leading to the removal of Joseph Estrada in 2001, followed by his arrest; a mutiny against the government of Goria Arroyo in 2003; and the continuing separatist conflict in Mindanao.[105]

For the Philippines and for Filipino families, international remittances have become a major vehicle of support. There is some contention as to how much of this benefits the poor directly, though on balance it seems likely that more flows directly to the relatively affluent urban areas. Growth and capital formation have remained sluggish for the most part but it seems more likely that this is attributable to extraneous factors, rather than to any obvious growth inhibiting effects of the remittances themselves.

5.3   IN PERSPECTIVE: MIGRATION REGIMES AND GLOBAL REMITTANCES

Having reviewed the evidence from several countries in some detail, it is time to attempt to place this evidence in perspective. How unique are these experiences and what do they exhibit in common?

Factors Shaping the Amounts Remitted

As noted in Section 5.1, the determinant of remittances may broadly be divided into the effects of the type of migration involved and the influence of the macroeconomic setting.

Migrant types

In a recent review, Black (2003: 2) notes:

> it is possible to say with some confidence that remittances are likely to be higher
> in situations where the migrant leaves broadly for economic rather than political
> or social reasons, where they have temporary rather than permanent resident
> status, where they are young, but married with family left behind at home, and that
> remittances will increase as emigrant wages increase – although at a certain point,
> further increases in wage levels do not seem to translate into higher remittances.

Although there is a general presumption that temporary migrants remit more
than their permanent counterparts, most of the more formal evidence appears
to be based on the related issue of duration of residence, and the results are
ambiguous.[106] In reviewing the evidence, Glytsos (2001) reports findings both
of a negative association between amount remitted and duration of absence
(which Glytsos dubs a 'permanent settlement syndrome'), and of cases with
a positive association ('return illusion' in Glytsos's terminology).[107] Our
case study areas reflect this diversity, though a clear theme that emerges is
the importance of remittances from the temporary migration to the Gulf
states and more recently within East Asia, both in absolute terms and as a
proportion of workers' earnings while away. Among these contract workers,
evidence from the Philippines indicates that remittances tend to rise initially
with duration of stay then ultimately decline, though few workers stay for so
long. At least relative to migrants' earnings, the evidence from India suggests
a much greater propensity to remit among the temporary workers in the
Gulf than among the more permanent settlers in the US.[108] There are also
indications that remittances to Albania decline after the migrant has been
away for some time. Glytsos (1997) undertakes one of the few attempts to
compare remittances of temporary and permanent migrants more directly.
In particular, this study looks at remittances during the period 1960–93 from
Greek migrants to Australia, who are largely permanent, and from Greek
migrants to Germany, most of who were temporary movers in the early years
but amongst whom permanent settlement became more common. Glytsos
confirms that the temporary migrants remitted a higher portion of their
incomes. In an alternative approach, Merkle and Zimmerman (1992) explore
data on 721 individual migrants in the German Socioeconomic Panel and find
that neither remittances nor savings are significantly impacted by duration
of stay in Germany, given the income and various personal characteristics of
the migrant. However, remittances (but not migrant savings) are significantly
lower, the longer the migrant reports intending to stay in Germany.

Koser and Van Hear (2002: 5) note that 'Most … remittances are sent
by economic migrants rather than by asylum seekers and refugees', which
is in agreement with Black's summation on migration for political reasons.

However, Koser and Van Hear go on to note that some conflict-torn countries have indeed been the recipients of significant remittance inflows, highlighting the cases of Sri Lanka and Somalia. In particular, Koser and Van Hear (2002) describe a process of transfers from a 'wider diaspora' to a 'near diaspora', especially the near diaspora in camps in countries of first asylum, who in turn act as conduits passing remittances to kin in the home country. More generally, it may be noted that reported remittances sent to the various developing countries in 2000 were uncorrelated with the number of refugees from those countries, once the level of total net out-migration from each country is controlled for.[109] As Koser and Van Hear note, remittance data are likely to be particularly incomplete for countries in conflict or countries that produce asylum seekers. This would tend to bias downward any measured correlation between the number of refugees and reported remittances. In other words, the lack of an observed negative correlation across countries suggests that any notion that refugees remit less, on average, is far from confirmed. Certainly this would be consistent with the finding that Albania reports very large remittances indeed, though there is no indication how much of these remittances emanate from the recognized refugees. Similarly, it was noted in Section 5.2 that Vietnam is now receiving significant levels of remittances from the US, though in this case the remittances go unrecorded.

Not surprisingly, there is little evidence to indicate whether irregular migrants remit as much as comparable documented migrants. Not only is undocumented movement much more difficult to observe but there is a common presumption that undocumented workers use informal, unrecorded remittance channels more frequently.[110] To the extent that legal migrants command higher pay and have less difficulty sending remittances, one might well expect larger transfers from regular migrants. On the other hand, this would be mitigated where documented migrants are assimilated more fully into the host country setting. Certainly, even recorded remittances to countries such as Albania and Moldova are indeed massive, relative to their economies, despite the preponderance of undocumented migration.

A study by Faini (2002) examines gross reported remittances received in relation to the extent of brain drain from those remittance-receiving countries.[111] This study controls for the stock of migrants abroad as a percentage of home country population, and for income per capita in the home country. Faini (2002: 7) concludes, 'Two facts stand out. First, as expected, remittances are an increasing function of the stock of migrants. Second, and more crucially, remittances decline as the share of migrants with a tertiary education goes up. The first result is in line with expectation, the second … is more surprising.' Given the complexity of the relationship between education and remittances outlined in Section 5.1, Faini's finding with respect to the brain drain is entirely plausible. For instance, Faini notes that although highly skilled migrants earn more, they also move more permanently and are often accompanied by their families, both of which features may tend to diminish remitting. In addition, however, the cross-country evidence appears to be quite sensitive to the specific data adopted. Thus Figure 5.12 plots the logarithm of gross reported remittances received per capita for forty-two developing countries in 2000, against the logarithm of the extent of brain drain to the US from each of these countries.[112] The two measures are (significantly) positively correlated, as depicted by the best-fit line drawn through the data. Moreover this association does not change if controls are introduced for income per capita in the home country, net migration rate from the home country, size of home country population, and the number of recognized refugees from each country.

There is, then, conflicting evidence about the average patterns of remittances across countries with respect to the extent that migration is highly skilled. However, it is also clear from Figure 5.12 that there is a good deal of variation across countries in any such association. This diversity in behavior is exemplified from some of our case studies. Rough calculations indicate that Moroccans in the US remit somewhat less per person than do Moroccans in Europe, despite the very high educational qualifications of Moroccans in the US. In the context of Tunisia, this is supported by Jellal (2002) who examines micro data on remittances and finds that the percentage of a migrant's income remitted is negatively correlated with skill level of the migrant. In India, it

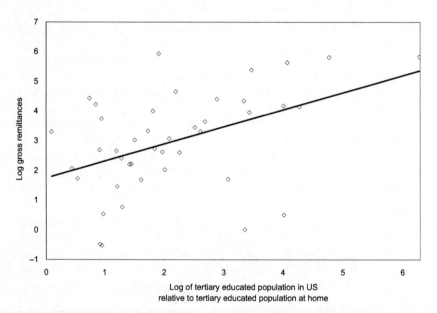

Figure 5.12   Gross remittances received against brain drain to US: 42 developing countries, 2000

seems remittances per migrant may have been approximately comparable from the Gulf and from the US, despite the much higher education and income levels of those in the US. On the other hand, in the Philippines, estimates by Rodriguez (1996) demonstrate that remittances from contract workers rise with the level of education, both in absolute terms and relative to predicted earnings of the migrant, though even here remittances then decline among university graduates as compared to those with only college education. Overall, it may perhaps be fair to say that it remains unclear whether the highly educated remit more, though they may well remit a smaller portion of their earnings than do the unskilled.

Lastly, before turning to macroeconomic factors shaping remittances, it may be noted that most of the evidence from our case study areas and elsewhere indicates smaller amounts remitted by women than by men. It is less clear whether women remit a smaller portion of their earnings, however. Indeed, Rodriguez found precisely the opposite in the Philippines, namely that although women contract workers remit less this represents a higher portion of their earnings.

Macroeconomic factors

Swamy (1981) actually provides a comparison of the importance of the gender composition of migration in shaping remittances, as opposed to the role of macroeconomic factors. 'Swamy (1981) found that, for a pooled sample of three Mediterranean countries over 18 years, the "ratio of females to the total migrant labor population of each nationality has a significant negative coefficient, suggesting that demographic factors may be far more important in determining the changes in the value of per capita remittances than are financial variables".'[113] Swamy is able to make this comparison, without resort to normalizing for differences in scales of effects, because her results indicate that the financial variables have no discernible influence in either direction. Straubhaar (1986b) supports Swamy's finding with respect to financial variables. Expressing official remittances to Turkey during 1963–82 in terms of real purchasing power, Straubhaar finds no association with the real exchange rate, nor with the difference in the real interest rates, between Turkey and Germany. Rather, Straubhaar concludes that Turkish remittances have responded to changes in government in Turkey and hence to political confidence. The importance of such findings lies in the apparent impotence of policy to induce remittances through manipulation of either the exchange rate or the interest rate: 'Contrary to conventional belief it turned out that the incentives to attract emigrants' remittances have not been very successful.'[114] However, not all analysts concur. For example, Elbadawi and Rocha (1992) maintain that the absence of any correlation between interest rate differentials and remittances, as reported by Swamy, may reflect a spurious correlation between interest rate changes and other events.

The counter-evidence on interest and exchange rates is, however, very mixed and not always truly appropriate. Several studies point to greater remittances as the foreign rate of interest rises relative to the home country interest rate.[115] Although this is plausible in terms of the wealth effect of overseas returns on assets as described in Glytsos (2001), the implication is that offering premium returns on home country assets to attract additional remittances would prove counter-productive. Indeed, where the home country interest rate is explored as a separate argument, as opposed to its difference from overseas rates, the evidence suggests that the home country rate is again irrelevant.[116]

Several studies have shown that a higher black market premium on foreign exchange rates diminishes official remittances.[117] Although such findings are of interest in their own right, it remains unclear from this whether total remittances, the sum of official and unrecorded remittances, actually increase as the black market premium evaporates. Moreover, of the few contributions that have systematically studied the effects of market exchange rate depreciation on official remittances, the results are mixed. Glytsos (1988), finds that depreciation of the drachma against the Deutsche Mark, between 1960 and 1982, tended to decrease remittances from Germany to Greece, presumably reflecting the greater ease of achieving given real payments in Greece. In contrast, 'The experience of other countries shows that the foreign exchange rate is positively related with average remittances.'[118] Theory predicts ambiguity in the effect of the exchange rate on remittances and the limited evidence seems to confirm this ambiguity. Indeed, in the case of Morocco, as we have seen in Section 5.2, depreciation of the exchange rate was found by Faini (1994) to diminish dollar remittances in the immediate future but to increase these remittances over time. Yet a further difficulty remains to be adequately dealt with in this sphere. Remittances may not only be affected by the exchange rate but in turn the real exchange rate may be affected by remittances, as may the premium on the black market. Indeed, the tendency for remittances to contribute to appreciation of the exchange rate is a key part of the economic consequences of remitting, at least in some contexts.

Economic Consequences of Remittances

The general discussion of the economic consequences of remittances may readily be divided into two: the effects on poverty and inequality; and the influences upon investment, growth and macroeconomic stability.

Inequality and poverty

Within the literature on the consequences of remittances for inequality, a further distinction must be made. Most of the contributions examine only the impact effects on inequality; whether rich families or poor families receive more remittances. A smaller number of contributions go further and look at inequality across families, given adjustments within the family induced by remittances, such as labor force participation adjustments and asset accumulation. An even smaller subset recognizes the (local) multiplier effects of spending from remittances. On the other hand, distribution within the family seems to have been rather neglected.

Overall, 'The evidence on the impact of remittances on income inequality is mixed.'[119] Indeed, we have seen that it is even controversial within some of our case study countries. Early results for the Philippines in 1983 suggested that the impact effect of remittances were fairly neutral with respect to inequality, whereas data from 1991 indicate that the main beneficiaries were from the top income deciles, especially in urban areas. Stark *et al.* (1986) hypothesize exactly the opposite evolution over time and find supporting evidence from two villages in Mexico. In particular, Stark *et al.* suggest that, as long as international migration is confined to an elite few, the effects of remittances add to pre-existing inequality; but as network effects spread information about migration opportunities and lower the costs of moving, migrants become drawn from a wider social spectrum and remittances prove equalizing. To what extent the Philippine results contradict this, as opposed to simply reflecting non-comparable data sets and samples in the two periods, is difficult to judge, though mass departure on contract was well underway by the time of the first survey in 1983.

Within the rural sectors of both Egypt and Pakistan, Adams (1991, 1998) finds that remittances sharpen inequality. Measuring incomes inclusive of remittances Adams notes, in the case of Egypt, that the poorest quintile of households produce a proportionate share of still-abroad migrants, the richest 40 percent of households produces more than their share, but the second and third quintiles are under-represented. 'It is these variations in the number of migrants produced by different income groups – and not differences in either migrant earnings abroad or marginal propensities to remit – that cause international remittances to have a negative effect on rural income distribution.'[120] In the context of Pakistan, Adams (1998) notes that the lack of remittances sent to poorer rural families may also reflect inability to finance international migration and hence under-representation of the poorest among the migrants.

In contrast, Taylor and Wyatt (1996) find an impact effect of remittances (81 percent of which are from the US) within rural Mexico that reduces inequality marginally. Moreover, the effect of remittances on household incomes is shown to depend upon the initial assets of the household. Possessing more animals (a liquid asset) diminishes the impact of remittances on family income, whereas possessing non-marketable land rights enhances the income effect of remittances. Taylor (1992) uses this to demonstrate that, whereas in the short run remittances sharpen inequality once the induced effect of remittances on farm income is accounted for, in the long run the income distribution becomes more equal through the liquidity provided for capital accumulation (and particularly of livestock). Data from the same Mexican villages are used by both Stark *et al.* (1986) and Adelman *et al.* (1988) to illustrate that remittances equalize income distribution across families within a given village, the latter study being one of the first to incorporate simulated multiplier effects of spending out of remittances. Moreover, Stark *et al.* (1986) go on to argue that any initial inequality in the distribution of remittances across villages tends to become diffused over time, through trickle-down effects in the labor market. On the other hand, Milanovic (1987) found no support for this tendency to greater equality through trickle-down from remittances in national data on Yugoslavia for 1978, 1983 and 1988. Indeed, in this Yugoslav context remittances are reported to have sharply increased inequality, again apparently because it was the relatively well off who tended to migrate. Similarly, in Kerala, it has already been noted that the evidence suggests that the poorest do not go to the Gulf, though at least across districts with different propensities to migrate it seems inequality has not been exacerbated.

The evidence on the inequality effects of remittances is indeed mixed. However, this is far less true of findings with respect to poverty. Although some aspects of the emigration–remittance pattern may potentially exacerbate poverty (see Chapter 8) since remittances per se are unlikely to lower anyone's income, poverty rates are correspondingly unlikely to be worsened. Indeed claims of poverty relief from the impact of remittances are fairly universal in our case study countries and elsewhere.[121]

Lastly, an additional, potentially important consequence of remittances for inequality within the family should be noted. As Glytsos (2002a: 17) surmises, 'As one of the social implications, which may have further repercussions on development, remittances enable young migrants to set up households earlier, increase the independence of women in and out of the household, and, by reducing fertility, have an impact on demographic changes.' To a large extent this aspect of female empowerment has been neglected, at least amongst economists. Yet, as Chimhowu *et al.* (2003) note, the economic implications may be important. In particular they emphasize that a large number of the remittance-receiving households are female-headed and women represent a growing portion of migrants. Where these two patterns enable greater control by women over spending, the authors cite evidence that more is spent on education and on health. In contexts such as Sri Lanka, Indonesia and the Philippines, the potential for empowerment of women through extensive migration may be proving important. In other contexts, such as Albania, this appears to be far less true to date.

Investment and growth

The effects of remittances on macroeconomic expansion are no less contentious than are the effects on inequality. The World Bank's *Global Development Finance Report* puts a positive spin on the expansionary effects; 'If remittances are invested, they contribute to output growth, and if they are consumed, then also they generate positive multiplier effects.'[122]

The *Global Development Finance Report* goes on to cite the case of high savings out of remittances in Pakistan, which we have already reviewed. Our other case studies indicated signs that remittances may indeed have served to accelerate investment in Morocco and perhaps in India. More generally, Glytsos (2002b) estimates a simple dynamic, simultaneous model of aggregate investments, consumption, imports and the feedback of these components through GDP, for each of seven Mediterranean countries from about 1969 to 1993. Simulating the direct and indirect effects of remittances on incomes and hence on investment through this framework, Glytsos finds that over a six-year period investment rises with remittances in six out of the seven countries, and in four of these investment rises by more than the initial amount remitted. Similarly, León-Ledesma and Piracha (2001) find a significant positive association between remittances and aggregate investments in eleven transition economies in Eastern Europe during 1990–99, controlling for such factors as GDP per capita, the real rate of interest and inflation.[123] In a related vein, Lucas (1987) estimates a positive effect of remittances from foreign workers in the South African mines upon cattle accumulation and on crop productivity in the principal recruiting nations; Woodruff and Zenteno (2001) argue that remittances from the US have financed much of the micro-enterprise development in urban Mexico;[124] while McCormick and Wahba (2003) point to the role of remittances in small enterprise development in Cairo.

The evidence on multiplier effects from remittance spending, particularly from housing construction, is also substantial.[125] All of these studies tend to agree that the multiplier effects are quite large. However, this result ought not to be too surprising, for it seems the possibility of limited capacity thwarting domestic expansion is not a feature of these simulations; rather it is assumed that limited aggregate demand is the principal constraint on output. Yet, in practice, it seems that in some contexts additional remittances have served to drive up relative prices of land and housing, perhaps indicating a lack of excess capacity, though it is less clear that remittances have commonly fueled sustained inflation.[126] Certainly we see little sign of inflation engendered by remittances in our case study countries.

Nonetheless some reservations must be expressed; there are also reasons to anticipate that remittances may actually slow economic expansion. First there is the issue which arose in the course of discussing both Albania and Moldova of a situation similar to Dutch disease in which the inflow of remittances causes a real appreciation, or at least postpones depreciation, of the exchange rate. The limitations which this may impose on export performance can readily limit output and employment, though surprisingly little attention seems to have been granted to this aspect in the empirical literature. Second, the role of remittances in accelerating urbanization, or the contraction of agriculture through labor withdrawal, arose in the contexts of both Albania and Morocco.

More generally, it has been hypothesized that the income from remittances may permit remaining family members to reduce their work effort, which Chami *et al.* (2003) set out to test. This study looks at cross-country GDP growth data, both in the cross-section and in panel form over time. A number of controls are allowed for in alternative specifications investigated, most consistently the portion of GPD invested, private capital inflows, and a series of regional dummy variables are inserted. The primary interest of the study is, however, the statistically significant, negative association which is found between GDP growth and inflows of Worker Remittances (though Compensation of Employees is excluded from the measure of remittances). Of course, such cross-country studies of growth are notoriously sensitive to the precise list of controls introduced, and the range permitted in this study is relatively narrow.[127] On the other hand, the inclusion of a control for investment in the home country means that any growth generated by investment, stimulated by additional remittances, goes unrecognized. Nonetheless, the result is provocative. The authors interpret their result as stemming from labor effort effects, which are appropriately hypothesized to affect the level of output. In the transition to empirical exploration, however, the study turns away from analysis of output levels to examine the rate of growth of output instead. Whether a negative correlation between the rate of change of capital productivity and the level of remittances reflects an influence through labor effort is unclear; it might, for instance, even reflect the effects of an overvalued exchange rate. Perhaps more importantly, it can be exceedingly difficult disentangling whether remittances cause slower growth, or whether slower growth causes more migration and possibly greater remittances per migrant. Chami *et al.* (2003) do note the reverse correlation, namely that remittances are found to be greater, the lower is income in the home country, relative to that in the US, controlling for the difference in interest rates between the two countries which proves to be irrelevant.[128] In other words, this additional finding indeed confirms the difficulty in disentangling the effects of remittances on growth from those of growth and economic performance on remittances.

The issue of whether remittances diminish growth, given investment levels, is thus contentious. On the other hand, there is evidence, at least in some contexts, that remittances have enabled greater rates of investment and hence growth. More certainly, remittances probably raise income levels and not merely those of remittance recipients, though again there may be exceptions where over-valued exchange rates result. Finally, the increments to average incomes appear to be sufficient to outweigh any detrimental effects to income distribution in most contexts, in the sense of resulting in widespread poverty alleviation.

On Policies to Affect Both the Amounts Remitted and their Economic Consequences

Notwithstanding the ambiguities in the evidence, both with respect to the role of financial measures in affecting remittances and the macroeconomic benefits from remittances, most governments have not shied away from efforts to stimulate additional remittances. On the other hand, efforts to redirect the uses of remittances to more productive ends are much rarer.

Indeed, it is not clear that efforts under the latter category are always warranted.[129] A number of countries have attempted to redirect remittance spending by taxing these remittances:

> in most cases this has failed with the main effect being to channel the remittances through non-official channels. In 2002, Sri Lanka announced that it would impose a 15 percent tax on the US$1.2 billion remittances received each year. However, it had to quickly withdraw the measure when there was a mass outcry.[130]

India has offered preferential access to imports of capital goods and raw materials for returning migrant workers who set up or expand business establishments. Pakistan has had a similar scheme, which has also been open to overseas Pakistanis, with particular incentives for setting up units in backward areas, as well as permitting investments in export processing zones. Clearly both are intended to increase the rate of investment out of remittances, yet by lowering the relative costs of capital both schemes may have biased expansion away from much needed job creation. In any case, at least in India 'according to the available fragmentary evidence, so far their overall impact has been rather insignificant'.[131] In addition, a number of governments have developed programs in business counseling and training, and in entrepreneurship training, which are aimed at returning migrants and will be taken up in Chapter 7, though they are also a means of channeling the resources of returning migrants into investments. Complaints about lack of appropriate infrastructure to complement investments out of remittances are common, such as those noted in the contexts of Albania and Indonesia. On the other hand, it is not clear that decisions with respect to either levels of infrastructure investments, or the geographic dispersal of those investments, ought to be dictated by the availability of local remittances (though chronic under-investment may indeed be a handicap). Nonetheless, a specific scheme has been designed to do precisely this in Mexico. Hometown associations have become common among Mexican migrants in the US, raising funds for their communities of origin. 'Migrant hometown associations remit an estimated $60 million a year for infrastructure improvements in their hometowns, and their contributions are matched by federal and state governments.'[132] This scheme has apparently been quite successful in promoting infrastructure development, though it also raises issues with respect to inequality of these developments across communities.[133]

Although such schemes to affect spending out of remittances are rare, policy schemes intended to enhance the amounts remitted are very common. At least four classes of such policies may be distinguished: mandatory remittance requirements; financial incentives offering premium exchange rates, interest rates and tax breaks; lowering the costs and other barriers to formal transfers; and regulation of informal intermediaries.

Most attempts to impose mandatory remittances from contract workers, such as those introduced at early stages in Bangladesh, Pakistan, the Philippines and Thailand have quickly failed, simply diverting more recruiting to unofficial channels.[134] Such schemes have succeeded in ensuring high levels of recorded remittances only in contexts where the option of unofficial recruiting was effectively closed off, as in the case of Korean workers who were typically on contract directly to Korean construction companies, or the compulsory deposits required of foreign mine workers in South Africa during colonial times where all recruiting has been channeled through a single agency to ensure monopsony control.[135]

Schemes offering financial incentives to remit through official channels are extremely widespread. Some of these schemes have been described in the context of our case studies, and more general accounts are provided in Russell (1986) and in Puri and Ritzema (1999). Russell (1986: 690) notes of the 'policy measures introduced by countries sending labor to the Middle East ... there are no known systematic evaluations of their efficacy'. It is not clear that this has changed in the interim. The foregoing discussion of the ambiguity of the effects on remittances of exchange rate changes, and of any effects of interest rate differentials, should clearly indicate ambivalence towards using such instruments. Yet many governments appear in less doubt, at some potential cost to their constituents. Among the common devices deployed are access to foreign currency accounts (with permission to repatriate) and foreign currency denominated bonds. However,

> A major limitation of foreign currency accounts as a tool for stimulating remittances is that they, by their very nature, are attractive only to migrants belonging to professional and higher-skilled categories who earn relatively higher incomes ... Generally, one finds that none of the incentive schemes address all factors that lead to the leakage of remittances into informal channels.[136]

Again, there are exceptions, and the Bangladeshi Wage Earner Scheme appears to have been one. Under this scheme, workers remittances in foreign exchange could be sold at auction where the premium over the market exchange rate was around 30 percent in the early 1990s; the buyers of foreign exchange were then entitled to certain imports, which were restricted and again commanded high premiums. In other words, it was the highly distorted trade and exchange rate policies in place that rendered the Wage Earner Scheme successful in attracting official remittances and these attractions have since been largely disbanded.[137] Similarly El-Sakka and McNabb (1999: 1501) attribute some of their findings on the sensitivity of Egypt's official remittances to changes in the black market premium, and to the domestic interest rate, and to major distortions in both markets;

> pegging both interest rates and exchange rates contribute to the dollarization problem. Unrealistic interest rates encourage migrants to remit their earnings in the form of real assets or to keep them in the form of foreign currency, usually US Dollars. As a consequence, substantial deposits of foreign exchange – usually held by private agents – will not be available to the government.

Perhaps in consequence of such ambiguities and limitations, much of the recent attention among commentators (if not governments) has shifted to lowering the costs and barriers to official remittance channels.

> Here, the policy implications are perhaps clearer: remittances are likely to increase if legislative barriers and fiscal costs of financial transfers can be reduced; the latter is likely to be facilitated by the introduction of more market players and modes of transmission, better provision of reliable information to migrants on the costs of transfer, and generally better and more credible supervision of the sector to ensure the transparency and reliability of transfers.[138]

Ratha (2003: 165) notes that 'The average cost of transferring remittances to Central and South America is in the range of 13 percent, and often exceeds 20 percent.' One reason for these exorbitant fees is the small amount transferred on a typical occasion, incurring high fixed costs. This issue has come to attract a good deal of attention within the Americas recently: in 2001, the US amended the Electronic Fund Transfer Act to require clearer disclosure of terms; US banks have increasingly recognized identification cards issued by Mexican consulates, both to documented and irregular migrants, as sufficient to open a bank account, and other South American governments are contemplating similar schemes; moreover various links between financial intermediaries are being explored, such as the links established by the International Remittance Network involving Citibank and some credit union cooperatives, and thoughts of 'partnerships between leading banks and the government post office network in countries that do not have banks with extensive branch networks in rural areas'.[139] Increased competition in the funds transfer market is beginning to lower the exorbitant mark-ups that have prevailed, yet rates remain high to date.

Azad describes parallel difficulties in remitting to Bangladesh and to the rural areas in particular:

> The remitters encounter various problems in sending their remittances, especially to the remote areas of the country, through official channels. The process of sending remittances through banks is slow and complicated. There is a lot of paper work and documentation, which the workers find it difficult to accomplish. Lack of knowledge of banking procedures is also a hindrance in sending remittances through the banks. There is also the risk of the remittance documents ... getting lost in transit. On the other hand, the process of sending money through informal channels is simpler, safer and quicker ... While it takes about 13 days in receiving remittances sent through the banks, it takes at most three days for beneficiaries to receive remittances through informal channels.[140]

Despite these advantages of the informal remittance system there is a common concern to divert transfers from informal to formal channels. In part these concerns stem from the role of the informal system in financing smuggling, laundering money from narcotics trade, and as a suspected conduit of funds for 'terrorist' organizations. The last of these has resulted in particular efforts to monitor informal transfers since September 11, 2001, which has slowed and perhaps diminished informal remittance flows globally and not just from the US. For example, the resultant temporary drop in remittances to Morocco in 2002 has already been noted in Section 5.2, while Hugo (2003a) reports an initial surge in remittances to Pakistan, in anticipation of tighter future monitoring, as well as major concerns in the Philippines under threat of sanctions from the Financial Action Task Force.

The Asia-Pacific Group on Money Laundering (2003: 19) notes that 'International efforts to control alternative remittance systems have until recently been haphazard and lacking in commitment.' The group recommends a two-pronged approach; tighter regulation of intermediaries and greater efforts to identify those intermediaries. Neither is likely to prove easy. Moreover, such efforts run the usual regulatory danger of hampering the operations of the well-intentioned while driving the less well-intentioned more deeply underground. Diminishing harmful, illegal activities is clearly a desirable goal; whether diverting funds from the informal to formal channels (and potentially reducing overall transfers in the process) is equally desirable is far less obvious. Diverting funds would place more tax money and more foreign exchange at the disposal of government. Ultimately, however, whether diverting remittances to formal channels represents a social improvement, over leaving these funds in the hands of migrants and their families, depends very much upon how each government spends the additional resources.

5.4   CLOSING REMARKS

The interactions between home and host countries generate not only quite different migration regimes but also quite different remittance regimes, and the two are very interdependent. Temporary migration to the Gulf has generated massive remittances over an extended period. The expansion of temporary labor migration within East Asia has also spawned large, though predominantly unrecorded remittances. For Turkey and the Maghreb countries, a mix of recorded and unofficial remittances provide a critical resource, and some of the countries of Eastern Europe have become utterly dependent for day to day living on remittances from undocumented migrants. Very few refugees in camps command the resources to remit at all, yet global evidence suggests no lower rates of remittance to countries generating large numbers of recognized refugees. The wider diaspora appears to be an important part of this story, with resettled refugees and asylum seekers in the higher income countries remitting home, possibly though the near diaspora in camps in third countries. Recognition of the importance of remittances as a source of external finance has evolved rapidly among the developing countries of the western hemisphere where, by 2000, gross reported remittances exceeded 40 percent of the current account balance and a quarter of the inflow of direct investments. Of all countries in the world, the US is the largest single source of reported remittances, but relative to the stock of migrants the EU sends more and the GCC states far more. Moreover, Mexico's reported remittance inflows amount to almost a third of the US reported outflows and most of the evidence points to a relatively low rate of remittance compared to the very high earnings of the highly skilled from the rest of the developing world residing in North America. The upshot of these regimes is that, on average, the lower income developing countries receive a higher portion of their incomes from remittances than do the middle income countries, although remittances received per capita are lower among the poorer countries.[141]

Within countries, the evidence on whether the impact effect of remittances tends to equalize the income distribution is mixed, though accounting for multiplier effects of remittance spending, both within and across villages, seems to tip the balance toward a more equalizing effect. Similarly, although remittances seem to be a significant source of investments in some countries this is not the case in others. One suspects that much of this difference in inducement to invest reflects the overall attractiveness of investing in any given economy, but this remains to be tested. Whether remittances accelerate economic growth, through investments or otherwise, remains a matter of dispute and the evidence is again mixed. However, remittances clearly do raise income levels for many, and not necessarily only the recipients of remittances once multiplier effects of spending and the associated stimulus to labor markets are accounted for. In consequence, there is widespread recognition of the role of remittances in alleviating poverty.

Policy efforts to divert remittances toward more productive uses are rare and may, in any case, not be warranted everywhere. Policy efforts to stimulate remittances, on the other hand, are common though not always effective. Little evidence emerges to support the notion that higher interest rates, offered to those who remit, encourage larger flows. There is some evidence to suggest that depreciation of the market exchange rate can encourage greater recorded transfers, though this is hardly ground for an exchange rate policy. Narrowing the premium on the black market for foreign exchange also appears to enhance reported remittances, though whether total remittances are enhanced is far more dubious. The developing countries are coming under increasing pressure to shrink and to regulate the informal transfer system, though such efforts may prove a mixed blessing for the developing countries and their poorer populations.

Global remittances, both formal and perhaps informal, have grown rapidly in recent years and remittances have proved a stable source of finance, certainly in relation to private capital flows but also in relation to official development assistance. Despite attempts to localize jobs and to expel irregular migrants in the GCC states, and despite two Gulf wars, remittances from the Middle East have continued to expand. In Southeast Asia, there is some evidence to indicate that informal remittances may actually have increased during the East Asia crisis. Yet, in other contexts concerns for the continuation of current remittances are real. To the extent that skill bias in the immigration policies of the industrialized countries continues, remittances could be harmed, perhaps particularly so if the industrialized countries compete with each other by offering more permanent settlement and family accompaniment to the highly skilled. Meanwhile, the inability of irregular migrants to move back and forth, in Europe and elsewhere, is forcing greater permanence and ultimately may result in declining remittances.

NOTES

1.   See Russell (1986: Table 1) on the benefits and costs of international remittances.
2.   Ratha (2003: 157). The total of $72.3 billion is the sum of Workers' Remittances and Compensation of Employees on current account plus Migrants' Transfers on capital account in the IMF's *Balance of Payments Yearbook*. Workers' Remittances are meant to be transfers by migrants who are employed, or intend to remain employed, for more than a year in another economy in which they are considered residents; Compensation of Employees includes wages, salaries and other benefits of border, seasonal and other non-resident workers. In 2001, Workers' Remittances reported as inflows to the developing countries totaled US$57.1 billion and Compensation of Employees was $15.4 billion. (The slight discrepancy in these totals from the *Balance of Payments Statistics*, as compared to the World Bank report, results from data updates in the latter.) In practice, it seems

clear that the distinctions between these two categories are far from strictly observed. For example, the Philippines reports most of their official remittances as Compensation of Employees, whereas most of their migrants are working abroad for more than a year in any given spell. In principle, remittances should include only that portion of compensation of employees that is transferred home. Bilsborrow *et al.* (1997) accordingly point out that adding together compensation and remittances, which has become the norm, may well result in some double counting. Additional difficulties with the official data include treatment of cash and goods brought home by returning migrants, the latter frequently being defined as imports rather than remittances even if the migrant is bringing gold. The third category of remittance, Migrants' Transfers on capital account, is reported by only a few countries (though they are comparatively large in the case of Russia, for example).

3. Direct investment, remittances and balance on goods and services from IMF *Balance of Payments Statistics* and *International Financial Statistics*. ODA from Ratha (2003: statistical appendix). Both direct investment and remittances are measured net (inflows minus outflows) to the set of developing countries included in the IMF data, but after subtracting the four included GCC states (data on Qatar and UAE are not available). Remittances are defined as the sum of Workers' Remittances and Compensation of Employees. ODA refers to 'Total net ODA flows from DAC countries, multilateral organizations, and non-DAC countries' (World Bank 2003c: 200). World Bank (2003c), *Global Development Finance: Striving for Stability in Development Finance*, Washington DC: World Bank.

4. Ratha (2003: 157).

5. The data on remittances are derived from the IMF *Balance of Payments Statistics* 2002 and are defined on the same basis as the World Bank study. GDP per capita is measured in purchasing power parity US\$, as is GDP in the denominator on the vertical axis. Only countries reporting positive remittances received are included.

6. In both the lower and upper panels the line is estimated simply by ordinary least squares. In the upper panel the associated t-statistic for a zero null hypothesis on the slope is 1.79 whereas in the lower panel this t-statistic is 2.71.

7. Remittances ought really to be related to the stock of migrants rather than net flow, but stock data are not available. The finding of a weaker association with net flow in the earlier 1990s may well then reflect a weaker association between the earlier flow and the accumulated migrant stock, perhaps as a result of higher return migration from the earlier period.

8. This refers to the largest positive and negative residuals in an ordinary least squares regression of net remittances on net annual migration from 1990 to 1995 and from 1995 to 2000. The two migration variables are jointly, though not separately significant. Neither GDP per capita nor population (as another control for size) of the home country proves significant if included in the analysis. On the other hand, migration and remittances ought to be represented as jointly determined, and to this extent the simple results presented here are probably biased.

9. These informal systems possess a variety of names in different parts of the world. El Qorchi *et al.* (2003: 1) list some of these names: *fei-ch'ien* (China), *hui kuan* (Hong Kong), *hundi* (India), *hawala* (Middle East), *padala* (Philippines), and *phei kwan* (Thailand).

10. El Qorchi *et al.* (2003: 34).

11. For a review, see Glytsos (2001).

12. For a more comprehensive review of the following arguments, see Lucas and Stark (1985), and the survey in Rapoport and Docquier (forthcoming).

13. See Cox (1987), Bruce and Waldman (1990) and Coate (1995), among others.

14. Poirine (1997) emphasizes the role of loan arrangements in his study of remittances to Samoa and Tonga from Australia.

15. See Van Hear (2003), for a summary statement on refugees and remittances.

16. See the discussions in Faini (1994), and Garson (1994).

17. On this 'portfolio' approach, in which exchange rate uncertainties play a central role, see Katseli and Glytsos (1989), and Wahba (1991).

18. On the other hand, 'The consideration of investment profitability in the host country is particularly pertinent in more recent years, in view of the fact that migrants are increasingly establishing their own businesses' (Glytsos, 2002a: 14).

19. This potential feature plays a central role in a recent IMF study by Chami *et al.* (2003), to which Section 5.3 returns.

20. See Stark *et al.* (1986).

21. Adelman *et al.* (1988), Taylor (1992).

22. On the other hand, effects through induced tightening in the labor market and of additional foreign exchange mean that benefits are not entirely confined to the specific region.

23. Compare the discussion of the effects of official capital flows in Eaton (1988).

24. For an early statement of these ideas, see Stark and Levhari (1982).

25. The emphasis on the dual roles of remittances, in financing capital formation and the trade deficit, has led to comparisons with the earlier two-gap models depicting similar roles for aid. Yet care needs to be taken not to perceive the savings-investment and foreign exchange roles as entirely independent. See the general critique of the two-gap approach in Bruton (1969) and of its application to remittances in Glytsos (2002a).

26. Quibria (1996), McCormick and Wahba (2000).

27. Workers' Remittances per migrant are higher from the US than from the EU, while Compensation of Employees per migrant are greater from the EU. To the extent that these categories are correctly reported this would reflect a greater relative importance of remittances from temporary workers in the EU as compared to the US.

28. As with Canada, Singapore does not report remittances.

29. Remittances again refer to Workers' Remittances plus Compensation of Employees. No data on remittances are available for Bulgaria, Macedonia and Ukraine in 1995. In addition, the IMF *International Financial Statistics*, at the time of writing, reports no data on exports from Moldova or on GDP for Belarus, Macedonia and the Ukraine in 2000 and 2001. All of the averages in Table 5.4 are adjusted accordingly. However, data on GDP are not reported at all for Albania. Throughout, GDP is measured in local currency units in each year and dollar remittances are converted at the official market exchange rate.

30. See Chapter 2 on patterns of migration from Albania.

31. King *et al.* (2003: 1).

32. World Bank (2000b: 2).

33. King et al. (2003: 3).

34. King et al. (2003: 22).

35. King et al. (2003: 48).

36. These reported patterns are based on 26 in-depth interviews among Albanian migrants in the UK. The sample, while not random, is nonetheless intended to be typical of Albanian migrants in the UK.

37. King *et al.* (2003: 3–4). Korovilas (2003b), suggests a greater degree of small business start-ups financed out of remittances from Greece, based on his 1996 interviews, a finding that is supported more generally by Konica and Filer (2003).

38. King *et al.* (2003: 34, 49).

39. In Figure 5.4 remittances prior to 1992 are represented by Other Private Transfers. After 1992 remittances are measured as the sum of Workers' Remittances and Compensation of Employees from the IMF *Balance of Payments Statistics*. All other data are from the IMF *International Financial Statistics*. Albania takes unusual steps to include transactions through the parallel cash market and goods imported by migrants as well as

transfers through commercial banks in estimating reported remittances (see IMF, 2000). Nonetheless, Korovilas (2003b) undertakes some rough calculations based on assumed days of work, wage rates and proportion of earnings remitted, and suggests that the official figures may under-report actual flows by more than 40 percent. The 1996 household survey examined in Konica and Filer (2003), indicates total remittance receipts some 38 percent higher than the estimate by the Bank of Albania and almost exactly double the IMF estimate.

40. Inflation was more rapid during 1997 and 1998, following the turmoil associated with the collapse of a huge pyramid scheme. Korovilas (2003b), attributes the existence of the pyramid scheme to the presence of remittances. However, this attribution rests on noting that expenditures on the scheme could not have been afforded without the income from remittances. Certainly investment in these schemes, out of remittances or otherwise, proved a serious mistake, but this is not quite the same as blaming the scam on remittances.

41. Sleptova (2003: 21).

42. Sleptova (2003: 22, 24).

43. Remittance data are from the IMF *Balance of Payments Statistics*. Workers' Remittances form only a tiny part of the remittance data, most of which are reported as Compensation of Employees. The latter are based on reports from the Migration Office, foreign embassies and banks and 'take into account the number of employees, their salaries, and the duration of labor contracts' (IMF, 2000: 262). All additional data are from IMF *International Financial Statistics*. GDP and Gross Fixed Capital Formation are converted to US$ at the average market exchange rate.

44. See the World Bank *Moldova Country Brief* for 2003.

45. See Khachani (1998).

46. Morocco reports only Workers' Remittances, including 'bank transfers, postal money orders, and foreign banknotes paid into the banking system' (IMF, 2000: 265) and recorded in the Statement of Exchange Transactions. No Compensation of Employees is reported.

47. The regression actually pools annual data on Morocco, Portugal, Tunisia, Turkey and Yugoslavia, with fixed effects representing the different countries. In addition to the logarithm of the real exchange rate and the difference in domestic and destination country interest rates (adjusted for expected devaluation), the regressions also control for income at home and abroad, the stock of migrants overseas and lagged remittances.

48. See the descriptions of these arrangements in Garson (1994). Currency exchange restrictions have been particularly tight in Algeria, resulting in much smaller recorded remittances per migrant. See also Safir (1999).

49. See Box 1 in Garson (1994), for a general description of the types of incentives introduced in various Maghreb countries.

50. World Bank (2003b: 6). Conversely, Khachani (2004), also attributes the 60 percent increment in remittances in 2001 to the introduction of the euro and to uncertainty following September 11. In particular, Khachani notes that reported remittances increased sharply not only from Europe during 2001, but also from the US (+144.1%), from Kuwait (+216%) and from Qatar (+117.1%) in terms of dirham.

51. Derived by comparison of data on remittances from France (Garson, 1994), with totals from *International Financial Statistics*.

52. World Bank (2003b).

53. Remittances from Garson (1994); consumer price index for France from *International Financial Statistics*; migration data from Giubilaro (1997).

54. Clearly it would be preferable to examine the remittance data in terms of migrant stocks rather than flows, and to explore the role of undocumented migrants also, but data are lacking. Khachani (1998), argues that the propensity to remit from France to the Maghreb

is higher than to other regions because of the lack of assimilation of Maghreb peoples in France, the migration of family members notwithstanding.

55. Leichtman (2002: Table 4), cites data from the Moroccan Ministère des Affaires Étrangères indicating that some 94 percent of Moroccans overseas were in Europe and 5 percent in North America in 1997. On the other hand, the World Bank (2003b), reports 90 percent of remittances were from Europe and 3.9 percent from North America in 1999.

56. Glytsos (1998: n.p.).

57. See also Wahba (1996) and Soudi and Teto (2004), for support of this position. On the other hand, Khachani (2004) notes the tendency for remittances to be invested in the somewhat more prosperous regions, in part because of lack of infrastructure in poorer areas.

58. A person is deemed, by the Government of India, to be of Indian origin if he or she was born in India or has at least one grandparent, or parent, born in undivided India.

59. The data in Figure 5.8 are derived from Reserve Bank of India statistics at http://www.rbi. org.in/, together with data from Nayyar (1994: tables 9 and 10). The data for the dollar area and for total transfers reproduce the Reserve Bank data, after deducting contra-entries for PL480 imports in the early years. The portion attributed to Europe and Australia include all non-sterling OECD remittances and a portion of the sterling transfers too. Data for the Gulf include part of the sterling transfers plus a part of the non-sterling (non-OECD) transfers. The portions attributed to each region follow Nayyar (1994). In 1996–97 the basis of reporting private transfers was revised substantially, resulting in a sharp jump in dollar area transfers which is not shown in Figure 5.8. At the time of writing, the most recent data available on the RBI web for Invisible Transactions by Region are for 1996–97.

60. US Census Bureau at http://www.census.gov/population/www/socdemo/foreign.html/. Note that foreign-born population is a narrower definition than Persons of Indian Origin, presumably explaining the smaller US numbers.

61. Nayyar (1994: 63).

62. Nayyar (1994: 63). Indeed, Nayyar argues that most of the policy incentives to remit have benefited this group rather than unskilled migrants going to the Gulf.

63. These problems are noted in the Report of the Committee on the Indian Diaspora (Government of India, 2001).

64. Nayyar (1994: 73).

65. Nayyar (1994: 74).

66. More generally, this proves robust to controlling for the level of GDP and for last year's rate of investment.

67. See Zacharia *et al.* (1999, 2002).

68. Zacharia *et al.* (1999: 23).

69. Zacharia *et al.* (2002).

70. Nayyar (1994: 73–4). See the evidence in Gulati and Mody (1983).

71. The data are from Nair (1998: table 8.12). Nair notes the absence of a rank correlation across districts but it is also true that the measures are uncorrelated.

72. See Nair (1998), and Isaac (1993).

73. Nair (1998: 267).

74. Nair (1998: 279).

75. Data on Kerala's net domestic product at constant prices are derived from Reserve Bank of India statistics at http://www.rbi.org.in/. See Chapter 2 for data on recruitment of contract workers from India to the Gulf. An ordinary least squares regression of the logarithm of net domestic at constant prices product provides:

$$-79.8 + 0.093 \text{ LM} + 0.045 \text{ YR} \qquad \text{No. Observations} = 18$$
$$(16.77) \ (3.86) \qquad (17.80) \qquad R\text{-squared} = 0.98$$

where LM indicates the logarithm of recruitment lagged one year and YR indicates the time trend. T-statistics for a zero null-hypothesis are shown in parentheses and standard errors are heteroskedasticity consistent. The general nature of this result also proves fairly robust to alternative specifications.

76. Data from IMF *Balance of Payments Statistics*, which include only Workers Remittances and no Compensation of Employees in the case of Pakistan.

77. Data on the black market exchange rate premium are from El Qorchi *et al.* (2003: table A2.4), and from Cowitt (1984).

78. See Amjad (1989).

79. The survey was conducted jointly by the Asian Research Team for Employment Promotion of the International Labor Organization and by the Federal Bureau of Statistics in the Government of Pakistan.

80. Azam (1991: table 3).

81. See Azam (1991).

82. Azam (1991).

83. Amjad (1989: 21). See also Burki (1988).

84. Note that although this points to the relatively well-off rural families benefiting from remittances, most of the truly wealthy live in town. In addition, Adams's (1998) measure of relative family poverty includes the remittances themselves; to a limited extent, the rich may appear rich precisely because they receive remittances. However, the level of remittances does not appear to be sufficiently large, even for the high income households, to alter the general conclusion.

85. See Hugo (2003a) and Cohen (2003).

86. Hugo (2002a: table 36).

87. Nayyar (1997: table 8).

88. Hugo (1995).

89. Hugo (1998).

90. Hugo (2003a: 34–5).

91. Bagasao (2003).

92. I am most grateful to the Commission on Filipinos Overseas for supplying this table.

93. National Statistics Office at http://www.census.gov.ph/.

94. In contrast, the US Census Bureau (2002b) estimates 1.2 million people in total in the US, whether permanently or otherwise in 2000, who were born in the Philippines.

95. See also Go (2002), for comparable estimates.

96. From 1990 to 2001, Workers' Remittances comprised less than 8 percent of the reported total, with Compensation of Employees comprising the remainder.

97. The black market premium on foreign exchange, on which these estimates are partially based, averaged about 6 percent from 1974 through 2000, with a spike to 50 percent in 1983 and the disappearance of any discrepancy since 1996 (El Qorchi *et al.*, 2003; Cowitt, 1984). Nonetheless, concerns about money laundering through Philippine financial organizations brought the Paris-based Financial Action Task Force to the brink of imposing sanctions in March 2003.

98. Alburo (1993).

99. Note that this survey does not incorporate permanent emigrants but focuses on contract and other temporary workers. See also Rodriguez and Horton (1995).

100. Rodriguez (1996) and Hugo (2003a).

101. Alburo (1993) also supports this position.

102. See the 2002 Survey of Overseas Filipinos at http://www.census.gov.ph/.

103. Rodriguez (1996: S430).

104. Saith (1997: 34–5). The results refer to a 1991 study (for sources, see Saith, 1997). For supporting evidence on the rural areas, see Rodriguez (1998).

105. External factors have contributed too, in recent years, including the impact of El Niño, the SARS epidemic, and the regional crisis. In the mid-1990s there was a brief period of respite, during which direct investment, GDP and export growth accelerated, but this was also a period of appreciation in the real exchange rate.

106. The temporary–permanent dichotomy of status and duration of stay are not necessarily correlated. Indeed, the correlation may be particularly weak if the distinction refers to intent; many migrants who believe they will return home find themselves staying for longer than they intended.

107. For example, Glytsos (1988) finds a positive association between time away and remittances from Germany to Greece but a negative association from the US to Greece. Elbadawi and Rocha (1992) as well as Merkle and Zimmerman (1992) find negative associations for remittances to several Mediterranean countries. On the other hand, Brown (1997) rejects the notion of any decay in remittance with time away in analyzing remittances to Samoa and Tonga. O'Neil (2003a: 11) recognizes this diversity: 'There are remittance "life cycles" and they vary across cultures, countries, and economic conditions.'

108. In contrast, Stern (1998: tables 19 and 20) reproduces data from the Bank of Thailand that would indicate far higher remittances per worker from the US than from the Gulf. However, these data refer to the period of suspended recruitment from Thailand to parts of the Gulf and may not be representative. Indeed, the reported remittances from the US appear to jump upwards from 1988 to 1990 simultaneously with the decline from the Middle East.

109. More specifically, this refers to the regression of net remittance receipts on net migration from each country as discussed in connection with Table 5.2. If these results are extended to include a measure of the stock of refugees from each of the 76 developing countries included, that measure has a tiny, statistically insignificant coefficient associated with it. This remains true if remittances, migration and refugees are measured per capita, and no matter whether net or gross remittances are considered. No simple non-linear connection with the number of refugees could be detected either. Data on the numbers of refugees are from UNHCR, and 54 of the 76 countries are reported to be the country of origin of some refugees.

110. See, for example, Economic Resource Center for Overseas Filipinos (2002).

111. Remittances are examined both per capita and relative to GDP across 33 and 38 developing countries respectively.

112. Faini (2002), adopts the measure of brain drain tabulated by Carrington and Detragiache (1999). In Chapter 4, some limitations of this measure have been noted. The alternative measure depicted in Figure 5.12 refers to data comparable to those on brain drain to the US in Chapter 4.

113. Russell (1986: 685). The quoted passage is from Swamy (1981: 36).

114. Straubhaar (1986b: 737).

115. See, for example, El-Sakka and McNabb (1999) on Egypt, or Katseli and Glytsos (1989) on Greece.

116. See Katseli and Glytsos (1989). This is also supported by the findings of Faini (1994).

117. See, for example, Chandavarkar (1980), Elbadawi and Rocha (1992), El-Sakka and McNabb (1999) and other references reviewed in Glytsos (2001).

118. Glytsos (1988: fn7). See the references cited therein.

119. Ratha (2003: 164.)

120. Adams (1991: 10).

121. Adams and Page (2003a), examine panel data on poverty headcounts and poverty gaps,

across countries, with varying numbers of time series observations on each country. The study controls for GDP per capita and inequality (as represented by the Gini coefficient) in each country–time period. Even given these controls, poverty is estimated to diminish significantly, the larger are either remittances received relative to GDP, or the stock of migrants reported in the OECD countries relative to total home population. The authors note that the estimated effect is small, but note that since the controls already include both the level and distribution of income, 'rather than express surprise at the small magnitudes of the elasticity of poverty reduction with respect to the migration and remittance variables, we should be surprised that they are significant at all' (Adams and Page, 2003a: 14). The authors go on to speculate that the fact they find an effect may reflect the nature and timing of the data. It is also difficult disentangling the effects of migration on poverty from the effects of poverty on migration (which they estimate to be zero), at least within the confines of the ordinary least squares approach adopted.

122. Ratha (2003: 164).

123. On the other hand, since both remittances and investment are measured relative to GDP this may introduce a degree of spurious correlation.

124. Woodruff and Zenteno (2001: abstract) 'use a survey of more than 6000 small firms located in 44 urban areas of Mexico. We focus on one important source of investment capital for Mexican entrepreneurs: earnings from migration by the owner or family members working in the United States. We estimate that remittances are responsible for almost 27% of the capital invested in microenterprises throughout urban Mexico. Within the ten states with the highest rate of migration to the United States, we estimate that more than 40% of the capital invested in microenterprises is associated with remittances.'

125. See, for example, Stahl and Habib (1989) on construction in Bangladesh, Adelman and Taylor (1990) on Mexico, Kandil and Metwally (1990) on Egypt, Glytsos (1993) on Greece, and Zarate (2002) on Mexico at the national level.

126. See Looney (1990) who argues that remittances fueled inflation in some of the Arab countries in the 1980s and counter claims for Asia by Stahl and Arnold (1986). Another possible sign of lack of demand driven expansion is when most remittances simply result in additional imports. See, for example, Handoussa (1991) on Egypt.

127. See, for example, Levine and Renelt (1992).

128. The authors then use these two measures as instrumental variables in re-estimating the growth equation though it would seem the choice of instruments may not be felicitous, particularly given the insignificant role of interest rate differentials in the first stage.

129. Athukorala (1992, 1993), is critical of the Asian experience in this sphere: 'The findings cast doubt on the viability and effectiveness of "migrant-specific" policy initiatives and point to the need for an economy-wide approach encompassing appropriate exchange-rate and financial policies' (Athukorala, 1992: 511).

130. Hugo (2003a: 33).

131. Puri and Ritzema (1999: 15).

132. *Migration News*, July 1, 2003 at http://migration.ucdavis.edu/mn/index.php.

133. Complex issues are also raised with respect to funding under the *Oportunidades* program aimed at aiding communities according to their levels of income; it is unclear to what extent each scheme implicitly taxes the other.

134. Abella (1992).

135. On the Korean case see Puri and Ritzema (1996); on South Africa see Lucas (1985, 1987).

136. Puri and Ritzema (1996: 13,14).

137. The black market exchange rate premium in Bangladesh fell from over 270 percent in 1988 to zero in 1998. See El Qorchi *et al.* (2003). Bangladesh nonetheless has continued to introduce various additional incentive schemes. See Azad (2003: 15).

138. Black (2003: 3).

139. Ratha (2003: 165). More generally, see Suro *et al.* (2002), on the remittances system within the Americas.

140. Azad 2003: 16). The issue of risk in official transfers has also been noted in the case of India.

141. For Africa (excluding the Maghreb) reported gross remittances amounted to more than 62 percent of direct investment. On average this represented about US$13 per capita among the fifteen reporting countries in 2000. (Twenty-seven African countries included in the IMF *Balance of Payments Statistics* for 2002, report no remittances in 2000, although eight of these report receipts in either 1998 or 1999.) In comparison, the four major countries of South Asia reported receipts of about US$10 per capita in 2000.

6. The Diaspora and Transnational Networks

> In an age of swift and cheap transportation and communication, emigration no longer represents the break with the home country that it once did. And in this context, social and economic capital can no longer be neatly segregated analytically. Many students of migration agree that these transnational networks are today the most important developmental resource associated with international migration. (Newland, 2003: 6)

Transnational networks play a two-way role in international migration. On the one hand, family, friends or other contacts overseas ease the process of relocating, serving to sustain and amplify specific migration streams once initiated. An account of this role and some of the difficulties in measuring its importance are discussed in Chapter 2. On the other hand, as transnational networks become established they may also play a role in shaping developments in the home country. Again, these links and influences prove difficult to measure, but there is nonetheless growing evidence of their significance. The purpose of the present chapter is to outline the mechanisms through which transnational networks are supposed to contribute to developments at origin, and to review some of the supporting evidence. Yet it seems equally important to note when international migration does not appear to lead to such advantages for the home country.

Section 6.1 sets the stage by describing the nature and formation of some of the transnational networks that are attracting so much attention. Section 6.2 then turns to the role of international migration, and of social and business networks, in promoting both international trade and international capital flows, describing the hypothesized mechanisms underlying these links and the evidence. Section 6.3 addresses the closely related issue of transnational knowledge networks, the circulation of knowledge workers, and their roles in diffusing technical progress between nations. Section 6.4 briefly notes some of the other key influences that a diaspora can have upon developments in the home country, by affecting foreign policy, the pressures for reform, and issues of security. The chapter closes by returning to the quote at the outset, and asking where we stand on whether transnational networks are the most important developmental resource associated with international migration.

6.1   ON THE NATURE OF TRANSNATIONAL NETWORKS

Globalization is leading traders and investors into contexts that are increasingly unfamiliar, where opportunities are not always apparent and the rules of business are not always transparent. International migrants often possess better and more reliable information about their own origins, and hence facilitate transactions in this increasingly complex setting. However, these advantages can be considerably enriched and strengthened in contexts where contact between the migrant and home remains dense. Through such contacts, the migrant may not only be the source of new information about the home setting, but be well placed to evaluate the reliability of this information. Repeated transactions within the family also assume a special importance when legal enforcement of contracts remains rudimentary. The bonds between family members, reinforced by the potential for social sanctions, offer advantages to at least three forms of contracting: in reaching and enforcing agreements between family members themselves; in identifying more trustworthy contracting partners for others; and in the potential for family members to enforce contracts with others, on behalf of absent kin and their allies, especially where legal systems are ponderous, ineffective or rudimentary.[1]

Some observers argue that transnational networks are becoming increasingly dense.[2] This might be anticipated, as the demands of globalization increase, and as communication and travel are facilitated. As travel back and forth becomes more frequent it would not be surprising to see continued contact. Yet such physical movements may not be essential to the process. Migrants may have many reasons for wishing to maintain their contacts with the old country, even if they rarely visit. Such reasons may range from nostalgia to altruism toward family members remaining at home, to an intent ultimately to return home or to find a spouse from the home setting, to possession of property in the home community, to concerns with maintaining contact for reasons of religious and ethnic identity.

The manifold reasons for maintaining contacts also spawn a wide variety of mechanisms through which contacts are maintained.[3] Whereas unskilled workers are typically portrayed as relying largely upon kin-based networks, middle class migrants are depicted as selecting different networks depending upon the purpose, while professional migrants tend to rely more on colleagues, fellow alumni and more formal organizations.

To some extent these transnational networks become established and sustained by initial social networking in the new country. Such networks are well documented among less skilled workers.[4] However, Saxenian also documents the evolution of a plethora of ethnic-based associations among foreign-born professionals in Silicon Valley, where Chinese and Indian immigrants form the largest groups and are best organized, though more recently Korean, Japanese, Filipino and Singaporean organizations have also evolved. 'As their communities grew during the 1970s and 1980s, these immigrants responded to the sense of professional and social exclusion by organizing collectively.'[5] The initial roles of such networks are typically local, providing immigrants with labor market information, mentoring, professional contacts, 'angel' investment loans, and a safety net. However, as the networks evolve their international roles and activities expand too, sometimes evolving into more formal transnational associations. Meyer and Brown (1999) thus list more than forty formal, technology associations designed to connect thirty countries to their highly skilled nationals abroad.

A broad variety of transnational networks exist, playing different roles. Yet this very variety also renders difficult any testing for the significance of the economic contribution of the many networks. The relevant concept of community varies from context to context. Although accounts of national diasporas abound, the nation-state may not be the relevant unit to consider in analyzing the evolution and role of networks. For instance, Saxenian (1999: 31) documents exclusionary ethnic divisions within the Chinese technology community in Silicon Valley. Alumnae relationships also appear to be important, such as those among graduates of India's Institutes of Technology or Taiwan's elite engineering universities, creating cliques within a nationality, as can differing vintages of arrival from certain countries.

This diversity and overlap renders difficult the choice of ways in which to represent networks empirically. Nonetheless an empirical literature is emerging, examining at least some of the purported economic benefits of transnational networks. In particular, the burgeoning evidence linking transnational networks and merchandise trade is considered in the following section, together with the more rudimentary evidence on implications for financial capital flows, before turning to knowledge networks thereafter.

6.2 NETWORKS, TRADE AND CAPITAL MOVEMENTS

Transnational business and social networks are posited to play two major roles in promoting bilateral trade and capital movements. First, migrants possess some natural advantages in overcoming inadequate information about trading and investment opportunities in their home countries. The migrant may simply alert traders and investors to possibilities of which they are unaware. Through network contacts, the migrant is also more likely to become aware of newly emerging opportunities. Perhaps most importantly, though, the migrant may be able to lower reputation barriers against trade in goods and services and against investment opportunities, essentially offering his or her own reputation in the new country as collateral. Second, as discussed in the previous section, the migrant may be well placed to enforce contracts, whether in trade or invested funds, through a network of contacts at home.

Trade

The potential for international migration to swell trade with the old country has long been recognized. However, much of the early attention focused on exports of specialty items, reminders of a previous lifestyle demanded by the diaspora, and on tourism by returning natives. More recently, international trade economists have turned their attention in the direction of transnational networks, in part to explain the 'mystery of the missing trade', or why 'Nations appear to trade too much with themselves and too little with each other'.[6]

There is abundant evidence that trade diminishes (sharply and perhaps exponentially) with distance.[7] In consequence, much of the trade of large countries never crosses international boundaries, resulting in a high ratio of internal to international trade. Transport costs do not appear to be the main culprit. Transport costs are typically too low to account for the sharp distance profile of declining trade. Moreover, most forms of transport involve high fixed costs of loading and unloading, with relatively small costs per additional mile; as a result, transport costs would not result in the exponential decline in trade with distance, as commonly depicted. Instead, recent speculation has turned to the diminishing density of networks with distance, in part reflecting the influences of geography on migration, as a potential explanation.

There have been some important recent attempts to explore these ideas empirically. Rauch and Trindade (2002) examine global, bilateral trade patterns, in 1980 and 1990, using an extended gravity model.[8] The cross-product of ethnic Chinese population shares, in each pair of trading partner countries, is found to increase trade significantly. The authors suggest that this reflects the role that the Chinese business network plays in promoting trade generally. But the study also goes further, enquiring into the role played by these networks. In particular, the authors argue that any contract enforcement effect of networks should be common to all commodity groups. On the other hand, acquiring reliable information about differentiated or heterogeneous goods is depicted as more difficult than is obtaining trustworthy perceptions of more homogeneous goods; there is simply a greater variance of attributes among the former. Hence, information comes to play a greater role in shaping trade in differentiated heterogeneous goods, and the study shows that the cross-product of ethnic Chinese population shares enhances trade more in heterogeneous commodities than in homogeneous categories. In other words, this result is interpreted as indicating a considerable quantitative effect of networks on informational barriers, in addition to any contribution through contract enforcement. In fact, the estimated effects in the study by Rauch and Trindade are very large indeed. 'For trade between countries with ethnic Chinese population shares at the levels prevailing in Southeast Asia, the smallest estimated average increase in bilateral trade in differentiated products attributable to ethnic Chinese networks is nearly 60%.'[9] Whether this surprisingly large figure partially represents some spurious unobserved effect, such as high interregional trade within Southeast Asia in particular, or whether some mis-measurement is involved by representing the interaction of the Chinese communities in a simple linear form, is unclear. Nonetheless, the study is highly provocative in suggesting an important, and perhaps very large, effect of transnational business networks in promoting merchandise trade.

Saxenian (1999) notes the special importance of highly skilled migrants as a conduit to trade promotion, arguing that Asian-born, US-based engineers and scientists play a key role in the world of high-tech trade, by acting as middlemen. Yet the principles of comparative advantage do not vanish in the process:

> Silicon valley remains the center of new product definition and design and development of leading-edge technologies, whereas Taiwan offers world-class manufacturing, flexible development and integration, and access to key customers and markets in China and Southeast Asia ... However, these economic gains from specialization and trade would not be possible without the underlying social structures and institutions provided by the community of Taiwanese engineers, which insures continuous flows of information between the two regions. (Saxenian, 1999: 62)

This case study thus illustrates that skilled migration enabled exploitation of Taiwan's comparative advantage both in manufacturing and within the Asian trading system; advantages that might otherwise have remained neglected.

Similarly, Head and Reis (1998) also confirm that highly skilled migrants have a larger impact on Canadian trade than do less skilled migrants. In particular, Head and Reis estimate an extended gravity model of Canadian import and export patterns, using panel data from 1980 to 1992 on bilateral trade with 136 trading partners. Their estimates suggest that a 10 percent increase in the accumulated stock of permanent immigrants from a typical country is associated with a 1 percent increase in Canadian exports to that country and a 3 percent increase in imports from that country.[10] Head and Reis then proceed to interact these responses of trade with the type of migrant and region or origin of the immigrant. The elasticity of response of trade to skill-based migration proves significantly greater than for family-based, refugee or business immigrants, and the import response proves largest for immigrants from East Asia. Combining these two additive effects, the estimates suggest that 'East Asian independent immigrants have an export elasticity of 0.29 and an import elasticity of 0.74.'[11] In other words, a doubling of skilled immigration into Canada from East Asia is reported to be associated with a 74 percent increase in Canadian imports from East Asia. This latter estimate is clearly very large indeed, though as Head and Reis note the estimate is probably biased upward by spurious correlation between rising immigration and trade integration which could not be fully represented in the model.[12]

Thus, the burgeoning empirical evidence points to a significant role for migrants in promoting bilateral trade with their home nations, that highly skilled migrants may be particularly critical in this trade promotion, and that both contract enforcement and information transmission may play distinct roles in this process.[13] Nonetheless, some reservations persist as to the potential for other, unobserved phenomena to be stimulating both trade and migration. Moreover, the extent to which migration enhances trade, or whether trade enhances migration, is difficult to discern. Overall the estimated effects seem improbably large, though perhaps indicative of a very real underlying phenomenon. Given the large and growing movement of highly skilled people from Asia to both Canada and the US, this may suggest an important and sizeable feedback effect on the sending countries. For some of the Asian economies, any such growth in their exports can prove particularly valuable, both as a correction to years of neglect of exports (in India and China, for example) and as a source of valuable foreign exchange.

Financial Capital Flows

Migrants and their associated networks may also serve as a potential stimulus to international capital flows. First, emigrants may be relatively likely to invest in their own country of origin, because they are better placed to evaluate investment opportunities and possess contacts to facilitate this process. Not all such investments from the diaspora are reported as migrants' transfers on capital account. Second, an emigrant may also encourage foreigners to invest in the emigrant's home country. Successful direct investment frequently demands a local facilitating partner; emigrants are well placed to identify more trustworthy and competent partners. Returned migrants, known to the foreign investor, may even take on this role of being the local counterparts themselves.[14] In addition, exposure to nationals from a particular country may alter perceptions of doing business with that country, again encouraging foreign investment.[15]

The potential role of networks in promoting international capital flows assumes greatest importance in dynamic industries, where information commands the highest premium. As Saxenian (1999: 54–5) notes, 'The scarce resource in this new environment is the ability to locate foreign partners quickly and to manage complex business relationships across cultural and linguistic boundaries. This is particularly a challenge in high-technology industries in which products, markets, and technologies are continually being redefined – and where product cycles are routinely shorter than nine months.'

In contrast to trade, systematic empirical evidence on links between financial capital flows and transnational networks has yet to be developed. A recent paper by Mody *et al.* (2003) offers a potential vehicle for such development. The authors hypothesize that industry-specific expertise in a country enables multinationals headquartered within that country to screen overseas investment projects more accurately. On the other hand, it is argued that greater corporate transparency in the target investment country diminishes the value of such expertise. Mody *et al.* then present estimates of an extended gravity model for direct investment flows from 12 source countries to 45 host countries during the 1980s and 1990s. Measures indicating protected creditors' rights and a high debt–equity ratio are both shown to diminish the relative importance of direct investment. The authors argue that this reflects the advantages of multinationals, with their specific knowledge and internal financing, in contexts where capital market operations are not so transparent. Moreover, countries that have a greater concentration across categories of exports are shown to undertake more outward direct investment, which the study interprets as reflecting the effects of greater specialized knowledge, granting an advantage in evaluating direct investment prospects. Although the authors do not raise the issue, it would seem that international migrants and their transnational networks might be particularly well placed to be a source of the specific expertise at the heart of this framework.

BOX 6.1   THE BAMBOO NETWORK AND NON-RESIDENT INDIAN INVESTORS

The Overseas Chinese Affairs Commission (2003) estimates more than 35 million ethnic Chinese living outside of China in 2002: 27 million live in Southeast Asia (7.3 million in Indonesia, 7 million in Thailand, 5.9 million in Malaysia and 2.6 million in Singapore), 4.5 million in North America, and a million each in Peru and Russia. The Government of India (2001: xi) reports 'the Indian Diaspora numbers over 20 million' listing nearly 17 million 'persons of Indian origin' and citizens living overseas in December 2001, of whom some 4 million are Indian citizens (see Table 5.6). More than 3 million Indian citizens are in the GCC states, the US 2000 census reports a million people born in India, while Canada and the UK both have about a million persons of Indian origin. A 'person of Indian origin' is defined to be anyone born in India or to have at least one grandparent, or parent, born in undivided India. The definition of the ethnic Chinese is far less clear, yet whichever concept is adopted, both the Chinese and Indian diaspora are large.

Investments in China by its diaspora have been massive, whereas India's diaspora has invested far less in India. During the decade to 2000, total foreign direct investment in China amounted to US$318 billion. By 1999, 48 percent of the total assets of 'foreign funded enterprises' were in 'enterprises funded by entrepreneurs from Hong Kong, Macao and Taiwan'. In contrast, foreign direct investment in India during the same period was US$17 billion of which 15 percent was realized from non-resident Indians although an additional net inflow of nearly US$15 billion into various deposit schemes occurred from non-resident Indians (rising to an average of US$2.5 billion per year during 2000–2002).

This gap in investments occurs despite some similarities: both countries possess a substantial diaspora of which a significant portion are professionals or business people in higher income countries; both countries possess large reserves of low cost labor; and both have been undergoing economic reforms. However, the economic settings in China and India provide quite different incentives for foreign investors. Since Deng Xiaoping's 'open door' policy initiative in 1978, China has actively encouraged foreign investors, offering very favorable tax rates and investing heavily in infrastructure in Special Economic Zones. Powerful political forces in India oppose foreign investment in general and the approval process consequently remains ponderous and opaque, though some relatively minor concessions are available to non-resident Indian investors. More generally, economic reforms in China have been quite profound, despite a lack of significant political reform. Democratic India has proceeded more tentatively and haltingly with industrial deregulation and trade liberalization, initiated in the 1980s but furthered since 1990. India's growth has accelerated from the lack-luster performance of the 1960s and 1970s, averaging 3.4 percent annual growth in GDP per capita from 1981 to 2000, yet this pales alongside the remarkable 8.4 percent growth in China's GDP per capita over the same period.

Foreign investment in China has both contributed to and been encouraged by the strong growth record. The concentration of these foreign investments in the coastal plain areas partly reflects the location of the Special Economic Zones and Open Coastal Cities. However, this geographic focus of investments also reflects the origins of much of the Chinese diaspora. Economic growth in these coastal regions has far exceeded that of the interior, yet the benefits of this development have been shared through expanded internal migration from other regions. The job creation from Chinese diaspora investments played a key role in this diffusion of benefits. In contrast to direct investments in China from the industrialized nations, those from the diaspora 'were mostly labour intensive production geared towards export' (Li and Li, 1999: 40). Both in mainland China and elsewhere throughout Southeast Asia, in the transnational activities of the Chinese diaspora, 'Kinship ties are extremely important and family control over firms is the rule ... The massive cross-investments among these nations are evidence of a new but poorly understood economic power ... The bamboo network ... Although ethnic Chinese trading circles have existed on a cross-border basis for many centuries, the exodus of millions of Chinese citizens during and after the Communist Revolution of 1949 was responsible for the rapid expansion of this entrepreneurial network' (Weidenbaum and Hughes, 1996: 53, 8).

Box 6.1 presents some background information on the 'Bamboo network' among overseas Chinese entrepreneurs and on non-resident Indians. Whereas the Chinese diaspora has been a very major source of direct investments in China, the Indian diaspora has not.[16] Since neither context is particularly transparent, any explanation of the difference must lie elsewhere. In particular, the extremely profitable opportunities that have opened up in China, combined with a welcoming attitude and incentives to foreign investors, contrasts sharply with India's general fear of multinationals and slower economic expansion. The Chinese diaspora has undertaken massive investments in China largely because it has been very profitable to do so. Nonetheless, the concentration of these investments in the hands of overseas Chinese entrepreneurs may well reflect their specific knowledge, perhaps combined with network advantages in enforcing contracts and in obtaining and evaluating specific information.

6.3 KNOWLEDGE NETWORKS AND TECHNOLOGY DIFFUSION

One of the key elements in the recent discussion of the potential for a brain gain resulting from international migration of the highly skilled is the argument that migrants establish knowledge networks that transmit new ideas and technologies back to their home country. The ideas underlying this are decomposed here into five steps: (i) the importance of technological improvements to economic development among the poorer countries; (ii) the role of international diffusion of ideas and technologies within these improvements; (iii) the part that international migration plays in the establishment and maintenance of transnational knowledge networks; (iv) the contribution of knowledge networks and of international migration more generally to the international diffusion of ideas; (v) the circumstances under which a home country is well placed to take advantage of new technologies diffused from overseas. None of these steps is without controversy, and evidence on the last three is particularly weak.

The Role of New Technologies in Economic Development

The relative contribution of productivity improvements to growth, as opposed to investments in capital and skills, is both a matter of some dispute and of considerable inter-country variation. In particular, the relative role of productivity improvements proves quite sensitive to how well labor and capital input measures are corrected for quality upgrading, suggesting that significant parts of productivity enhancements are not disembodied but require investments for their realization.[17] These difficulties notwithstanding, Easterly and Levine (2001) review the extensive cumulative evidence on the role of productivity improvements in growth differences across countries and present, as a stylized fact, their conclusion that it is productivity differences and improvements, rather than factor accumulation, that account for most of the differences in income levels and growth across countries. Yet even if one grants this stylized fact, it must be recognized that these productivity improvements, which simply reflect the residual growth not accounted for by measured factor accumulation, can embody many components, ranging from the impacts of policies that might enhance or inhibit efficient use of resources to the evolution and adoption of new products and processes. In the end, new ideas cannot be quantified; as Krugman (1991: 53) notes, 'they leave no paper trail by which they can be measured and tracked'. Instead, empirical work in this sphere relies upon measures of research inputs, such as research expenditures, and correlates of ideas, such as patents taken out or cited. Evenson and Westphal (1995) review estimates of the rate of return to research expenditures and note that the average return on agricultural research in the developing regions far exceeds that in the developed regions; the very few studies of returns to industrial research in the developing regions indicate a lower but still very rewarding return. Basic industrial research in the lower income countries is, however, hardly intensive. To the extent that the lower income countries are exposed to new technologies, those technologies are largely initially evolved overseas.

International Diffusion of Technology

The notion that technologies diffuse across international boundaries, resulting in technology convergence in the absence of sustained new technological developments that are geographically concentrated, has been recognized for some time.[18] Systematic empirical contributions to this field are, however, more recent.

A series of papers have shown that total factor productivity growth (the residual growth not accounted for by measured factor use) in the OECD countries is significantly related to the stock of scientists and engineers available and to the rate of expenditures on research and development, both within the respective OECD country and within other member countries.[19] Moreover, these cross-country effects have been demonstrated to diminish strongly with distance.[20] On the other hand, this distance effect is estimated to have diminished over time, possibly indicating the role of accelerated communications in facilitating technology movements. In other words, significant international diffusion of new technologies is indeed observed, at least amongst the industrialized nations, and is geographically localized though localization of learning may be diminishing over time.

On the other hand, this empirical literature has not managed to disentangle the factors underlying this diffusion process. A number of vehicles may be envisioned: multinational corporations may simply elect to transplant their technology offshore to lower production costs; technologies may be leased out in return for royalties; or trade in commodities embodying advanced technologies may spur attempts to copy or may enable reverse engineering. Of particular interest in the present context, however, is the role of international migration of the highly skilled in this process of technology diffusion.

The observation that spillover effects diminish with distance between nations does not really help to distinguish between these components. As Keller (2002) notes, one cannot tell how much of this is due to the diminution of bilateral trade as opposed to the reduction of direct foreign investment with distance.[21] To this should be added that we also cannot tell how much is due to less migration and hence less dense knowledge networks over greater distances. Keller does, however, note that possessing a common language is estimated to enhance estimates of bilateral technology diffusion significantly, though in turn this may again reflect enhanced trade, investment flows or the knowledge networking between countries with related languages, with or without or other forms of interaction.

This burgeoning literature on technology diffusion across countries is illuminating and promising but so far has failed to incorporate the developing regions, and the role of knowledge networks within these transmission processes remains almost entirely unexplored.

The Nature of Knowledge Networks

The concept of a knowledge network is rather nebulous. Meyer and Brown (1999) identify forty-one such networks attached to thirty different countries. Each of these networks seeks to link highly skilled nationals overseas with colleagues at home in various ways. Many involve local associations of skilled expatriates, which have been formed in the host countries, as well as various internet-based organizations that make systematic efforts to promote contact with colleagues at home and even undertake development efforts.[22] A few examples, drawn from our case study areas, may suffice to illustrate:

- The Silicon Valley Indian Professionals Association states that a key part of its mission is 'to contribute towards cooperation between the United States and India in high technology areas'. Partly in view of the recent economic downturn in the US information technology industry, however, their annual event in November 2003 is 'focused on business and careers opportunities with respect to India Outsourcing. The sessions will be accompanied by "Job Fair" to find career opportunities in India.'[23]
- The IndUS Entrepreneur group was formed in 1992 and has several chapters in India as well as the US, UK, Singapore and Switzerland, tying together experienced entrepreneurs and start-up managers with a core group of angel investors, though not explicitly focused on links with India.[24]
- The recently revived Philippine Brain Gain Network 'is a business network of talented engineers, scientists and organizations focused on increasing the competitiveness of the Philippine economy in world markets through application of advanced information and bio technologies ... seeks to counter the "brain drain" by reconnecting the expatriate Filipino Network to collaborators in the Philippines.'25

A quite different type of knowledge network, also included in the list of Brown and Meyer, is the UNDP Transfer of Knowledge through Expatriate Nationals program, which placed 5000 volunteers on assignments in 49 developing countries during its first twenty years after inception in 1977.[26]

Each of these examples, including the UNDP program, involves migrants who have become relatively settled in their new country. However, short-term movements of knowledge workers have apparently risen also, offering yet another vehicle for technology diffusion.[27] For example, in India the practice of 'body-shopping' (in which local recruiters provide information technology workers overseas on a short-term, just-in-time basis) has expanded, and there has also been rapid growth in the intra-company transfer of personnel, often on a short-term basis.[28] Moreover, students returning from overseas training frequently maintain contacts with fellow alumnae either informally or through more formal network associations. Thus, Regets (2001) notes the strong positive correlation between the number of US doctorates received by natives of a country and the percentage of that country's internationally co-authored articles that are with a US-based author. A number of interpretations of such a correlation are feasible, but it may suggest a role for returned students as vehicles of contact and hence information transmission.

With increasingly effective international communications and travel, international migration may be far from essential to the maintenance of knowledge networks. However, international migrants are probably more often involved in such knowledge networks than are persons who have never migrated. Both features are illustrated, to some extent, in Table 6.1, which reports the responses to a survey representing some 542 000 individuals, ages 75 or less, who earned a science or engineering doctorate in the US through academic year 1994.[29] Both the US and foreign-born scientists and engineers report that their work is much less likely to benefit from long-term relocation of six months to two years, as opposed to using long-distance communication and short-term visits. Moreover, respondents born in the US are more likely to report that their work does not and would not benefit at all from visits (either short- or long-term) or from long-distance communication with foreign colleagues than are foreign-born respondents. The extent to which the reverse pattern holds, whereby overseas scientists and engineers abroad benefit from contacts with US-based colleagues, remains undocumented.

Table 6.1 Reported benefit to work from contacts outside of US among US science and engineering doctorates

Place of birth	Long-distance communication			Short-term visits			Long-term visits		
	A great deal	Some-what	Not at all	A great deal	Some-what	Not at all	A great deal	Some-what	Not at all
US	26.1	39.6	34.3	17.7	37.9	44.4	7.9	19.0	73.1
Non-US	29.4	40.4	30.1	23.3	40.1	36.6	12.3	24.2	63.4

Source: National Science Foundation, Division of Science Resources Studies, 1995 Survey of Doctorate Recipients; special unpublished tabulation prepared by N. Kannankutty, 5/1/01.

Knowledge Networks, Migration and Technology Transfer

There is ample evidence of a wide variety of knowledge network forms and of international movement of the highly skilled, and of scientists and engineers in particular, both on a long-term and short-term basis. There is far less evidence of the actual transfer of technology that results. Saxenian (1999: 60) maintains that the US–Taiwan 'transnational community has accelerated the upgrading of Taiwan's technological infrastructure by transferring technical know-how and organizational models as well as by forging closer ties with Silicon Valley ... management practices in Hsinchu companies are more like those of Silicon Valley than of the traditional family-firm model that dominates older industries in Taiwan.' In later work, Saxenian (2002) goes on to describe a comparable positive role played by the Indian diaspora in the expansion of the Indian software industry. Other observers are more skeptical, at least of the Indian case; 'It should be emphasized that India's success in software is principally the result of domestic entrepreneurs and domestic capabilities. The role of the Indian diaspora and international human capital flows from India simply highlights additional mechanisms that are important in understanding sectoral growth processes'[30] (see Box 6.2 on the development of India's software industry).

Quantifying and even testing these ideas more formally has proved largely elusive to date. A very recent exception is a paper by Agrawal *et al.* (2003) which demonstrates that within the US and Canada, a patent taken out by an inventor is more likely to be cited, not only in the current location of the inventor, but also in locations in which the inventor previously resided.[31] Moreover, this co-location effect is found to be particularly strong across different fields. The interpretation placed on these findings by the authors is that the social capital established by an inventor, in their initial location, facilitates subsequent diffusion of the inventor's ideas. Within a specific field, researchers are likely to interact through conferences and papers, diminishing the role for social capital in diffusing ideas, though this is less true across fields. At least within North America, it seems that knowledge spillovers are geographically localized but that researcher migration can significantly ameliorate this concentration. International evidence along these lines is sorely lacking.

BOX 6.2   DEVELOPMENT OF INDIA'S SOFTWARE INDUSTRY

The first recorded software exports from India occurred in 1974. By 1980, software exports equaled US$4 million growing to US$131 dollars in 1990, over a billion dollars in 1997, and estimated to have surpassed US$10 billion during 2002–2003.

Entrants to the software industry comprised both existing firms that diversified (such as Wipro which was already established in the computer hardware sector) and start-ups (such as Infosys which was created by seven managers who broke away from another start-up). Although some of the initial impetus to the industry arose from the need to service local hardware, the main stimulus to the phenomenal growth has clearly stemmed from the export market. Outsourcing by US firms has been particularly important, amounting to some 60 percent of the export market in the late 1990s.

In this process, India has two major advantages: the abundant supply of relatively low cost software engineers and facility with

English. Salaries range from perhaps a third of the US salary for software developers to less than 10 percent for basic programmers. In the early stages, many of the software engineers were transplants from other branches of engineering. Subsequently, higher education in the information technology fields has proliferated. Thousands of private training institutions have appeared, with accreditation supervised through the Department of Electronics, and a number of multinationals have started their own authorized training centers. In addition, many of the engineering colleges now offer courses and fields in computer sciences, and combined private and government initiatives have enabled the foundation of a series of Indian Institutes of Information Technology.

State governments have come to compete with each other in attracting software firms. The provision of infrastructure is particularly critical and a system of some 35 Software Technology Parks has emerged with various combinations of central, state and private sector sponsorship. Nonetheless, in India's software industry the lead has clearly been taken by the private sector, followed by partial public training and infrastructure support. This profile contrasts sharply with India's heavy industry developments in an earlier era, when the commanding heights were reserved for the public sector alone, and it is no coincidence that the software industry's emergence coincided with the major shift toward a more liberal environment for business and trade beginning in 1991.

The rapid growth of the software industry in India is no doubt a success story in terms of foreign exchange earnings and in remuneration for engineers and venture capitalists. The implications for overall employment creation and ultimate poverty reduction are less apparent. There may be close to half a million IT professionals employed in India, yet this figure is small in relation to a total labor force of more than 330 million. It is unclear quite how large are the multiplier effects of spending by the nouveau riche IT professionals and of backward linkages from software training and other service sectors, but they would need to be very major indeed to impose any serious impact on India's poor. Rather, Arora and Athreye (2001) suggest that the principal means of impact on India's overall development may lie in productivity improvements, derived from copying the software sector's model of entrepreneurship and governance.

The links between evolution of the software industry and India's diaspora are essentially three-fold. First, is the role of knowledge networking with overseas professionals, either individually or through such organizations as the Silicon Valley Indian Professionals

Association. On the other hand, 'the Indian software industry is overwhelmingly engaged in routine, low-level design, programming, and maintenance services' (Saxenian, 2000: 5); contacts with overseas professionals and their experiences with the latest ideas and techniques may thus not have been so important. Second, one source of IT professionals in India has been the return of nationals with experience in the US and elsewhere. No reliable indications of the extent of this return appear to be available; nonetheless, it seems the rate of return migration has generally been low, but may have accelerated with the recent downturn in the US sector. Third, and perhaps more importantly, persons of Indian origin are reputed to have been instrumental in removing the reputation barriers to trade, encouraging their American employers to explore outsourcing of software from India. Indeed, the successes with software outsourcing may have reduced reputation barriers to trade in other services too and we are now witnessing service sector job displacement from the US to India in a much wider range of service fields, which may ultimately impact employment patterns in India much more deeply.

On the Capacity to Benefit from Knowledge Transfers

There is much discussion of the role of knowledge networks in the promotion of development in some of the tigers of East Asia and in such contexts as Ireland and Israel. The same discussions do not arise with respect to the lowest income countries. In fact it seems that for technology transfer through migrants and their networks to be a significant factor in economic development at home, three basic sets of conditions must hold: the migrants must be employed in sectors, occupations and countries that grant access to useful information; a knowledge network must emerge in some form, permitting transfer of that information; the home country must be in a position to take advantage of the new information.

Although the emergence of knowledge networks has attracted a good deal of attention, the potential for the home country to benefit has not, and the latter may be far more critical in determining the outcome. In modeling technology transfers among the OECD countries, Eaton and Kortum (1996) present evidence consistent with wider, bilateral technology gaps between economies, granting greater potency to those new ideas that are generated in the more technologically advanced nation. In essence, the potential for productivity improvements through catch-up dominates in this framework, given the rate of technology diffusion. On the other hand, Evenson and Westphal (1995) emphasize the critical roles played by the recipient country's capacity to adapt incoming technologies to local circumstances, as well as the country's technological infrastructure, which includes a functioning system of intellectual property rights. On these latter grounds, it seems likely that the lowest income countries would not be well placed to adapt and adopt the latest technologies emerging from the OECD nations, even where diffusion of these ideas occurs. Perhaps the role of technology gaps in this transfer process is therefore not monotonic over a broader spectrum of income levels; wider gaps in technology may render transfer more effective when both countries possess relatively sophisticated technologies, but render transfer less effective between nations at extremely different levels of technology.

The existing empirical work on total factor productivity does indicate that the prior level of technology positively affects speed of progress from given research inputs. In other words it is more difficult for countries with less productive technologies to add to those technologies for themselves. To the extent that new ideas are an important force in growth, as opposed to adoption of pro-growth development strategies or investments in skills and capital, the lower income countries may then be compelled to rely largely upon diffusion of these new ideas from the higher income countries. If, in addition, innovation in one country has a greater impact on countries at a similar level of technology, this would suggest that migration of scientists and engineers is both less likely to reduce new know-how generated at home and less likely to transfer back useful foreign technologies to the lower income countries.

The rate of brain drain from the Philippines to the US is very large, yet there is little discussion of technology transfer to the Philippines, the role of the Philippine Brain Gain Network notwithstanding. India has developed a very large and very successful software sector, but it may be argued that the main impetus came from domestic entrepreneurs not from overseas, the role of the Silicon Valley Indian Professionals Association notwithstanding. To the extent that non-resident Indians played a key part in the expansions in Bangalore and Hyderabad it seems to have been in lowering the reputation barriers to entry, permitting initial exports, rather than in transferring knowledge. Indeed, most of the discussion of technology transfer to the home country from overseas nationals, resulting in a brain gain, arises among the relatively higher income countries, which possess the capacity to process and take advantage of these technologies.

6.4   THE DIASPORA, POLITICS AND SECURITY

It would be misleading to leave this discussion of the influences of a diaspora on economic development in the home country without, at least briefly, touching upon the role that a diaspora sometimes plays in shaping politics and the state of security within the home country. Both may impact economic development.

Where the overseas community is large or notably wealthy in relation to the home electorate, the diaspora may retain significant influence on politics in the home country through absentee voting, lobbying and 'donations'.[32] In addition, the diaspora may be able to exert indirect political influence through lobbying efforts with their host country government. Alternatively, the diaspora may affect decisions in their home country through threats or acts of violence. Certainly a number of overseas communities have been a source of funds, arms, or even armed support, for separatist or insurrectionist movements.[33] Countries of refuge, including the US on several instances, have armed refugees and actively supported armed conflict against the home country. Individuals, ethnic groups and dissidents, exiled from their home state, commonly organize to threaten the stability or hegemony of their home country.[34] In some cases, organized gangs have come to operate transnationally, and the negative experiences of migrants while abroad is often cited as one of the roots of rising fundamentalism, which has become a source of concern in both host and sending countries.

The objectives of these many interventions obviously vary very considerably. In some instances, migrants support 'self-determination and independence for their minority kinfolk at home ... also ... the case of migrants supporting democratization movements against autocratic regimes in their home countries. In the former case are the demands by the Irish, Sikhs ... Armenians ... and others for self-determination. In the latter case are the demands by Chinese, Filipinos, Cubans and South Koreans for democratization in their homelands' (Weiner, 1993: xviii). Other instances are less magnanimous, involving self-aggrandizement or profit.

The economic consequences are equally mixed. Where interventions by the diaspora lead to violence or civil war, the local economy is normally harmed, at least in the short run. The evidence on whether successful attempts to promote democratization accelerate economic development is mixed. Either way, such interventions are likely to diminish the willingness of the home country's ruling elite to interact with their diaspora, in turn reducing the odds of benefiting through the modes of economic interaction described in this chapter.

Lever-Tracy *et al.* (1996) argue that the influence of the overseas Chinese investors has been critical in promoting economic reform, though without political reform, within China. On the other hand, non-resident Indians did contribute to ending the Emergency declared by Mrs Gandhi, though the economy returned to its previous lack-luster performance thereafter; the more fundamental economic reforms came to India after 1990 with little participation from the Indian diaspora. Perhaps the most revealing of our specific case study areas is, however, that of the Philippines. Shain (1993: 305) argues that,

The anti-Marcos campaign of Filipinos abroad was one of the most successful and multifaceted diasporic efforts to unseat a nondemocratic regime ... shortly after her inauguration as President of the Philippines, Corazon Aquino went to San Francisco to pay tribute to the Filipino-Americans for their contribution to the struggle for democracy. She encouraged them to take an active role in American politics in support of the homeland's economic interests.

As we have seen, little economic benefit came to the Philippines from this transition.

6.5   WHERE DO WE STAND AND WHAT ARE THE POLICY IMPLICATIONS?

The evidence does suggest that countries can benefit from their diasporas in various ways. However, the routes through which the major benefits are channeled, and even whether any obvious benefits are actually observed, varies very much from context to context. The Indian software industry benefited from a well-placed diaspora in the US reducing reputation barriers to trade. China has benefited from ethnic Chinese entrepreneurs overseas who invested on a large scale in the home regions within China, creating large numbers of jobs and expanding export performance. Taiwan has benefited from migration and reverse migration to Silicon Valley, leading to knowledge networks that have advanced the high-tech industries in Taiwan in ways that are appropriate to Taiwan's comparative advantage.

To a large extent, it seems the differences in these mechanisms reflect differences in the home country economies far more than they reflect differences in migration regimes. The expansion of India's software industry grew largely out of domestic initiatives and was founded on an abundance of highly trained and under-employed engineers, in a context where trade in general had been overtly discouraged and hence reputation barriers to trade were endemic. Non-resident Indians have not invested in India on the same scale as have the overseas Chinese in China, because India has not welcomed foreign investment in general and China offers more rewarding financial prospects.[35] Both India and China have probably enjoyed only small technology gains from their diasporas, in part because of the lack of what Evenson and Westphal (1995) call technological capital and in part because of their technology gap in relation to the OECD regions. It is the higher income countries, such as Taiwan, Korea, Ireland and Israel, that have been able to take most advantage of technology transfers from their diasporas, again reflecting the state of the home country economy rather than the skill base or location of the diaspora. Meanwhile, most of the low income countries are left out of this virtuous cycle; although the relative rate of brain drain (at least to the US) tends to be higher among the poorer countries, few of these countries are well positioned to experience any of the beneficial forces of brain gain. The Philippines has one of the highest rates of emigration and of brain drain in the world; the resultant diaspora did contribute to the overthrow of the Marcos regime but there has been no subsequent improvement in economic performance and no signs of any brain gain effects.

The extent to which migrants enhance trade flows, foreign investments by others or themselves, and transfers of technology, may be susceptible to policy interventions.[36] Yet the efficacy of such interventions remains poorly understood. A number of countries do offer incentives to overseas nationals to invest in the home country. China offers substantial tax breaks and infrastructure support to foreign investors in general and investment has been massive, yet the link between these incentives and realized investments remains unclear. Non-resident Indians are permitted to invest, subject to approval, in a wider range of real estate options than are other foreign investors, allowed greater equity participation in civil airlines, and to acquire a greater range of immovable properties. However, the Report of the High Level Committee on the Indian Diaspora[37] 'also observed that there are major irritants still extant in the actualization of these policies', though the committee did not speculate on the efficacy of removing these irritants as a stimulant to the relatively low rate of investments from non-resident Indians. However, Bagasao (2003: 4) does comment on related efforts in the Philippines:

> Over the past 20 years, the Philippines has gradually built up legislation designed to tap the resources of its extensive diaspora. These laws invariably contain incentives and privileges in cases they invest, donate, purchase real property or open a local enterprise in areas that normally are reserved for Filipino citizens ... Unfortunately no monitoring system has been designed to measure how effective these laws have been in attracting expatriate capital, neither do we also see extensive evidence showing that large numbers of migrants have taken advantage of these incentives. On the contrary, potential returnees have decided to abandon plans of retiring, working or investing in the Philippines after getting disenchanted with bureaucracy and unstable policies.

Fostering contacts with the overseas diaspora, and especially the intelligentsia, may facilitate the emergence of more active knowledge networking. Actively encouraging and supporting the formation of transnational associations involving researchers at home and abroad may complement such efforts. Yet how effective government efforts prove in this vein remains uncertain. First, some of the more active formal networks appear to have emerged from private initiatives and not from government sponsored efforts. Second, it is far from clear how effective these networks ultimately prove as vehicles for realized improvements in productivity at home.

Are transnational networks the most important developmental resource associated with international migration today? There are indications that migration of highly skilled people may prove important in overcoming prevailing barriers to trade in a world where reliable information is scarce. Yet, given the current policy environment, the more general answer must surely be no. To the extent that positive feedback effects through trade, investment and technology transfer are observed, it tends to be through networking with the highly skilled, not through the unskilled. Yet the highly skilled migrate in large numbers only to North America. Nonetheless, for some countries the diaspora indeed plays a major role. For some of the poorest countries this appears to be far less true. Indeed, it is in some of the poorer countries that parts of their diaspora are more actively involved in promoting or supporting instability and violence at home.

NOTES

1. Greif (1993) develops this idea in the context of medieval Maghribi traders.
2. See, for example, Kotkin (1993) who attributes a major role in the process of economic globalization today to 'Global Tribes', or the review of the field in Portes *et al.* (1999).
3. See the summary in Vertovec (2002) on dimensions along which differences in networks have been described. On the other hand, Kofman (2000) notes the lack of attention that has been paid to gender relations in this process.
4. See the accounts in Portes (1995) for example.
5. Saxenian (1999: 21).
6. Rauch (2001: 1177). See, for example, Trefler (1995) who raises the mystery of the missing trade.
7. Leamer and Levinsohn (1995) survey much of this evidence on 'gravity' models of trade. Bergstrand (1985) provides a classic example.
8. The following control variables are included in the regressions: ratio of GNP and populations of the bilateral pair, distance between principal cities, whether the countries share a land border, an index of remoteness of both countries, extent to which the pair share a common language and colonial tie, and membership in the European Economic Community or European Free Trade Area.
9. Rauch and Trindade (2002: 116).
10. In a prior, similar study of US trade and immigration, Gould (1994) estimates the effect of immigration on US exports to be larger than on US imports, but this study does not distinguish types of immigrants or regions of origin as in Head and Reis (1998).
11. Head and Reis (1998: 59).
12. On the other hand, it seems that the figure implied by the estimates is actually much larger still (some 110 percent rather than 74 percent), once an appropriate interpretation of the dummy variables is applied.
13. See also Lloyd (1996) on trade and migration between Asia and Australia.
14. See the case study of Hewlett-Packard in India described in Saxenian (1999: 62–3).
15. Kapur (2001: 16) describes the mentoring role that The IndUS Entrepreneur (a group of Indian IT entrepreneurs and professionals) has played, boosting 'confidence of overseas investors about India's potential despite India's innumerable problems'.
16. Huang (2003) raises questions about how much of the 'foreign' investment entering China through Hong Kong and Taiwan is actually by foreigners. Some may represent investments by nationals, routed to take advantage of particular advantages granted to foreign investors.

Nonetheless, investments by the diaspora are certainly vast and Lever-Tracy *et al.* (1996) suggest that the Chinese experience in attracting such large investments from its diaspora may prove unique. Yet the experience of Taiwan denies this uniqueness. A substantial two-way flow of direct investments occurs between the US and Taiwan, both in general and in the investment relationships between Silicon Valley and the Hsinchu-Taipei region in Taiwan in particular. Saxenian (1999: 61) quotes a Taiwanese investor, 'When we invest we are also helping bring entrepreneurs back to Taiwan. It is relationship building ...'.

17. See, for example, Young (1995) on controversies with respect to measurement.

18. Vernon (1966) describes how the international diffusion of technology erodes any temporary edge possessed by the inventing nation in his discussion of the product cycle. Krugman (1979) offers a more formal treatment.

19. Coe and Helpman (1995), Eaton and Kortum (1996, 2002).

20. See Keller (2002).

21. On the effect of distance in reducing direct investments see, for instance, Brainard (1997). See also Portes and Rey (1999) on gravity models in international equity movements more generally. The role of trade as the main vehicle of technology transfer has proved controversial; see, for example, Coe and Helpman (1995), Keller (1998) and Lumenga-Neso *et al.* (2001).

22. In contrast, Meyer and Brown (1999: 5) describe, and include in their list of 41 networks, a category of student-scholarly networks that assist students abroad and encourage a dialogue between scholars but 'have a limited scope in terms of activities and contributions to the country of origin'. Examples include Chinese Scholars Abroad and the Moroccan Association of Researchers and Scholars Abroad.

23. http://www.sipa.org/.

24. 'TiE, a not-for-profit global network of entrepreneurs and professionals, was founded in 1992 in Silicon Valley, California, USA. Although its birth name, The Indus Entrepreneurs, signifies the ethnic South Asian or Indus roots of the founders, TiE stands for Talent, Ideas and Enterprise. It is an open and inclusive organization that has rapidly grown to more than forty chapters in nine countries. TiE endeavors to cultivate and nurture the ecosystems of entrepreneurship and free-market economies everywhere, as it sees this to be the single most powerful instrument of prosperity' http://www.tie.org/; see also the description of TiE in Kapur (2001).

25. http://www.bgn.org/.

26. http://www.undp.org.lb/tokten.

27. Koser, Khalid and John Salt (1997), 'The Geography of Highly Skilled International Migration', *International Journal of Population Geography*, 3 (4), 285-303.

28. On body-shopping in India, see Aneesh (2001). In 1980, the US issued 38 600 L1 (intra-company transferee) visas; by 1990 the number was 63 200 and in 2002, 313 700 L1 visas were issued. Both body-shopping and intra-company transferees have also been used to circumvent immigration controls; body shopping has apparently led to claims that workers are needed for jobs that do not exist, and dummy corporations have been established to take advantage of intra-company transfer facilities.

29. I am grateful to Nirmal Kannankutty of the NSF for preparing this table. The table originally appeared in Lucas (2001a).

30. Kapur (2002) at http://www.people.fas.harvard.edu/~dkapur/images/dk_causes.pdf. See also the comparative discussion of the role of the diaspora and developments in the software industries in India, Ireland and Israel in Kapur and McHale (2002) who emphasize our general inability to reach conclusions at this stage.

31. On the geographic localization of citations in the US see Jaffe *et al.* (1993).

32. See Levitt (2001) and Sheffer (2003) for example.

33. See the examples listed in Weiner (1993: ix).

34. Weiner 1993: 12).

35. The footloose direct foreign investments in East and Southeast Asia have been sensitive to cost conditions, and to labor costs in particular, as well as exchange rate formation and corporate tax rates within the target countries. These investments have also been quite sensitive to political stability in the target economies. See Lucas (1993).

36. See the recent report prepared for USAID by Johnson and Sedaca (2004).

37. Government of India (2001: 429).

7. Repeat and Return Migration: A Habit or 'There and Back Again'*

Most of the early economics literature on migration was couched in terms of an abiding decision to invest in relocation for the remainder of one's life.[1] Yet even international migrants frequently return home, not merely to visit but often to settle, though sometimes only to emigrate once again. Moreover, this pattern is not new; the New England puritans made the arduous journey back and forth across the Atlantic with surprising alacrity and later, 'between 1908 and 1957 about 15.7 million persons immigrated to the United States and about 4.8 million aliens emigrated'.[2] Nonetheless, 'In the contemporary world ... international circular migration is occurring on an unprecedentedly large scale, involving a greater cross-section of groups and taking a wider variety of forms than ever before.'[3]

The distinction between persons admitted on a temporary basis versus permanent settlers is far from synonymous with return and one-way migrants respectively. Although there is a correlation between these two dichotomies, some 'temporary' migrants never leave and some 'permanent' settlers turn around and depart quite quickly. Moreover, those who leave, no matter whether temporarily or permanently admitted, may not be returning home but moving on to a third destination: step, rather than return, migration. In addition, a high level of turnover may exist among migrants, with a great deal of back and forth movement, yet the resultant stock of persons present in the host country can be far from temporary.

From the perspective of the migrant-sending countries, higher turnover has both positive and negative potential implications for economic development. On the one hand, the countries of origin may gain through the greater remittances, and perhaps other forms of contribution, from migrants whose absence has not yet lapsed into lack of concern for those at home. On the other hand, too high a turnover may limit overseas earnings, to the extent that these rise with duration of stay, and may also restrict the experiences and newly acquired skills often supposed to enrich the potential contributions of returning sojourners. A high turnover may also make it easier for the host country to export the unemployment effects of shocks, resulting from recessions or other crises, imposing the costs of adjustment on poorer sending countries instead. Yet, in practice, the stock of 'temporary' migrants does not prove easy for hosts to adjust.

Suffice to say, for the moment, that the economic development implications of return migration are shaped by the extent, context and composition of return, as well as by the activities taken up by migrants on return. The discussion in this chapter is organized accordingly, addressing these two major components in the following sections respectively.

7.1 EXTENT, CIRCUMSTANCES AND COMPOSITION OF RETURN MIGRATION

As with other migration patterns, return migration represents the intersection of choices by migrants and their families and of controls and incentives imposed by receiving and sending countries. Although early economic theories neglected the issue, there are many quite rational reasons for migrants freely to choose to return home.

Perhaps the most obvious is a change in circumstances at destination or origin, either at a macro level or in the idiosyncratic experiences of individual migrants. The former might well encompass the onset of a recession in the host country, particularly rapid economic improvement in the country of origin, conflict resolution at home, or escalating violence overseas.[4] For the individual migrant myriad changes of circumstances can readily prompt return, ranging from the measured process of ageing to far less expected events, perhaps requiring unanticipated resumption of responsibilities at home.[5] However, a number of economic theories have also been put forward to rationalize return migration even without such reversals, and within these perhaps two major categories of explanation may be discerned: target saving and failed aspirations.[6]

Target saving migrants are viewed as planning their return from the outset. The sojourn overseas is the phase in this strategy during which the migrant saves prodigiously for subsequent return.[7] Given a limited duration of high income earning while abroad, target savers are normally represented as having higher saving propensities than foreign counterparts or even fellow nationals not contemplating return; some, but not necessarily all, of the savings may be remitted while away.[8] At least three reasons for return migration being a part of this strategy, as opposed to simply enjoying the accumulated savings abroad, have been modeled. The first category simply emphasizes preferences for consumption at home, or more generally depicts preferences for specific locations. As income is accumulated by migrants, they become better able to afford their choice of where to live.[9] A second motivation for return is derived from greater buying power at home out of the accumulated assets. This purchasing power advantage may reflect either cheap price levels in the home country in general or some specific living opportunities open to the returning migrant, such as accommodation and care offered by waiting kin.[10] Thirdly, return may be motivated by higher returns at home on skills acquired while abroad, relative to the returns abroad.[11] Again these differences in returns may either be general or more specific to the migrant, as in the case that skills need to be complemented by local knowledge and contacts. Yet return migration is not always planned at the outset. Some returns simply reflect failed initial plans.[12] Migrants seeking their fortunes overseas may run out of resources to continue the search; over time a migrant's true ability may be revealed to foreign employers and prove inadequate;[13] or the migrant may have been deluded about the real opportunities abroad.[14]

Theories based on altered circumstances, target saving or failed aspirations, each view return migration as voluntary. This may not be the case. Temporary entry permits expire, even 'permanent' visas may be withdrawn, undocumented migrants may be apprehended, asylum seekers rejected and refugees repatriated. On the other hand, there is no necessary association between the legal basis of entry and the incidence of return. Host country critics of temporary worker programs point to their tendency to become permanent, both in the sense of inability to diminish the stock of migrants and in the lack of turnover of workers. On the other hand, where crossing borders without documentation is difficult, dangerous and costly, the lack of legal, temporary entry can result in lengthier stays by irregular migrants whose return home is discouraged by the costs of repeat entry. Moreover, return of 'permanent' settlers is not uncommon, occasionally reflecting incentives and encouragement offered by the home countries.

Systematic evidence on the extent and composition of return migration is difficult to glean. There is less evidence still on the contribution of the several factors shaping the choice to return, the effects of controls and policy incentives. In part this reflects the paucity of our data. If the data on international migration are generally poor, the recording of return migration is far worse. For example, censuses that ask only place of birth and of current residence never recognize circular migration in the interim, leave alone the incidence of many repeat migrations. Nonetheless, some important aspects of the process of return migration can be discerned from the various contexts and these are organized here under two main headings: the case of unskilled guest, seasonal and undocumented workers, and the return of highly skilled persons and of permanent settlers.[15]

Guest, Seasonal and Undocumented Workers

In a number of contexts, both in our case study areas and elsewhere, guest worker programs permit legal entry of temporary, largely unskilled and semi-skilled workers, for a specified period. This permission may range from a single season of work to several years. Some hypotheses as to why migrants may wish to remain only temporarily have been listed in introducing this section, but what of the demand side of this phenomenon? What is the nature of demand for relatively unskilled migrant workers and why does this take the form of temporary entry?

Many of the tasks undertaken by unskilled migrant workers offer wages and working conditions that local workers in the higher income countries are unwilling to accept. If the migrants did not fill these tasks, adjustments would no doubt take place along three dimensions: first, wages in these jobs would rise and perhaps a few local workers would begin to find the tasks more acceptable; second, the methods of production in any given activity would begin to shift, adopting techniques that use more equipment and skilled workers, rather than demanding large inputs of unskilled workers; third, the patterns of production themselves would begin to adjust, with contraction and closures in activities requiring more intensive use of unskilled labor. Generalizations about the potential for adjustment along each of these three lines are not possible, since much will depend upon the structure and initial conditions of production in each host country. For example, the last dimension, altering the pattern of production, no doubt varies very considerably across sectors: some manufacturing sectors can prove very footloose, especially when outsourcing of selected activities is a viable option; at the opposite extreme extraction industries are essentially tied to the location of mineral deposits; some services may be traded while others, such as care of the elderly, are more difficult to trade unless the elderly themselves can be exported![16]

Some of these activities generate temporary demands for labor. This is particularly true of seasonal agriculture, tourism, and contexts where construction is concentrated in months with less inclement weather or involves a specific major project. In contrast, the turnover of workers in manufacturing and many service industries can impose significant costs on employers. These costs may include the process of worker selection, revelation of mismatches after hiring, training and inability to induce effort among workers who know their employment will be short-lived. Nonetheless, the host state may attempt to impose restrictions requiring temporary stays to avoid permanent settlement of migrants and their families who are deemed unwanted. These conflicting interests can pit employers against the state, though sometimes employers are mollified by lower benefit requirements mandated for migrant workers, thus lowering the overall cost of labor.

From the host country perspective guest worker schemes are also envisioned as offering a mechanism to meet temporary overall labor demands, increasing labor recruiting in times of shortages and expelling workers in the event of a downturn. In this fashion, the host can shift the burden of unemployment cycles offshore. Reality does not always match this scenario, raising two distinct aspects of the permanence of 'temporary' workers: the extent of turnover and return of individual migrants within a given stock, and the ability of host countries to reduce the overall stock of temporary migrants both over a short cycle and upon intended cessation.

Critics of guest worker programs point to both sides of the labor market in arguing that subsequent cut-backs in the number of temporary workers can prove difficult. On the supply side, the growth in migrant networks makes it easier for subsequent workers to move, families become accustomed to the absence of migrants and adjust their work patterns and even location to deal with this, and there is less incentive for job creation in the home country. On the demand side, production of labor-intensive items is encouraged in the host country, as are methods of production that continue to rely on less skilled labor inputs. Whether the overall stock of temporary workers can effectively be reduced, once a program is well established, presumably then depends very much upon the root of change as well as upon the balance of these supply and demand forces. Legislation to cut back the number of temporary work visas issued, perhaps motivated by growing xenophobia, faces opposition from employers. If enacted, such legislation may simply result in a shift from legal to undocumented migration. On the other hand, there may be a shift in labor demand by employers, possibly reflecting a recession in their industry. The extent to which this shift is likely to translate into lower wages, versus a reduction in the import of temporary workers, depends very much on how responsive is the supply of migrant workers to wage cuts, as well as to any institutional barriers to such cuts.

So what does the limited evidence show? How permanent are temporary worker movements? How much turnover occurs? Do we see effective reductions in the stocks of temporary workers? Who returns and how long do they stay abroad? Four settings are examined here. The US–Mexican case is looked at very briefly first, in part because it raises some important questions, followed by Europe, the Gulf, and then East Asia.

Mexican Migration to the US

During World War II, the US introduced the *bracero* program to admit temporary agricultural laborers from Mexico to meet labor shortages, which partly emanated from conscription of American employees. After the war, the program continued and grew very substantially under lobbying from US farmers who adapted both cropping and farming techniques to the availability of cheap labor. The *bracero* program was formally repealed in 1964, but Martin and Teitelbaum (2001: 123) argue that,

> Today, scholars largely agree that the 22 years of *bracero* employment created the conditions for the subsequent boom of unauthorized Mexican migration. To minimize transportation costs, U.S. employers had encouraged prospective *bracero* workers to move to Mexico's sparsely populated northern region, thereby

swelling Mexican border cities that offered little local employment. Meanwhile, workers seeking American jobs had learned they could save the large fees and bribes normally paid to *bracero* recruiters in Mexico by simply crossing the border illegally. Blending in with the legitimate *braceros*, they could find a job.

Just how much migration would have occurred anyway, in the absence of the *bracero* program, given the widening income gap between the US and Mexico, remains unclear. Certainly migration from Mexico had a very substantial history well before the *bracero* program.

Indeed, the US and Mexican labor markets, particularly in those US states bordering Mexico, have been quite thoroughly symbiotic. Although this is not new, the numbers involved have grown rapidly and the stock of Mexicans in the US, legally or otherwise, is probably around 8 million. Yet the available evidence also suggests that turnover and return to Mexico is common from within this stock, though with some important variations. For example, Reyes and Mameesh (2002: 580–81) find:[17]

> three patterns of migration for undocumented migrants across U.S. destinations: semi-permanent and permanent migration to urban areas; temporary migration to agricultural areas; and sojourner, or cyclical, migration to border regions ... The findings of this study reiterate the importance of economic opportunities as an important predictor of not only migration to, but also length of stay in, the United States. Dynamic regions not only attract more immigrants, but they also attract a more permanent population of migrants.

Partly out of concern for future irregular migration, 'in 1997, the bipartisan U.S. Commission on Immigration Reform reported to the president and Congress with a unanimous voice that adoption of a new temporary worker program "would be a grievous mistake"'.[18] However, in January 2004, President Bush proposed a new initiative granting amnesty to many workers illegally in the US, offering them three-year temporary work visas, with a possibility of extension on proof of employment, though ultimately requiring return home. Whether such a program would substitute for irregular migration or tend to swell the ranks of the undocumented remains a matter of political dispute, though the announcement effect has spurred a surge in attempted border-crossings in anticipation of an amnesty.

Europe

In contrast to the US, Canada, Australia and New Zealand, Europe has never sought to attract permanent settlers. Instead, labor migrants to Europe are admitted almost entirely on a temporary basis, requiring several years of legal, temporary residence prior to attaining any rights of settlement.[19] Following the demise of the guest worker programs in 1974, return migration has indeed been a significant feature of this system.[20] This is brought out for the case of Germany in Figure 7.1.[21] From 1975 through 1985, foreign population outflow was actually reported to exceed the inflow to Germany.[22] In part, the returns from Germany after 1983 and also from France after 1975 may have reflected financial incentive programs put into place to encourage departure, though as Dustmann (1996) notes in describing these programs, it is difficult to judge their efficacy given that a significant portion of beneficiaries might have returned anyway.[23] After the mid-1980s, the surge in inflows from the transition economies and other asylum seekers again came to dominate outflows from Germany. Moreover, the turnover pattern for non-EU migrants closely mirrors the overall pattern, at least during the 1990s in Germany, and by 1997–98 the outflows both of all foreigners and of non-EU nationals again exceeded the corresponding inflows, though both net flows again reversed thereafter (see Figure 7.1). On the other hand, the extent of turnover of non-EU population in Germany since 1990 has been much higher than for the four other European countries where somewhat comparable data are available: whereas non-EU population outflows averaged over 73 percent of inflows to Germany from 1990 to 2001, in Belgium the corresponding ratio was 49 percent, for Denmark and Sweden the ratios were about 25 percent, and for the Netherlands 19 percent. Where social register data are available, a far more complete picture of return migration patterns may be obtained. For example, analysis of such data by the Government Institute for Economic Research in Finland, tracing the cohort of migrants arriving in 1990, indicates that slightly over 30 percent of those who had entered Finland for one year or more had left Finland after ten years, almost half of these having left within

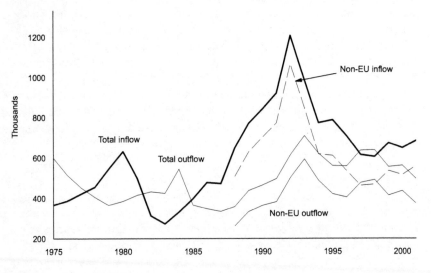

Figure 7.1   Foreign population inflow and outflow: Germany, 1975–2001

the first three years.[24] However, these averages mask considerable differences by region of origin; among those from other OECD countries, more than 60 percent had left Finland after ten years, whereas from Estonia the cumulative return was just over 20 percent, and from Russia and the refugee countries only slightly over 15 percent had returned.

Despite the continuing relative importance of return migration from Germany during the last quarter of the twentieth century, the reported stock of foreign population (including people born in Germany of foreign parents) has continued to grow, from less than a million in West Germany in 1960 to 3 million in 1970, about 4.5 million in 1980, and nearly 7.5 million in unified Germany in 2000, as family reunification has led to more permanent settlement. The fact that the early guest worker programs thus led to far more permanence than was intended by the host states is widely recognized.[25] In consequence, by 2000, official estimates recognized 2 million Turkish nationals in Germany; in France there are over a million Maghrebi nationals (see Table 2.2).

But did the guest worker system lay preconditions for the subsequent expansion of irregular migration, as claimed by some critics of the *bracero* program in the US? Certainly irregular migration to Western Europe has expanded since 1974. However, despite the lack of reliable data, it seems the former recruitment countries are not necessarily the source of most clandestine workers in the EU. Such countries as Albania and Moldova were never part of the guest worker system. Thus, it would seem difficult to make a case that early recruiting systems caused supply responses in the sending countries that ultimately led to clandestine movements in Europe. Did adjustments in the nature of employment in Europe during the guest worker years induce later pressures to employ undocumented workers? The guest workers, prior to 1974, were employed very largely in the industrial sector, whereas this does not appear to be the case for the majority of today's undocumented workers, so such a case could only be made on the grounds of guest worker migration having kept down wages more generally. Certainly, the availability of cheap labor led critics to complain that the guest worker system was slowing investments and mechanization of industry: 'Japan [was] getting robots while Germany [got] Turks.'[26] Whether the general availability of unskilled labor during the guest worker period ultimately restructured European employment such as to spur subsequent undocumented migration remains a matter of speculation, though in the context of Europe, where downward wage flexibility is considerably less than in the US, such a spur appears relatively unlikely. Certainly, there appears to be some presumption that expansions in current systems of legal admission of temporary migration will discourage the use of undocumented workers.[27]

In fact, in Germany there has been some revival of temporary labor programs. Agreements were signed with Hungary, Poland and Yugoslavia during 1988–90. Under these arrangements, firms in the labor supplying countries undertake a specific piece of work in Germany and workers are provided as part of the project. Initially a ceiling of 95 000 was set on the number of project workers to be admitted on this basis, though the ceiling was subsequently lowered to 50 000 in 1992, and during 2002 about 45 000 workers were admitted on this basis. In contrast to the early guest worker program, it seems that return has been far more strictly observed under these project worker programs.[28] Temporary project workers admitted to Germany in this fashion are subject to the German minimum wage but do not contribute to the German unemployment and pension schemes, which keeps down total labor costs. An indication of the changing face of the European migration system, however, is that during 2002 Germany also admitted almost 300 000 workers for up to ninety days of seasonal work in agriculture, forestry and hotels. Almost all of these seasonal workers admitted to Germany were from Poland, though there is also a special provision for Czech commuters to work in Germany.

In the UK too, a sharp increase has occurred in the number of temporary workers admitted in recent years, rising from 30 000 in 1995 to 137 500 in 2002. More than 60 percent of temporary workers admitted in 2003 were non-EU nationals. Since 1945, the UK has had a Seasonal Agricultural Workers Scheme designed largely to allow short-term farmwork by foreign students. During 2003 about 20 000 persons were admitted on this basis, plus another 39 000 working 'holiday makers'. Rising concern to address the growing number of asylum seekers arriving from Iran, Turkey and East Europe has also led to a new program, issuing renewable 12-month work permits to nationals of these countries, ages 18 to 25, for work in specific sectors (including agriculture, food processing, hotels and construction). During 2004 this program is supposed to admit 10 000 workers from Turkey, 10 000 from Iran and 20 000 from East Europe with 25 000 of these filling seasonal farm jobs. In practice, most of the documented seasonal agricultural workers in Britain are recruited through about 5000 'gang masters' who reportedly skim about a quarter to a third of the total pay as a contract fee.

The growth in use of seasonal workers in Germany, Italy and the UK during the 1990s is brought out in Figure 7.2, albeit for different definitions of seasonal workers in each case.[29] Moreover, somewhat comparable short-term labor programs exist throughout the European Economic Area. For example:

• Austria places a ceiling of 8000 on the average number of seasonal workers permitted to be employed in the country in any one month. However, turnover in these positions appears to be very rapid, so that the number of visas issued for this program is more than six times the ceiling level, though some of the visas presumably are issued for re-entry of the

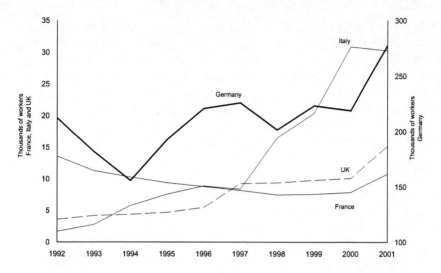

Figure 7.2   Inflows of seasonal workers: France, Germany, Italy and UK, 1992–2001

same person. Prior to July 2002, these permits applied only to work in agriculture and tourism, but new regulations now permit work in other sectors. Permits are now for six months, with extension for another six months, though workers are then required to leave Austria for a minimum of two months.

• Spain has bilateral labor recruitment agreements with Bulgaria, Ecuador, Morocco, Poland and Romania. Contract workers are admitted for a year or more, persons ages 18–35 can be employed for up to 18 months, and seasonal workers are allowed on contracts of up to nine months. These workers participate fully in the Spanish social security and health systems.

• In February 2003, Portugal and Ukraine signed an agreement allowing an estimated 200 000 undocumented Ukrainians in Portugal to become legal seasonal workers.

• In 2003, Greece recognized seasonal workers from Albania and Bulgaria entering for up to six months of work, as well as Egyptians employed in the Greek fishing industry for up to nine months.

• Among the Scandinavian countries, Norway admits about 15 000 non-EU seasonal workers, mostly from Poland and the Baltic countries, and in 2003 the period of permitted stay was doubled to six months. In Finland, the number of short-term work visas issued grew from about 7000 in 1999 to over 14 000 in 2002, some 59 percent of the total number of visas were issued to non-EU migrants.[30]

Europe's tradition of reliance on temporary labor importation thus continues and has expanded in a number of directions in recent years, including growing use of cross-border workers as well as seasonal employees. Moreover, at least some of the European governments see such programs as mechanisms for limiting clandestine movements. Indeed, in a few instances, attempts have been made to institutionalize this: Italy has signed a bilateral agreement with Romania to take contract workers in exchange for readmission of illegal migrants and Spain has similar arrangements with Morocco and Ecuador.

The Gulf

Since contracts (commonly issued initially for two years) can normally be renewed without returning to the country of origin, the duration of stay among workers migrating to the GCC states can vary substantially, though in the end there is no permanent settlement. After adjusting for the under-representation of longer term migrants inherent in any survey of returnees, Mahmud (1989) estimates an average stay in the Middle East among Bangladeshi workers of just under 4 years, with 22 percent staying 1–2 years or less and 13 percent staying more than 5–6 years. Similarly, Addleton (1992) reports that 56 percent of returning Pakistani workers in the early 1980s had been abroad for 4 or more years, with white-collar and professional workers staying longer while most production workers returned after less than 4 years. Addleton also reports that most Pakistani workers were returning only with reluctance, usually because of contract expiration, premature termination of employment, or compulsory repatriation. Only a few returned for family reasons or ill health. Indeed, Pasha and Altaf (1987) model optimal choice of duration of stay for Pakistani workers and conclude that only truly massive wage cuts in the Gulf would induce significant voluntary net return migration. Figure 7.3 offers a more recent depiction of duration of stay in the Gulf among workers who had returned to Kerala.[31] Among the 722 respondents who provided this information in a 1998 survey, the mean length of stay reported was nearly 7.4 years and 20 percent had been in the Gulf for 12 or more years.

Yet despite these images of extended periods of stay, the Gulf states have experienced periodic net out-migration, achieved both through cut-backs in recruiting as well as through contract non-renewal and compulsory returns. For example, estimates for both Pakistan and Sri Lanka indicate substantial net return migration from the Middle East by the mid-1980s, following the decline in oil prices.[32] Net return migration again became very substantial following the first Gulf war in 1991, as already noted in the context of discussing remittances to Kerala. Meanwhile, expulsions of unauthorized workers run to approximately 400 000 a year from Saudi Arabia alone and an amnesty during 1996–98, when political commitment to 'Saudization' of employment increased, resulted in more than a million 'voluntary' returns.

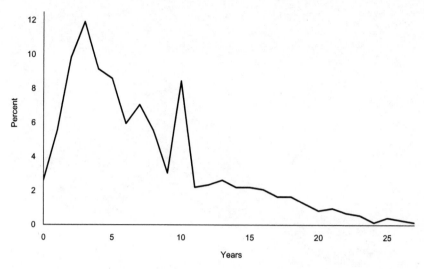

Figure 7.3 Duration of stay in Middle East among returned migrants to Kerala

The guest worker system in the Gulf states is utterly temporary in that settlement of individuals is effectively impossible. Only the very highly paid are entitled to bring family members to join them and the minimum salary cut-off for such permission has been steadily raised. Moreover, the member states have managed to export the impact of their economic and other crises, imposing much of the burden of adjustment on the sending states. Yet in the long run, the Gulf has also become utterly dependent on the continuation of the temporary labor system.

East Asia

Dependence on the use of temporary low skilled labor has clearly grown in the higher income economies of East Asia too, both in the form of contract labor and of irregular employment. Although permanent settlement is almost certainly rare, at least among the unskilled migrants, some settlement does occur. As Hugo (2003b: 3) notes:

In the Peninsular Malaysian context, it is interesting to compare the situation on the northern and southern borders. In the north there is a longstanding pattern of circular migration of Thais across the border to work in Malaysia facilitated by a local regime, whereby such movement is not inhibited by officials. There is little permanent settlement of Thais in northern Malaysia. On the other hand, there are increasing restrictions on Indonesians seeking to work in Malaysia, so once they get in there is a greater tendency to seek to settle permanently. While the distance between home and work is not very great, their migration is necessarily undocumented, so visiting home is expensive and there is a danger of being

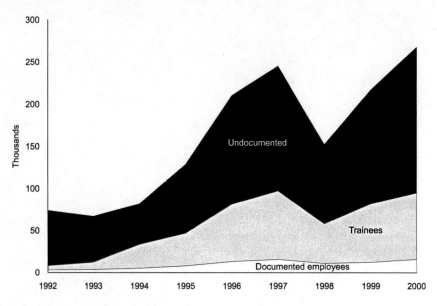

Figure 7.4   Foreign workers in Korea by legal status during the East Asia crisis

detected. Hence return visits are infrequent and migrants may have opted to bring their families to Malaysia.

Based on a village survey in East Indonesia, Hugo (1998) offers one of the few insights into the duration of stay among these circulating workers within East Asia. Of those who had returned to the village from Sabah in Malaysia, about a fifth had been away for two or more years during their last migration; among those still away but with family present in the village to report on them, a quarter had been away for ten or more years, and on both counts, women migrants were less numerous and stayed away for shorter periods.

This village survey was conducted prior to the financial crisis in 1997–98, which hit three of the principal labor importing countries in the region (Korea, Malaysia and Thailand), and had at least indirect effects on others (with temporary economic stagnation in Hong Kong and Japan, though any effect on Singapore was far less apparent). Manning (2002: 372) argues that during the crisis, 'labour receiving countries tried to cut back on *stocks* of migrants with limited success, although policies had more success in stemming the *flows* of migrants'. Yet the evidence seems mixed. In Korea, more than 53 000 undocumented workers (about a third of the estimated total) left the country under an amnesty program in 1998 and the rate of separation of foreign trainees accelerated with slack demand. The number of contract workers reported going to Korea from the Philippines fell by nearly a third in 1998 compared to 1997, but then almost doubled in 1999 and the stocks of both trainees and undocumented workers rebounded almost immediately. This is well illustrated in Figure 7.4; the ability to adjust quickly during the year of crisis in 1998 is apparent as both undocumented workers were expelled and 'training' was curtailed. Yet both had fully recovered within two years. Indeed, Figure 7.4 could well stand as a caricature of East Asian labor migration, dominated by unskilled workers, either undocumented or in disguise, and offering considerable flexibility to the host country. Malaysia also restricted new recruiting in 1998, announced an amnesty and attempted to ensure that foreign workers, retrenched from the manufacturing sector, either left the country or relocated to the still thriving plantation sector. By the end of 1999, the restrictions on recruiting in Malaysia had been lifted. In Thailand, the number of arrests of illegal migrants is reported to have increased sharply and the official estimate of the stock of illegal foreign workers fell from 987 000 in 1998 to 664 000 in 1999. In Hong Kong, the rate of growth of the stock of foreign domestic helpers did diminish, though this slowdown started before the crisis, and the number of Filipino domestic helpers is reported to have increased from 131 000 in 1995 to 143 000 in 1999, while the number of Indonesians grew from 16 000 to 41 000 in the same interval.

The reported stocks of foreign workers in Korea and Thailand diminished quite sharply in 1998 and 1999 respectively. On the other hand, the picture in Hong Kong clearly supports Manning's depiction of limited stock adjustment. In Malaysia it is more difficult to tell. Nonetheless, even in Korea, the stock of undocumented workers quickly rebounded and Debrah (2002: 1) argues that 'this brought home to the labour-receiving countries in Pacific Asia that although their labour migration policies are built on the concept of "temporariness", in reality it might be difficult if not impossible to avoid the use of migrant workers'. While this may be correct, it is not altogether clear that this experience alone could substantiate such dependence. Not only had demand conditions in the labor receiving countries shifted dramatically with the crisis, but conditions in some of the major labor supplying countries had altered even more dramatically. The rapid return to use of foreign labor may not have reflected intransigence in demand for these workers alone, but also their enhanced willingness to migrate even at lower wages.

Real wages fell in each of the four labor importing countries hit by the crisis. No doubt this partially explains the temporary dip in reported remittances to both the Philippines and Thailand, though exchange rate uncertainty may well have been a contributing factor too, despite concerns over falling incomes of family left at home (see Figure 7.5).[33] On the other hand, Hugo (2003a) notes that informal remittances to parts of East Indonesia may actually have increased during the crisis, in part because of the massive depreciation of the rupiah.

Meanwhile, cuts in real wages in Indonesia were far deeper than in any

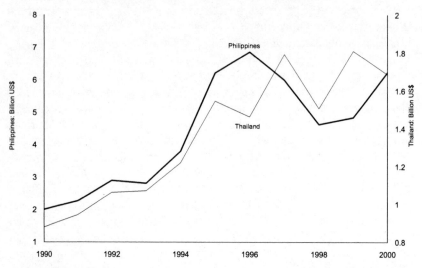

Figure 7.5 Official remittances to the Philippines and Thailand during the East Asia crisis

of the migrant receiving countries and Indonesian workers were desperate to find overseas work.[34] In the Philippines too, real wages fell, at least in the capital region, and open unemployment increased. In the balance, recruitment of overseas contract workers did not decline in the East Asia region as a whole during the crisis, as may be seen in Figure 7.6.[35]

Highly Skilled Workers and Return of 'Permanent' Settlers

One of the elements of supposed brain gain from departure of the highly skilled stems from their return with newly acquired skills, or at least with enriching experiences. The following section looks at the post-migration experiences of these highly skilled persons, as well as those of unskilled returnees. First, however, the present section considers both the extent and context of return of the highly skilled. Some evidence is also included on the return of 'permanent' settlers more generally, given that permanent settlers tend to be the more highly skilled, though the converse is not necessarily the case, given the growth in temporary movement of highly skilled intra-company transferees and of various kinds of Mode 4 service employees, as well as students.[36]

The US is the dominant destination among highly skilled migrants, and in Chapter 4 it was noted that among foreign scientists and engineers who had received their doctorates from US universities in 1994–95 while on temporary visas, about half were still in the US by 1999.[37] Finn (2001) notes

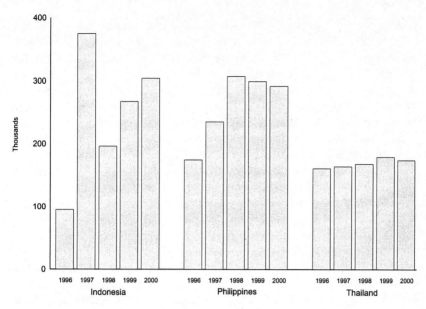

Figure 7.6   Flow of contract workers to East Asia from Indonesia, the Philippines and Thailand during the East Asia crisis

that the overall stay rate for this 1994–95 cohort was unusually low, in large part because many Chinese students were excluded from the figure having become permanent residents prior to graduating (a direct consequence of the Tiananmen Square incident in June 1989), and Chinese students generally have the highest stay rate. In fact, it seems that the stay rate of these scientists and engineers rose during the 1990s; of the 1989 cohort, Finn reports 49 percent were still in the US two years after graduating, whereas 69 percent of the 1997 cohort were still in the US after two years (including those who were permanent residents at graduation). Perhaps most importantly, for present purposes, the stay rates in the US are particularly high among nationals of the low income countries.

Borjas and Bratsberg (1996: 165) reach a similar conclusion about US permanent residents more generally, that 'Immigrants tend to return to wealthy countries that are not too far from the United States.' Nonetheless there is considerable inter-country variation in this average pattern, and the return rate calculated for African nationals, for example, is higher than for Europeans.[38] In a related study, Borjas (1989) infers departure from the US, based on attrition from a longitudinal survey, and argues that it is the 'failures', the least successful scientists and engineers, who leave the US. Inferring emigration from attrition in a panel survey is quite risky, given that high attrition rates from such surveys are common. However, social register data permit Edin *et al.* (2000) to trace individual immigrants to Sweden from 1970 to 1990 and to observe their subsequent emigration with much greater confidence. On average, within five years, more than a quarter of the immigrants to Sweden had emigrated. However, this study finds a higher rate of emigration among the earlier economic migrants largely from the Nordic area and other OECD countries, than among the refugees arriving in the later period, predominantly from non-OECD countries. Edin *et al.* also show that, within both waves of migrants, those who were relatively less successful economically in Sweden were more likely to leave.[39]

A few countries, particularly in East Asia, have set up programs to induce students and highly skilled professionals to return home. Efforts to encourage repatriation have been coordinated by the Ministry of Science and Technology in Korea and by the National Youth Commission (NYC) in Taiwan. In both Korea and Taiwan, government support for development of research centers and high tech clusters has played a key role in this strategy. In Korea, this initiative really began in 1966 with the establishment of the Korea Institute for Science and Technology followed by several other R&D institutes and engineering schools, concentrated in the Seoul Science Park and Daeduk Science Town. In Taiwan too, the government set out 'to improve and strengthen the institutions of higher learning'[40] and to support such centers as the Hsinchu Science Park. In both contexts these facilities have succeeded in attracting repatriates: 'In 1996, 82 companies in the Hsinchu Science Park (or 42 percent of the total) were started by returnees from the United States, primarily from Silicon Valley, and there were 2563 returnees working in the park alone.'[41] By 2000 the number of returnees working in Hsinchu Science Park had reached 5025. Nonetheless it remains unclear to what extent employment of repatriates in these facilities merely attracted those who would have returned anyway. Moreover, there is an issue as to whether the research generated in the public research institutes proved as productive as that in the private sector, though Yoon (1992) asserts that there were considerable spillover effects from the public research, even to the extent of being critical in instigating serious private R&D in Korea. Within the Korean public research institutes, repatriates have been offered premium salaries, though this has also led to internal problems of resentment (see Yoon, 1992). Taiwan's NYC has also been able to offer some financial incentives to returnees, in the form of travel subsidies, as well as assistance with job placement and business investments (obtaining loans, production locations and facilities).[42]

By 1992 some 100 000 self-financed students had left the People's Republic of China, most studying in the US, but almost none had returned (Engelsberg, 1995). Moreover, the Chinese Academy of Science 'sent over 7500 of its personnel as visiting scholars and graduate students from 1978 to 1991, approximately 50 percent of whom had returned by 1991'.[43] In 1984 ten post-doctoral research stations were established, growing to 145 stations by 1989, yet as of June 1989 these had attracted only 140 returnees in total (40 percent of all returned PhDs at that stage). In consequence the PRC government introduced a series of incentives to return, including a new service center for returnees set up in 1989, allocations for housing of returnees and duty free purchases of computers and automobiles, and offers of return air fares for self-financed students. Nonetheless the various incentives gave rise to mounting 'study-abroad fever' and to resentment among those unable to study abroad (Chang and Deng, 1992). Offering increased incentives became difficult and policy makers resorted to sticks as well as carrots in designing incentives to return. For example, some provinces and institutions introduced fines imposed on families of students failing to return on time. Moreover, attempts were made to restrict departure to categories of students more likely to return, including a minimum of five years' work experience prior to departure for certain categories of students and imposing training fees on those departing before meeting work requirements. In the Special Economic Zones, employers have been better placed to offer greater financial incentives to returnees, in part because of the greater competition in these zones. But in 1989, tighter controls were also introduced on job assignments of returnees, and Engelsberg (1995) notes that this clearly discouraged return.

The combined result of both carrots and sticks has been very limited return to the People's Republic. For instance, the US National Science Foundation (2001) reports that of 16 550 Chinese recipients of doctorates in science and engineering from US universities between 1988 and 1996, 85 percent planned to stay in the US at the time of receiving their doctorate (of these, 20 percent had firm offers of employment in the US, 36 percent had firm offers of post-doctorates, and the remaining 44 percent planned to stay despite having no firm offer). A part of the reluctance to return in the first half of the 1990s clearly reflected the aftermath of Tiananmen, though Zweig (1997) found, based on 273 personal interviews with former residents of China in the US in 1993, that economic factors were part of the reason for this failure to return also, including housing as well as earnings and lack of job mobility in China, as well as fear of not being able to leave China again. Nonetheless there is some evidence that return to China has begun to increase, though only very modestly as indicated in Figure 7.7.[44] In a sample of 185 returnees in Shanghai, Keren *et al.* (2003) found that 78 percent considered themselves to be permanently settled in China, while 16 percent were considered 'temporary returnees' among whom 71 percent still owned property overseas and 27 percent of the entire sample retained either permanent residence status or citizenship overseas.

In concluding a study of return migration of the highly skilled to Bangladesh, China, Taiwan and Vietnam, Iredale *et al.* (2003:185) note that 'The role of the government in facilitating return migration is as important

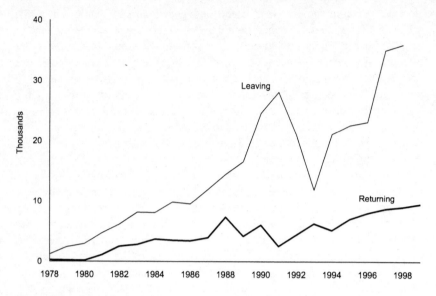

Figure 7.7   China: estimates of students leaving for study abroad and returning, 1978–99

as the economic, social and political environment of the country.' In practice, discerning how much of the relatively high return to Taiwan is attributable to government efforts versus spectacular growth of the Taiwanese economy is difficult. The same may be said of the slight, recent increase in return to China. In the context of Vietnam, Anh (2003) describes the employment guarantees that the government of Vietnam has offered to returning students as well as financial state support in the forms of travel expenses and housing. Moreover, the number of highly skilled people returning to Vietnam has now begun to increase very modestly, though recent returnees are reported to have benefited less from these government incentives than did the smaller contingent returning before 1995. An interesting contrast is provided by Indonesia, where the return rate of students from study abroad has been extraordinarily high. As in several other countries, Indonesian students who are funded by the state are required to work for a specified period at home or to repay the costs, though attempts to circumvent this rule appear uncommon, suggesting that it is not a binding constraint in compelling student return. On the other hand, return to Bangladesh among its highly educated diaspora appears minimal; Rozario and Gow (2003: 61) 'highlight the potential impact returnees could make if their number was higher, but more importantly if Bangladesh was ready for them'.

7.2   THE ASSIMILATION OF RETURN MIGRANTS

This last remark leads into the issue of what awaits migrants, both skilled and unskilled, upon return to their home country. Reintegration has many components, including issues of psychological and social readjustment upon return. For present purposes, however, the focus will be purely upon economic reintegration and assimilation in the home country labor market in particular.

Before turning to the evidence, in the contexts of South Asia, Southeast Asia and East Europe in particular, it is worth pausing to note two general difficulties that arise in interpreting this evidence. First, re-entry often involves a process of searching for the 'right' opportunity. In other words, labor market assimilation is a dynamic process and evidence on the state of employment of returnees should accordingly be seen in relation to how long the migrant has been home. Second, is the question of an appropriate benchmark against which to judge the earnings or employment status of returnees. Both the process of migration and the process of return are selective; only certain types of people tend to go and only some of them return. This raises the question as to whether it is fair to compare the earnings of returnees with earnings of those who never left; rather the question is how much would the returnees have earned if they had never left? Very few studies make appropriate adjustments for these two issues, in looking at the employment situation among returnees.

South Asia

Only small numbers of highly skilled people return to reside in South Asia and very little is known of the experiences of these select few. Instead, the dominant stream of circular migrants in South Asia is clearly the relatively low skilled workers returning from the Persian Gulf.

Pakistan

In the first decade after the first oil crisis, Pakistan was the largest source of workers going to the Middle East from Asia, supplying more than a quarter of total Asian contract workers. By the early 1980s, more than 100 000 workers were returning each year. The ILO-ARTEP national survey in 1985–86 counted 17.4 percent of returned migrants unemployed and actively looking for work, with another 4.2 percent voluntarily unemployed and apparently hoping to return to the Gulf. In fact, 'Rates of unemployment were positively related to the level of education, skill classification and financial savings . . . the high unemployment rate for return migrants did not necessarily reflect the overall employment imbalances in the economy. It seems that to a considerable extent the high degree of unemployment among return migrants could be attributed to their relatively comfortable financial situation whereby they could afford to prolong the waiting period while looking for a suitable job.'[45] Arif (1996) uses the ILO-ARTEP survey data to look more explicitly at these dynamics of transition into employment after return. However, Arif (1996: 807) notes that the data do not distinguish whether unemployed returnees initially withdrew from the labor force; in consequence, 'reported duration of unemployment is interpreted as the "period without a job"'. Nearly two-thirds of those without a job had been home for less than two years and non-employment fell sharply and fairly steadily during the first 12–18 months after return. Nonetheless some longer-term non-employment did persist: 60 percent of those actively seeking work at the time of the survey had been non-employed for more than a year; 28 percent had been non-employed for than two years. Given the time since returning home, the odds of not being employed were generally greater for those with higher levels of education, who had not been working prior to migrating, had professional or clerical posts overseas, had been abroad for longer, and had larger accumulated savings at the time of return. All of these factors tend to suggest that a good deal of the non-employment involved a considerable element of choice.

The same, ILO-ARTEP survey revealed that nearly a third of all emigrants who had returned during 1975–85 had set themselves up in their own business. Kazi (1989: 160) notes, 'Despite the fact that a large proportion of the entrepreneurs were new entrants into the field, the rate of business failure was not high. The rate was 15 percent for urban and 11 percent for rural areas.' On the other hand, Azam (1991: 63) notes that 'Most of the business ventures were less than a year old at the time of the survey, which made it difficult to evaluate their prospects.' More recent analyses of these same data have shown the key role that savings while overseas played in this process of transition from wage employment prior to migration into self-employment, notably in urban businesses, upon return.[46]

The Government of Pakistan has made some effort to encourage this process. A Non-Repatriable Investment Scheme permits overseas Pakistanis to import machinery and equipment at reduced duty rates to establish manufacturing enterprises, with higher rebates for projects in underdeveloped areas. 'The impact of these schemes has not yet been assessed. However, according to the available fragmentary evidence, so far their overall impact has been rather insignificant.'[47]

Azam (1991) also notes the findings of a 1988 study of 78 returned motor mechanics, welders and operators and their employers in Pakistan. The employees in this study reported having acquired new specific skills while abroad, but both the employees and employers reported that these new skills were of no use on return. The employers did report a superior work performance from the returned migrants, as compared to workers who had never been overseas, though it is unclear whether this reflected better work habits learned abroad or simply selection of more dynamic workers as migrants in the first place.

India

In Kerala, various surveys indicate extremely varied levels of unemployment among returned workers from the Gulf, ranging from 60 percent in 1985 and 50 percent in 1987 to 20 percent in 1992–93, while a 2001 survey shows 8 percent seeking work though about a quarter of those considered to be of working age had dropped out of the labor force.[48] Whether this represents an improving trend is unclear because the average time since return from the Middle East differs across the various studies. Overall, Kerala has the highest unemployment rate in India, which may partly explain the high average unemployment indicated by these various studies. On the other hand, Zachariah *et al.* (2001) argue that those who were unemployed prior to departure stay abroad for longer, which may mean that observed returnees are among the more employable locally. Nonetheless, these authors paint a fairly bleak picture of the employment of returned migrants in Kerala in 2001, with little effective occupational switching, an average age upon return that makes deployment of any newly acquired skills less likely, and most returnees having spent all of their earnings fairly quickly.

Sri Lanka

About two-thirds of Sri Lankans going overseas for work are women. Some surveys taken during the 1980s indicated that the unemployment rate of female returnees was far lower than among males. However, for both men and women, the unemployment rate appeared very high in these surveys, though Rodrigo and Jayattissa (1989) raise serious doubts about the quality of these data. Nonetheless, in 1982, the Sri Lankan government attempted to deal with these low employment levels.

> Sri Lanka was the first labour-exporting country in Asia to launch an entrepreneurship development programme for return migrants . . . This initiative showed that return migrants belonging to higher occupational categories are suitable for an orientation program of this type leaving out unskilled return migrants. Second, the possibilities for guiding candidates into business are limited unless accompanied by measures to facilitate the access to capital. Third, the ability to identify and develop a project, as well as managerial skills needed to run a business, cannot be imparted only through a program of class instruction.[49]

Bangladesh

The study by Rozario and Gow (2003) provides a rare glimpse into return migration of the highly skilled to South Asia. The authors note both the small number of highly skilled returned migrants in Bangladesh and the absence of any sampling frame from which to draw a random sample. Nonetheless their survey of 108 highly qualified individuals, returned largely from Australia but also from the UK, US and India, suggests a high level of employment, mostly on salary, in managerial positions within large organizations, in the private sector.

Southeast Asia

Although it is apparent that a good deal of return migration is occurring in Southeast Asia, at least of relatively unskilled workers coming back both from the Middle East and from other parts of East Asia, not much information is available about these returnees.

Philippines

The government of the Philippines, in cooperation with some non-governmental organizations, has put in place a series of mechanisms to aid the reintegration of returning migrants, ranging from training and business development assistance to housing loans, counseling and information provision.[50] However, no evaluation of the efficacy of these programs appears to have been undertaken, though early take up on some of these efforts appears to have been quite minimal.[51]

Tan (1993) provides a particularly eloquent account of skill acquisition among overseas Filipinos and the usefulness of these fresh abilities in the Philippines, with respect to several major occupational groups:

- [Almost a quarter of Filipino workers contracted abroad from 1990 to 2000 were sea-based workers.] Our overseas seamen man larger and more modern ships and freighters than exist here ... They come home regularly but mainly for vacations ... No HC [human capital] *is* transmitted by these workers. (Tan, 1993: 322–3)

- Our overseas doctors and nurses in the West and in the Middle East work with more state-of the-art equipment. Our construction workers and mechanics on American bases are assisted by motorized tools and equipment. (Tan, 1993: 322)

- In the case of overseas domestic helpers, 28 percent are college graduates who might have been school teachers ... and some 23 percent [possess] some formal vocational training ... While the overseas domestics do acquire some OJT [on the job training] in housework, they are deskilled ... overall. For those who go back to teaching, there is a loss ... since their teaching experience has been interrupted. (Tan, 1993: 323)

- The musicians and entertainers that work in many Asian cities are a different breed altogether. (Tan, 1993: 324)

Vietnam

In Vietnam 'The Government encourages those who have savings to set up their own small or medium-sized business. They are offered enterprise management courses and facilitated access to bank loans.'[52] However, once again it is unclear that any evaluation of these schemes exists and Anh (2003) notes that the majority of returned highly skilled migrants to Vietnam are not employed in business but in universities, research institutions and state administration, albeit mostly in management roles. The rigid state salary scales also poses a problem in attracting returnees:

> For those working in state-owned enterprises for the first time, they receive a starting salary at the first level. Many returnees expressed concern about this salary system. Many cities and provincial authorities are pioneering ways of attracting highly-skilled workers and talent by offering accommodation support, allowances, etc. However, these measures are unlikely to be successful due to the lack of resources and poor implementation in practice. (Anh, 2003: 154)

The net results appear to be little or no gain in pay upon return to Vietnam from the sojourn abroad.

East Europe

The extent of return migration to East Europe remains very poorly documented. Kulu and Tammaru (2000) note that in the first six years after re-independence in Estonia some 1100–1200 ethnic Estonians returned to Estonia. This return rate was lower than in the 1970s, and was higher from the former Soviet Union, relative to the diaspora there, than from the west. Nearly 40 percent of those returning during the first half of the 1990s spoke Estonian poorly or not at all, though Kulu and Tammaro argue that reintegration has proved easier for Estonians returning from the west, who have tended to settle in urban parts of Estonia, than among those returning from the former Soviet territories, whose settlement is more dispersed. However no information is provided on the employment situation or earnings of either group. Moreover there appears to be no evidence on the return experiences of the substantial numbers of Estonians working on a seasonal or temporary basis abroad since 1990, especially in Finland. Indeed, one of the few contexts where information is available about the employment experiences of migrants returning to East Europe since 1990 is in Albania.

Albania

The newly emergent migration from Albania in the 1990s has featured fairly high rates of return, both by choice and compulsion. From a 1996 survey, Konica and Filer (2003: 4) estimate that '61 percent of Albanians who left the country since 1990 had returned by the summer of 1996. Among those who returned, about half were sent back by authorities in the destination country and half opted to return voluntarily'. Those returned by the authorities had been away on average for about six months, while those returning voluntarily had been away for a year. Family members reported to be still away had been out of Albania for an average of two years. As the World Bank study by De Soto *et al.* (2002: 44–5) summarizes, 'Twenty-five percent acknowledge that the household member on migration has left permanently ... Most migration is for periods of less than six months ... Usually the same members of the household go forth and back. Fifteen percent of those who emigrate have left at least six times since 1990.'

Thus De Coulon and Piracha (2002: 2) argue that 'Evidence suggests that a large number of Albanian migrants fall into the category of temporary (or guest) workers. In Greece, of those who received a temporary white card in the regularisation programme in 1998, only 54% proceeded to the second phase of application one year later to obtain a permanent green card.' De Coulon and Piracha go on to compare earnings of returnees with those who never left, in this case controlling for selection in the initial process of leaving Albania. They find that 'return-migrants are negatively selected compared to stayers in Albania ... had the stayers migrated (and then returned) they would have earned more than twice the wages of return migrants'.[53] However, 'The benefits for migrants, once they return, translate into access to better positions on the job ladder, but not in increased rewards for ... age and education. The return migrants on average earn more than the stayers'.[54]

7.3   TOWARDS CONCLUSIONS

Although reliable historical perspectives are not available, it seems that circular migration has increased globally. Not only have various forms of guest worker programs expanded, but rotation of highly skilled persons is occurring more frequently too, both on short-term bases and after a period of settlement.

The vast majority of guest workers return home, though the duration of stay can be substantial in the interim. The lengths of stay depend in part upon the fixed costs of re-entry and the odds of being able to return abroad again. Intensive repeat migration is prevalent in the border areas of Mexico and among seasonal workers in the EU; Albanians who return voluntarily have been away only a year on average; but stays in the Gulf average some four to five years; and tightening of controls on irregular migration in Malaysia is reported to have led to more permanent settlement from Indonesia.

Returning guest workers typically have high saving rates while away, enabling early retirement or extended job search on return. The early experiences of returning guest workers from the Gulf and from Germany consequently indicated high non-employment rates, though some of these summary measures may have reflected relatively short intervals since returning and the dynamics of the re-entry process. A number of countries have, nonetheless, created various facilities intended to aid reintegration into home country employment; there are some indications that these packages have proved utterly ineffective, though little or no formal evaluation of these mechanisms has taken place.

The notion that migrants gain skills and experience, which can enhance their earnings on return, receives mixed reviews. The experiences of the very large numbers of overseas Filipinos appear unlikely to prove helpful on return. In Vietnam, rigid pay structures thwart any advantages for the burgeoning trickle of returnees. On the other hand, estimates indicate that Albanians who have been abroad earn more than those who never went, despite the fact the stayers would apparently have earned even more abroad than those who actually left. Lack of entrepreneurial experience and access to credit are commonly cited as constraints faced by returnees attempting to make a transition into non-farm self-employment, though evidence on the failure rate of these enterprises is far from complete. McCormick and Wahba (2001: abstract) do however:

> find evidence supporting the hypotheses that both overseas savings, and the duration of stay overseas increase the probability of becoming an entrepreneur amongst literate returnees to Egypt. Amongst illiterate returnees, overseas savings alone increase the probability of becoming an entrepreneur. The results for literates suggest that skill acquisition overseas may matter more substantially than overcoming a savings constraint in explaining how overseas opportunities influence entrepreneurship on return. For illiterates, who usually accept menial positions overseas that offer little opportunity for learning, the opposite obtains.

Among migrants admitted legally on a longer-term basis to the OECD countries, fairly high departure rates are reasonably well documented. However, departures are far more prevalent among migrants from the other OECD countries; return to the lower income countries, having gained entry as an immigrant in a high-income country, is rarer. Moreover there are some indications that on average those who return have been among the less successful overseas. A number of programs have been established with the intent of encouraging return of the highly skilled, including students abroad. Again, however, no serious evaluation of the efficacy of these efforts appears to have been undertaken despite their high costs in terms of resources, resentment created, and inducement to go overseas to take advantage of the incentives.

The return of migrants is certainly perceived positively by most sending and host countries, though too rapid return also has disadvantages to both. For the migrant supplying nations, shorter sojourns abroad probably limit some of the social costs of absent parents and spouses, though high turnover raises the incidence of the many fixed costs associated with going. The intent to return sustains connections, expanding remittance transfers and possibly other forms of gain transmitted from a more involved diaspora; too rapid return limits the resources accumulated by the migrant and hence diminishes these transfers. In the host countries, rapid turnover imposes higher costs on employers (except in seasonal or short-term work) and prevents social assimilation. On the other hand, very short-term residents are often net fiscal contributors to their hosts' coffers, which is of growing interest given the ageing and associated social security problems faced in many of the industrialized nations. In addition, more rapid turnover may enhance the ability to adjust the stock of foreign workers in the event of a downturn, though the evidence on this is mixed. For example, during the East Asia crisis efforts to reduce the presence of foreign workers seems to have focused on expulsion of irregular employees rather than return of contract workers; recruitment within the region from Indonesia, the Philippines and Thailand hardly paused (though recruitment from Bangladesh did). In contrast, the Persian Gulf states have proved capable of fairly rapid expulsion of large numbers of workers in the face of crises, such as the Gulf conflict of 1991 when the involuntary return of large numbers of workers imposed severe adjustment problems on some of the migrant source areas, despite the prevalence of contract renewals and visa trading, which have resulted in protracted stays.

Net migration to Germany followed the German business cycle both during the early guest worker program and thereafter until 1990, enabling Germany to shift some of the consequences of these cycles offshore.[55] Yet, despite high turnover throughout, the early guest worker system in Europe clearly resulted in more permanent settlement than most European countries anticipated and wanted. Subsequent efforts to reduce the stocks of foreign nationals, by offering financial incentives to return, proved ineffective: the incentives were simply too small. The more recent revival of labor contracting and use of seasonal labor in Europe appears to be resulting in less permanent domicile. In any case, irregular migrants can become fairly permanent too, as among some of the urban-based Mexicans in the US, and indeed such permanence tends to be reinforced by an inability to come back yet again. Whether temporary and irregular migrants are substitutes or complements appears mixed. Critics of the newly proposed guest worker program in the US claim that the earlier *bracero* program induced subsequent undocumented movement, though some expansion in irregular migration would surely have occurred anyway. Certainly some of the European countries today are either assuming that expanded legal entry will reduce the numbers of asylum seekers and irregular movements, or exploring bilateral deals to regularize recruiting in return for efforts to reduce irregular migrations.

The OECD countries show little inclination to permit permanent entry of unskilled foreign workers. The future implications of migration from the developing countries for economic development in those countries of origin, and specifically for their poor, will consequently hinge critically upon the continued evolution of temporary worker programs. In a few contexts, conscious decisions have been taken to reduce long-term reliance on imported labor, though such decisions were not always realized. Attempts to localize jobs in the Gulf in the mid-1990s did not come to fruition; termination of the *bracero* program did not mean an end to demands for Mexican workers in the US; cessation of guest worker recruiting did not witness an end to use of unskilled foreign labor in Europe. On the other hand, when some of the South African mining houses elected around 1971 to curtail more than a century of foreign mine labor recruiting, to upgrade technology and localize jobs, more than half a million miners went from being 62 percent foreign to 62 percent domestic within six years, though at a cost of tripling in real wages.[56] Agricultural subsidies currently play a key role in enhancing demands for temporary guest workers in many of the industrialized nations; protectionism to avert outsourcing could come to play a similar role. Meanwhile, technology in many spheres is becoming increasingly skill-intensive, permitting diminished reliance on less skilled workers, though in such areas as care for the elderly the potentials for both substitution and outsourcing may well prove limited.

NOTES

* J.R.R. Tolkien, *The Hobbit or There and Back Again*, George Allen and Unwin Ltd., 1937.

1. See Sjaastad (1962) for example.
2. Dustmann (2001: 229) citing evidence from Jasso and Rosenzweig (1982). See also Piore (1979).
3. Hugo (2003b: 1).
4. Rapid economic progress in Ireland has generated very substantial return migration and, more recently, significant immigration, resulting in positive net migration into Ireland in the second half of the 1990s.
5. Obviously a wide range of changing circumstances for individuals exists. A particular variant that has attracted some attention in the literature is the departure of others from the home community, improving the migrant's perception of their relative deprivation upon return. See, for example, Stark and Taylor (1991).
6. For an excellent survey see Dustmann (2001).

7. Dustmann (2003) notes that rising wages may reduce migrants' choice of length of stay by enabling earlier completion of target saving, and presents supporting evidence from German data.

8. Galor and Stark (1990), Merkle and Zimmermann (1992).

9. Hill (1987), Djajić and Milbourne (1988), Raffelhüschen (1992).

10. See, for example, Fan and Stretton (1985).

11. Dustmann (2001).

12. 'Guestworkers are more likely to return home when they lose access to German jobs … immigrants in Germany migrated for employment and continue to stay so long as they have in employment in Germany … The odds of returning are high during the first 5 years since arrival in Germany and after retirement' (Constant and Massey, 2003: 650).

13. See Katz and Stark (1987).

14. See Blejer and Goldberg (1980), on migrants returning from Israel.

15. While recognizing the many vexing issues associated with the return and resettlement of refugees, no attempt is made to consider these here.

16. On the growing role of migrant workers in caring for the elderly and for children, see OECD (2003: Box 1.2).

17. Reyes and Mameesh (2002) warn that both their own and virtually all prior work on return to Mexico draws upon a sample of persons observed in Mexico, a sample which is naturally biased toward those more likely to have returned. See also Lindstrom (1996).

18. Martin and Teitelbaum (2001: 131).

19. In the UK context, Dobson *et al.* (2001: 22) note, 'Some indication of the propensity of work permit holders to settle more permanently can be derived by comparing the number accepted for settlement with the number of long-term work permits issued four years previously. The comparison suggests that in the period 1986–99 around a quarter of long-term work permit holders have applied for and been accepted for settlement.'

20. Indeed, Böhning (1984), estimates that more than two-thirds of all guest workers admitted to Germany and in excess of 80 percent of those admitted to Switzerland returned, indicating a high level of turnover in the earlier period also.

21. OECD *Trends in International Migration.*

22. The same pattern occurred in Switzerland. See Dustmann (1996).

23. France does not report outflow data.

24. I am most grateful to Dr Aki Kangasharju of the Government Institute for Economic Research, Helsinki, for sharing these results, derived from data provided by Statistics Finland.

25. See Castles *et al.* (1984), and Werner (2000), for example.

26. Quoted in Martin and Teitelbaum (2001: 125), from Martin (2004), edited by Wayne A. Cornelius, Takeyuki Tsuda, Philip L. Martin and James F. Hollifield. The implications for subsequent growth performance in both contexts are clearly complex. However, it may be noted that from 1970 to 2002, Germany's GDP per capita grew at 2.35 percent per year on average, while the East Asian miracle growth in Japan averaged 2.71 percent; a fairly small though non-trivial gap. (Based on GDP volume indices and population data from the IMF *International Financial Statistics.*)

27. See, for instance, UK Government (2002).

28. See, Werner (2000).

29. Data from OECD (2003). The varying definitions are: France, 'Number of contracts with the Office des Migrations Internationales' (which excludes EU nationals); Germany, 'Workers recruited under bilateral agreements'; Italy, 'Agricultural seasonal workers entering Italy with a work authorization'; UK, 'Seasonal workers under the special Seasonal Agricultural Workers Scheme. Including readmissions' (OECD, 2003: 381).

30. I am grateful to Dr Aki Kangasharju of the Government Institute for Economic Research

for help with data from the Foreign Ministry of Finland, Directorate of Immigration.

31. I am grateful to Professor K.C. Zachariah of the Centre for Development Studies, Trivandrum, for providing these measures.

32. On Pakistan see Addleton (1992); on Sri Lanka see Rodrigo and Jayatissa (1989).

33. IMF *Balance of Payments Statistics.* Reported remittances for Indonesia refer almost entirely to transfers from the Gulf and are therefore not shown.

34. See Fallon and Lucas (2002).

35. Indonesia from Soeprobo (2004); Philippines from Go (2002); Thailand from Chalamwong (2002).

36. Mode 4 refers to World Trade Organization provisions on the temporary movement of personnel associated with international trade in services.

37. Directly comparable data are not available on graduates from most European universities, though Johnson (2001) notes that return rates among doctoral graduates from French universities in 1998 were only 28 percent in the natural sciences and 20 percent in engineering. In contrast, Johnson also reports that the return rate from the UK universities was far higher in the same year.

38. The statistical obstacles in reaching such conclusions are considerable: return is inferred from a comparison of the profile of the foreign-born population in the 1980 census with the inflow of permanent residents since 1971 though, as the authors note, it may be misleading to infer that anyone has returned home merely because they have left the US, and some strong assumptions are necessary to deal with non-permanent resident inflows.

39. 'Australia tends to be categorised purely as an immigration country, but in fact, it also is a country of significant emigration ... Former settlers have formed a major part of the outflow' (Hugo 2002b: 306). This 'permanent' outflow of former settlers, as recorded by the Australian Department of Immigration and Multicultural Affairs, averaged around 20 000 per year during the 1990s and the majority of permanent departures (including the Australian-born) have been professionals and managers though whether these are the less successful migrants, as in Sweden, is unknown. On out-migration from Germany, see Constant and Massey (2003).

40. Chang (1992: 38).

41. Saxenian (1999: 58 fn. 9). Yoon (1992), reports 908 repatriates employed in public R&D institutes in Korea between 1968 and 1989.

42. See Tsay (2003), for greater detail on Taiwan's efforts to induce return.

43. Engelsberg (1995: 114).

44. The data for Figure 7.7 are from Guochu and Wenjun (2002: table 4), which include estimates for both self-supported students as well as those sent by government and other units. In 1999, the number of students estimated leaving China was 80 000, which is not depicted to preserve the scale in earlier years.

45. Kazi (1989: 179).

46. Arif and Irfan (1997), Ilahi (1999).

47. Puri and Ritzema (1999: 15).

48. Nair (1998) and Zachariah *et al.* (2001).

49. Puri and Ritzema (1999: 15–16).

50. See IOM (2003b: 148–150).

51. Athukorala (1993), Puri and Ritzema (1999).

52. IOM (2003b: 182).

53. De Coulon and Piracha (2002: 22).

54. De Coulon and Piracha (2002: 22).

55. Zimmermann (1995).

56. Lucas (1985).

8. Poverty, Inequality and the Social Impacts of Migration

In considering the consequences of alternative migration regimes for development, it is important to recognize that improvements in average incomes within the countries of origin by no means guarantee betterment for all. In the midst of overall economic development, pockets of poverty may well be left behind; indeed poverty may even be deepened for some. Obviously, the incidence of absolute poverty can only become worse in the face of growth in average incomes if the share of income going to the poor declines. For the most part, the evidence suggests that economic growth dominates, resulting in few cases of rising poverty incidence despite overall growth.[1] Nonetheless the issues remain as to the effects of migration upon inequality, whether some groups are left behind in any gains from migration, and indeed whether some are made absolutely worse off. These issues are taken up in Section 8.1. In addition, however, the process of international migration has widespread social ramifications within the countries of origin, beyond any effects on economic performance, and not all of these ramifications are necessarily positive; again some may be hurt in the midst of aggregate economic progress. A full treatment of the impact of international migration upon family structures and norms, and upon society and polity more generally, is well beyond the scope of this volume, though Section 8.2 of this chapter at least notes some of the more important implications.

8.1 MIGRATION, INEQUALITY AND POVERTY

The consequences of emigration for income inequality across families may be thought of as being driven by three major elements: the income classes from which migrants are drawn; the patterns of remittances according to income classes; and the various indirect effects of migration upon non-migrating groups. Given these interrelated components, defining a counterfactual against which to compare becomes ambiguous. Whereas some studies refer to a baseline of household income before migration, others are founded on post-migration incomes, either before or after adjusting to receipt of remittances. The differences can be quite considerable.

The conventional wisdom is that the poorest do not emigrate from most contexts. However, it seems that much of the evidence in support of this notion refers to remittance patterns, rather than migration itself. Yet remittance patterns across income classes may reflect selectivity with respect to migration, or remittances, or both. Nonetheless, there are good reasons to suppose that the poorest may indeed be constrained from emigrating, by lack of finances to afford costly moves, by lack of sufficient education to qualify for overseas recruiting, and by lack of access to appropriate social networks as a result of their social class and geographic location. What does the evidence from some of the case area countries indicate?

Case Study Countries

Upon reviewing the evidence with respect to Bangladesh, Siddiqui (2003:3) notes, 'It is assumed that the extreme poor people are more likely to migrate to other parts of the country ... Some rural poor people also migrate internationally. Little data are available on the proportion of international migrants that is poor.' In his earlier review, Mahmud (1989: 79) concurs: 'There are hardly any reliable estimates of the pre-migration level of earnings of migrants' households.' However, Mahmud goes on to cite two 1980 studies that 'suggest that migrants are drawn from a more affluent background compared to others in the same skill-category ... migrants' families derive nearly a quarter of their income from sources other than remittances. The weight of evidence thus supports the hypothesis that emigration helps only the relatively better-off families to move further up the income scale.'[2] Mahmud argues that it is the cost of migration which represents the chief barrier to the poorest from migrating in Bangladesh, noting that these costs tend to be higher for the poor 'which is perhaps indicative of their greater vulnerability to exploitation by recruiting agents. The most common means of meeting these costs is sale or mortgage of land, which therefore precludes the landless.'[3] However, Siddiqui (2003: 3) notes 'the poor also migrate. They do so by acquiring work visas through relatives, friends and neighbours. In these cases, migrants do not have to purchase the visa and the employer occasionally pays for the air fare.'

'It is well known that eight states in India – Kerala, Karnataka, Andhra Pradesh, Punjab, Gujarat, Goa, Maharashtra and Tamil Nadu – most of them maritime states on the west – account for almost the entire outflow of migrants to the Middle East.'[4] These eight states are among the eleven states with the highest income levels in India (see Figure 8.1).[5] To some extent, these states probably have higher incomes because of prior migrations. On the other hand, the fact that these are the higher income states in India does not mean that few people live in poverty there. The head count ratio of people living in poverty within these states as of 1999–2000 is estimated to average nearly

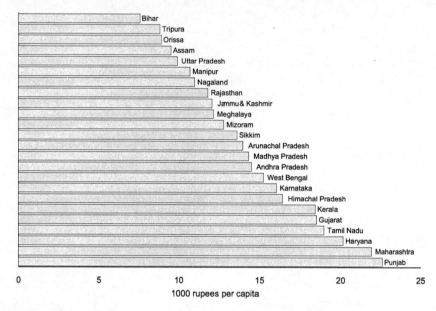

Figure 8.1   Net domestic product per capita: states of India, 2000

23 percent, or about 90 million people, with rural poverty incidence ranging from over 35 percent in Maharashtra to about 6.4 percent in Punjab.[6] Kerala probably provides about half of India's workers going to the Gulf, and here the head count ratio of poverty is estimated to be 10.5 percent in urban areas and 14.4 percent in rural areas. Of the emigrants from Kerala, Nair (1998: 267) notes 'Most are poor, with few assets at time of first migration. However, the proportion of the extremely poor (i.e. without land assets, housing facilities and employment was negligible) ... it is the not-so-extremely poor and not-so-extremely rich which participate actively in the emigration process.'

From Pakistan, as already noted in Chapter 3, most migrants to the Gulf have originated from rural areas and a disproportionate number of migrants have been drawn from the relatively poor, rain-fed agricultural portions of Northwest Frontier Province and Punjab in particular. A 1986 study showed that 'Between 70 and 80 percent of the migrants had a premigration income of less than Rs1,000 per month, which put them among the low- or low-middle income groups ... it was not the poorest who benefited from the overseas migration, but rather those belonging to the lower-middle income groups.'[7] Nonetheless this implies that 70 to 80 percent of the migrants had pre-migration incomes less than the average monthly earnings in manufacturing at the time.[8] Adams (1998) looks at remittances received from abroad in relation to income classes of households and notes that the portion of income derived from external remittances rises steadily with income: whereas the

20 percent of rural families with the lowest incomes received only 1 percent of their incomes from external remittances the richest 20 percent derived nearly 14 percent of their incomes from foreign remittances. However, as Adams notes, the data from which these results are derived were not meant to be representative of rural Pakistan as a whole and to a limited extent some of the richer households may appear rich precisely because they receive remittances, these transfers being included in the measure of income class.[9] Certainly, given the apparent profile of migrants, the strength of Adams's regressive findings seems surprising and Gazdar (2003) concludes that the impact of migration to the Gulf now has a 'moderate' impact on the poor though it was 'high' in his view at an earlier stage. Alderman (1996) also notes that the rain-fed areas from which many migrants are drawn experience high agricultural variability and that these communities have high rates of financial savings; in offering a potential for consumption smoothing through episodes of inclement weather, the strategy of international migration and associated remittances may well thus offer relief from transitory episodes of poverty in addition to any longer term impacts on more chronic forms of poverty.

Saith (1997) argues, based on families reporting income from abroad as their main source of income, that most contract workers leaving the Philippines are drawn from the higher income regions surrounding Manila.[10] On the other hand, substantial internal migration also occurs from the poorer, outer islands toward these higher income regions, though Saith expresses some skepticism about how much of this internal migration is either induced by emigration or results in subsequent step migration overseas following internal relocation. Thus, Saith (1997: 32) concludes 'that … at least as far as the direct effect of migration is concerned, the benefits accrue disproportionately to the richer regions, sectors and classes'. Yet Cox and Jimenez (1995) argue, based on evidence from the same Family Income and Expenditure Survey for 1988, that private transfers in the Philippines are strongly equalizing. In particular, the results of Cox and Jimenez indicate that incomes of the poorest 20 percent of households rise by 63 percent (79 percent in urban areas and 46 percent in rural areas) while incomes of the richest 20 percent of households decline by 6 percent. This last result clearly reflects the fact that the study by Cox and Jimenez combines all forms of private transfers, including remittances from overseas as well as internal transfers, though it is unclear how much of the stark contrast in results, as compared to Saith, stem from inclusion of internal transfers and how much arises from differences in methodological approach (such as the basis of family income on which income class is defined). The issue is important because, as Cox and Jimenez go on to note, to the extent that private transfers decline with family income levels, any public efforts at poverty alleviation would prove less than fully effective, as remittances would tend to decline and offset the public transfers. For example, Cox and

Jimenez calculate that if sufficient poverty relief were made available to eliminate all initial poverty in the Philippines then, after private transfers adjust, about 48 percent of urban families and 94 percent of rural families would remain below the poverty line. However, Rodriguez (1998) notes that in reaching these conclusions, Cox and Jimenez define income class of the household simply based on observed incomes after omitting remittances. In other words, it is implicitly assumed that all other components of household incomes are unchanged by the fact of remittance receipts. Moreover, as Rodriguez emphasizes, this does not represent the overall effect of migration and remittances unless the migrant would have contributed nothing to household income had he or she not migrated. To adjust for this, Rodriguez compares incomes across households with and without migrants and hence simulates what the income of a comparable family with no migrant would have been.[11] Based on this procedure, Rodriguez estimates that a migrant raises average per capita household income by about 6.5 percent, compared to the projected household income had the migrant remained at home.[12] In the process, inequality of household incomes rises slightly, with the Gini of inequality rising by 1 to 2 percentage points. Nonetheless it seems unlikely that absolute poverty incidence would be increased by this slight sharpening of inequality. Given the exceedingly poor performance of the Philippine economy, and especially the lack of job creation at home, the option of migration and remittance has almost certainly been poverty alleviating, at least in the short run, though the benefits from international migration appear to have gone disproportionately to the relatively well off. On the other hand, it is plausible that over the longer run the option of emigration has postponed domestic reforms that might have led to more domestic employment creation, an issue to which we shall return.

Several studies of migration from the Gulf to Thailand in the early 1980s, cited in Tingsabadh (1989), indicate that the mean family income of migrants was above the average for Thailand at the time. However, Figure 8.2 depicts the most detailed of these studies, which reports the fraction of migrants originating from households in various income ranges, defined by household income prior to migrating.[13] According to these estimates, perhaps some 45–50 percent of migrants were from families below the poverty line prevailing at that time.

Adams and Page (2003b) note that the countries of the Middle East North Africa (MENA) region combine exceptionally low poverty levels with relatively even distributions of income. 'Two factors account for this situation: international migration/remittances and public sector (government) employment. Since the early 1980s international migration to the Persian Gulf and Europe has helped boost the incomes of the poor in the Middle East.'[14] For example, in Morocco the head count of poverty fell from 26 percent in 1984–85 to 13.1 percent in 1990–91 then rose again to 19 percent by 1998–99.[15] Here,

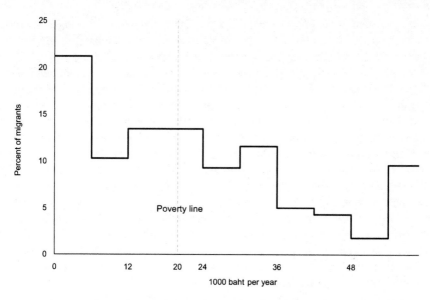

Figure 8.2   Migrants by household income before going abroad: Thailand, 1981

Adams and Page (2003b: 2037, 2040) note 'in Morocco the lack of change in the overall Gini coefficient means that falling poverty is mainly a result of the 21% increase in real mean per capita expenditures' and 'the rapid increase in remittance income coincided with substantial reductions in the poverty headcount in Morocco and Tunisia'.

In Albania 'There are some significant differences between those who want to migrate and those who actually succeed in doing so. A major difference is in wealth – either in cash or in informal social capital. Those with wealth are more likely to succeed in leaving and sending remittances home. Those without it are forced to stay at home and cope some other way. It can be expensive to migrate.'[16] Nonetheless migration from Albania has undoubtedly offered a major vehicle of poverty relief during a very painful transition, either directly or indirectly by opening opportunities for internal migration out of the deeply impoverished northern regions. 'Whether people are relatively prosperous because they migrate, or they migrate because they are relatively prosperous, the perception among Albanians is that if you migrate you have the opportunity to become more wealthy.'[17]

Poverty Reduction, Pockets of Poverty and Poverty Imposed

Whether inequality increases or diminishes with migration and remittances appears to vary across our case study countries. Davies and Wooton (1992) offer a potential explanation for the diversity of these results. In this framework, a critical distinction is made between whether skilled and unskilled workers are 'friends' or 'enemies': if friends then increasing employment of either category raises the wage of the other; if enemies then increased employment of either lowers the wage of the other. The distinction between the two arises from the technology embodied in the range of goods produced. When skilled and unskilled workers are friends, emigration of either category of labor generates greater income equality. When they are enemies, emigration of skilled workers harms unskilled workers while raising wages of remaining skilled workers and thus exacerbates inequality. Systematic testing of these ideas remains to be undertaken. Meanwhile, unraveling how much of the observed variation is attributable to the different methods and counterfactual scenarios posed, remains problematic. No doubt some of the variation is, however, quite real.[18] Yet despite the range of findings with respect to the distributional consequences, perhaps a consensus does emerge that poverty has been reduced by the migration–remittance experience in most, and possibly all, of the contexts examined.

The migration–remittance nexus may be particularly effective in addressing issues of transient poverty. First, migration may prove a viable option in the face of sudden crisis or economic downturn. Massive refugee flows have resulted from the onset of violence and associated poverty in the last two decades, though not all of these incidents have proved to be transient. Migrations, both internal and international, also resulted from the onset of the East Asia financial crisis.[19] Moreover, there is evidence that remittances move counter-cyclically, thus offering relief during recessions, perhaps motivated by altruism during times of crisis but also stimulated by exchange rate depreciation.[20] On the other hand, to the extent that remittances are indeed motivated by altruism, and hence concerns for loss of income at home, a trade-off may emerge with other private or public efforts at poverty alleviation. As public relief kicks in, remittances become less necessary and consequently diminish. Estimates of the extent of trade-off involved vary considerably from context to context, though there is a consensus that the trade-off is considerably less than 100 percent, so remittances are indeed poverty alleviating even in contexts with complementary public relief efforts.[21]

This is not to deny that pockets of poverty can prove quite resilient to substantial emigration streams. Given the key role of networks in amplifying migration, some communities, villages or specific families may well remain bystanders amidst an exodus. Cumulative inertia sets in.[22] Villages with little or no initial migration can become increasingly isolated from any direct benefits of international migration and possibly of internal migration too. For these communities, any poverty alleviation from migration must rely upon trickle-down effects, which remain poorly documented. That some communities may be bypassed is not a criticism of prevailing migration regimes, only a note that whereas migration and remittance generally contribute to poverty alleviation they are very unlikely to eradicate poverty. Migration alone will not suffice.

The departure of migrants may not only leave behind pockets of poverty but can, in principle, deepen absolute poverty. As discussed in Chapter 3, this is certainly possible in contexts where migrants possess skills that prove hard to replace and where the absence of those skills diminishes the productivity of workers remaining at home. At least within our case study areas there appears little sign of this, though the issue has certainly arisen over the last few years in South Africa.[23] However, an additional possible context in which absolute poverty may be deepened by migration remains to be noted. In particular, virtually all of the foregoing discussion has focused on poverty incidence across families, but migration can also exacerbate poverty within families.[24] The incidence of such impoverishment is particularly difficult to measure. It is clearly not sufficient to note whether families of absent migrants are poor. Ideally one needs to know the well-being, prior to migration, of those left behind. This typically requires information on the pattern of sharing within the family before the migrant left. Are the wife and children really worse off with the migrant away, or did the father simply consume most of the family's income before leaving too? Given the difficulties in measuring individuals' consumption within the family, there is a dearth of systematic testing of this potentially important issue. Nonetheless a clear potential for impoverishment exists: absence may permit or induce a family head to renege on a prior commitment to support a spouse or children at home, and the departure of children may impoverish elderly parents, where the absent children curtail their prior responsibility of support.[25]

8.2 NOTES ON SOME MAJOR SOCIAL IMPLICATIONS OF MIGRATION

These last remarks begin to hint at a range of changing attitudes and family structures that may potentially be ushered in by the migration process. The absence of family members and the exposure to new experiences abroad can reshape social developments and not merely economic development at home. Any extended discussion of the potential social implications of international migration is well beyond the scope of the present study. Yet to omit mention of some of the issues that arise would leave an imbalanced and incomplete impression of the overall consequences of migration for developments at home. A few very brief remarks on the role of a diaspora in domestic politics and in affecting security in the home country have already been offered in Chapter 6. But many other issues remain unmentioned.

A number of health related issues arise from international migration.[26] These range from concerns for the mental health of migrants, to the lack of healthcare workers as a result of their emigration, and the potential for the spread of diseases through migration. The last of these has become particularly acute with the spread of HIV-AIDS which has been clearly shown to have followed international truck routes in Africa and concern continues over the links between international mobility and transmission of HIV-AIDS.[27] By way of example of mental health issues, Addleton notes: 'Psychologists in Pakistan coined the term "Dubai Syndrome" to describe some of the costs associated with migration to the Gulf: "The syndrome is defined as a sense of disorientation resulting from the harsh working conditions, social isolation, culture shock and sudden acquisition of (relative) wealth in the UAE, which together produce psychosomatic disorders . . . The victim feels isolated and guilty for leaving his family . . . "'.[28] Although both of these issues, HIV-AIDS and psychosomatic disorders, raise very serious concerns, they are also distinct in an important respect. The 'costs' identified by Addleton in describing the psychological impacts of migration are largely borne by the migrant and his or her family. To the extent that the migrant is aware of these potential problems they may be weighed in the decision whether to risk the undertaking. HIV-AIDS is different in this respect: the costs can spread far beyond the migrants' families, raising major social concerns requiring societal and indeed multinational solutions.

Addleton's reference to family separation raises other issues besides health effects. Although international migration is most common among relatively young adults, by no means all remain single. Many, and in some contexts most, are married and have children.[29] Family accompaniment is relatively rare, except among more highly skilled migrants. In some instances, the resultant separation can be for extended periods. The average tour to the Gulf is probably four to five years and the costs of visits home are high. Irregular migrants everywhere are effectively restricted from visiting home by the costs, risks and dangers of re-entry. On the one hand, the absent spouse and parent may be a key source of additional financial resources for those left at home, provided the absentees do not fail to remit. On the other hand, such protracted separation can take its toll on family cohesion and the raising of children.

Discerning the effect of absence on family structure is very difficult. As Buric notes in an early study of international migration from Serbia, 'The divorce rate is high in migrant families, but those whose marriages were unstable to begin with were more likely to work abroad.'[30] Where migration opens new economic opportunities for women, increased financial independence may also permit them to escape a failed marriage. Indeed, as Constable (2003) describes in the context of Filipina women in Hong Kong, international migration can offer the opportunity to exit a marriage in societies that deny divorce. Thus, international migration may be associated with marital dissolution for several reasons, not merely because of the effects of extended conjugal separation.

Examining the effects of parental absence upon the education and other outcomes of child-rearing presents similar difficulties: perhaps the absent parents would have been more irresponsible in raising their children anyway, or perhaps they are absent for unobserved reasons and circumstances that also result in low attainment of the children. In fact the correlations between parental absence and attainment of children prove rather mixed, depending upon the context. For example:[31]

> In relation to children, the most glaring effect of migration has been to cause disturbance in the family's educational or child rearing functions. The presence of grandparents acts to reduce this problem; in rural environments, grandparents have been particularly important. (Buric: 1973, abstract, with reference to Serbia)

> Overall, the impression is that migration is not necessarily disruptive for the development of the children left behind, particularly if it is the mother whom remains in the home. The effect depends mostly on the extent of involvement of the extended family. (Battistella and Conaco, 1998: 220, with reference to the Philippines)

The mixed effects ought not to be too surprising. On the one hand, remittances from the absent migrant may help to finance continued schooling. For instance, the preliminary results from an on-going study in the Philippines indicate that more children from migrant families, than from other families, are enrolled in private schools.[32] Similarly, Yang (2004) finds that both Filipino boys and girls, ages 10–17, in families hurt by a negative exchange rate shock to migrant members abroad during the 1998 financial crisis, became significantly less likely to attend school. On the other hand, the lack of parental supervision and influence may affect performance at school; extended family members may not fill the role of the absent parent adequately. Indeed, in Pakistan during the 1970s and 1980s, 'as many as a million wives were separated from their husbands for long periods of time. Many more children were growing up without fathers present in the households. Although extended family systems sometimes helped cushion families against some of the more adverse effects of migration, they could not postpone the impact of rapid change forever. In some cases at least, extended families themselves became the casualties of change.'[33]

One of the more important elements of change in global migration has been the growing mobility of women, both in the context of family migration and alone.[34] The effects that this has had on the empowerment or disempowerment of women remains poorly understood. Thus Hugo (2000: 287) 'pointed to the general neglect of women's empowerment issues in demographic research and this is nowhere more evident than in research into migration'. This neglect is a pity. Indeed, both the increasing migration of women and the migration of men may play a part in women's empowerment. The absence of men abroad can leave job openings that present new, empowering opportunities for women, or simply create a power vacuum that might, in principle, be occupied by the women who remain at home. Yet such shifts in power may be rare. King *et al.* (2003: 4) report that despite the massive recent male migration from Albania, control remains firmly male dominated: 'Although migration and remittances were not found to be reshaping patriarchal gender relations, they were, in some cases, changing generational relationships, with decision-making on the use of the remitted capital passing from the male family elders to the migrant sons.' As De Soto *et al.* (2002: 46) add on the Albanian case: 'Households without men are perceived to be vulnerable and have fewer members to do the same amount of work ... women are feeling much greater psychological stress, in part due to the migration of men in their household.'

Perhaps where women migrate for work the balance of control over family spending may be more greatly affected, which suggests an interesting line of research yet to be systematically explored, examining the effects on consumption and investment patterns of the family in relation to the portion of remittances originating from female migrants. Indeed, overseas women workers are often the dominant earners in the family. Yet, as Hugo points out, not all overseas experiences of women are empowering:

> There can be no doubt that, while migration often results in women gaining a range of new freedoms, in some cases the opposite can occur ... Disempowerment is especially prevalent when women move as undocumented migrants so that recruiters and employers hold power over them ... The growing practice of trafficking in women migrants ... results in violation of their human rights ... Migrant women are frequently in vulnerable situations which result in disempowerment.[35]

Perhaps, in the end, one of the most powerful effects of international migration arises, however, through changing attitudes more generally. The effects are mixed.[36] For women migrants, a sojourn overseas means exposure to new cultures and life-styles, which may result in new freedoms being asserted. Yet among male migrants from Pakistan, Addleton (1992: 155, 158) notes, 'For some, migration strengthened family ties and traditional ways of thinking. For others the migration experience led to a complete break with the past ... Attitudes toward religion are also suggestive of the more complex conflicts engendered by the migration experience.' Many observers attribute the rise in fundamentalism at least partially to expanded migration.[37] Addleton argues that the changes brought about by the mass migrations to the Gulf undermined the center in Pakistan. Rising fundamentalism is having more global impacts and may ultimately reshape international migration.

NOTES

1. See, for example, Ravallion (2001) and the review of evidence in Lucas and Salem (2002).

2. Mahmud (1989: 79).

3. Mahmud (1989: 79).

4. Nair (1998: 260).

5. Data on state-wide net domestic product are from the Reserve Bank of India at http://www.rbi.org.in/ and refer to 1999–2000, though the Reserve Bank notes that data are strictly comparable across states. Population data are from the 2001 census at http://www.censusindia.net/. Goa is not shown in Figure 8.1 given that net domestic product is not available for 1999–2000, however, by 1997–98 Goa had by far the highest income of any state.

6. Deaton, Angus S. and Alessandro Tarozzi (2000), 'Prices and Poverty in India', Princeton: Research Program in Development Studies, Princeton University, at http://www.wws.princeton.edu/%7Edeaton/papers.html. This estimate is based on a detailed regional analysis of poverty in India, derived from the 1999–2000 National Sample Survey, by Kijima and Lanjouw (2003). In particular, the figures in the text refer to the estimates in the Appendix and exclude Goa. The head count ratio is based on a poverty line developed by Deaton and Tarozzi.

7. Azam (1991: 56).

8. Moreover the *Pakistan Economic Survey* reports that an unskilled laborer in construction in Lahore earned about Rs39 per day in 1986 and gross national income per capita was Rs5585 per year.

9. See the discussion in Chapter 5.

10. See Chapter 3.

11. Rodriguez (1998) notes a number of difficulties in making such adjustments, including the fact that the decision to migrate may well be correlated with unobserved features of the household, biasing the results.

12. Though note that this includes only the migrants' remittance in the former and their full earnings, in principle, in the latter. Barnham and Boucher (1998: abstract) explore an alternative approach, in which 'Potential home earnings of migrants are imputed, as are the earnings of non-migrants in migration households, in order to construct no-migration counterfactuals.' In the context of Bluefields, Nicaragua, Barnham and Boucher find that migration combined with remittances exacerbate inequality adopting this method.

13. Data are from the original study in Peerathep (1982) and the discussion of this in Tingsabadh (1989). I am most grateful for personal correspondence with Professor Tingsabadh clarifying some issues with respect to these data.

14. Adams and Page (2003b: 2027). Adams and Page support their argument with a regression analysis of poverty levels, around 1990, among fifty developing and transition economies. They note that given GDP per capita and income inequality (as represented by a Gini coefficient) poverty levels are lower where remittances received are greater relative to GDP. Given these controls, poverty levels are significantly lower in the MENA countries than in the remaining developing countries. Moreover, the negative association between poverty levels and remittances is even greater in the MENA region than elsewhere. (See Chapter 5 for a discussion of some of the issues that arise in interpreting these results, in commenting on the closely related work in Adams and Page, 2003a.)

15. Adams and Page (2003b).

16. De Soto *et al.* (2002: 42).

17. De Soto *et al.* (2002: 46).

18. For a general review see Skeldon (2003).

19. See Fallon and Lucas (2002) and Chapter 7.

20. See Ratha (2003).

21. The principle, known as Riccardian equivalence in economic theory, suggests that private and public transfers may fully offset one another. The evidence, at least from the developing and transition economies, suggests otherwise. See Cox and Jimenez (1990, 1992, 1995), Cox *et al.* (1997) and Taylor (2000).

22. On cumulative inertia see Chapter 2. See also Hulme *et al.* (2001) and Kothari (2002) on the exclusion of the extremely poor.

23. See, for instance, Kirov (1999).

24. See Bryceson (2000) and Kothari (2002).

25. See, for example, the evidence in Schrieder and Knerr (2000) on Cameroon.

26. The Migration Health website of IOM at http://www.iom.ch/en/who/main_service_areas_migration.shtml provides comprehensive coverage.

27. See the proceedings of the Fifteenth International Aids Conference, Bangkok, July 11–16, 2004. For references and discussion on the emigration of healthcare workers, see also Chapter 4.

28. Addleton (1992: 156). The quote by Addleton is from Ahmed (1984). Addleton also cites similar accounts from Kerala.

29. See, for example, Rodrigo and Jayatissa (1989) and Samarasinghe (1998) on Sri Lanka; Azam (1991) on Pakistan.

30. Buric (1973: abstract).

31. See also, amongst others: on El Salvador, Edwards and Ureta (2003) on India, Bharat (1986) on Indonesia, Hugo (2002c) and on Pakistan, Addleton (1992: chapter 9).

32. I am extremely grateful to Dr Maria Asis for a personal communication sharing these preliminary results from the study, conducted by the Scalabrini Migration Center, of 1443 children ages 10–12.

33. Addleton (1992:156).

34. See Zlotnik (2003).

35. Hugo (2000: 302–3). See also the series of discussion papers prepared for the Consultative Meeting on Migration and Mobility and How this Movement Affects Women, Malmo, Sweden, December 2–4, 2003 at http://www.un.org/womenwatch/daw/meetings/consult/Sweden03.htm.

36. In a study comparing attitudes toward the status of women in Turkey, Day and Içduygu (1997: 343) find that 'Returned migrants tend to be concentrated at the more "progressive", less "traditional" end of the spectrum.' Close kin and friends of migrants were ranked next most progressive and 'all others' in the control group ranked most traditional. However, Day and Içduygu also argue that these differences more closely reflect selectivity in recruitment for work abroad than any socialization effects from the migration experience.

37. Keddie (1998).

PART C

Conclusions: Policy Choices and the Political
Economy of Migration Regimes

9. Who Benefits from International Migration? Beyond Economic Development at Origin

To begin to understand the political economy of international migration regimes it is first essential to weigh who is likely to gain and who loses in the process. In doing so, it is necessary now to go beyond the issues of economic development within the countries of migrants' origins, which have been the subject of Part B. Many of the policy decisions that ultimately shape the nature of international migration lie in the hands of the countries of immigration and it is time to incorporate consideration of the winners and losers from immigration too. Section 9.2 of this chapter addresses these issues. However, in outlining the impacts of migration upon economic development at origin in the foregoing chapters, little attention has been directed to the presumed gains for the migrants themselves. This is redressed in Section 9.1 and, in particular, attention is directed to the fees imposed by middlemen.

9.1 CONSTRAINED MIGRATION: WHO EXTRACTS THE RENTS?

Among the many groups who may be helped or hurt by the migration process, the migrants themselves presumably do gain. For many, and perhaps most migrants this also means that their average earnings or incomes are raised by migration, though a number of caveats may be noted with respect to this: where the major motive for migration is to escape violence the migrant may well be leaving behind a better livelihood; the migrant may have anticipated higher incomes which fail to materialize; risk-averse migrants may well choose to move to a setting with lower average but less risky pay; where the migration decision is taken by the family, the individual migrant may encounter a lower standard of living, no matter whether this occurs in the context of accompanying a spouse overseas or of a younger generation dispatched abroad by parents. These caveats notwithstanding, in a broad sense migrants or their families clearly believe they will gain from migration (with the clear exception of trafficking and contemporary slavery), and for many this embodies a gain in average incomes.

In simulating the global impacts from a small increment to temporary migration, Walmsley and Winters (2003) find huge gains to the migrants themselves (both from developed and developing regions) driven almost entirely by the massive prevailing and sustained wage gaps between countries. Freeman and Oostendorp (2000) undertake a particularly careful analysis of these wage gaps, comparing pay within occupations across 150 countries from 1983 to 1998. Even after adjusting these wages for differences in the cost of living across countries, Freeman and Oostendorp (2000: 16) confirm that 'there remains huge cross country variation in the payment to workers in the same occupation'. For instance, the median wage in the high income countries is estimated to be 4.8 times higher, and that in the upper middle income countries 2.1 times higher, than the median wage in the low income countries, within the same occupations.[1] The extent of gap in pay actually received by migrants is less clear. At least in the US, migrants initially earn less than natives of similar age, gender and with similar amounts (if not quality) of education, though any pay disadvantage appears to have been eliminated within ten years.[2] Irregular migrants probably earn less still than comparable documented migrants. Moreover, in some contexts, wages appear to differ quite substantially by country of origin. For example, Shah (1998b) estimates that the average pay of unskilled, male migrants in the Jaleeb Al-Shayookh district of Kuwait in 1995, ranged from 48 Kuwaiti dinars among Bangladeshi and Sri Lankan workers to 92.9 for Pakistanis and 101.5 for Indians.[3]

Suffice to say that the premium earned by overseas migrants from the developing countries is typically very large and in many instances extends to wages being several times greater than at home.[4] In effect, however, access to these lucrative posts is rationed and, as always, rationing leads to facilitating payments: migrants must incur not only the dislocation of leaving home and often family too, but also significant financial outlays. In particular, three classes of costs may be distinguished here: the costs of obtaining legal entry, the costs of irregular entry, and the costs of remitting to home.

Given the attempts to limit entry, the lack of inter-state arrangements for the recruitment of temporary workers, and the general difficulties in obtaining information about openings overseas, labor migration has become increasingly commercialized in the hands of private recruiters.

> Private firms serving as recruitment intermediaries today account for 80 to 90 percent of labour migration flows ... from Asian countries. They probably account for a significant share of migration flows in other regions as well, but the documentation of this phenomenon is generally poor so that it is not possible to say with confidence how global it has become ... The market for recruitment services has grown especially in the more technologically advanced economies where the

labour requirements of industries are more complex. In the United Kingdom, for example, the number of agencies engaged in placement services rose from 5,000 at the beginning of the 1980s to 13,500 at the beginning of the 1990s.[5]

Frequently these arrangements involve more than one agency; private recruitment companies in the sending countries link up with job brokers in the destination countries. Together, these private services have been quite instrumental in the overall expansion of temporary labor migration flows. Fees are charged to the employer, the recruited worker, or both. However, in the face of an excess supply of migrants wishing to move it seems likely that most of the incidence of these fees falls on the migrants (either directly or in the form of lower wages) no matter who actually pays the fees. A number of countries, notably in Europe and the UAE, have prohibited agencies from charging fees to workers but this proves almost impossible to enforce: the demands for the services of private recruiters are simply too great. 'Alternatives to fee-charging job intermediaries are unfortunately not very attractive. Public employment offices are generally far less effective in finding job offers abroad than their private counterparts, hence most job-seekers tend to go to private intermediaries despite the risk of fraud and the very high fees that they normally charge.'[6]

Data on these charges are scant, though a few indications exist within our case study areas. Figure 9.1 shows the major components of the cost of going

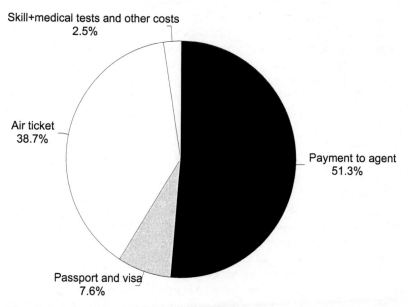

Figure 9.1   Components of costs of going abroad: Thailand, 1984

abroad as reported by the Thailand Department of Labor for 1984.[7] The total cost estimated at that time was 43 518 baht, as compared to an estimated annual income of migrants' households before going abroad of 43 043 baht in a 1986 study.[8] As Figure 9.1 shows, the agents' fees amounted to slightly more than half of this cost, or approximately a half year's worth of family income prior to migrating. Stern (1998) reports that by 1996, agencies were demanding 200 000 to 250 000 baht simply as an advance payment for recruitment to Japan from Thailand and about half this for Taiwan, when the average monthly wage in urban private industry was 6156 baht.[9] In 1998, Zachariah *et al.* (1999: 11) estimate 'An average emigrant from Kerala spent Rs 44 000 for going abroad.' In 1997–98 the average daily wage for a man in paddy farming in Kerala was about 104 rupees and 150 rupees for an urban, first class carpenter. No clear breakdown of this total emigration cost is available in the case of Kerala, though Zachariah *et al.* (1999) do note that among those who paid an agent's commission the average charge was 14 000 rupees (though this is less than half of the amount reported paid in visa fees among those reporting visa costs).

Table 9.1 shows estimates of the costs of obtaining visas to work in Kuwait, as reported in Shah (1998b) from a survey of 800 male workers in the Jaleeb Al-Shayookh district of Kuwait in 1995. Among those who paid for a visa the average reported prices were high, ranging from US$654 for an unskilled worker from Sri Lanka to US$1733 for unskilled workers from Bangladesh. Averaging across those who paid and those who did not, the typical payment for an unskilled worker from Bangladesh amounted to 81 percent of an annual salary in Kuwait. At the opposite extreme, the cost of a visa for a skilled Indian worker amounted to less than 4 percent of his salary. Figure 9.2 shows these same data, displaying the average cost of obtaining a visa by the source of that visa and country of origin.[10] The three sources refer to private recruiting agents, visas obtained directly from employers and government bureaus, and visas obtained through friends and relatives. Extremely few visas were in fact reported obtained through government bureaus. Across the four countries, on average, a visa obtained directly from the employer costs the worker about US$632 less, and a visa obtained through friends and relatives about US$168 less, than if the visa is obtained through a private recruiting agency.[11] On the other hand, given the source of visa, the costs of obtaining a visa are highest from Bangladesh, followed by Pakistan, with costs from India and Sri Lanka significantly lower than both. In other words, the poorer the country, the higher the recruitment cost, which is quite consistent with Abella's (1997) characterization of recruitment costs determined by the gap in pay available and the length of the queue of potential workers waiting for the chance to migrate. That these high fees are not competed away by other recruiting agencies seems to reflect a distinct lack of competition in the recruiting sector, with barriers to entry perhaps

Table 9.1 Visa costs in Kuwait by country of origin, 1995

	Country of origin							
	Bangladesh		India		Pakistan		Sri Lanka	
	Unskilled	Skilled	Unskilled	Skilled	Unskilled	Skilled	Unskilled	Skilled
Paid for visa (%)	92.0	72.0	36.0	19.0	87.0	76.0	92.0	88.0
Visa cost if paid (US$)	1733.0	1617.0	1116.0	1292.0	1294.0	1036.0	654.0	671.0
Monthly salary (K. dinar)	48.7	100.0	101.5	166.9	92.9	159.4	48.2	79.7
Visa cost/annual pay (%)	81.4	29.0	9.8	3.7	30.1	12.3	31.0	18.4

Source: Shah (1998b: Tables 2.4, 2.5 and 2.8).

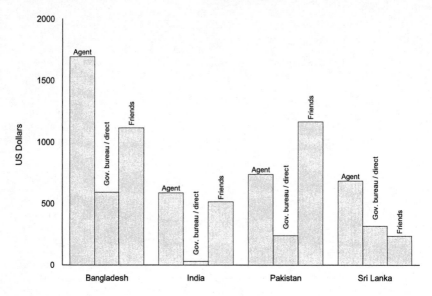

Figure 9.2   Cost of visas reported by South Asian male migrants in Kuwait by source of visa and country of origin, 1995

partially enforced by the importance of reputation among job brokers in the labor-receiving countries.

Commercialization of documented labor migration has grown and the fees associated with this are high and, in the face of excess supply of migrant labor, those costs are borne almost entirely by the migrants themselves. An alternative is to bypass the legal channels of migration and attempt undocumented entry. However, this route is far from free either. Beyond the personal risks of arrest, injury or even fatality involved in border crossings, and indeed partly because of these risks, irregular migration has also become highly commercialized with 'an emerging pattern of increasing professionalization'.[12] Indeed, 'There is evidence to suggest that traffickers and smugglers are behind a substantial proportion of irregular migration, though how much can at best only be guessed.'[13]

> These 'migration merchants' ... range from legal travel agencies to sophisticated transnational human smuggling rings operating in half a dozen countries ... Today, even modest 'mom and pop' smuggling operations operating in remote areas of the world have the resources to get an unauthorized migrant across the US border, often by contracting out some of the more complicated activities to larger transnational rings.[14]

As Salt and Stein (1997) note, these smuggling operations may be character-

ized as a market, along similar lines to that depicted by Abella (1997) for
legal recruiting, with a price driven partly by the potential gains, either to
smuggled aliens who willingly participate, or to merchants in the case of
trafficking. Naturally, any information about these costs is very piecemeal,
but Salt (2001) summarizes some of the amounts reported incurred in being
smuggled into Europe and into North America.[15] Figure 9.3 shows these fees
paid to smugglers against GDP per capita in 2000, for various countries of
origin.[16] The fees paid for entry to North America tend to be greater than fees
for entry to Europe and both decline significantly with higher income levels
in the country of origin.[17] In other words, despite the obvious limitations of
these measures, they again suggest a scenario in which smugglers are able to
charge higher fees where the gap in potential earnings is greater.

No matter whether a recruiter or smuggler is paid, the fixed costs of initial
entry are very high, amounting to several months or even more than a year
of potential earnings at destination.[18] To the extent that these are payments
to nationals of the country of origin they represent within country transfers,
albeit probably very regressive ones, though no doubt a significant portion
of the payments also winds up going to foreigners. The fixed cost nature
of these fees also obviously discourages rapid return; given that the cost is
incurred the migrant must typically remain sufficiently long to repay the debt
and back and forth movement is effectively ruled out when each cost of entry
is exorbitant.

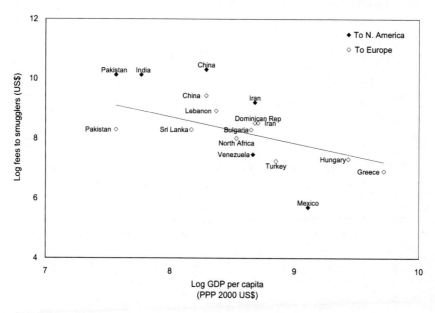

Figure 9.3   Fees paid to smugglers: entry to Europe and North America

The high fees required to send remittances impose another form of substantial taxation upon migrants' gains. IADB (2004) notes that in the Latin America and Caribbean (LAC) region, most remittances went through informal channels as late as 1990. Since then, more formal channels have evolved and the costs of transmitting through these formal channels have declined somewhat. For instance, the IADB (2004: 12) estimates that 'Before 2000, the average cost of sending remittances to LAC was about 15% of the value of the transaction.' However, by February 2004, IADB estimates that 7.9 percent of an average US$200 remittance to Latin America and the Caribbean went in transfer fees. However, these fees ranged from less than 5.5 percent in the case of Ecuador to just over 12 percent to Cuba with fees showing a weak negative association with income levels across countries in the region. On average, fees remain 'astronomical in comparison with the costs of bank transfers among industrial countries'[19] and perhaps especially so in the lower income countries where bank competition remains weak. In consequence, remitting migrants clearly prefer the cheaper, informal banking system though the future prospects for this informal sector are unclear as discussed in Chapter 5.

The combined fees extracted from migrants by various agents clearly can be very substantial. These fees also vary a great deal though there are indications that each component tends to impose a higher cost on migrants from lower income countries, even in absolute terms. For migrants from lower income countries, the overall effect is a very significant drain upon their net gains. For instance, if an unskilled worker pays 80 percent of his first year income to recruiting agents (see Table 9.1), goes to the Gulf for four years, remits half of his earnings and pays 15 percent commission on his remittances, this would amount to an average tax of 27.5 percent. This is a significant imposition, though probably far above the median rate. Despite the exorbitant fees that prevail it remains clear that most migrants indeed gain and gain, a good deal.

9.2   WINNERS AND LOSERS: DESTINATION COUNTRY PERSPECTIVES

At least to some extent, the attitudes of natives to the arrival of fresh migrants are shaped by the perceived consequences for incomes of the prior residents. Two components attract most attention. The first is the impact that migrants may have on wages or employment levels of prior residents, and hence also on profits accruing to business owners. The second group of concerns revolves around the fiscal implications of immigration.

Labor Market Effects of Immigration

The theory of labor market reactions to immigration is well developed but essentially mirrors the case of emigration already sketched in Chapter 3 and does not bear much repetition here. Suffice to say that immigration is generally hypothesized to reduce demand for comparable native workers, resulting in either diminished wages or employment levels for these competing workers. For other types of workers and business owners the effects are ambiguous. For those who benefit from enhanced pay, immigrants are commonly termed 'friends' in this literature; for those who are hurt, immigrants are termed 'enemies'. The 'standard' theory shows that every factor has at least one 'friend', such that some prior residents always gain from immigration.[20] Any additional employment resulting from immigration obviously expands total output while tending to lower pay of directly competing workers. The result is a net gain for the remaining income recipients already in the country: some gain and some lose (particularly directly competing workers) but on average there is a gain. Where the number of people affected by lower wages as a result of the immigration is large relative to the number of migrants, 'income transfers from immigration exceed the net welfare gains. This result explains why distributional effects are at the center of policy debates over immigration controls.'[21]

These distributional effects and the consequent different political positions were well illustrated in the *New York Times* coverage of President Bush's recommendation of a new guest worker program which would regularize and admit largely unskilled workers on a temporary basis.

> 'The president's proposal will help big corporations who currently employ undocumented workers' Howard Dean, the Democratic presidential hopeful, said in a statement ... John J. Sweeney, president of the A.F.L.-C.I.O., said the plan deepened 'the potential for abuse and exploitation of these workers while undermining wages and labor protections for all workers.' The view that the proposal would hurt American workers was shared by one of the leading groups that want to keep strict limits on immigration, the Federation for American Immigration Reform ... Business groups said the plan would help the economy by ensuring employers access to needed workers ... Immigrants are Divided on Bush Proposal.[22]

Given that some groups gain while others lose, immigration may not be supported politically despite net overall economic gains. This may occur because groups that are hurt possess disproportionate political power, or because groups who in fact would gain are uncertain of this advantage, or simply because the majority feel they would lose despite substantial gains for a small minority.[23]

The economic theory of who gains and who loses, of who is likely to support and oppose immigration on economic grounds, is then well developed. But what does the evidence actually show with respect to the impact of immigration on host country labor markets? This has been the subject of a very extensive, and on-going literature over the last couple of decades.[24] Most of these contributions rely upon the geographical variation within the host country in concentration and composition of the immigrant population to explore the impact of immigration on local wages. The earlier studies tended to rely simply upon the cross-sectional variations in the concentration of migrants, asking whether wages are lower in cities or areas with more immigrants. These studies are subject to an obvious flaw that immigrants' selection of location is likely to be determined partly by local labor market conditions. In response, three major approaches have been taken. The first looks at substitution between natives and immigrants, while a second approach examines changes in wages of original residents, in both cases studying effects within a specific city or region, over time, as the number of immigrants varies.[25] However, both of these first two approaches are subject to a common problem: where internal out-migration accompanies the local arrival of immigrants, the effect of immigration upon the labor market is likely to be diffused beyond the specific location.[26] The third approach is to represent immigrants' choices of location more explicitly as part of the analysis.[27]

Despite these methodological differences, a remarkable uniformity emerges among the several surveys of this literature.

> the American labor market adjusted well to immigration flows, absorbing immigrants into local area work forces with little redistributive losses to natives. (Abowd and Freeman, 1991: 20)

> Despite the popular belief that immigrants have a large adverse impact on the wages and employment opportunities of the native-born population, the literature on this question does not provide much support for this conclusion. (Friedberg and Hunt, 1995: 42)

> most studies in the literature find only small effects of immigration on labor market outcomes of natives. (Lalonde and Topel, 1997: 826)

Most of this literature examines impacts on the US labor market. In Europe, labor markets tend to be less flexible, so any effects of immigration on labor market outcomes for prior residents are more likely to impact employment levels rather than wages. However, in Europe also the conclusion appears to be that any effects have been minimal. For example, based on their study of employment effects of immigration to Germany during 1985–89, Pischke and Velling (1997: 594) conclude, 'Our results indicate no detrimental effects of immigration.' Similarly, summarizing a study of the APEC region, Lloyd and Williams (1996: 8) note 'As is the case in the majority of analyses of the economic effects of immigration ... that while any effects on income depend both on the characteristics of the country and the characteristics of the immigrants, such effects are likely to be small at the aggregate level'.

Fiscal Effects of Immigration

The potential contribution of immigrants to the fiscal balance of their host country has attracted increasing attention in recent years, in view of population ageing in the OECD countries and the consequent pending social security crises. Naturally, whether and how much migrants contribute net to the fiscal coffers of their hosts depends very much upon the composition of migration. Uniform answers should not be expected.

On the tax side, the contribution of immigrants obviously depends upon income and hence the correlates of income, such as the migrant's age and education. In addition, however, tax collection is no doubt lower from irregular migrants than from comparable documented migrants, while some countries impose only a basic tax on very short-term migrants. On the expenditure side, much depends upon whether working migrants are accompanied by family since most (though not all) countries confine benefits to dependants present in the host country. Whether migrants return home for retirement matters too, as does the life expectancy of migrants if they remain in the country of immigration.

Empirical examination of the net fiscal contribution of immigrants has become increasingly complex, moving from static snapshots of whether migrants pay more taxes than they receive in benefits at any moment in time, to longer-term perspectives embracing migrants' descendants and attempted simulation of the effects of immigration on the wider economy. The literature is now very extensive, encompassing a wide range of higher income countries.[28] Not surprisingly, the results vary a good deal, not only from country to country but also according to the precise approaches taken. Nonetheless it is probably fair to say that most agree that immigration, even along current lines, can contribute to fiscal alleviation of the pending social security problems. Within this, results on whether less skilled migrants prove net fiscal contributors prove mixed. Thus, Lee and Miller (2000: 353) writing on the US case, note that the higher fertility levels of immigrants mean that even immigration of less skilled migrants 'temporarily eases the projected fiscal burden of the retiring baby boomers in a few decades'. On the other hand, Wadensjö (2000) finds a contrast between Danish immigrants from 'western' and 'non-western' countries in this respect; the second generation among the latter group continues to be a net fiscal drain according to this study, so that any higher fertility presumably detracts from alleviation. In Germany,

the overall net payments of foreigners aged between 10 and 45 are on average 25% lower than those of natives of identical age. In the last three decades of their life, net receipts of foreigners are approximately 40% lower as compared to those of Germans. The differences in average life-cycle tax payments between German natives and foreigners can be attributed to a number of reasons. On average, the foreigners presently living in Germany are less qualified and work in less qualified jobs with lower average earnings than natives. Foreigners exhibit a higher savings rate and frequently avoid early retirement to complete the minimum contribution period required to become eligible for social security benefits.[29]

Certainly there is widespread agreement that highly educated migrants generally contribute more to the fiscal balance, even taking into account the dynamic effects of their dependants. Indeed, a few studies indicate that highly targeted immigration, focusing on the highly skilled of prime working age, could completely eliminate the projected social security crisis though other observers disagree with this position (not to mention whether such targeting is truly feasible). More generally, 'Perhaps the most important conclusion, on which most analysts agree, is that the overall fiscal consequences of altering the volume of immigration would be quite small and should not be a major consideration for policy.'[30]

Summing Up: The Political Economy and Politics of Immigration

Although attitudes of natives to the arrival of fresh migrants may be partially shaped by consequences for their incomes, the empirical evidence suggests this is more a matter of perception than fact. Although economic theory for the most part predicts net economic gains to prior residents, though with much larger redistribution effects among these residents, the wage effects on which these predictions are founded have proved difficult to isolate: the effects of immigration on wages and employment of prior residents appear to be small. The considerable recent attention to the potential for immigration to resolve the pending social security crisis indicates relatively small, but generally positive, fiscal impacts of immigration.

To some extent the contrast between political perception and the economic evidence may reflect differences in time horizons. The investigation of fiscal effects has become very far sighted: 'Although the future is highly uncertain, it is clear that the consequences of immigration can be assessed only over very long time horizons. Some U.S.-born children of immigrants arriving today will still be alive 130 years from now.'[31] Whereas this may be clear analytically, voters' opinions may be shaped by far more myopic considerations. Similarly, and indeed rather remarkably, almost all of the economic theory of the gains and distributional effects of immigration is derived in the context of a long-run model, with or without international trade: the short-run framework, in which workers and business owners care far more about the specific sector in which they make an income, has been relatively neglected. In practice, lobbying by business very much reflects the short-term concerns of entrepreneurs to access cheap, sometimes qualified, labor for their particular sector; unions care about the position of their own members rather than about 'labor' in more nebulous terms.

Nonetheless, we cannot escape the fact that the evidence generally indicates small wage and employment effects and small, possibly mixed, fiscal effects even in the shorter term. Either our evidence is wrong or political opposition to immigration is not ultimately founded on economic grounds, but out of concerns to preserve some sense of national, ethnic or racial identity. In turn, the latter raises the gamut of questions about multi-culturalism versus social assimilation in shaping tolerance toward immigrant communities and in the enrichment of local cultures.

NOTES

1. See Freeman and Oostendorp (2000: Figure 4).
2. See the surveys by Borjas (1994) and by Lalonde and Topel (1997).
3. Such wide disparities in pay would suggest three possibilities: that there really are skill differences across communities, that a strong preference exists for men of particular nationalities, or that the market is somehow segmented and rationed even among Kuwaiti employers.
4. See, for instance, the references in Chapter 2, Section 2.3.
5. Abella (1997; 1, 2). See also, ILO (1997: chapter 5). The South African mining industry has experienced a century of recruiting through such licensed agencies, the largest of which changed names a number of times but in latter days became known as the Employment Bureau of Africa. See Lucas (1985).
6. Abella (1997: 2). De Soto *et al.* (2002: 40) recount the experiences of one Albanian migrant: 'When we decide to leave, we form a group of three to six persons. Last time, we were caught in the vicinity of the village where we were going to work. We were beaten badly. To travel from here to Greece, you have to pay L 12 000. Besides, you must have some additional money to afford food expenditures.' As of 2000, 12 000 Lek was about US$85 at the official rate.
7. Tingsabadh (1989: Table 10.8).
8. The study is by Sumalee and cited in Tingsabadh (1989).
9. Source for the data on wages is Chalamwong (2002).
10. The source of data for Figure 9.2 is Shah (1998b: Tables 2.3 and 2.5). In particular, the average amount reported spent on obtaining visas in Table 2.5 is adjusted for the proportion of people paying for visas according to Table 2.3.
11. The first difference is statistically significant; the second difference is not. These results refer to a regression analysis of the costs as depicted in Figure 9.2 on dummy variables representing the four countries and dummies for the three visa sources.
12. Susan Martin (2000: 1).
13. Salt (2001: 24).
14. Kyle and Liang (2001: 4).
15. These measures, which are typically based on reported experiences of a few individuals, are reproduced in IOM (2003a: Table 17.21). 'Smuggling fees may also be determined

by the level of auxiliary services provided by the trafficker, such as fake identification documents, job brokering, visas, etc.'

16. Where a range of costs is indicated, the midpoint is shown in Figure 9.3. For the North Africa region, GDP refers to a simple average for Algeria, Morocco and Tunisia.

17. An ordinary least squares regression with the logarithm of smuggling costs as dependent variable generates:

$$15.78 - 0.88 \text{ LY} + 14.76 \text{ NA} - 1.72 \text{ LY*NA}$$

$$(4.65) \quad (2.31) \quad\quad (1.83) \quad\quad (1.76) \quad\quad\quad\quad \text{No. obs} = 17: \text{Adj.R sq.} = 0.58$$

where LY indicates natural logarithm of GDP per capita at origin and *NA* is a dummy variable representing entry to North America as opposed to Europe. T-statistics are shown in parentheses and standard errors are heteroskedasticity robust. The regression line shown in Figure 9.3 refers to the coefficient on LY for Europe.

18. The fees paid to smugglers for entry to the US or Canada from China, India and Pakistan are reported to exceed US$25 000.

19. Ratha (2003: 165). See also the report by Bair (2003) on Latin American remittances and access to the banking system.

20. See the survey of this literature in Ruffin (1984: 262–3) for sufficient conditions for this property to hold. There are competing hypotheses. For instance, Lundborg and Segerstrom (2002) develop a theoretical model in which technology in the 'North' is driven in part by migration from the 'South'. Migration not only lowers wages of competing workers in the North, but increases competition among technologies and hence diminishes rents accruing from these technologies. It is then possible, though not certain, that all prior residents in the 'North' lose.

21. Lalonde and Topel (1997: 818).

22. *New York Times*, Thursday, 8 January 2004, pp. A20–A21.

23. On the last of these see Benhabib (1996).

24. For a recent reexamination see Borjas (2003).

25. See, for example, Lalonde and Topel (1991) and Goldin (1994).

26. Filer (1992).

27. This last approach thus uses instrumental variables to represent these choices, though the selection of appropriate instruments is, as always, difficult. For an early application, see Altonji and Card (1991).

28. Amongst others see: on Austria (Keuschnigg *et al.* 1999); Denmark (Wadensjö, 2000); Germany (Bonin *et al.* 1999 and 2003); Spain (Collado *et al.* 2002); Sweden, Ekberg (1999); US, Auerbach and Oreopolis (2000), Lee and Miller (2000) and Storesletten (2000); US, Japan and EU, Fehr *et al.* (2004).

29. Bonin *et al.* (1999: 84–5).

30. Lee and Miller (2000: 353).

31. Lee and Miller (2000: 353).

10. Migration Regimes and Economic Development: Policy Implications

Policy options open both to lower income, migrant-sending countries and to higher income countries can reshape migration streams. The options are, however, quite distinct in the two sets of nations and are considered separately here. Although there is considerable room, and perhaps need, also for bilateral and multilateral accords in this nexus, it is the policies adopted by the individual nations, and the interactions between these chosen strategies, that carry most force in shaping both migration outcomes and their development consequences.

10.1 DEVELOPMENT AND MIGRATION: POLICIES IN THE COUNTRIES OF ORIGIN

Most international migrants would prefer to stay at home if only jobs were available and personal safety secured. In the end, this preference is probably the major reason why more people do not move, despite huge income gaps between home and potential destination areas. In this sense, mass out-migration is, to a substantial extent, a reflection of the failure of migrants' home countries to create jobs and to prevent violence. The lack of peace may well stem from the instability or aggression of neighboring countries rather than from home itself. On the other hand, pursuing a development strategy that creates jobs and raises the demands on domestic labor is often far more firmly within the terrain of the home country's policy makers.

As late as the end of the 1980s, the Washington Consensus was that a lack of appropriate job creation in the developing countries simply arose from badly designed trade protection within those countries. In this view, all one needed to do was to 'get prices right' and development with job creation would ensue. The experiences of the 1990s, with the painful outcomes in some of the transition economies in particular, but also the series of financial crises in East Asia, several countries in Latin America and in Turkey, substantively qualified this view. Although trade reform is still generally seen as a key and often necessary component of reform for economic development, trade reform alone rarely suffices. Macroeconomic stability, public support for basic education and healthcare, reform and regulation of the financial system, establishing transparency in the legal and regulatory systems, perhaps privatization, and the ability to constrain crime and maintain peace, now figure prominently on the list. The complexity of this agenda poses a major challenge to the governments of many of the lower income countries. Some are succeeding, some far less so.

For a number of the major migrant source countries within our four case study areas, lack of wage and employment growth remain, or indeed have become, a problem: this is clearly true, for instance, of Bangladesh, Sri Lanka and the Philippines, Algeria and Morocco, Albania and Moldova.[1] Others have begun to grow more rapidly and a number of these have made the transition to become major migrant destinations themselves. These include the newly industrialized economies of East Asia (Brunei, Hong Kong, Korea, Malaysia, Singapore, Taiwan) but also the countries of Southern Europe (Greece, Italy, Spain, Portugal). Within the last 30–40 years many of these countries were significant sources of out-migration but a transition has occurred. Still other countries remain at the margin of any such transition. Thailand is both a major host to Burmese migrants and an important source of migrant labor, largely to the higher income countries of the region. From India, migration to the Gulf and to North America has continued to grow rapidly, even as the economy has begun to grow more significantly. But, at the same time, migration into India from Bangladesh and other neighboring countries is also massive. Relative to Bangladesh, incomes in India are high. Yet, how much widespread employment and consumption growth has been enjoyed in India with the speedier GDP growth in the 1990s remains in dispute (as reflected in the 2004 election outcomes). In consequence, mass migration from India continues.

For countries that have proved unable to generate jobs and wage growth at home, the migration option offers a critical safety valve. The migrations to the Gulf, within East Asia, to Europe from non-OECD countries, and to the US from Mexico are largely of low skill or unskilled workers. Many are drawn from low income countries and from poor households within these countries, even if the very poorest rarely migrate. The nature of the safety valve is at least two-fold. First, the departure of significant numbers of unskilled workers alleviates pressures on the home country labor markets. In some contexts (such as Pakistan and the Philippines from our case studies), there are hints that this may have led to higher wages for those left behind; elsewhere labor withdrawal may simply have led to higher employment for nationals at home (Bangladesh, Albania). Either way, workers at home gain. The second element of the safety valve is derived from the remittances sent home.

Certainly many governments are quite preoccupied with maximizing remittance earnings, actively seeking or negotiating to facilitate migration and designing schemes to encourage remittances from the resultant diaspora. For the low income countries, on average, reported remittances amounted to 1.9 percent of GDP in 2001. For a number of countries, this ratio was far higher. Within our study areas, remittances amounted to 7–10 percent of GDP in Sri Lanka, the Philippines and Morocco and 15–17 percent in Albania and Moldova. For Jordan and Lesotho remittances were close to a quarter of GDP.[2] In these countries, remittances obviously represent a major source of livelihood and of poverty alleviation. The efficacy of policy efforts to induce additional remittances remains poorly documented and understood. Such efforts typically fall into three categories: offering foreign currency denominated, repatriable bank accounts and bond issues; premium interest rates for remitters; and premium exchange rate schemes. The indications are that the first of these largely benefit more affluent migrants, and no serious evaluation of whether these programs actually induce additional transfers appears to exist. Such evidence as we have on premium interest rates suggests that they are entirely ineffective. On the other hand, the exchange rate does indeed seem to matter to the amounts remitted. This is not to suggest that governments should intervene to manipulate their market exchange rates solely to promote remittances. Rather it is an indication that such schemes as the Wage Earner Scheme in Bangladesh may well have been quite effective in realizing remittances, though it is difficult to disentangle how much of the additional, recorded remittances simply represented diversion of informal remittances into the recorded flows.[3]

Whether remittances accelerate or retard domestic production remains a matter of some dispute. In a number of contexts, there are emerging indications that remittances enhance domestic investment levels. Elsewhere, spending from remittances acts as a catalyst for economic expansion. Offsetting factors include reduced labor supply in families supported by remittances, though in labor surplus economies this should hardly be a concern. As with any financial inflow, remittances may or may not be deployed to generate further expansion, yet in the interim they certainly permit raised living standards. Some remittance recipients elect to enjoy their transfers in terms of additional consumption, some invest in their children's education, homes and other assets, while others use the remittances to reduce their participation in the labor force. A number of critics complain that too little investment results and that policies should be designed to correct this. Yet the grounds for intervention in these private decisions are not well founded. A government may appropriately decide to stimulate overall investment levels but why should investment by remittance recipients be specifically targeted? To a large extent the same may be said of decisions by returning migrants to retire (perhaps temporarily) on their remittance income. On-going efforts by home governments to address this latter 'problem' remain without serious evaluation and anyway are probably misguided. A free choice to remain out of the labor force should surely not warrant correcting.

On the other hand, attempts to promote migrant labor and hence ensuing remittances do face a serious policy dilemma, given that most governments with contract labor systems have expressed a concern to protect the rights, safety and terms of work of their overseas workers. Several diplomatic confrontations have arisen over highly publicized cases of abuse in recent years, and the government of the Philippines has been particularly active in negotiating bilateral agreements on terms of employment. However, as always, where attempts to improve conditions of work raise labor costs, or even lead to confrontation, they are also likely to restrict the demand for workers. Hence the dilemma. In the context of international recruitment a trade-off in terms and level of recruitment may prove particularly acute, since attempts by one home government to enforce better conditions for their workers may simply switch recruiting to less well regulated countries of origin. An additional, related concern arises with respect to private recruitment agencies, which are commonly regulated in an attempt to restrict fraud and trafficking. Such regulation must, however, be weighed against the tendency to drive recruiters abroad, to divert more labor into irregular, unmonitored channels, possibly with even worse standards than if no regulation occurred, and to limit competition in the legal recruitment market at home. The last element is of particular concern given the extremely high fees that the limited number of recruiting agents are able to extract at present.

The brain drain continues to attract attention in the international arena though less so in domestic policy discussions. Two major elements of cost are traditionally associated with the brain drain. The first refers to losses imposed on others by the departure of highly skilled workers. The departure of any productive inputs normally leads to losses for those who remain at home. However, the withdrawal of highly skilled professionals is often presumed to impose unusually high losses, either in terms of job creation for workers remaining at home or in terms of specific outputs forgone. The latter range from limited healthcare, to diminished learning as teachers depart, to lack of institutional development, leadership and technological development. The second major element of cost is the sunk cost of public investment in education of emigrants and the inability to tax the earnings of this elite group. The evidence with respect to both elements is extraordinarily thin.

In thinking about policy options with respect to the brain drain, the emigration of all highly skilled, highly educated persons is simply too nebulous to be amalgamated: any costs imposed on others by emigration of elite groups may impose very real and substantial costs in some settings yet be seen as a blessing elsewhere. In the Philippines, for instance, where college education is largely privately funded, families apparently consciously invest in their youngsters to gain access to overseas posts, either to provide support for themselves through remittances or simply for the betterment of their offspring. Moreover, the last few years have witnessed growing discussion of the processes of brain gain, through which a nation can benefit from its highly skilled diaspora even from afar. Three main channels for potential gain have emerged in discussion: the role of overseas nationals in acting as middlemen in promoting trade; the expansion of financial inflows, not merely from the diaspora but from others spurred by information provided by the diaspora; and the transfer of technology through creation of knowledge networks. Apart from a small, but interesting body of evidence on the links between migration and international trade, the empirical support for brain gain effects remains thin and tentative. Moreover, the discourse refers mostly to the relatively welloff 'developing' economies; the case that the lower income countries have gained significantly from their brain gain has yet to be made.

The brain drain seems high on the list of migration policy concerns in only a few countries today. Yet this surely does not stem from any common belief in processes of brain gain. Rather, migration offers an important safety valve not only for unskilled, underemployed workers but, in many contexts, for skilled workers too. Where open unemployment of the highly skilled, and of recent college graduates in particular, poses a threat to political stability, governments understandably become concerned to find opportunities to occupy these graduates.[4] An alternative, adopted in a number of contexts, is that government simply absorbs the surplus in public service employment, though this clearly imposes very real costs both in financial terms and possibly in the form of bloated and less competent bureaucracy. Elsewhere, governments discretely facilitate emigration.

Where the loss of highly skilled people is considered to pose a public problem, the options open to the home country policy makers are few. Restricting emigration ought not to be an option to deal with the brain drain, being a basic human right, and fortunately very few countries have elected to attempt such restrictions. Instead, a number of countries (and some international agencies) have introduced programs to encourage return of overseas professionals. Yet such strategies can be very costly, in terms of sufficiently attractive salaries, fixed costs of establishing research centers, resentment of these privileges by those who stayed at home and hence increased incentives to depart. Moreover, the limited evidence points to skills acquired abroad proving of very limited relevance, especially in the lower technology settings of the poorer countries.

Perhaps the major alternative that remains is reforming public funding for higher education, particularly where the sunk cost of educating departing migrants is the principal cause of concern. Certainly overseas tertiary education is very costly and the evidence shows that the return rate of students is lower among the poorer countries than among the middle income developing countries. On the other hand, a significant portion of foreign training costs are borne by the host countries, and the technical training provided cannot be emulated in the developing regions. Similarly, the costs of tertiary education at home, relative to incomes, are highest in the low income countries. While the private rewards to this privileged education at home and abroad are high, and enjoyed largely by the children of wealthy families, the social returns are much lower. It is nonetheless entirely feasible that private and public spending on the education of departing migrants represent a worthwhile investment: an investment in the export of educated migrants in return for their remittances.

Yet, in the end, this cycle of migration and remittance as a safety valve, whether for unemployed college graduates or under-employed, less skilled workers, breeds dependence. The pressure to design and commit to a development strategy that creates employment, the incentive to evaluate the public structure of college financing, even the necessity to deal with containing violence, are postponed by the migration option. Moreover, this cycle can become self-fulfilling. For example, the lack of jobs at home may be partially caused by an over-valued exchange rate; the lack of jobs spawns emigration and the resultant remittances help prop up the exchange rate. In countries such as Albania and Moldova the evidence points in this direction; massive remittances have clearly provided vital poverty relief in the short run during a period of extremely painful transition, yet dependence on continued migration and remittances may well postpone both the need and means to generate jobs at home.

10.2   MIGRATION AND DEVELOPMENT: POLICIES IN THE COUNTRIES OF DESTINATION

Beyond the broad development performance and strategy of the lower income countries, the major policies determining the important features of today's global migrations from low to high income countries lie largely in the hands of the host countries. As these host nations make their policy determinations that shape migration, the development implications for the countries of origin are rarely considered.

Migration Policies

Migration is generally not perceived as a policy instrument wielded by the high income countries to achieve or affect development in the sending countries. Rather, it should not be surprising that the migration policies of the industrialized countries are determined almost entirely in their own interest. There are exceptions. Small numbers of refugees are resettled and asylum seekers recognized. Yet for the most part the strategy is clearly to confine refugees to the developing countries in which they first arrive; the select few who gain entry to the industrialized countries are often among the better educated and wealthiest of the refugees. Indeed recognition or denial of asylum status and the select listing of safe countries often effectively form a part of foreign policy, again pointing away from altruism as the main motive, even in admitting refugees.

Controls and migration pressures: domestic concerns

Despite overriding self-interest, the development connection with migration nonetheless arises. Ultimately, the concern to contain the extent of migrant arrival can only partially be realized through imposition of border controls and sanctions against apprehended irregular migrants and their employers. Even the most draconian attempts to erect barriers to entry are never fully effective. Economic development in the regions of origin, notably economic development that results in job creation and wage increments, does diminish migration pressures. The theoretical arguments are clear that suggest the opposite, that economic development may increase migration pressures particularly among the lower income nations, but do not seem to be supported by the evidence in today's world. The industrialized countries thus have a self-interest in the economic development of migrant source countries, if only because these developments affect the migration pressures to come. Indeed, these concerns are often quite explicit, as in the mandate of Europe's High Level Group on Asylum and Migration and in the design of the NAFTA agreement. Yet the reverse, the impact of migration upon economic development at origin, rarely shapes or even informs migration policy design.

Instead, the attitudes toward migrant arrival in the industrialized countries are shaped by quite different concerns. The evidence on the impacts of immigration upon wages and employment levels of natives is quite uniform in finding only very small effects. Most of this evidence refers to the US, but the limited evidence on Europe concurs. In turn, this suggests that the impacts of immigration both upon overall incomes among prior residents and upon the distribution of those incomes across different classes are quite negligible. On the other hand, this evidence does not appear to have ameliorated popular perceptions of economic threat from competition for jobs and of resultant gains to employers; these perceptions underlie much of the policy formation, the mounting evidence notwithstanding. The evidence also points to the existing set of migrants in most industrialized countries being net contributors to the fiscal coffers over the balance of their lives after migration. Indeed, there has arisen considerable interest in the potential to resolve the pending ageing and associated social security crisis through immigration of younger, tax-paying migrants. However, most simulations suggest that the prospects of such a resolution are dim. The net fiscal contributions of less skilled workers appear mixed, though where migrants are admitted temporarily to work, and are neither accompanied by family nor remain into their old age, the contributions seem clear. Indeed, the tendency of lower paid migrants to continue work beyond minimum retirement age helps to extend this contribution. Prospects of resolving the social security crisis seem brighter if more migrants are highly skilled and also leave any family members at home. However, to attract the highly skilled in today's competitive environment typically requires admission of their dependants, which dampens the net fiscal improvement.

There is a common presumption that admission of highly educated migrants adds more to incomes of natives than admission of low skill migrants, even beyond any effects on fiscal contributions. This is the mirror image of a brain drain effect. However, as with the brain drain, the evidence is controversial. Although there is widespread agreement that higher levels of education in a population are correlated with more rapid economic growth, which causes which remains contentious. Even if the causality runs from higher education to more rapid growth, the issue of who captures the benefits of the additional growth remains unsettled: do prior residents really gain from spillover effects of highly educated immigrants in promoting growth or do most of the additional returns accrue to the migrants themselves? Similarly, although social outcomes with respect to such elements as public health, involvement in civic life, freedom from crime, or a cleaner environment, are also correlated with education levels, again whether education is the causal factor is disputed.

Despite this lack of resolution on the economic advantages and disadvantages of migration, and of skilled versus unskilled migrants in particular, many of the industrialized nations are actively and increasingly seeking to attract highly skilled permanent settlers and less skilled workers on a temporary basis.

> There is a renewed interest in the recruitment of new immigrant workers in many OECD countries. The phenomenon of population ageing explains part of this trend. Although the management of flows remains a high priority, a number of OECD countries are seeking to attract skilled and highly skilled foreign workers and are making access to the labour market of foreign students after graduation easier. These changes are not limited to skilled labour. Some countries are also seeking out less skilled workers, especially in agriculture (the United States, Australia, Spain and Greece), construction, care giving for the elderly and other business and household services (Italy, Portugal, United Kingdom). Evidence of these flows is visible in the increasing share of temporary labour migration in total flows ...[5]

These patterns are not confined to the OECD countries alone: a number of the non-OECD, higher income countries of East Asia and in the Persian Gulf have exhibited similar preferences. In the process, the economic development impacts of these migration streams are shaped, to a large extent, by the nature of these chosen migration regimes.

Development impacts   A key component in the economic impacts of migrants' departures on the economy of the home country is the propensity of these migrants to remit. Although our evidence on the determinants of international remittances is far from sound, largely owing to the paucity of data, it seems probable that remittances tend to rise with the level of migrants' earnings, with the intent to return home, with the incidence of leaving immediate family members behind, and with the legality of migration. There seems little question that of the four migration regimes selected for closer study here, remittances per migrant are by far the highest from the GCC states. The migrants in the Gulf are very largely unskilled or low skilled workers, who stay on average some four to five years, leaving their families behind. In this context, the saving and remittance rate out of earnings has been quite extraordinary and these remittances have played a major role in shaping living standards in each of the major labor supplying countries in Asia. The fact that these are predominantly low skill workers, often coming from lower income settings within their home countries (though typically not the poorest), has meant that the most immediate benefits of these remittances have fallen on relatively poor households. From Europe, remittances to such countries as Morocco, Albania and Moldova have obviously been extremely important also, these three countries being among the thirteen countries worldwide with the highest reported remittance inflows relative to GDP in 2001.

In the Americas a number of policy initiatives are under way to lower the costs of remitting through formal channels and to induce additional transfers. Although the costs of remitting have come down in the last decade, they remain high. In part this reflects the fixed costs of numerous small transfers. However, the exorbitant fees also reflect high mark ups and the lack of competition. In view of this, on-going efforts to promote competition and greater transparency in the remittance market are certainly to be commended.[6] The system of Home Town Associations, established among Mexicans in the US, is also designed both to promote greater transfers and to direct their use toward investment in public infrastructure. However this scheme, which involves matching federal funds from the Mexican government, may well prove quite regressive because public support is diverted to communities already enriched by transfers from the US. Irregular migrants generally have more difficulty transferring funds through formal channels, if only because they lack identification to effect the transfer. For many years, Mexican consulates in the US have issued their own identity cards, to both legal and irregular migrants, and these cards are increasingly accepted as sufficient to open a bank account and hence to make transfers. Yet any form of identity card is potentially subject to abuse and therefore controversial. Indeed the Mexican consulate cards were 'Designed originally to help police identify persons involved in accidents (or crime).'[7] The recent proposal to introduce national identity cards in the UK has consequently met with concerted criticism from civil liberties groups.

Within East Asia a large part of both migration and remittances have been irregular. For example, despite the presence of well over a million Indonesians in East Malaysia, Indonesia reports only remittances from the Middle East: both migration to and remittances from East Malaysia go unrecorded. Indeed, the system of informal transfers is quite global: the *hundi, hawala, padala, phei kwan* and *fei-ch'ien* networks are simply cheaper and faster than remitting through formal channels. Current efforts among the industrialized countries to curtail and regulate the informal banking network that transmits these informal remittances thus raises very serious concerns. The chief objective in restricting this extensive network is to close a channel through which terrorist units are thought to transfer funds internationally. It seems doubtful that this effort will prove effective in seriously restricting terrorist funding: there are too many alternatives. Limiting informal remittances may also channel more remittances into the formal system, which could have the benefits of diminishing capital flight from the developing countries, perhaps reducing contraband trade, and enhancing tax revenues to the home governments. However, these efforts are also very likely to reduce total remittances significantly and to reduce remittances to poorer households in particular.

'At the end of the 1990s and in 2000, most OECD countries introduced specific measures to facilitate the recruitment of skilled foreign workers.'[8] The competition to attract the highly skilled is intensifying and is likely to continue, though to date the US has clearly been the dominant outlet for the brain drain. Moreover, the proportion of college-educated people in the US, relative to the stock of such persons at home, is generally higher among the poorer nations. By 2000, more than 40 percent of the US foreign-born adult population possessed a tertiary education and about three-quarters of these were from the developing and transition countries. Although well over half of the foreign-born college-educated adults in the US possess degrees from American universities, a significant transfer of invested public resources from the home country may nonetheless be involved: in the secondary education of these migrants, in any first degrees obtained at home prior to attending a US university, or even in partial funding of the US degree. In a few instances the industrialized countries have shown some sensitivity to these potential costs of the brain drain, though this sensitivity does not always translate into restraint. For example, 'Britain's National Health Service in 2001 promised not to "actively recruit" nurses from developing countries such as South

Africa. Without active recruitment, 1500 of the 13 000 foreign nurses who arrived in the UK between April 2001 and April 2002 were from South Africa; the number of foreign nurses in the UK doubled in the past three years.'[9] More generally, the attempts to attract highly skilled migrants to the OECD countries show little concern for the potential costs to the nations of origin and various proposals for schemes to compensate the lower income countries have been stymied. Yet blanket criticism of the higher income countries is not warranted in this regard either. Preventing highly skilled persons from taking advantage of migration, simply because of their country of origin, is discriminatory. Moreover, the deployment of these personnel is often far from effective at home; indeed, the withdrawal of unemployed professionals, sometimes called a 'brain overflow', can be a political blessing and possibly an economic one too, if these professionals then remit from abroad.

Study abroad is one of the primary vehicles of entry to the higher income countries for the highly skilled and the number of foreign students has grown rapidly in most of the OECD countries. Indeed, as the OECD (2003: 35) notes, 'One of the most striking features of the recent changes in international migration flows is the emergence of a "new" category of admissions: foreign students.' In each of the OECD countries, a major portion of the cost of training this expanding set of foreign college students is provided by the governments of the host countries. To a large extent, these subsidies are justified domestically on the grounds of attracting, training and selecting the brightest people from abroad for subsequent employment in the OECD host country. Where students return home, or elsewhere abroad, subsidies may still be justified to tax-payers in the host countries: subsidizing a returning elite promotes future goodwill and business contacts. Nonetheless, critics question the merits and extent of these public subsidies; criticism that has been amplified by recent concerns for security threats from a large foreign student presence.[10] Certainly the choices that the OECD nations make with respect to willingness to issue visas to foreign students and to admit students to state universities also have important development implications for the countries of origin, though rather mixed implications. On the one hand, it is clear that study abroad is a key factor in promoting and permitting the brain drain. On the other hand, denying a high quality education to students from the lower income countries may also retard development potential. The latter may be particularly critical where those students actually return home, though the evidence shows that the stay rate of students in the US is particularly high from the lower income countries.

Both in the context of high skilled migrants and of the diaspora and their remittances, return migration assumes a central importance in the development implications of sojourns overseas. Without an intent to return home, links with the diaspora evaporate over time: remittances and the stimuli to trade, capital flows and technology transfer die. Students and other highly skilled people who settle permanently abroad, and are able to bring their family or form a family abroad, contribute little to their home countries. The migrants themselves probably benefit more from permanent settlement, but those left at home do not.

Across four case study regimes: lessons and dilemmas

The four migration regimes that formed our case study areas have exhibited contrasting outcomes with respect to migration patterns and levels, and hence with respect to development implications among the countries of origin.

Permanent settlers   Traditionally, both Canada and the US have been among the small set of countries seeking permanent settlement of migrants. This has never been true of Europe, East Asia or the Gulf. The opportunity to settle clearly benefits the lucky few migrants who achieve this status. On the other hand, the ultimate alienation from the home country among permanent settlers also restricts feedback on those left behind. Links with the home country decline eventually; by the second generation, remaining commitments are few. Immigration to the US and Canada has risen steadily over the last half century. But, in recent years, even the US has increasingly emphasized various forms of temporary admission categories and may move further in this direction, though the motives for this shift lie not in concerns for development in the countries of origin.

Temporary workers   Across the four regimes, admission of temporary workers poses a number of dilemmas:

1. Return: A major concern in most of the host countries is the ability to return workers admitted on a temporary basis. Although the early guest worker programs in Europe had high turnover levels, that guests came to stay became notorious. The European states lacked the political will to deport reluctant returnees and to deny family reunification; financial incentives, later offered to encourage return, proved too little. Management of the newer guest worker programs in Europe, perhaps particularly the process of subcontracting short-term projects, appears to be leading to higher return rates. In contrast, the Gulf states have never really been bothered with settlement among their contract workers from Asia. Some stay for quite extended periods, but only a very few highly skilled migrants really settle.
2. Permanence of temporary programs: Access to foreign labor generally alters the structure and nature of production in the host countries; entrenched interests of domestic employers (not to mention any complementary domestic workers or consumers) then render termination of these programs politically costly. This has been a common feature

across each of the four regimes. In the Gulf, periodic attempts to localize jobs have largely failed. In East Asia, the realities of the 1998 financial crisis brought home a growing dependence on foreign labor. In the US, critics assert that ending the *bracero* program simply accelerated irregular migration, in part because of adjustment to foreign labor presence. In Europe, both some manufacturing sectors and various forms of agriculture are highly dependent on access to migrant workers. In most of these contexts, the future dependence on foreign temporary labor is intimately tied to trade policy: the continued protection of labor-intensive manufacturing and maintenance of massive agricultural subsidies. The prospects for sustained and expanded migration, particularly of unskilled workers, from the lower income countries is thus critically tied to the trade policies of the industrialized countries, a feature to which the following section returns. Nonetheless, even in the face of trade policy reform, the demand for relatively unskilled labor will continue, and probably grow, in fields such as childcare and care for the elderly. In the Gulf, a good deal of the more recent migration has been to supply such services and the migration of women has grown in the process.

3. Exporting shocks: The capacity to export temporary workers in times of shock potentially offers relief to the host countries. A 'beggar-thy-neighbor' strategy, this shifts the burden of adjustment to the lower income countries of origin. The reality is that most of the democracies have shown very limited ability, or political will, to export temporary labor during shocks. The East Asia crisis generated very limited return migration and, in any case, the stock levels very soon recovered. Yet remittances fell during this period of shock, and evidence from the Philippines indicates that this may have led to such factors as reduced school attendance and additional child labor. On the other hand, the Gulf states have shown much greater ability to adjust recruitment, and even to return workers on current contracts, during both financial and armed conflicts. The resulting adjustments have imposed significant costs on the sending countries: the recession in Kerala following the 1991 Gulf crisis was quite deep. Yet recovery has generally been rapid in these cases too. Temporary migration schemes thus do impose a greater risk on the sending countries, but the resultant downturns appear often to be brief.

4. Duration of stay: In the Persian Gulf, the average duration of stay among contract workers has been some four to five years; many stay far longer. In contrast, Europe has significantly increased its use of seasonal and very short-term migrant labor. These differences in duration of stay impact the economic feedback on the sending countries. Very short periods of stay generally mean very low pay for the migrant worker and hence limited remittances; very long periods of stay can result in a declining commitment to support those at home. Rapid turnover among migrant workers also has

implications for employers in the host countries: in particular, temporary workers in permanent jobs tend to be costly; turnover requires training and sorting, and may prove disruptive. In the design of temporary work programs, careful consideration should thus be given to the duration of permitted stay. It matters to host employers and to developments at home.

5. Family accompaniment: The strict resistance to family accompaniment among the GCC states, except for the highly skilled, does much to explain willingness of migrants to return. Moreover, the separation of families promotes remittances and the Gulf has been by far the largest source of remittances per migrant. On the other hand, the separation of families can take its toll on marital relationships as well as the upbringing of children. Yet the additional remittances promote the education of children left at home; the small amount of available evidence suggests remittance receipts more than offset absence of a parent, particularly in societies where extended families step in for support. A further concern, however, is the potential for conjugal separation to worsen the spread of HIV-AIDS, as solitary migrants turn to casual and commercial sex.

6. Assimilation and migrants' rights: The cultural assimilation of migrants poses a serious dilemma for the host countries. Failure to assimilate often leads to continued xenophobia and resentment of migration in the host country population. Successful assimilation discourages return migration. Attempts at acculturation are also open to criticism for failing to appreciate the richness of a multicultural society. A similar dilemma occurs with migrants' rights. Denying the right to vote, the acquisition of citizenship and access to state benefits ostracizes the migrant community and keeps them from integrating. Offering these rights increases the desire to stay and migration pressure more generally. Within the EU this has led to particular difficulties of coordination, given that citizenship in any of the Schengen countries bestows the right to work in all. Meanwhile, the range of foreigners entitled to vote in local elections in EU varies considerably across member countries. In the US, integration of the Hispanic community of temporary migrants into the US schooling system remains contentious and debates over bilingual education continue to rage. In the GCC states these issues hardly arise: there are essentially no state benefits for foreigners and acquiring citizenship is simply impossible. The GCC states are frequently criticized for the lack of rights granted to migrant workers. Yet there is a trade off. Offering better working conditions, better pay, improved rights and access to state benefits would improve the lot of migrants, but may well reduce their numbers as the perceived costs to employers and host states rise.

7. Dependence at origin: Not only do host states tend to become dependent upon on-going temporary work programs but the same may be said of the home countries too. Families in the sending countries adjust their

life styles to the migration opportunity. Home governments postpone efforts to deal with job shortages and lack of foreign exchange as long as continued export of labor and remittance receipts look reasonably sure. The Philippines has developed a massive system of rotating labor abroad, and remittances sustain those at home. The result has been a failure to design policies for job creation within the Philippines. Indeed, such failures become a by-product of the migration–remittance nexus, not only because of postponed policy adjustments, but because of endogenous economic responses. There are, for instance, indications of upward pressure on wages in the Philippines from migration, which limits domestic demands for labor. Similarly, remittances place upward pressure on the exchange rate, restricting export performance and hence job creation in the export related sectors. The dilemma for the migrant-receiving countries resides in the continued migration pressures with continued dependence.

Irregular migrants All four regimes generate large numbers of irregular workers. This reflects a combination of the pressures on migrants to enter illegally despite the high costs and risks of doing so, the willingness and desire of domestic employers to hire irregular workers, and the inability or reluctance of states to protect their borders and to evict over-stayers. In the US, the overwhelming majority of undocumented migrants are from Mexico, despite militarization of the border. Many of the huge number of rejected asylum seekers remain within the EU without documents. Moreover, the long eastern border and Mediterranean coastline are almost impossible to seal. In the Gulf, most of the irregulars are over-stayers to whom the states turn a blind eye in deference to employers. In East Asia, this deference to employers has permitted not only substantial numbers of over-stayers but widespread employment of 'trainees'.

In comparison to their regular counterparts, the irregular migrants probably contribute less to economic development at home. First, larger fees are abstracted by middle men to smuggle undocumented migrants over the border than are required of regular migrants. Second, these high entry fees and risks deter back and forth movement, eventually loosening ties with home. Third, it is more difficult for irregular migrants to remit, at least through official channels.

Irregular movements in the context of all four of the migration regimes thus probably contribute less to economic development at home. Substituting regular migration programs instead would, in this sense, clearly be preferable. In addition, such substitution would reduce the proliferation of criminal activities of smugglers, not to mention enhancing the rights and well-being of the migrants. The notion of a more formal guest worker program was floated in the US in January 2004. In March 2004, Korea established a guest worker program. The UK has expanded its Special Agricultural Workers Scheme precisely with the intent of reducing asylum applications. Malaysia has announced a series of amnesties, such as that during the 1998 crisis, intended to legalize some of the huge irregular labor force present in the country. In the mid-1990s, several GCC states offered amnesties to their over-stayers too.

Amnesties have a distinct moral hazard problem: migrants attempt to enter without documents in the anticipation of being granted amnesty. The US experienced a surge in border crossings after the hint of an amnesty in January 2004. More generally, however, there is a question of whether guest worker programs substitute for, or exacerbate, irregular migration. Opinions differ and evidence is sparse. Ending the bracero program in the US may have escalated irregular migration from Mexico; such a case seems more difficult to make in Europe.

Highly-skilled migrants   In contrast, the role of highly skilled migrants differs significantly across our four regimes. The chief destination of most highly skilled migrants is North America and the US in particular. The competition for the highly skilled is heating up, with most of the European countries and several of the East Asian countries attempting to attract these footloose movers. The loss of healthcare workers in some parts of the world probably imposes very real and large costs in humanitarian and financial terms; the withdrawal of healthcare professionals from Sub-Saharan Africa is probably particularly onerous. On the other hand, some of our case study countries, such as India and the Philippines, almost certainly gain from the export of highly skilled people. Perhaps the lesson to be drawn is that selective restraint can be important to development prospects when recruiting highly skilled people, though few countries have displayed such restraint.

Training foreign students has not only become a big business in its own right, but also serves as a major vehicle for attracting high achievers to stay and work. The US has traditionally been the dominant attraction, but the European, Japanese and Australian universities have escalated foreign student recruiting dramatically and the EU-15 now have more foreign students (in general and from non-OECD countries) than the US and Canada combined. Again, however, there is a dilemma with respect to curtailing such programs. On the one hand, foreign students tend to stay, especially from the lower income countries, resulting in a loss to the developing countries of some of their best and brightest. On the other hand, few developing countries can offer a comparable education. The obvious answer is to offer the opportunity for this specialized training but simultaneously to seek ways of encouraging return home. Yet the latter is not in the interest of the host countries and there is mounting evidence that, on average, it is the least successful migrants who return home.

Of the four regimes, migration to the Gulf has surely had the largest positive impact on economic development in the sending countries. Most of the workers are unskilled, many are now women, all return home, and remittances are enormous. Some of this success comes at a high cost to the migrants who must leave their families behind, remain ostracized from local society, and possess few rights and little protection. Yet most of the migrants report that they would willingly go again, if they could.

Trade, Aid and Migration: Towards Policy Cohesion

The set of industrialized country policies that impact economic development in the lower income regions is by no means confined to migration policies. Trade, aid and any investment policies of the richer nations (not to mention peace-keeping efforts) can have profound effects upon the economic performance of the developing countries and hence upon future migration. For the most part, these policy elements are not coordinated amongst the industrialized countries, or even within a single nation where they are typically the responsibilities of rather disparate ministries. A few countries are clearly far more committed to doing something about economic development in the poorer parts of the world than are others, though the expression of this varies; while some of the industrialized countries provide greater amounts of aid, others are more open to trade with the developing countries, and some admit low skilled migrants, temporarily, on a legal basis.[11] Very few (if any) of the industrialized countries see migration as an instrument of development for the lower income countries. On the other hand, multilateral negotiations have drawn increasing attention to the development opportunities thwarted by trade protectionism among the rich nations, and aid is at least meant to enhance those opportunities. Whatever the intent, migration, trade, aid and investment flows are all intimately linked; they shape economic development to a significant extent and hence future migrations.

The links between migration and trade, and hence trade policies of the industrialized countries, are the subject of continuing debate. There is mounting evidence that international migration may stimulate trade between the host and home countries. The earlier emphasis was on the trade effect arising from migrants' specific demands for goods from home. More recently this has given way to increasing emphasis on the importance of migrants, and especially highly skilled migrants, as middlemen in promoting trade. To date, the evidence remains confined to a somewhat narrow set of contexts: US bilateral trade enhanced by bilateral migrations, Canadian trade with Asia is amplified by Asian migration to Canada, cross-border ethnic Chinese communities facilitate mutual trade, and India's IT engineers overseas helped to stimulate growth of India's software exports. How much wider spread these effects will prove (for instance whether migration from Africa has served to stimulate trade with Sub-Saharan Africa) remains to be explored.

Meanwhile, the more contentious aspect of the trade–migration nexus is whether trade liberalization and expansion serve to reduce or exacerbate migration pressures. Trade theory allows for both possibilities (see Box 10.1).[12] Theory may help us to organize our thoughts but it provides no clear answers. Meanwhile, 'serious policy debate almost always starts from the presumption that trade and migration are strong substitutes', 'Mexican migration into the USA was a major consideration during the NAFTA negotiations ... Western Europe trade initiatives with Central and Eastern Europe are prompted significantly by fears of large-scale migration'.[13] Perhaps, in the end, this presumption is not too unreasonable, despite the ambiguities. Migration pressures tend to be greatest where the gaps in relative factor endowments are particularly large and it is precisely in these contexts that the long-run, theoretical approach that is outlined first in Box 10.1 tends to dominate. Whereas scale economy effects and variations in technology may drive the intra-industry trade patterns that pervade trade among the richer nations, the net trade between north and south is more commonly characterized by contrasting factor abundance, suggesting that trade and migration may well indeed be substitutes between the richer and poorer nations.

BOX 10.1   DOES MORE TRADE MEAN LESS MIGRATION? NOTES ON THE AMBIGUITY OF TRADE THEORY

The crux of the dichotomy in predictions as to whether trade and migration are substitutes or complements resides in the source of the gains from trade between nations. Where the major forces underlying these gains are differences in the availability of key inputs to production, trade and migration act as substitutes in the long run. Countries with large amounts of labor relative to their invested capital have a cost advantage in exporting items that use labor particularly intensively. In this scenario, the expansion of trade then raises wages in the labor abundant country, thus mitigating pressures to emigrate from the low wage setting. If instead, trade patterns are driven primarily by differences in demands for goods in various countries, the result is effectively the same. The country that has a strong preference for things that require a lot of labor in production would have high wages before opening to trade, simply because of the effective demand for labor to produce those goods. Opening to trade and importing the labor-intensive goods would then diminish the demands for labor in the high wage country, satisfying the demands for labor-intensive goods through trade rather than through migration. In contrast, where the principal driving forces of trade are differences in technologies between nations, opening to trade magnifies wage gaps and thus intensifies migration pressures. What matters here is which set of countries have the relative technological advantage in more labor-intensive activities, and which are the nations with superior technology in product lines that place lesser demands on labor. Opening to trade will stimulate migration from the latter to the former. Lastly, gains from trade may stem from scale economies. When larger is better, a country can enjoy a cost advantage in trade simply as a result of a larger concentration of that industry within their borders. Even if countries have similar labor availability relative to capital, similar demand patterns and similar technologies, a wage gap may nonetheless then emerge as a result of trade and industrial specialization; wages will be greater in the country that happens to expand the industry that is initially more labor-intensive and vice versa, though this pattern of specialization may reflect little more than historical accident.

This theoretical literature is quite prolific, ambiguous with respect to outcomes, and focuses on the longer run. The more immediate effects of trade liberalization are quite different with respect to their implications for earnings gaps, though no less ambiguous. In the shorter term, entrepreneurs are unable or reluctant to alter many of their productive inputs rapidly as prices shift under changed trade regimes. Unskilled labor inputs are often one of the easiest to change quickly. Imagine the effect of this, then, if the industrialized countries alter their openness to trade with the lower income countries. In the developing regions the terms of trade shift; the prices of some export goods rise, the exchange rate may well respond and the prices of imported goods thus alter too. Some industries enjoy rising prices and want to hire more labor while other industries are laying off workers. Whether wages or unemployment do the adjusting depends very much on labor market flexibility, though ambiguity for the real buying power of workers' wages is heightened further by the fact that some consumer prices are rising while others may be falling. The standard trade theory of these adjustments thus indicates that short-term effects of trade reform, either by the home, developing economies, or by the richer nations, may either diminish or sharpen the effective earnings gaps and hence the pressure to migrate in the near future.

To the extent that this is true, protectionist policies on behalf of both the host and home countries contribute to the lack of labor market improvements in the developing countries and consequently result in added incentives to migrate. The need for trade policy reforms in the migrant-sending countries has already been noted, as has the necessity of accompanying any such reforms with appropriate supporting strategies. Nonetheless the protectionism of the industrialized nations vis-à-vis exports from the lower income countries, especially protection on the more labor-intensive items, exacerbates the inability to create jobs in the sending countries. The multi-fibre agreement, a major offender, is finally scheduled to disappear next year, though import taxes on garments and textiles remain high. Not only has this protection on the textile and apparel industries in the north restricted increased development of these labor-intensive sectors in the south and thus contributed to migration push, but at least in the US the apparel and textile sectors have been among the major employers of immigrant workers thus contributing to migration pull.[14] Various agricultural subsidies, both explicit and implicit, have proved a major sticking point in multilateral trade negotiations and many of these blatantly harm agricultural development and some of the poorer people within the developing regions. Among the many implicit forms of such subsidy is the supply of aid in the form of food. As Philip Martin (2002: 8) notes:

> In most developing countries, 40 to 60 percent of the labor force is employed in agriculture, and farm goods are a major export. Most migration-receiving countries protect their farm sectors, generally by guaranteeing their farmers higher-than-world prices for commodities they produce, and then sometimes donating or subsidizing the sale of the excess produced in world markets, which depresses prices. Between the late 1980s and the late 1990s ... the producer support equivalent (PSE) level of subsidy for the farm sector in the US, Japan and the EU rose from about 4 times ODA to 5 times ODA.

However, it is not only protectionism in merchandise trade that affects migration outcomes: trade in services matters also. Both in the Uruguay Round and at Doha, market-opening commitments to trade in services occupied much of the attention. Mode 4 of trade services, recognized by the resultant General Agreement on Trade in Services, encompasses migration explicitly, covering the temporary international movement of individuals engaged in providing services. However,

> The limited Mode 4 commitments that have already been made pertain almost totally to highly skilled personnel, in particular to the category of intra-corporate transferees who are basically an adjunct to foreign direct investment. These commitments, at present, have limited utility for developing countries because their 'comparative advantage' lies in low and medium-skilled services ... Developing countries stand to gain the most from the liberalization of trade in services ... Within the GATS, Mode 4 is unquestionably the most politicized of all the four modes of service supply.[15]

At the time of writing, any progress toward expanding coverage of Mode 4 commitments appears to have halted, following the collapse of discussions at Cancun.

The industrialized countries have been hesitant, and reluctant to commit to trade reforms that could accelerate development in the poorer regions of the world. Meanwhile, the level of aid commitment varies very considerably across the OECD members, with only a handful of countries (Denmark, Luxembourg, Netherlands, Norway, Sweden and soon Belgium) meeting the 0.7 percent of Gross National Income target adopted by the UN. In fact, ODA as a fraction of GNI fell during the 1990s, and by 2001 reported remittance receipts of the developing countries exceeded total ODA. Both remittances and aid represent transfers, most of which are from residents in the higher income countries to the developing countries, but remittances are clearly regressive relative to aid: remitters are typically poorer than the tax payers who finance aid.[16]

The targeting and effectiveness of aid in alleviating poverty remain a matter of controversy. The tying of aid, granting aid in kind rather than cash, and the use of aid as an instrument of foreign policy all limit the ability of bilateral aid in promoting growth and poverty relief. Targeting aid toward countries with 'sound institutions' may have improved the efficiency of aid delivery, sharpened transparency as to the ultimate beneficiaries, and offered a bargaining chip in promoting a transition toward sound governance. Yet such targeting can also divert funds from the world's poorest.[17]

Both trade and aid policies of the high income countries affect economic development in the poorer regions, yet both may prove fairly blunt instruments for promoting development.[18] Trade policies of the industrial countries are circumscribed by the trade strategies adopted in the lower income countries. Aid may even serve to harm job creation in some instances, through financing a postponement of critical reforms, by propping up the exchange rate and deterring export expansion, and by depressing export prices through venting of surplus farm produce.[19] Nonetheless, greater donations of aid and openness to trade with the developing regions are generally to be commended; for the most part they do serve to relieve poverty incidence. As a by-product migration pressures are diminished. Yet this does not imply that trade and aid should be deployed as instruments targeted to the reduction of migration.

> it would be a mistake to make aid conditional on measures which aim to limit out-migration. Withdrawing aid to countries which fail to limit out-migration would simply plunge them further into poverty; threatening such a withdrawal would force developing countries to spend scarce resources on border controls rather than poverty reduction, would undermine any notion of partnership, and would simply succeed in pushing more migrants into the arms of smugglers and traffickers. Development assistance or the threat of its withdrawal must never be used as a tool for migration management.[20]

Not everyone agrees. For example, the terms of reference of Europe's High Level Working Group require them to conduct assessments of 'aid and development strategies in the battle to limit economic migration'.[21] More generally, there are indications that aid may indeed be targeted toward the higher migration countries. Figure 10.1 shows ODA receipts per capita against net out-migration rates for 77 developing countries.[22] Only countries with positive aid receipts and positive net out-migration are shown. Among these countries, there is a clear positive association between the two measures, an association which is also depicted.[23] Moreover, the correlation evident in Figure 10.1 is not merely a result of higher aid going to poorer countries which also have higher out-migration rates: the association persists even controlling for income levels among these countries.[24] Nor does this appear to reflect aid commitments to conflict-torn countries that generate large out-migrations of refugees; again the association persists even controlling for the numbers of refugees per capita originating from each country. There is a good deal of variability in this association, as may be seen in Figure 10.1. Among the outliers with notably low levels of aid, given their rates of out-migration and income levels, are Mexico, India, China, Nigeria and Iran. Several of our case study countries with particularly high out-migration rates also receive less aid than the norm for their income level; these include the Philippines, Indonesia, Thailand and Bangladesh. At the opposite extreme, above-normal levels of aid went to such countries as Macedonia, Tunisia, Laos, Bulgaria and Poland. Obviously many factors besides poverty and migration shape aid patterns across countries. Nonetheless, on average, high out-migration

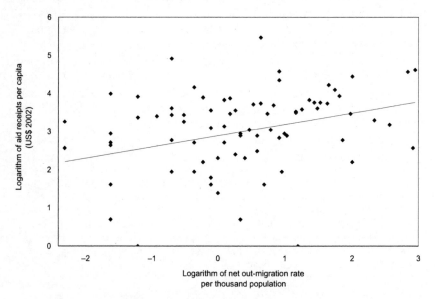

Figure 10.1   Aid recipients per capita against net out-migration rate: 77 developing and transition economies with reported, positive, net out-migration, 1995–2000

developing countries did receive more aid per capita in 2002, both in general and given their income levels and numbers of refugees generated. The extent to which this reflects a concerted effort to contain migration pressures is open to speculation.

Industrial country policies are certainly in need of greater cohesion. Aid, trade, capital flows and migration are intimately linked. At present, policies designed to affect one component often conflict with policies that are aimed elsewhere within this nexus. Protectionist policies that harm job creation in the developing world and simultaneously stimulate industries that employ (irregular) migrants in the industrialized countries are at odds with concerns to control migration of less skilled workers. The same may be said of the recent trend to limit ODA. If concerns over migration pressures serve as a catalyst to expand aid and to open trade generally this may not be a bad thing. On the other hand, the effect could instead be greater preferential treatment in aid and trade, diverting such efforts away from poor areas that generate less migrants perhaps simply because of their geography. Attempts to cajole governments in the lower income countries to control out-migration, using threats of discontinued aid or inducements of expanded trade opportunities are very unlikely to succeed: emigration controls are probably no more effective than immigration controls and would violate a basic human right. Cohesion is important: targeting blunt instruments clumsily is not. This is a fine line to tread.

10.3   IN CLOSING

Global migration across borders has grown, though no faster than world population. The last century witnessed a transition in which these movements became increasingly subject to control. The right to emigrate is widely recognized; the right to immigrate is not and the high income countries appear as elite clubs with restricted entry. Yet everywhere admission controls fail, resulting in irregular entry, albeit at high cost. The term 'unwanted' migration has passed into common parlance. Yet international migration can be, and for the most part is, a positive force for both receiving and sending countries.

The arrival of working migrants raises the total incomes of those already present. Some lose and some gain. The latter dominate but may be outvoted. Although most international migrants would prefer to stay at home if only jobs were available and personal safety secured, the latter conditions are far from being met. In the interim, the migration option offers a critical safety valve for unskilled workers, for unemployed skilled workers who pose a threat at home, and for refugees fleeing very real violence. Although middlemen skim a significant portion of the gains from entry restrictions, migration offers substantial gains. The experience is not always pleasant. Certainly many migrants face significant risks in crossing borders, then face abuse and resentment from xenophobes. Yet most report that they would repeat the experience: the gains are simply too large to resist.

The element of return in migration is key to the economic effects on those who remain at home. The intent to return sustains commitment to those left behind, which is critical to the process of remitting; the sharing of the migrants' gains. Everywhere the high income countries emphasize their preference for temporary migration. In the Gulf, migration has always been temporary but the numbers have expanded. In East Asia, most of the movement remains irregular and temporary. Europe has never intended that migrants should settle and is exploring new versions of temporary unskilled labor contracting and even attempting to attract the highly skilled on temporary visas. The US continues its reliance on circular migration of irregular migrants and substantially expanded temporary admissions of highly skilled personnel in the 1990s.

In this concern for return migration there is, then, a concurrence of interests between the poor and rich economies, between the sending and receiving nations, though the motives differ. For the lower income countries the dominant concern is the continued contact and support received from migrants who intend to return home. For the migrant-receiving nations, the preference for temporary admission is driven largely by a reluctance to integrate, despite the lessons of history on the tremendous gains that have resulted from the mingling and melding of cultures.

NOTES

1. On the links between out-migration, failure to create appropriate employment and an inward looking trade strategy in the Philippines, see Abella (1993).
2. Ratha (2003: Figure 7.4).
3. See Athukorala (1993: 115).
4. Hugo (1996), describes this as a situation of 'brain overflow' in parts of the Asia-Pacific region.
5. OECD (2003: 16).
6. See, for example, the US National Credit Union Administration website on the US Wire Transfer Fairness and Disclosure Act of 2001 at http://www.ncua.gov/legislation/107-HR1306.htm.
7. Ratha (2003: 166).
8. OECD (2003: 27).
9. *Migration News*, 1 July 2003 at http://migration.ucdavis.edu/.
10. See, for example, Borjas (2002).
11. See, for instance, the Commitment to Development Index and its components, compiled and published by the Center for Global Development at http://www.cgdev.org/rankingtherich/home.html.

12. For surveys see Ethier (1996) and Venables (1999).

13. Ethier (1996: 66, 50).

14. See, for example, Collins (1991).

15. Sands (2004: 1–2).

16. I am grateful to Susan Martin for drawing my attention to this point.

17. See, however, Dollar and Levin (2004), who argue that those aid agencies that have focused on sound institutions and policies have also been more poverty focused.

18. Lucas (1999).

19. See, for example, Ranis (1994) on the Philippines; Schiller (1994) on Turkey; Molle (1996), on East Europe, and van Wijnbergen (1986) on the exchange rate effect.

20. UK (2004: 92).

21. Van Selm (2002: 4).

22. Data on ODA per capita are from the World Bank World Development Indicators 2004, and net migration measures are from UN (2002a) and refer to 1995–2000.

23. In contrast, among the aid-recipient countries that experienced net in-migration no clear association between aid and rates of migration is apparent.

24. An ordinary least squares regression on cross country aid data, for 77 countries that received ODA in 2002 and also experienced net out-migration between 1995 and 2000, generates:

$$\log (AID) = 5.342 - 0.313 \log (GDP) + 0.288 \log (MIG) + 0.013 \, RFG \quad \text{No. observations} = 77$$
$$\quad\quad (5.01) \quad (2.23) \quad\quad\quad (2.93) \quad\quad\quad (1.09) \quad\quad R\text{-squared} = 0.17$$

where AID is ODA received per capita in US$ in 2002, GDP is measured per capita at PPP prices in 2000, MIG is net out-migration per thousand population during 1995–2000, and RFG is the number of refugees originating from each country per thousand population in 2002. T-statistics for a zero null hypothesis are shown in parentheses and standard errors are heteroskedasticity robust.

References

Abassi, Nasreen (1987), 'Urbanization in Pakistan, 1951–81', Research Report Series No. 152, Islamabad: Pakistan Institute of Development Economics, April.

Abella, Manolo I. (1992), 'Contemporary Labour Migration from Asia: Policies and Perspectives of Sending Countries', Mary M. Kritz, Lin Lean Lim and Hania Zlotnik (eds), *International Migration Systems: A Global Approach*, Oxford: Oxford University Press, pp. 263–78.

Abella, Manolo I. (1993), 'Labor Mobility, Trade and Structural Change: The Philippine Experience', *Asian and Pacific Migration Journal*, **2** (3), 249–68.

Abella, Manolo I. (1995), 'Asian Labour Migration: Past, Present and Future', *ASEAN Economic Bulletin*, **12** (2), 125–38.

Abella, Manolo I. (1997), 'The Recruiter's Share in Labour Migration', paper presented at the Conférence sur les Migrations Internationales à la Fin du Siècle: Tendances et Questions, Barcelona, May 7–10.

Abowd, John M. and Richard B. Freeman (1991), 'Introduction and Summary', in John M. Abowd and Richard B. Freeman, *Immigration, Trade and the Labor Market*, Chicago: University of Chicago Press.

Acemoglu, Daron and Joshua Angrist (2001), 'How Large are Human-Capital Externalities? Evidence from Compulsory Schooling Laws', *NBER Macroeconomics Annual 2000*, **15**, 9–59.

Acma, Bulent, 2002, 'Economic Consequences of International Migration: Case Study of Turkey', paper presented at the Conference on Poverty, International Migration and Asylum, Helsinki, September 27–28.

Adams, Richard H. Jr (1991), 'The Effects of International Remittances on Poverty, Inequality, and Development in Rural Egypt', Research Report No. 86, Washington DC: International Food Policy Research Institute.

Adams, Richard H., Jr (1998), 'Remittances, Investment, and Rural Asset Accumulation in Pakistan', *Economic Development and Cultural Change*, **47** (1), 155–73.

Adams, Richard H., Jr (2003), 'International Migration, Remittances and the Brain Drain: A Study of 24 Labor-Exporting Countries', World Bank Policy Research Working Paper 3069, Washington DC: World Bank, June.

Adams, Richard H. Jr and John Page (2003a), 'International Migration,

Remittances and Poverty in Developing Countries', Policy Research Working Paper 3179, Washington DC: World Bank, December.

Adams, Richard H. Jr and John Page (2003b), 'Poverty, Inequality and Growth in Selected Middle East and North Africa Countries, 1980–2000', *World Development*, **31** (12), 2027–48.

Addleton, Jonathan S. (1992), *Undermining the Centre: The Gulf Migration and Pakistan*, Oxford: Oxford University Press.

Adelman, Irma and J. Edward Taylor (1990), 'Is Structural Adjustment with a Human Face Possible? The Case of Mexico', *Journal of Development Studies*, **26** (3), 387–407.

Adelman, Irma, J. Edward Taylor and Stephen Vogel (1998), 'Life in a Mexican Village: A Sam Perspective', *Journal of Development Studies*, **25** (1), 5–24.

Agrawal, Ajay K., Iain M. Cockburn and John McHale (2003), 'Gone But Not Forgotten: Labor Flows, Knowledge Spillovers, and Enduring Social Capital', National Bureau of Economic Research Working Paper No. 9950, Cambridge MA, National Bureau of Economic Ressearch, September.

Ahmed, Akbar S. (1984), 'Dubai Chalo: Problems in the Ethnic Encounter between Middle East and South Asia Muslim Societies', *Asian Affairs*, **15** (3), 273.

Alburo Florian A. (1993), 'Remittances, Trade and the Philippine Economy', *Asian and Pacific Migration Journal*, **2** (3), 269–83.

Alburo Florian A. and Danilo I. Abella (2002), 'Skilled Labour Migration from Developing Countries: Study on the Philippines', International Migration Papers, No. 51, Geneva: International Labour Office.

Alderman, Harold (1996), 'Saving and Economic Shocks in Rural Pakistan', *Journal of Development Economics,* **51** (2), 343–65.

Altonji, Joseph G. and David Card (1991), 'The Effects of Immigration on the Labor Market Outcomes of Less-Skilled Natives', in John M. Abowd and Richard B. Freeman, *Immigration, Trade and the Labor Market*, Chicago: University of Chicago Press.

Amjad, Rashid (1989), 'Economic Impact of Migration to the Middle East on the Major Asian Labour Sending Countries: An Overview', in Rashid Amjad (ed.), *To the Gulf and Back: Studies on the Economic Impact of Asian Labour Migration*, New Delhi: ILO–ARTEP.

Aneesh, Aneesh (2001), 'Rethinking Migration: High-Skilled Labor Flows from India to the United States', in Wayne A. Cornelius, Thomas J. Espenshade and Idean Salehyan (eds), *The International Migration of the Highly Skilled: Demand, Supply, and Development Consequences for Sending and Receiving Countries*, San Diego: Center for Comparative Immigration Studies, University of California.

Anh, Dang Nguyen (2003), 'Vietnam: Emergence of Return Skilled Migration', in Robyn Iredale, Fei Guo and Santi Rozario (eds), *Return*

Migration in the Asia Pacific, Cheltenham, UK and Northampton, MA, USA: Edward Elgar.

Arif, Ghulam M. (1996), 'Period without a Job after Returning from the Middle East: A Survival Analysis', *Pakistan Development Review*, **35** (4) Winter, 805–20.

Arif, G.M. and M. Irfan (1997), 'Return Migration and Occupational Change: The Case of Pakistani Migrants Returned from the Middle East', *Pakistan Development Review*, **36** (1), 1–37.

Arora, Ashish and Suma Athreye (2001), 'The Software Industry and India's Economic Development', *WIDER Discussion Paper No. 2001/20,* World Institute for Development Economics Research, United Nations University, Helsinki.

Asencio, Diego C. (1991), 'Foreword', in Demetrios G. Papademetriou and Philip L. Martin (eds), *The Unsettled Relationship: Labor Migration and Economic Development*, New York: Greenwood Press.

Asia-Pacific Group on Money Laundering (2003), 'Consideration and Adoption of the APG Alternative Remittance Regulation Implementation Package', APG Annual Meeting, APG Secretariat.

Athukorala, Prema-Chandra (1992), 'The Use of Migrant Remittances in Development: Lessons from the Asian Experience', *Journal of International Development*, **4** (5), 511–29.

Athukorala, Prema-Chandra (1993), 'Improving the Contribution of Migrant Remittances to Development: The Experience of Asian Labour-Exporting Countries', *International Migration*, **31** (1), 103–23.

Athukorala, Prema-Chandra and Chris Manning (1999), *Structural Change and International Migration in East Asia: Adjusting to Labour Scarcity*, Melbourne: Oxford University Press.

Auerbach, Alan and Phillip Oreopolis (2000), 'The Fiscal Impact of US Immigration: A Generational Accounting Perspective', in James Porterba (ed.), *Tax Policy and the Economy*, **14**, Cambridge MA: MIT Press.

Azad, Abul Kalam, 'Importance of Migrants' Remittance for Bangladesh Economy', paper presented at the International Conference on Migrant Remittances: Development Impact, Opportunities for the Financial Sector and Future Prospects, London, October 9–10.

Azam, Farooq-I (1986), *Pakistani Return Migrants from the Middle East: Resettlement and Related Issues*, Geneva: International Labour Office.

Azam, Farooq-I (1991), 'Labour Migration from Pakistan: Trends, Impacts and Implications', *Regional Development Dialogue*, **12** (3), 53–73.

Azam, Farooq-I (1998), 'International Migration Dynamics in High and Low Migration Districts of Pakistan', in Reginald Appleyard (ed.), *Emigration Dynamics in Developing Countries. Vol. II: South Asia*, Aldershot: Ashgate Publishing pp. 147–75.

Bagasao, Ildefonso (2003), 'Migration and Development: The Philippine

Experience', paper presented at the International Conference on Migrant Remittances: Development Impact, Opportunities for the Financial Sector and Future Prospects, London, October 9–10.

Bair, Sheila C. (2003), 'Improving Access to the US Banking System among Recent Latin American Immigrants', report prepared for the IADB Multilateral Investment Fund, Center for Public Policy and Administration, University of Massachusetts, Amherst.

Barnham, Bradford and Stephen Boucher (1998), 'Migration, Remittances, and Inequality: Estimating the Net Effects of Migration on Income Distribution', *Journal of Development Economics*, **55** (2), 307–31.

Barro, Robert J. (1991), 'Economic Growth in a Cross-Section of Countries', *Quarterly Journal of Economics,* **106** (2), 407–44.

Barro, Robert J. (1999), 'Inequality, Growth and Investment', National Bureau of Economic Research Working Paper No. 7038, Cambridge MA, March.

Barro, Robert J. and Jong-Wha Lee (1993), 'International Comparisons of Educational Attainment', *Journal of Monetary Economics*, **32** (3), 363–94.

Barro, Robert J. and Xavier Sala-i-Martin (1992), 'Regional Growth and Migration: A Japan–US Comparison', National Bureau of Economic Research Working Paper No. 4038, Cambridge MA, March.

Battistella, Graziano and Cecilia Concaco (1998), 'The Impact of Labour Migration on the Children Left Behind: A Study of Elementary School Children in the Philippines', *Sojourn*, **13** (2), 220–41.

Bean, Frank D., Thomas J. Espenshade, Michael J. White and Robert F. Dymowski (1990), 'Post-IRCA Changes in the Volume and Composition of Undocumented Migration to the United States: An Assessment Based on Apprehensions Data', in Frank D. Bean, Barry Edmonston and Jeffrey S. Passel (eds), *Undocumented Migration to the United States: IRCA and the Experience of the 1980s*, Washington DC: Urban Institute Press, pp. 111–58

Beine, Michel, Frédéric Docquier and Hillel Rapoport (2001) 'Brain Drain and Economic Growth: Theory and Evidence', *Journal of Development Economics*, **64** (1), 275–89.

Benhabib, Jess (1996), 'On the Political Economy of Immigration', *European Economic Review*, **40** (9), 1737–43.

Bergstrand, Jeffrey H. (1985), 'The Gravity Equation in International Trade: Some Micro-Economic Foundations and Empirical Evidence', *Review of Economics and Statistics*, **67** (3), 474–81.

Berman, Eli and Zaur Rzakhanov (2000), 'Fertility, Migration and Altruism', National Bureau of Economic Research Working Paper No. 7545, Cambridge MA, February.

Bhagwati, Jagdish N. and Koichi Hamada (1974), 'The Brain Drain, International Integration of Markets for Professionals and Unemployment: A Theoretical Analysis', *Journal of Development Economics*, **1** (1), 19–42.

Bhagwati, Jagdish N. and Martin Partington (1976), *Taxing the Brain Drain*, Amsterdam: North Holland.

Bhagwati, Jagdish N. and Carlos Rodriguez (1975), 'Welfare Theoretic Analyses of the Brain Drain', *Journal of Development Economics*, **2** (3), 195–221.

Bharat, Shalini (1976), 'Single-Parent Family in India: Issues and Implications', *Indian Journal of Social Work*, **47** (1), 55–65.

Bils, Mark and Peter J. Klenow (2000), 'Does Schooling Cause Growth?', *American Economic Review*, **90** (5), 1160–83.

Bilsborrow, Richard E., Graeme J. Hugo, A.S. Oberai and Hania Zlotnic (1997), *International Migration Statistics: Guidelines for Improving Data Collection Systems*, Geneva: International Labour Office.

Bivins, Laura L. and Kala Krishna (2001), 'Transferability of Migration Licenses and the Distribution of Potential Rents', National Bureau of Economic Research Working Paper No. 8619, Cambridge MA, December.

Black, Richard (2003), 'Soaring Remittances Raise New Issues', *Migration Information Source*, San Diego: Migration Policy Institute, June.

Blejer, Mario I. and Itzhak Goldberg (1980), 'Return Migration – Expectations Versus Reality: A Case Study of Western Immigrants to Israel', in Julian L. Simon, and Julie DaVanzo (eds), *Research in Population Economics*, *Vol. 2*, Greenwich: JAI Press, pp. 433–49.

Blejer, Mario I., Harry G. Johnson and Arturo C. Prozecanski (1978), 'An Analysis of the Economic Determinants of Legal and Illegal Mexican Migration to the United States', *Research in Population Economics*, *Vol. 1*, Greenwich CN: JAI Press, pp. 217–31.

Böhning, W. Roger (1984), *Studies in International Migration*, New York: St Martin's Press.

Bonin, Holger, Bernd Raffelhüschen and Jan Walliser (1999), 'Germany: Unification and Ageing', *European Economy: Generational Accounting in Europe,* European Commission, Directorate-General for Economic and Financial Affairs.

Bonin, Holger, Bernd Raffelhüschen and Jan Walliser (2003), 'Can Immigration Alleviate the Demographic Burden?', *FinanzArchiv*, **57** (1), 1–21.

Borjas, George J. (1987), 'Self-selection and the Earnings of Immigrants', *American Economic Review*, **77** (4), 531–53.

Borjas, George J. (1989), 'Immigrant and Emigrant Earnings: A Longitudinal Study', *Economic Inquiry*, **27** (1), 21–37.

Borjas, George J. (1994), 'The Economics of Immigration', *Journal of Economic Literature*, **32** (4), 1667–717.

Borjas, George J. (2002), 'Rethinking Foreign Students: A Question of the National Interest', *National Review*, June 17, at http://www.nationalreview.com/.

Borjas, George J. (2003), 'The Labor Demand Curve is Downward Sloping: Reexamining the Impact of Immigration on the Labor Market', National Bureau of Economic Research Working Paper No. 9755, Cambridge MA, June.

Borjas, George J. and Berndt Bratsberg (1996), 'Who Leaves? The Outmigration of the Foreign-Born', *Review of Economics and Statistics*, **78** (1), 165–76.

Bourchachen, Jamal (2001), 'The Use of Censuses and Consular Statistics to Measure Migrations in Maghreb Countries', Working Paper No. 9, Conference of European Statisticians, ECE-Eurostat, Geneva, May 21–23.

Brainard, S. Lael (1997), 'An Empirical Assessment of the Proximity–Concentration Trade-Off between Multinational Sales and Trade', *American Economic Review*, **87** (4), 520–44.

Brown, Richard P.C. (1997), 'Estimating Remittance Functions for Pacific Island Migrants', *World Development*, **25**, April, 613–26.

Bruce, Neil and Michael Waldman (1990), 'The Rotten Kid Theorem Meets the Samaritan's Dilemma', *Quarterly Journal of Economics*, **105** (1), 155–65.

Bruton, Henry J. (1969), 'The Two Gap Approach to Aid and Development: Comment', *American Economic Review*, **59** (3), 439–46.

Bryceson, Deborah F. (2000), 'Rural Africa at the Crossroads: Livelihood Practices and Policies', Natural Resource Perspectives, No. 52, London: Overseas Development Institute.

Buchan, James, Tina Parkin and Julie Sochalski (2003), 'International Nurse Mobility: Trends and Policy Implications', WHO/EIP/OSD/2003.3, Geneva: World Health Organization.

Bundred, Peter E. and Cheryl Levitt (2000), 'Medical Migration: Who Are the Real Losers?', *The Lancet*, **356** (9225), 245–6.

Buric, Olivera (1973), 'A New Type of Incomplete Family: The One Whose Providers Have Gone to Work Abroad', *Sociologija*, **15** (2), 245–71.

Burki, Shahid J. (1988), 'Poverty in Pakistan: Myth or Reality', in T.N. Srinivasan and Pranab K. Bardhan (eds), *Rural Poverty in South Asia*, New York: Columbia University Press, pp. 69–88.

Burney, Nadeem A. (1989), 'A Macro-economic Analysis of the Impact of Workers' Remittances on Pakistan's Economy', in Rashid Amjad (ed.), *To the Gulf and Back: Studies on the Economic Impact of Asian Labour Migration*, New Delhi: ILO–ARTEP, pp. 197–222.

Carrington, William J. and Enrica Detragiache (1999), 'How Extensive is the Brain Drain?', *Finance and Development*, **36** (2), 46–9.

Castillo-Freeman, Alida J. and Richard B. Freeman (1992), 'When the Minimum Wage Really Bites: The Effect of the US-level Minimum Wage on Puerto-Rico', in George J. Borjas and Richard B. Freeman (eds), *Immigration and the Workforce: Economic Consequences for the United*

States and Source Areas, Chicago: University of Chicago Press, pp. 177–211.

Castles, Stephen, Heather Booth and Tina Wallace (1984), *Here for Good: West Europe's Ethnic Minorities*, London: Pluto Press.

Castles, Stephen, Heaven Crawley and Sean Loughna (2003), *States of Conflict: Causes and Patterns of Forced Migration to the EU and Policy Responses*, London: Institute for Public Policy Research.

Chalamwong, Yongyuth (2002), 'Thailand', in *Migration and the Labour Market in Asia: Recent Trends and Policies*, Paris: Organization for Economic Development and Cooperation.

Chami, Ralph, Connel Fullenkamp and Samir Jahjah (2003), 'Are Immigrant Remittance Flows a Source of Capital for Development?', IMF Working Paper WP/03/189, Washington DC: International Monetary Fund.

Chandavarkar, Anand G. (1980), 'Use of Migrants' Remittances in Labor-Exporting Countries', *Finance and Development*, **17** (2), 36–9.

Chang, Parris and Zhiduan Deng (1992), 'The Chinese Brain Drain and Policy Options', *Studies in Comparative International Development*, **27** (1), 44–60.

Chang, Shirley L. (1992), 'Causes of Brain Drain and Solutions: The Taiwan Experience', *Studies in Comparative International Development*, **27** (1), 27–43.

Chatterji, Monojit (1998), 'Tertiary Education and Economic Growth', *Regional Studies*, **32** (4), 349–354.

Chimhowu, Admos, Jenifer Piesse and Caroline Pinder (2003), 'The Socio-Economic Impact of Remittances on Poverty Reduction', paper presented at the International Conference on Migrant Remittances: Development Impact, Opportunities for the Financial Sector and Future Prospects, London, October 9–10.

Chin, Christine B.N. (2002), 'The "Host" State and the "Guest" Worker in Malaysia: Public Management of Migrant Labour in Times of Economic Prosperity and Crisis', *Asia Pacific Business Review*, **8** (4), 19–40.

Ciccone, Antonio and Robert E. Hall (1996), 'Productivity and the Density of Economic Activity', *American Economic Review*, **86** (1), 54–70.

Citizenship and Immigration Canada (2003a), *Immigration Overview: Facts and Figures*, Ottawa: Ministry of Public Works and Government Services.

Citizenship and Immigration Canada (2003b), *Statistical Overview of the Temporary Resident and Refugee Claimant Population: Facts and Figures*, Ottawa: Ministry of Public Works and Government Services.

Clark, Ximena, Timothy J. Hatton and Jeffrey G. Williamson (2002), 'Where Do Us Immigrants Come From? Policy and Sending Country Fundamentals', Working Paper No. 8998, Cambridge MA: National Bureau of Economic Research, June.

Coate, Stephen (1995), 'Altruism, the Samaritan's Dilemma, and Government Transfer Policy', *American Economic Review*, **85** (1), 46–57.

Coe, David T. and Elhanan Helpman (1995), 'International R&D Spillovers', *European Economic Review*, **39** (5), 859–87.

Cohen, Margot (2003), 'Overseas Bounty', *Far Eastern Economic Review*, **166** (2), 48.

Collado, M. Dolores, Iñigo Iturbe-Ormaetxe and Guadalupe Valera (2002), 'Quantifying the Impact of Immigration on the Spanish Welfare State', Instituto Valenciano de Investigaciones Económicas Working Paper WP-AD 2002–04.

Collier, Paul (1999), 'On the Economic Consequences of Civil War', *Oxford Economic Papers*, **51** (1), 168–83.

Collier, Paul and Anke Hoeffler (1998), 'On Economic Causes of Civil War', *Oxford Economic Papers*, **50** (4), 563–73.

Collins, Susan M. (1991), 'Immigrants, Labor Market Pressures, and the Composition of the Aggregate Demand', in John M. Abowd and Richard B. Freeman, *Immigration, Trade and the Labor Market*, Chicago: University of Chicago Press, pp. 305–18.

Commission for the Study of International Migration and Cooperative Economic Development (1991), 'Immigration and Economic Development', reproduced in Demetrios G. Papademetriou and Philip L. Martin (eds), *The Unsettled Relationship: Labor Migration and Economic Development*, New York: Greenwood Press, pp. 221–42.

Commission of the European Communities (2002), 'Integrating Migration Issues in the European Union's Relations with Third Countries', Communication from the Commission to the Council and the European Parliament COM(2002) 703 final, Brussels.

Constable, Nicole (2003), 'A Transnational Perspective on Divorce and Marriage: Filipina Wives and Workers', *Identities: Global Studies in Culture and Power*, **10** (2), 163–80.

Constant, Amelie and Douglas S. Massey (2003), 'Self-Selection, Earnings, and Out-Migration: A Longitudinal Study of Immigrants to Germany', *Population Economics*, **16** (4), 631–53.

Cowitt, Philip P. (ed.) (1984), *World Currency Yearbook*, Brooklyn: International Currency Analysis Inc.

Cox, Donald (1987), 'Motives for Private Income Transfers', *Journal of Political Economy*, **95** (3), 508–46.

Cox, Donald and Emmanuel Jimenez (1990), 'Achieving Social Objectives through Private Transfers: A Review', *World Bank Research Observer*, **5** (2), 205–18.

Cox, Donald and Emmanuel Jimenez (1992), 'Social Security and Private Transfers in Developing Countries: The Case of Peru', *World Bank Economic Review*, **6** (1), 155–69.

Cox, Donald and Emmanuel Jimenez (1995), 'Private Transfers and the Effectiveness of Public Income Redistribution in the Philippines', in Dominique van de Walle and Kimberly Nead (eds), *Public Spending and the Poor: Theory and Evidence*, Baltimore: Johns Hopkins University Press, pp. 321–46.

Cox, Donald, Emmanuel Jimenez and Wlodek Okrasa (1997), 'Family Safety Nets and Economic Transition: A Study of Worker Households in Poland', *Review of Income and Wealth*, **43** (2), 191–209.

Çuka, Elida, Harry Papapanagos, Natasha Polo and Peter Sanfey (2003), 'Labor Market Developments in Albania: An Analytic Overview', *Review of Development Economics*, **7** (2), 217–27.

Curran, Sara R., Filiz Garip, Chang Chung and Kanchana Tangchonlatip (2003), 'Migration, Cumulative Causation and Gender: Evidence from Thailand', paper presented at the Conference on African Migration and Urbanization in Comparative Perspective, Johannesburg, June 4–7.

Currie, Janet and Ann Harrison (1997), 'Sharing the Costs: The Impact of Trade Reform on Capital and Labor in Morocco', *Journal of Labor Economics*, **15** (2), S44–S71.

Davies, James B. (2003), 'Empirical Evidence on Human Capital Externalities', Working Paper No. 2003–11, Tax Policy Branch, Department of Finance, Ottawa: Government of Canada.

Davies, James B. and Ian Wooton (1992), 'Income Inequality and International Migration', *Economic Journal*, **102** (413), 789–802.

Day, Lincoln H. and Ahmet Içduygu (1997), 'The Consequences of International Migration for the Status of Women: A Turkish Study', *International Migration*, **35** (3), 337–71.

Deaton, Angus S. and Alessandro Tarozzi (200), 'Prices and Poverty in India', Princeton: Research Program in Development Studies, Princeton University, at http//www.wws.princton.edu/%7Edeaton/papers.html.

Debrah, Yaw A. (2002), 'Introduction: Migrant Workers in Pacific Asia', *Asia Pacific Business Review*, **8** (4), 1–18.

De Coulon, Augustin and Matloob Piracha (2002), 'Self-Selection and the Performance of Return Migrants: The Case of Albania', *Discussion Paper 0211*, Department of Economics, University of Kent, Canterbury.

Desai, Mihir, Devesh Kapur and John McHale (2001), 'The Fiscal Impact of the Brain Drain: Indian Emigration to the US', paper prepared for the Third Annual NBER–NCAER conference, Neemrana, India.

Desai, Mihir, Devesh Kapur and John McHale (2002), 'The Fiscal Impact of High Skilled Emigration: Flows of Indians to the US', at http://www. people.hbs.edu/mdesai/fiscalimpact.pdf.

De Soto, Hermine, Peter Gordon, Ilir Gedeshi and Zamira Sinoimeri (2002), 'Poverty in Albania: A Qualitative Assessment', World Bank Technical Paper No. 520, Europe and Central Asia Environmentally and Socially

Sustainable Development Series, Washington DC: World Bank.

DeVoretz, Don (2001), 'Canadian Immigration: Economic Winners and Losers', in Slobodan Djajić (ed.), *International Migration: Trends, Policies and Economic Impact*, London: Routledge, pp. 21–41.

Djajić, Slobodan (2001), 'Illegal Immigration Trends, Policies and Economic Effects', in Slobodan Djajić (ed.), *International Migration: Trends, Policies and Economic Impact*, London: Routledge.

Djajić, Slobodan and Ross Milbourne (1988), 'A General Equilibrium Model of Guest-Worker Migration: A Source-Country Specific Perspective', *Journal of International Economics*, **25** (3–4), 335–51.

Docquier, Frédéric and Hillel Rapoport (2003), 'Remittances and Inequality: A Dynamic Migration Model', Working Paper No. 167, Palo Alto: Center for Research on Economic Development and Policy Reform, Stanford University, June.

Dobson, Janet, Khalid Koser, Gail Mclaughlan and John Salt (2001), *International Migration and the United Kingdom: Recent Patterns and Trends*, London: Final report to the Home Office, December.

Dollar, David and Victoria Levin (2004), 'The Increasing Selectivity of Foreign Aid, 1984–2002', World Bank Policy Research Working Paper 3299, Washington DC: World Bank, May.

Dustmann, Christian (1996), 'Return Migration: The European Experience', *Economic Policy*, 22, 213–42.

Dustmann, Christian (2001), 'Why Go Back? Return Motives of Migrant Workers', in Slobodan Djajić (ed.), *International Migration: Trends, Policies and Economic Impact*, London: Routledge, pp. 229–42.

Dustmann, Christian (2003), 'Return Migration, Wage Differentials, and the Optimal Migration Duration', *European Economic Review*, **47** (2), April, 353–67.

Easterly, William and Ross Levine (2001), 'It's Not Factor Accumulation: Stylized Facts and Growth Models', *World Bank Economic Review*, **15** (2), 177–219.

Eaton, Jonathan (1988), 'Foreign Public Capital Flows', in Hollis Chenery and T.N. Srinivasan (eds), *Handbook of Development Economics Vol. 2*, Amsterdam: North-Holland, pp. 1305–86.

Eaton, Jonathan and Samuel Kortum (1996), 'Measuring Technology Diffusion and the International Sources of Growth', *Eastern Economic Journal*, **22** (4), 401–10.

Eaton, Jonathan and Samuel Kortum (2002), 'Technology, Geography and Trade', *Econometrica*, **70** (5), 1741–79.

Economic Resource Center for Overseas Filipinos (2002), 'Post-Conference Assessment Report', International Conference on Identifying Effective Economic Linkages between Overseas Filipinos and the Rural Communities in the Philippines held in Davao City, Philippines April 10–

12, report released from Geneva June 26.

Edin, Per-Anders, Robert J. LaLonde and Olof Åslund (2000), 'Emigration of Immigrants and Measures of Immigrant Assimilation: Evidence from Sweden', *Swedish Economic Policy Review*, **7** (2), 163–204.

Edwards, Alejandra Cox and Manuelita Ureta (2003), 'International Migration, Remittances and Schooling: Evidence from El Salvador', *Journal of Development Economics*, **72** (2), 429–61.

Ekberg, Jan (1999), 'Immigration and the Public Sector: Income Effects for the Native Population in Sweden', *Journal of Population Economics*, **12** (3), 278–97.

Elbadawi, Ibrahim A. and Robert de Rezende Rocha (1992), 'Determinants of Expatriate Workers' Remittances in North Africa and Europe', Working Paper WPS 1038, Washington DC: World Bank.

El Qorchi, Mohammed, Samuel Munzele Maimbo and John F. Wilson (2003), 'Informal Funds Transfer Systems: An Analysis of the Informal Hawala System', Occasional Paper No. 222, Washington DC: International Monetary Fund.

El-Sakka, M.I.T. and Robert McNabb (1999), 'The Macroeconomic Determinants of Emigrant Remittances', *World Development*, **27** (8), 1493–502.

Engelsberg, Paul (1995), 'Reversing China's Brain Drain: The Study-Abroad Policy, 1978–1993', in John D. Montgomery and Dennis A Rodinelli (eds), *Great Policies: Strategic Innovations in Asia and the Pacific Basin*, Westport: Praeger, pp. 99–122.

Ethier, Wilfred J. (1996), 'Theories about Trade Liberalization and Migration: Substitutes or Complements?', in P.J. Lloyd and Lynne S. Williams (eds), *International Trade and Migration in the APEC Region*, Oxford: Oxford University Press, pp. 50–68.

European Bank for Reconstruction and Development (1997), *Transition Report*, London: EBRD.

European Bank for Reconstruction and Development (2003), *Transition Report Update*, London: EBRD.

European Council on Refugees and Exiles (2001), *The Promise of Protection: Progress towards a European Asylum Policy since Tampere*, November.

European Council on Refugees and Exiles (2003), 'Asylum in the European Union: 2002–2003', at http://www.ecre.org/factfile/statistics.shtml.

Eurostat (2002), *European Social Statistics: Migration*, Luxembourg: European Communities.

Evans, Lynne and Ivy Papps (1999), 'Migration Dynamics in the GCC Countries', in Reginald Appleyard (ed.), *Emigration Dynamics in Developing Countries. Vol. IV: The Arab Region*, Aldershot: Ashgate Publishing, pp. 202–34.

Evenson, Robert E. and Larry E. Westphal (1995), 'Technological Change and Technology Strategy', in Jere Behrman and T.N. Srinivasan (eds), *Handbook of Development Economics Vol. 3A*, Amsterdam: North-Holland, pp. 2209–99.

Faini, Riccardo (1994), 'Workers' Remittances and the Real Exchange Rate: A Quantitative Framework', *Journal of Population Economics*, 7 (2), 235–45.

Faini, Riccardo (1996), 'Increasing Returns, Migrations and Convergence', *Journal of Development Economics*, 49 (1), Special Issue, 21–136.

Faini, Riccardo (2002), 'Migration, Remittances and Growth', paper presented at the Conference on Poverty, International Migration and Asylum, Helsinki, September 27–28.

Faini, Riccardo and Jaime de Melo (1995), 'Trade Policy, Employment and Migration: Some Simulation Results for Morocco', Centre for Economic Policy Research Discussion Paper No. 1198, London.

Faini, Riccardo and Alessandra Venturini (1993), 'Trade, Aid and Migrations: Some Basic Policy Issues', *European Economic Review*, 37 (2–3), 435–42.

Faini, Riccardo, Giampaolo Galli, Pitero Gennari and Fulvio Rossi (1997), 'An Empirical Puzzle: Falling Migration and Growing Unemployment Differentials among Italian Regions', *European Economic Review*, 41 (3–5), 571–9.

Fallon, Peter R. and Robert E.B. Lucas (2002), 'The Impact of Financial Crises on Labor Markets, Household Incomes and Poverty: A Review of Evidence', *World Bank Research Observer*, 17 (1), 21–45.

Fan, Yiu-Kwan and Alan Stretton (1985), 'Circular Migration in South-East Asia: Some Theoretical Explanations', in Guy Standing (ed.), *Labour Circulation and the Labour Process*, London: Croom-Helm, pp. 338–57.

Fehr, Hans, Sabine Jokisch and Laurence Kotlikoff (2004), 'The Role of Immigration in Dealing with the Developed World's Demographic Transition', National Bureau of Economic Research Working Paper No. 10512, Cambridge MA, May.

Feng, Zhang (2002), 'China', in *Migration and the Labour Market in Asia: Recent Trends and Policies*, Paris: Organization for Economic Development and Cooperation, pp. 127–39.

Fields, Gary S. (1994), 'The Migration Transition in Asia', *Asian and Pacific Migration Journal*, 3 (1), 7–30.

Filer, Randall (1992), 'The Impact of Immigrant Arrivals on Migratory Patterns of Native Workers', in George J. Borjas and Richard B. Freeman (eds), *Immigration and the Workforce: Economic Consequences for the Unites States and Source Areas*, Chicago: University of Chicago Press, pp. 245–69.

Finn, Michael G. (2001), *Stay Rates of Foreign Doctorate Recipients from U.S. Universities 1999*, Oak Ridge TN: Oak Ridge Institute for Science and Education.

Fischer, Peter A., Reiner Martin and Thomas Straubhaar (1997a), 'Should

I Stay or Should I Go?', in Tomas Hammar, Grete Brochmann, Kristof Tamas and Thomas Faist (eds), *International Migration, Immobility and Development: Multidisciplinary Perspectives*, Oxford: Berg, pp. 49–90.

Fischer, Peter A., Reiner Martin and Thomas Straubhaar (1997b), 'Interdependencies Between Development and Migration', in Tomas Hammar, Grete Brochmann, Kristof Tamas and Thomas Faist (eds), *International Migration, Immobility and Development: Multidisciplinary Perspectives*, Oxford: Berg, pp. 91–132.

Freeman, Richard B. (1993), 'Immigration from Poor to Wealthy Countries: Experiences of the United States', *European Economic Review*, **37** (2–3), 443–51.

Freeman, Richard B. and Remco H. Oostendorp (2000), 'Wages around the World: Pay across Occupations and Countries', National Bureau of Economic Research Working Paper No. 8058, Cambridge MA, December.

Friedberg, Rachel M. and Jennifer Hunt (1995), 'The Impact of Immigrants on Host Country Wages, Employment and Growth', *Journal of Economic Perspectives*, **9** (2), 23–44.

Gächter, August (2002), 'The Ambiguities of Emigration: Bulgaria since 1988', *International Migration Papers*, No. 39, Geneva: International Labour Office.

Galor, Oded and Oded Stark (1990), 'Migrants Savings, the Probability of Return Migration, and Migrants Performance', *International Economic Review*, **31** (2), 463–7.

Gammeltoft, Peter (2002), 'Remittances and Other Financial Flows to Developing Countries', *International Migration*, **40** (2), Special Issue, 181–211.

Garson, Jean-Pierre (1994), 'The Implications for the Maghreb Countries of Financial Transfers from Emigrants', in *Migration and Development: New Partnerships for Co-operation*, Paris: OECD.

Gazdar, Haris (2003), 'A Review of Migration Issues in Pakistan', paper presented at the Regional Conference on Migration, Development and Pro-Poor Choices in Asia, Dhaka, June 22–24.

Ghosh, Bimal (1998), *Huddled Masses and Uncertain Shores: Insights into Irregular Migration*, The Hague: Martinus Nijhoff.

Giubilaro, Donatella (1996), 'European Migration with Respect to the Maghreb and Turkey: The Social Policy Challenge', in Dan Corry (ed.), *Economics and European Union Migration Policy*, London: Institute for Public Policy Research, pp. 124–36

Giubilaro, Donatella (1997), 'Migration from the Maghreb and Migration Pressures: Current Situation and Future Prospects', International Migration Papers, No. 15, Geneva: International Labour Office.

Glytsos, Nicholas P. (1988), 'Remittances in Temporary Migration: A Theoretical Model and Its Testing with the Greek–German Experience',

Weltwirtschaftliches Archiv, **124** (3), 524–49.

Glytsos, Nicholas P. (1993), 'Measuring the Income Effects of Migrant Remittances: A Methodological Approach Applied to Greece', *Economic Development and Cultural Change*, **42** (1), 131–68.

Glytsos, Nicholas P. (1997), 'Remitting Behaviour of "Temporary" and "Permanent" Migrants: The Case of Greeks in Germany and Australia', *Labour*, **11** (3), 409–35.

Glytsos, Nicholas P. (1998), 'The Impact of Income Transfers on Growth', *Economic Research Forum for the Arab Countries, Iran and Turkey Newsletter*, **5** (4), article 04.

Glytsos, Nicholas P. (2001), 'Determinants and Effects of Migrant Remittances: A Survey', in Slobodan Djajić (ed.), *International Migration: Trends, Policies and Economic Impact*, London: Routledge, pp. 250–68.

Glytsos, Nicholas P. (2002a), 'The Role of Migrant Remittances in Development: Evidence from Mediterranean Countries', *International Migration*, **40** (1), 5–26.

Glytsos, Nicholas P. (2002b), 'A Macroeconometric Model of the Effects of Migrant Remittances in Mediterranean Countries', in Ismail Abdel-Hamid Sirageldin (ed.), *Human Capital: Population Economics in the Middle East*, Cairo: American University in Cairo Press, pp. 300–325.

Go, Stella P. (2002), 'The Philippines', in *Migration and the Labour Market in Asia: Recent Trends and Policies*, Paris: Organization for Economic Development and Cooperation.

Goldfarb, Robert, Oli Havrylyshyn and Stephen Magnum (1984), 'Can Remittances Compensate for Manpower Outflows', *Journal of Development Economics*, **15** (1–3), 1–17.

Goldin, Claudia (1994), 'The Political Economy of Immigration Restriction in the United States, 1890–1921', in Claudia Goldin and Gary D. Libecap (eds), *The Regulated Economy: A Historical Approach to Political Economy*, Chicago: University of Chicago Press, pp. 223–57.

Gonzalez, Eduardo T. (1995), 'Do Income Differentials Influence the Flow of Migrant Workers from the Philippines?' *Philippine Review of Economics and Business*, **32**, 79–97.

Gould, David M. (1994), 'Immigrant Links to the Home Country: Empirical Implications for US Bilateral Trade Flows', *Review of Economics and Statistics*, **76** (2), 302–16.

Government of India (2001), 'Report of the High Level Committee on the Indian Diaspora', http://indiandiaspora.nic.in/ Non-Resident Indians and Persons of Indian Origin Division, Ministry of External Affairs.

Greif, Avner (1993), 'Contract Enforceability and Economic Institutions in Early Trade: The Maghribi Traders' Coalition', *American Economic Review*, **83** (3), 525–48.

Grubel, Herbert G. and Anthony D. Scott (1996), 'The International Flow of

Human Capital', *American Economic Review*, **56** (2), 268–74.

Gudim, Anatol (2004), 'Case of Moldova: Mass Labor Migration as a Consequence of Inefficient Reforms', note prepared for the Workshop on International Migration Regimes and Economic Development, Expert Group on Development Issues, Swedish Ministry for Foreign Affairs, Stockholm, May 13.

Guest, Philip (2003), 'Bridging the Gap: Internal Migration in Asia', paper presented at the Conference on African Migration and Urbanization in Comparative Perspective, Johannesburg, June 4–7.

Gulati, I.S. and Ashoka Mody (1983), 'Remittances of Indian Migrants to the Middle East: An Assessment with Special Reference to Migrants from Kerala State', Working Paper No. 182, Trivandrum: Centre for Development Studies.

Gulati, Leela (1993), *In The Absence of Their Men: The Impact of Male Migration on Women*, London: Sage Publications.

Gunatilleke, Godfrey (1998a), 'The Role of Social Networks and Community Structures in International Migration from Sri Lanka', in Reginald Appleyard (ed.), *Emigration Dynamics in Developing Countries. Vol. II: South Asia*, Aldershot: Ashgate Publishing, pp. 71–112.

Gunatilleke, Godfrey (1998b), 'Macroeconomic Implications of International Migration from Sri Lanka', in Reginald Appleyard (ed.), *Emigration Dynamics in Developing Countries. Vol. II: South Asia*, Aldershot: Ashgate Publishing, pp. 113–46.

Guochu, Zhang and Li Wenjun (2002), 'International Mobility of China's Resources in Science and Technology and Its Impact', in *International Mobility of the Highly Skilled*, Paris: Organization for Economic Development and Cooperation, pp. 189–200.

Hadi A. (2001), 'International Migration and the Change of Women's Position among Left Behind in Rural Bangladesh', *International Journal of Population Geography*, **7** (1), 53–62.

Hamada, Koichi and Jagdish Bhagwati (1975), 'Domestic Distortions, Imperfect Information and the Brain Drain', *Journal of Development Economics*, **2** (3), 265–79.

Hammar, Tomas and Kristof Tamas (1997), 'Why Do People Go or Stay?', in Tomas Hammar, Grete Brochmann, Kristof Tamas and Thomas Faist (eds), *International Migration, Immobility and Development: Multidisciplinary Perspectives*, Oxford: Berg, pp. 1–20.

Handoussa, Heba Ahmad (1991), 'Crisis and Challenge: Prospects for the 1990s', in Heba Ahmad Handoussa and Gillian Potter (eds), *Employment and Structural Adjustment: Egypt in the 1990s*, Cairo: American University Press, pp. 3–21.

Haque, Nadeem Ul and Se-Kik Kim (1995), 'Human Capital Flight: Impact of Migration on Income and Growth', *IMF Staff Papers*, **42** (3), 577–607.

Hatton, Timothy J. and Jeffrey G. Williamson (1992), 'International Migration and World Development: A Historical Perspective', National Bureau of Economic Research Working Paper Series on Historical Factors in Long Run Growth, Cambridge MA.

Hatton, Timothy J. and Jeffrey G. Williamson (1994), 'What Drove the Mass Migrations from Europe in the Late Nineteenth Century?', *Population and Development Review*, **20** (3), 533–59.

Hatton, Timothy J. and Jeffrey G. Williamson (1998), *The Age of Mass Migration: Causes and Impact*, New York: Oxford University Press.

Hatton, Timothy J. and Jeffrey G. Williamson (2002), 'What Fundamentals Drive World Migration?', paper presented at the Conference on Poverty, International Migration and Asylum, Helsinki, September 27–28.

Head, Keith and John Reis (1998), 'Immigration and Trade Creation: Econometric Evidence from Canada', *Canadian Journal of Economics*, **31** (1), 47–62.

Hill, John K. (1987), 'Immigration Decisions Concerning Duration of Stay and Migratory Frequency', *Journal of Development Economics*, **25** (1), 221–34.

Huang, Yasheng (2003), *Selling China: Foreign Direct Investment during the Reform Era*, New York: Cambridge University Press.

Hugo, Graeme J. (1995), 'Labour Export from Indonesia: An Overview', *ASEAN Economic Bulletin*, **12** (2), 275–98.

Hugo, Graeme J. (1996), 'Brain Drain and Student Movements', in P.J. Lloyd and Lynne S. Williams (eds), *International Trade and Migration in the APEC Region*, Oxford: Oxford University Press, pp. 210–28.

Hugo, Graeme J. (1998), 'International Migration in Eastern Indonesia', paper prepared for East Indonesia Project, Department of Geography, University of Adelaide, January.

Hugo, Graeme J. (2000), 'Migration and Women's Empowerment', in Harriet B. Presser and Gita Sen (eds), *Women's Empowerment and Demographic Processes: Moving beyond Cairo*, Oxford: Oxford University Press, pp. 287–317.

Hugo, Graeme J. (2002a), 'Recent Labour Related Migration in Indonesia: Trends and Implications', first draft of a paper prepared for the Creating Socio-Economic Security as Poverty Eradication Project, Jakarta: International Labour Office.

Hugo, Graeme J. (2002b), 'Migration Policies Designed to Facilitate the Recruitment of Skilled Workers in Australia', in *International Mobility of the Highly Skilled*, Paris: Organization for Economic Development and Cooperation, pp. 291–320.

Hugo, Graeme J. (2002c), 'Effects of International Migration on the Family in Indonesia', *Asian and Pacific Migration Journal*, **11** (1), 13–46.

Hugo, Graeme J. (2003a), 'Asian Experiences in Remittances', draft chapter forthcoming in Donald F. Terry, Fernando Jiminez-Ontiveros and Steven

R. Wilson (eds), *Beyond Small Change: Migrants Remittances and Economic Development*, Baltimore: Inter-American Development Bank and Johns Hopkins University Press.

Hugo, Graeme J. (2003b), 'Circular Migration: Keeping Development Rolling?', *Migration Information Source*, June, San Diego: Migration Policy Institute.

Hugo, Graeme J. (2003c), *Migration and Development: A Perspective from Asia*, Geneva: International Organization for Migration.

Hui, Weng-Tat (2001), 'Foreign Manpower and Development Strategy in Singapore', in *Proceedings of the International Workshop on International Migration and Structural Change in the APEC Member Economies*, Chiba, Japan: Institute of Developing Economies, pp. 191–212.

Hulme, David, Karen Moore and Andrew Shepherd (2001), 'Chronic Poverty: Meanings and Analytical Frameworks', Working Paper No. 2, Institute for Development Policy and Management, University of Manchester.

Hurwitz, Agnès (2002), 'The Externalisation of EU Policies on Migration and Asylum: Readmission Agreements and Comprehensive Approaches', paper presented at the Conference on Poverty, International Migration and Asylum, Helsinki, September 27–28.

Iguchi, Yasushi (2002), 'Japan', in *Migration and the Labour Market in Asia: Recent Trends and Policies*, Paris: Organization for Economic Development and Cooperation.

Ilahi, Nadeem (1999), 'Return Migration and Occupational Change', *Review of Development Economics*, **3** (2), 170–86.

Ilahi, Nadeem and Saqib Jafarey (1999), 'Guestworker Migration, Remittances and the Extended Family: Evidence from Pakistan', *Journal of Development Economics*, **58** (2), 485–512.

Inter-American Development Bank (2004), *Sending Money Home: Remittance to Latin America and the Caribbean*, Washington DC: Multilateral Investment Fund.

International Labour Organization (1997), 'Protecting the Most Vulnerable of Today's Workers', Tripartite Meeting of Experts on Future ILO Activities in the Field of Migration, Geneva, April.

International Monetary Fund (2000), *Balance of Payments Statistics Yearbook Part 3: Methodologies, Compilation Practices, and Data Sources*, Washington DC: IMF.

International Organization for Migration (2000), *World Migration Report*, Geneva: IOM.

International Organization for Migration (2002), *Migration Trends in Eastern Europe and Central Asia: 2001–2002 Review*, Geneva: IOM.

International Organization for Migration (2003a), *World Migration 2003: Managing Migration Challenges and Responses for People on the Move*, Geneva: IOM.

International Organization for Migration (2003b), *Labour Migration in Asia: Trends, Challenges and Policy Responses in Countries of Origin*, Geneva: IOM.

Iredale, Robyn (2000), 'Migration Policies for the Highly Skilled in the Asia-Pacific Region', *International Migration Review*, **34** (3), 882–906.

Iredale, Robyn, Fei Guo, Santi Rozario and John Gow (2003), 'Conclusion', in Robyn Iredale, Fei Guo and Santi Rozario (eds), *Return Migration in the Asia Pacific*, Cheltenham, UK and Northamption, USA: Edward Elgar, pp. 181–9.

Isaac, T.M.T. (1993), 'Economic Consequences of the Gulf Crisis: A Study with Special Reference to Kerala', in Piyasiri Wickramasekera (ed.), *The Gulf Crisis and South Asia*, New Delhi: UNDP and ILO–ARTEP, pp. 59–102.

Islam, Muinul, H. Chowdhury, M. Salehuddin, J.P. Dutta, M. Ali and A.K. Hoque (1987), 'Overseas Migration from Rural Bangladesh: A Micro Study', Chittagong: Department of Economics, University of Chittagong.

Jaffe, Adam B., Manuel Tratjenberg and Rebecca Henderson (1993), 'Geographic Localization of Knowledge Spillovers as Evidenced by Patent Citations', *Quarterly Journal of Economics*, **108** (3), 577–98.

Jasso, Guillermina and Mark R. Rosenzweig (1971), 'Estimating the Emigration Rates of Legal Immigrants using Administrative and Survey Data: The 1971 Cohort of Immigrants to the United States', *Demography*, **19** (3), 279–90.

Jellal, Mohamed (2002), 'Transferts des Migrants Tunisiens et Qualification: Theorie et Evidence', *Revue D'Analyse Economique*, **78** (3), 397–410.

Johnson, Brett and Santiago Sedaca (2004), 'Diasporas, Émigrés and Development: Economic Linkages and Programmatic Responses', A Special Study of the US Agency for International Development, Trade Enhancement for the Services Sector Project, CARANA Corporation.

Johnson, Harry G. (1967), 'Some Economic Aspects of the Brain Drain', *Pakistan Development Review*, **7** (3), 379–411.

Johnson, Jean M. (2001), 'Mobility of S&E Students and Professional Scientists and Engineers', Panel on Human Resources in Science and Technology and Mobility of Scientists and Engineers, Fifth Inter-American Workshop on Science and Engineering Indicators, Montevideo, October 15–18.

Johnstone, D. Bruce (1998), 'The Financing and Management of Higher Education: A Status Report on Worldwide Reforms', a paper supported by the World Bank in connection with the UNESCO World Conference on Higher Education, Paris, October 5–9.

Kandil, M. and M.F. Metwally (1990), 'The Impact of Migrants' Remittances on the Egyptian Economy', *International Migration*, **28** (1), 159–80.

Kandil, M. and M.F. Metwally (1992), 'Determinants of the Egyptian Labour Migration', *International Migration*, **30** (2), 39–56.

Kapur, Devesh (2001), 'Diasporas and Technology Transfer', *Journal of Human Development*, **2** (2), 265–86.

Kapur, Devesh (2002), 'The Causes and Consequences of India's IT Boom', *India Review*, **1** (2), 91–110.

Kapur, Devesh and John McHale (2002), 'Sojourns and Software: Internationally Mobile Human Capital and High-Tech Industry Development in India, Ireland and Israel', draft paper, Harvard University.

Kassim, Azizah (2002), 'Malaysia', in *Migration and the Labor Market in Asia: Recent Trends and Policies,* Paris: Organization for Economic Development and Cooperation, pp. 231–55.

Katseli, Louka and Nicholas P. Glytsos (1989), 'Theoretical and Empirical Determinants of International Labour Mobility: A Greek–German Perspective', in Ian Gordon and A.P. Thirwell (eds), *European Factor Mobility Trends and Consequences*, London: St Martin's Press, pp. 95–115.

Katz, Eliakim and Oded Stark (1987), 'International Migration under Asymmetric Information', *Economic Journal*, **97** (387), 1987, 718–26.

Kazi, Shahnaz (1989), 'Domestic Impact of Overseas Migration: Pakistan', in Rashid Amjad (ed.), *To the Gulf and Back: Studies on the Economic Impact of Asian Labour Migration*, New Delhi: ILO-ARTEP, pp. 167–96.

Keddie, Nikki R. (1998), 'The New Religious Politics: Where, When, and Why Do "Fundamentalisms" Appear?' *Comparative Studies in Society and History*, **40** (4), 696–723.

Keller, Wolfgang (1998), 'Are International R&D spillovers trade-related? Analyzing Spillovers among Randomly Matched Trade Partners', *European Economic Review*, **42** (8), 1469–81.

Keller, Wolfgang (2002), 'Geographic Localization of International Technology Diffusion', *American Economic Review*, **92** (1), 120–42.

Keren, Luo, Fei Guo and Huang Ping (2003), 'China: Government Policies and Emerging Trends of Reversal of the Brain Drain', in Robyn Iredale, Fei Guo and Santi Rozario (eds), *Return Migration in the Asia Pacific*, Cheltenham, UK and Northampton, USA: Edward Elgar, pp. 88–111.

Keuschnigg, Christian, Mirela Keuschnigg, Reinhard Koman, Erik Lüth and Bernd Raffelhüschen (1999), 'Austria: Restoring Generational Balance', *European Economy: Generational Accounting in Europe*, European Commission, Directorate-General for Economic and Financial Affairs.

Khachani, Mohamed (1998), 'Migration from Arab Maghreb Countries to Europe: Present Situation and Future Prospects', *Economic Research Forum for the Arab Countries, Iran and Turkey Newsletter*, **5** (1), May, article 09.

Khachani, Mohamed (2004), 'Moroccan Migration to Europe: What Impact on the Economies of Countries of Origin?', in *Arab Migration in a Globalized World*, Geneva: International Organization for Migration, pp. 35–52.

Khadria, Binod (2002), 'Skilled Labour Migration from Developing Countries: Study on India', International Migration Papers, No. 49, Geneva: International Labour Office.

Kielyte, Julda (2002), 'Migration Movement in the Baltic States: Determinants and Consequences', paper presented at the Conference on Poverty, International Migration and Asylum, Helsinki, September 27–28.

Kijima, Yuko and Peter Lanjouw (2003), 'Poverty in India during the 1990s: A Regional Perspective', World Bank Policy Research Working Paper 3141, Washington DC: World Bank, October.

King, Russell (2003), 'Across the Sea and over the Mountains: Documenting Albanian Migration', *Scottish Geographical Journal*, **119** (3), 283–309.

King, Russell and Nicola Mai (2002), 'Of Myths and Mirrors: Interpretations of Albanian Migration to Italy', paper presented at the Annual Conference of the Association of American Geographers, Los Angeles, March 19–23.

King, Russell, Nicola Mai and Mirela Dalipaj (2003), *Exploding the Migration Myths*, London: The Fabian Society.

Kirov, Dotcho (1999), 'The Impact of International Migration on the Labor Market in South Africa', University of the North, South Africa at http://www.sba.muohio.edu/

Kofman, Eleonore (2000), 'The Invisibility of Skilled Female Migrants and Gender Relations in Studies of Skilled Migration in Europe', *International Journal of Population Geography*, **6** (1), 45–59.

Konica, Nevila and Randall K. Filer (2003), 'Albanian Emigration: Causes and Consequences', CERGE–EI Working Paper 181, Prague: Center for Economic Research and Graduate Education of Charles University.

Korovilas, James P. (2003a), 'The Economic Sustainability of Post-Conflict Kosovo', paper presented at the International Conference on Migrant Remittances: Development Impact, Opportunities for the Financial Sector and Future Prospects, London, October 9–10.

Korovilas, James P. (2003b), 'The Albanian Economy in Transition: The Role of Remittances and Pyramid Investment Schemes', paper presented at the International Conference on Migrant Remittances: Development Impact, Opportunities for the Financial Sector and Future Prospects, London, October 9–10.

Koser, Khalid and Nicholas Van Hear (2002), 'Asylum Migration: Implications for Countries of Origin', paper presented at the Conference on Poverty, International Migration and Asylum, Helsinki, September 27–28.

Kothari, Uma (2002), 'Migration and Chronic Poverty', Working Paper No. 16, Institute for Development Policy and Management, University of Manchester, March.

Kotkin, Joel (1993), *Tribes: How Race, Religion and Identity Determine Success in the New Global Economy*, New York, Random House.

Krugman, Paul (1979), 'A Model of Innovation, Technology Transfer, and the World Distribution of Income', *Journal of Political Economy*, **87** (2), 253–66.

Krugman, Paul (1991), *Geography and Trade*, Cambridge MA: MIT Press.

Kulu, Hill and Tiit Tammaru (2000), 'Ethnic Return Migration from the East and West: The Case of Estonia in the 1990s', *Europe-Asia Studies*, **52** (2), 349–69.

Kyle, David and Zai Liang (2001), 'Migrant Merchants: Human Smuggling from Ecuador and China', Center for Comparative Immigration Studies Working Paper No. 43, La Jolla, University of California at San Diego, October.

Lalonde, Robert J. and Robert H. Topel (1991), 'Labor Market Adjustment to Increased Immigration', in John M. Abowd and Richard B. Freeman, *Immigration, Trade and the Labor Market*, Chicago: University of Chicago Press, pp. 167–99.

Lalonde, Robert J. and Robert H. Topel (1997), 'Economic Impact of International Migration and the Economic Performance of Migrants', in Mark Rosenzweig and Oded Stark (eds), *Handbook of Population and Family Economics*, Amsterdam: North-Holland, pp. 799–850.

Leamer, Edward E. and James Levinsohn (1995), 'International Trade Theory: The Empirical Evidence', in Gene Grossman and Kenneth Rogoff (eds), *Handbook of International Economics Vol. 3*, Amsterdam: North-Holland, pp. 1339–94.

Lee, Ronald and Timothy Miller (2000), 'Immigration, Social Security, and Broader Fiscal impacts', *American Economic Review*, **90** (2), 350–54.

Leichtman, Maria A. (2002), 'Transforming Brain Drain into Capital Gain: Morocco's Changing Relationship with Migration and Remittances', *Journal of North African Studies*, **7** (1), 109–37.

León-Ledesma, Miguel and Matloob Piracha (2001), 'International Migration and the Role of Remittances in Eastern Europe', University of Kent Discussion Paper No. 01/13, Canterbury, University of Kent.

Lever-Tracy, Constance, David Ip and Noel Tracy (1996), *The Chinese Diaspora and Mainland China: An Emerging Synergy*, London: Macmillan Press.

Levine, Ross and David Renelt (1992), 'A Sensitivity Analysis of Cross-country Growth Regressions', *American Economic Review*, **82** (4), 942–63.

Levitt, Peggy (2001), *The Transnational Villagers*, Berkeley: University of California Press.

Li, Feng and Jing Li (1999), *Foreign Investment in China*, London: Macmillan Press.

Lindstrom, David P. (1996), 'Economic Opportunity in Mexico and Return Migration from the United States', *Demography*, **33** (3), 357–74.

Lloyd, P.J. (1996), 'Globalization, Foreign Investment and Migration', in P.J.

Lloyd and Lynne S. Williams (eds), *International Trade and Migration in the APEC Region*, Oxford: Oxford University Press, pp. 69–83.

Lloyd, P.J. and Lynne S. Williams (1996), 'Introduction', in P.J. Lloyd and Lynne S. Williams (eds), *International Trade and Migration in the APEC Region*, Oxford: Oxford University Press, pp. 1–12.

Loi, Cu Chi (2002), 'Vietnam', in *Migration and the Labour Market in Asia: Recent Trends and Policies*, Paris: Organization for Economic Development and Cooperation, pp. 309–36.

Long, Larry, C. Jack Tucker and William L. Urton (1988), 'Migration Distances: An International Comparison', *Demography*, **25** (4), 633–60.

Looney, Robert E. (1990), 'Macroeconomic Impacts of Worker Remittances on Arab World Labour Exporting Countries', *International Migration*, **28** (1), 25–44.

Lowell, B. Lindsay (2003), 'Skilled Migration Abroad or Human Capital Flight?', *Migration Information Source*, San Diego: Migration Policy Institute, June.

Lowell, B. Lindsay and Allan Findlay (2001), 'Migration of Highly Skilled Persons from Developing Countries: Impact and Policy Responses', International Migration Papers, No. 44, Geneva: International Labour Office.

Lucas, Robert E.B. (1975), 'The Supply of Immigrants Function and Taxation of Immigrants' Incomes: An Econometric Analysis', *Journal of Development Economics*, **2** (3), 289–308.

Lucas, Robert E.B. (1981), 'International Migration: Economic Causes, Consequences and Evaluation', in Mary M. Kritz, Charles B. Keely and Silvano M. Tomasi (eds), *Global Trends in Migration: Theory and Research on International Population Movements*, New York: Center for Migration Studies, pp. 84–109.

Lucas, Robert E.B. (1985), 'Mines and Migrants in South Africa', *American Economic Review*, **75** (5), 1094–1108.

Lucas, Robert E.B. (1987), 'Emigration to South Africas Mines', *American Economic Review*, **77** (3), 313–30.

Lucas, Robert E.B. (1993), 'On the Determinants of Direct Foreign Investment: Evidence from East and Southeast Asia', *World Development*, **21** (3), 391–406.

Lucas, Robert E.B. (1997), 'Internal Migration in Developing Countries', Mark Rosenzweig and Oded Stark (eds), *Handbook of Population and Family Economics*, Amsterdam: North-Holland, pp. 721–98.

Lucas, Robert E.B. (1999), 'International Trade, Capital Flows and Migration: Economic Policies towards Countries of Origin as a Means of Stemming Immigration', in Ann Bernstein and Myron Weiner (eds), *Migration and Refugee Policies: An Overview*, London: Pinter, pp. 119–41.

Lucas, Robert E.B. (2001a), 'Diaspora and Development: Highly Skilled

Migrants from East Asia', paper presented at the Conference on East Asia's Future Economy, Cambridge MA, October 1–2.

Lucas, Robert E.B. (2001b), 'The Effects of Proximity and Transportation on Developing Country Population Migrations', *Journal of Economic Geography*, **1** (3), 323–39.

Lucas, Robert E.B. (2004), 'International Migration to the High Income Countries: Some Consequences for Economic Development in the Sending Countries', *Annual Bank Conference on Development Economics*, forthcoming.

Lucas, Robert E.B. and Samira Salem (2002), 'Pro-Poor Economic Growth: A Review of Recent Literature', report submitted to USAID, Washington DC: Development Alternatives Inc. and Boston Institute for Developing Economies.

Lucas, Robert E.B. and Oded Stark (1985), 'Motivations to Remit: Evidence from Botswana', *Journal of Political Economy*, **93** (5), 901–18.

Lucas, Robert E.B. and Donald Verry (1999), *Restructuring the Malaysian Economy: Development and Human Resources*, London: Macmillan Press.

Lumenga-Neso, Olivier, Marcelo Olarreaga and Maurice Schiff (2001), 'On "Indirect" Trade-Related Research and Development Spillovers', Policy Research Working Paper 2580, Washington DC: World Bank Development Research Group.

Lundborg, Per and Paul S. Segerstrom (2002), 'The Growth and Welfare Effects of International Mass Migration', *Journal of International Economics*, **56** (1), 177–204.

Mahmood, Raisul Awal (1998), 'Bangladesh Clandestine Foreign Workers', in Reginald Appleyard (ed.), *Emigration Dynamics in Developing Countries. Vol. II: South Asia*, Aldershot: Ashgate Publishing, pp. 176–220.

Mahmood, Zafar (1990), 'The Substitutability of Emigrants and Non-Migrants in the Construction Sector of Pakistan', *Pakistan Development Review*, **29** (2), 123–36.

Mahmud, Wahiduddin, (1989), 'The Impact of Overseas Labour Migration on the Bangladesh Economy: A Macro-Economic Perspective', in Rashid Amjad (ed.), *To the Gulf and Back: Studies on the Economic Impact of Asian Labour Migration*, New Delhi: ILO–ARTEP, pp. 55–93.

Majid, Nomaan (2000), 'Pakistan: Employment, Output and Productivity', Issues in Development Discussion Paper No. 33, Geneva: International Labour Office.

Malakha, Irina (2002), 'External Migrations in Russia in 1992–2000: Evaluation of Educational Structure', paper presented at the Conference on Poverty, International Migration and Asylum, Helsinki, September 27–28.

Malmberg, Gunnar (1997), 'Time and Space in International Migration', in Tomas Hammar, Grete Brochmann, Kristof Tamas and Thomas Faist (eds), *International Migration, Immobility and Development: Multidisciplinary*

Perspectives, Oxford: Berg, pp. 21–48.

Mancellari, Ahmet, Harry Papapanagos and Peter Sanfey (1996), 'Job Creation and Temporary Emigration: The Albanian Experience', *Economics of Transition*, **4** (2), 471–90.

Manning, Chris (2002), 'Structural Change, Economic Crisis and International Labour Migration in East Asia', *World Economy*, **25** (3), 359–85.

Martin, Philip L. (2001), 'Trade and Migration: the Mexico–US Case', in Slobodan Djajić (ed.), *International Migration: Trends, Policies and Economic Impact*, London: Routledge, pp. 89–109.

Martin, Philip L. (2002), 'Migration and Development Linkages: Best Practices to Reduce Migration Pressures', paper presented at a Knowledge Network Meeting of the World Commission on the Social Dimension of Globalization, Geneva, December 16–17.

Martin, Philip L. (2004), 'Germany: Managing Migration in the 21st Century', in Wayne A. Cornelius, Philip L. Martin and James F. Hollifield (eds), *Controlling Immigration: A Global Perspective*, Stanford: Stanford University Press.

Martin, Philip L., Richard Chen and Mark Madamba (2000), 'United States Policies for Admission of Professional and Technical Workers: Objectives and Outcomes', International Migration Papers, No. 35, Geneva: International Labour Office.

Martin, Philip L. and Mark Miller (2000), 'Employer Sanctions: French, German and US Experiences', International Migration Papers, No. 36, Geneva: International Labour Office.

Martin, Philip L. and J. Edward Taylor (1996), 'The Anatomy of a Migration Hump', in J. Edward Taylor (ed.), *Development Strategy, Employment and Migration: Insights from Models*, Paris: OECD.

Martin, Philip L. and Michael S. Teitelbaum (2001), 'The Mirage of Mexican Guest Workers', *Foreign Affairs*, **80** (6), 117–31.

Martin, Susan F. (2000), 'Smuggling and Trafficking in Humans: A Human Rights Issue', paper prepared for conference on Best Practices for Migrant Workers, Santiago, June 19–20.

Martin, Susan F. (2002), 'Migration, Development and Socio-economic Integration', paper presented at a Knowledge Network Meeting of the World Commission on the Social Dimension of Globalization, Geneva, December 16–17.

Martin, Susan F., Andrew I. Schoenholtz and David Fisher (2002), 'Impact of Asylum on Receiving Countries', paper presented at the Conference on Poverty, International Migration and Asylum, Helsinki, September 27–28.

Massey, Douglas S. (2003), 'Patterns and Processes of International Migration in the 21st Century', paper presented at the Conference on African Migration and Urbanization in Comparative Perspective, Johannesburg, June 4–7.

Massey, Douglas S., Joaquín Arango, Graeme Hugo, Ali Kouaouci, Adela Pellegrino and J. Edward Taylor (1998), *Worlds in Motion: Understanding International Migration at the End of the Millennium*, Oxford: Clarendon Press.

McCormick, Barry and Jackline Wahba (2000), 'Overseas Employment and Remittances to a Dual Economy', *Economic Journal*, **110** (463), 509–34.

McCormick, Barry and Jackline Wahba (2001), 'Overseas Work Experience, Savings and Entrepreneurship amongst Return Migrants to LDCs', *Scottish Journal of Political Economy*, **48** (2), 164–78.

McCormick, Barry and Jackline Wahba (2003), 'Return International Migration and Geographical Inequality: The Case of Egypt', *Journal of African Economies*, **12** (4), Special Issue December, 500–532.

McCulloch, Rachel and Janet L. Yellen (1975), 'Consequences of a Tax on the Brain Drain for Unemployment and Income Inequality in Less Developed Countries', *Journal of Development Economics*, **2** (3), 249–64.

McCulloch, Rachel and Janet L. Yellen (1977), 'Factor Mobility, Regional Development, and the Distribution of Income', *Journal of Political Economy*, **85** (1), 79–96.

McMahon, Walter M. (1999), *Education and Development: Measuring the Social Benefits*, Oxford: Oxford University Press.

Merkle, Lucie and Klaus F. Zimmermannn (1992), 'Savings, Remittances and Return Migration', *Economics Letters*, **38** (1), 77–81.

Meyer, Jean Baptiste and Mercy Brown (1999), 'Scientific Diasporas, a New Approach to the Brain Drain', World Science Conference, Budapest, June, also available as Management of Social Transformation Discussion Paper No. 41, Paris, UNESCO.

Mghari, Mohamed (2004), 'Exodus of Skilled Labour: Magnitude, Determinants and Impacts on Development', in *Arab Migration in a Globalized World*, Geneva: International Organization for Migration.

Milanovic, Branko, 'Remittances and Income Distribution' (1987), *Journal of Economic Studies*, **14** (5), 24–37.

Mishra, Prachi (2003), 'Effect of Emigration on Wages in Developing Countries: Evidence from Mexico', seminar paper, New York: Department of Economics, Columbia University, April.

Miyagiwa, Kaz (1991), 'Scale Economies in Education and the Brain Drain Problem', *International Economic Review*, **32** (3), 743–59.

Mody, Ashoka, Assaf Razin and Efraim Sadka (2003), 'The Role of Information in Driving FDI Flows: Host-Country Transparency and Source-Country Specialization', draft, IMF and Tel Aviv University, April.

Molho, Ian (1995), 'Migrant Inertia, Accessibility and Local Unemployment', *Economica*, **62** (245), 123–32.

Molle, Willem (1996), 'The Contribution of International Aid to the Long-Term Solution of the European Migration Problem', in Dan Corry (ed.),

Economics and European Union Migration Policy, London: Institute for Public Policy Research, pp. 50–75.

Mountford, Andrew (1997), 'Can a Brain Drain be Good for Growth in the Source Economy?', *Journal of Development Economics*, **53** (2), 287–303.

Munshi, Kaivan (2003), 'Networks in the Modern Economy: Mexican Migrants in the U.S. Labor Market', *Quarterly Journal of Economics*, **118** (2), 549–99.

Nair, P.R. Gopinathan (1989), 'Incidence, Impact and Implications of Migration to the Middle East from Kerala (India)', in Rashid Amjad (ed.), *To the Gulf and Back: Studies on the Economic Impact of Asian Labour Migration*, New Delhi: ILO–ARTEP, pp. 343–64.

Nair, P.R. Gopinathan (1998), 'Dynamics of Emigration from Kerala: Factors, Trends, Patterns and Policies', in Reginald Appleyard (ed.), *Emigration Dynamics in Developing Countries. Vol. II: South Asia*, Aldershot: Ashgate Publishing, pp. 257–91.

Nayyar, Deepak (1994), *Migration, Remittances and Capital Flows: The Indian Experience*, New Delhi: Oxford University Press.

Nayyar, Deepak (1997), 'Emigration Pressures and Structural Change: Case Study of Indonesia', International Migration Papers, No. 20, Geneva: International Labour Office.

Newland, Kathleen (2003), 'Migration as a Factor in Development and Poverty Reduction', *Migration Information Source*, San Diego: Migration Policy Institute, June.

Nyberg-Sørensen, Ninna, Nicholas van Hear and Paul Engberg-Pedersen (2002), 'The Migration–Development Nexus: Evidence and Policy Options', *International Migration*, **40** (2), Special Issue, 3–43.

O'Neil, Kevin (2003a), 'Using Remittance and Circular Migration to Drive Development', *Migration Information Source*, San Diego: Migration Policy Institute, June.

O'Neil, Kevin (2003b), 'Remittances from the United States in Context', *Migration Information Source*, San Diego: Migration Policy Institute, June.

Organization for Economic Cooperation and Development (2001), *The Well-Being of Nations: The Role of Human and Social Capital*, Centre for Educational Research and Innovation, Paris: OECD.

Organization for Economic Cooperation and Development (2002), *Trends in International Migration: Continuous Reporting System on Migration*, Paris: OECD.

Organization for Economic Cooperation and Development (2003), *Trends in International Migration: Continuous Reporting System on Migration*, Paris: OECD.

Overseas Chinese Affairs Commission (2003), 'Top Twenty Countries by the Number of Chinese Population', at http://www.chicago.ocac.net/stat/english/, Statistics Office, Overseas Chinese Affairs Commission.

Papanek, Gustav F. (2003), 'Growth and Poverty in Sri Lanka: From Controls to Markets', Pro-Poor Economic Growth Research Studies, implemented by Development Alternatives, Inc. and Boston Institute for Developing Economies, under US Agency for International Development Contract No. PCE-I-02-00-00015-00.

Park, Won-Woo (2002), 'The Unwilling Hosts: State, Society and the Control of Guest Workers in South Korea', *Asia Pacific Business Review*, **8** (4), 67–94.

Pasha, Hafiz A. and Mir Anjum Altaf (1987), 'Return Migration in a Life-Cycle Setting: An Exploratory Study of Pakistani Migrants in Saudi Arabia', *Pakistan Journal of Applied Economics*, **6** (1), 1–21.

Passas, Nikos (1999), 'Informal Value Transfer Systems and Criminal Organizations: A Study Into So-Called Underground Banking Networks', The Hague: Wetenschappelijk Onderzoek–En Documentatiecentrum.

Peerathep, Roongshivin (1982), 'Some Aspects of Socio-Economic Impacts of Thailand's Emigration to the Middle East', ASEAN/Australia Population Project: Institutional Development and Exchange of Personnel.

Piore, Michael J. (1979), *Birds of Passage: Migrant Labor and Industrial Societies*, Cambridge: Cambridge University Press.

Pischke, Jörn-Steffen and Johannes Velling (1997), 'Employment Effects of Immigration to Germany: An Analysis Based on Local Labor Markets', *Review of Economics and Statistics*, **79** (4), 594–604.

Poirine, Bernard (1997), 'A Theory of Remittances as an Implicit Family Loan Arrangement', *World Development*, **25** (4), 589–611.

Portes, Alejandro, (ed.), (1995), *The Economic Sociology of Immigration: Essays on Networks, Ethnicity, and Entrepreneurship*, New York: Russell Sage Foundation.

Portes, Alejandro, Luis E. Guarnizo and Patricia Landolt (1999), 'The Study of Transnationalism: Pitfalls and Promises of and Emergent Research Field', *Ethnic and Racial Studies*, **22** (2), 217–37.

Portes, Richard and Hélène Rey (1999), 'The Determinants of Cross-Border Equity Flows', National Bureau of Economic Research Working Paper No. 7336, Cambridge MA, September.

Premi, Mahendra K. (1998), 'Impact of Internal Migration in India on the Dynamics of International Migration', in Reginald Appleyard (ed.), *Emigration Dynamics in Developing Countries. Vol. II: South Asia*, Aldershot: Ashgate Publishing, pp. 221–55.

Psacharopoulos, George and Harry Anthony Patrinos (2002), 'Returns to Investment in Education: A Further Update', World Bank Policy Research Working Paper 2881, September.

Puri, Shivani and Tineke Ritzema (1999), 'Migrant Worker Remittances, Micro-Finance and the Informal Economy: Prospects and Issues', Working Paper No. 21, Social Finance Unit, International Labor Organization.

Pyshkina, Tatiana V. (2002), 'Economic Consequences of the Migration of Labour from the Republic of Moldova', paper presented at the Conference on Poverty, International Migration and Asylum, Helsinki, September 27–28.

Quibria, M.G. (1996), 'Migration, Remittances and Trade: With Special Reference to Asian Developing Economies', in P.J. Lloyd and Lynne S. Williams (eds), *International Trade and Migration in the APEC Region*, Oxford: Oxford University Press, pp. 84–98.

Raffelhüschen, Bernd (1992), 'Labor Migration in Europe: Experiences from Germany after Reunification', *European Economic Review*, **36** (7), 1453–71.

Ranis, Gustav (1994), 'International Migration and Foreign Assistance: The Case of the Philippines', in W. Roger Böhning and Maryluz Schloeter-Paredes (eds), *Aid in Place of Migration*, Geneva: International Labour Office, pp. 177–201.

Rapoport, Hillel and Frédéric Docquier (forthcoming), 'The Economics of Migrants' Remittances', in Louis-Andre Gerard-Varet, Serge-Christophe Kolm and Jean Mercier Ythier (eds), *Handbook on the Economics of Giving, Reciprocity and Altruism*, Amsterdam: North-Holland.

Ratha, Dilip (2003), 'Workers' Remittances: An Important and Stable Source of External Development Finance', in *Global Development Finance: Striving for Stability in Development Finance*, Washington DC: World Bank, pp. 157–75.

Rauch, James E. (2001), 'Business and Social Networks in International Trade', *Journal of Economic Literature*, **39** (4), 1177–203.

Rauch, James E. and Vitor Trindade (2002), 'Ethnic Chinese Networks in International Trade', *Review of Economics and Statistics*, **84** (1), 116–30.

Ravallion, Martin (2001), 'Growth, Inequality and Poverty: Looking beyond Averages', *World Development*, **29** (11), 1803–15.

Ravallion, Martin and Lorraine Dearden (1988), 'Social Security in a Moral Economy: An Empirical Analysis for Java', *Review of Economics and Statistics*, **70** (1), 36–44.

Regets, Mark C. (2001), 'Research and Policy Issues in High-Skilled International Migration: A Perspective with Data from the United States', paper presented to the IZA Workshop on The International Mobility of Highly Skilled Workers, IZA Bonn, March 25–26.

Reyes, Belinda I. and Laura Mameesh (2002), 'Why Does Immigrant Trip Duration Vary across U.S. Destinations?' *Social Science Quarterly*, **83** (2), 580–93.

Rodrigo, Chandra and R.A. Jayatissa (1989), 'Maximizing Benefits from Labour Migration: Sri Lanka', in Rashid Amjad (ed.), *To the Gulf and Back: Studies on the Economic Impact of Asian Labour Migration*, New Delhi: ILO–ARTEP, pp. 255–95.

Rodriguez, Edgard R. (1996), 'International Migrants' Remittances in the Philippines', *Canadian Journal of Economics*, **29**, Special Issue, S427–32.

Rodriguez, Edgard R. (1998), 'International Migration and Income Distribution in the Philippines', *Economic Development and Cultural Change*, **46** (2), 329–50.

Rodriguez, Edgard R. and Susan Horton (1995), 'International Return Migration and Remittances in the Philippines', Working Paper No. UT-ECIPA-HORTON-95-01, Economics Department, University of Toronto.

Rozario, Santi and John Gow (2003), 'Bangladesh: Return Migration and Social Transformation', in Robyn Iredale, Fei Guo and Santi Rozario (eds), *Return Migration in the Asia Pacific*, Cheltenham, UK and Northampton, USA: Edward Elgar, pp. 47–87.

Rozelle, Scott, J. Edward Taylor and Alan deBrauw (1999), 'Migration, Remittances, and Agricultural Productivity in China', *American Economic Review*, **89**, 287–91.

Ruffin, Roy J. (1981), 'Trade and Factor Movements with Three Factors and Two Goods', *Economics Letters*, **7** (2), 177–82.

Ruffin, Roy J. (1984), 'International Factor Movements', in Ronald W. Jones and Peter B. Kenen (eds), *Handbook of International Economics Vol. 1*, Amsterdam: North-Holland, pp. 237–88.

Russell, Sharon S. (1986), 'Remittances from International Migration: A Review in Perspective', *World Development*, **14** (6), 677–96.

Russell, Sharon S. (2003), 'Migration and Development: Reframing the International Policy Agenda', *Migration Information Source*, San Diego: Migration Policy Institute, June.

Rybczynski, Tadeus M. (1955), 'Factor Endowment and Relative Commodity Prices', *Economica*, **22** (88), 336–41.

Safir, Nadji (1999), 'Emigration Dynamics in Maghreb', in Reginald Appleyard (ed.), *Emigration Dynamics in Developing Countries. Vol. IV: The Arab Region*, Aldershot: Ashgate Publishing, pp. 89–127.

Saith, Ashwani (1989), 'Macro-Economic Issues in International Labour Migration: A Review', in Rashid Amjad (ed.), *To the Gulf and Back: Studies on the Economic Impact of Asian Labour Migration*, New Delhi: ILO–ARTEP, pp. 28–54.

Saith, Ashwani (1997), 'Emigration Pressures and Structural Change: Case of the Philippines', International Migration Papers, No. 19, Geneva: International Labour Office.

Sala-i-Martin, Xavier (1995), 'Comment on 'European Migration: Push and Pull' by Zimmermann', *Proceedings of the World Bank Annual Conference on Development Economics 1994*, Washington DC: World Bank.

Salt, John (1997), 'International Movements of the Highly Skilled', Directorate for Education, Employment, Labour and Social Affairs, International Migration Unit Occasional Paper No. 3, OCDE/GD(97)169, Paris: OECD.

Salt, John (1999), 'Current Trends in International Migration in Europe', report to the Council of Europe, at http://www.social.coe.int/.

Salt, John (2001), 'Current Trends in International Migration in Europe', report to the Council of Europe, at http://www.social.coe.int/.

Salt, John and Jeremy Stein (1997), 'Migration as a Business: The Case of Trafficking', *International Migration*, **35** (4), 467–94.

Samarasinghe, Vidyamali (1998), 'The Feminization of Foreign Currency Earnings: Women's Labor in Sri Lanka', *Journal of Developing Areas*, **32** (3), 303–25.

Sands, Oonagh (2004), 'Temporary Movement of Labor Fuels GATS Debate', *Migration Information Source*, San Diego: Migration Policy Institute, June.

Sasikumar, S.K. (1995), 'Trends, Patterns and Characteristics of Indian Labour Migration to the Middle East During the Twentieth Century', *Indian Journal of Labor Economics*, **38** (2), 291–308.

Saxenian, Anna-Lee (1999), *Silicon Valley's New Immigrant Entrepreneurs*, San Francisco: Public Policy Institute of California.

Saxenian, Anna-Lee (2000), 'The Bangalore Boom: From Brain Drain to Brain Circulation?' http://dcrp.ced.berkeley.edu/faculty/anno/writings/.

Saxenian, Anna-Lee (2002), *Local and Global Networks of Immigrant Professionals in Silicon Valley*, San Francisco: Public Policy Institute of California.

Scanlan, Shivaun (2002), 'Report on Trafficking from Moldova: Irregular Labour Markets and Restrictive Migration Policies in Western Europe', Geneva: International Labour Office, May.

Schierup, Carl-Urik (1993), 'Prelude to the Inferno: Economic Disintegration and the Political Fragmentation of Yugoslavia', *Migration*, **19** (5), 5–40.

Schiller, G. (1994), 'Reducing Emigration Pressure in Turkey: Analysis and Suggestions for External Aid', in W. Roger Böhning and Maryluz Schloeter-Paredes (eds), *Aid in Place of Migration*, Geneva: International Labour Office, pp. 203–39.

Schrieder, Gertrud and Beatrice Knerr (2000), 'Labour Migration as a Social Security Mechanism for Smallholder Households in Sub-Saharan Africa: The Case of Cameroon', *Oxford Development Studies*, **28** (2), 223–36.

Seccombe, Ian J. (1988), 'International Migration in the Middle East: Historical Trends, Contemporary Patterns and Consequences', *International Migration Today*, **1**, Paris: UNESCO, 180–209.

Shah, Nasra M. (1998a), 'Emigration Dynamics in South Asia: An Overview', in Reginald Appleyard (ed.), *Emigration Dynamics in Developing Countries. Vol. II: South Asia*, Aldershot: Ashgate Publishing, pp. 17–29.

Shah, Nasra M. (1998b), 'The Role of Social Networks among South Asian Male Migrants in Kuwait', in Reginald Appleyard (ed.), *Emigration Dynamics in Developing Countries. Vol. II: South Asia*, Aldershot: Ashgate Publishing, pp. 30–70.

Shain, Yossi (1993), 'Democrats and Secessionists: US Diasporas as Regime Destabilizers', in Myron Weiner (ed.), *International Migration and Security*, Boulder: Westview Press, 287–322.

Sheffer, Gabriel (2003), *Diaspora Politics at Home and Abroad*, Cambridge: Cambridge University Press.

Siddiqui, Tasneem (2003), 'Migration as a Livelihood Strategy of the Poor: The Bangladesh Case', paper presented at the Regional Conference on Migration, Development and Pro-Poor Choices in Asia, Dhaka, June 22–24.

Simon, Julian L. (1995), 'Comment on 'European Migration: Push and Pull' by Zimmermann', *Proceedings of the World Bank Annual Conference on Development Economics 1994*, Washington DC: World Bank.

Sjaastad, Larry A. (1962), 'The Costs and Returns of Human Migration', *Journal of Political Economy*, **70** (5), Supplement, 80–93.

Skeldon, Ronald (2003), 'Migration and Poverty', paper presented at the Conference on African Migration and Urbanization in Comparative Perspective, Johannesburg, June 4–7.

Sleptova, Evghenia (2003), 'Labour Migration in Europe: Special Focus on the Republic of Moldova', Institute for Public Policy, Moldova Republic.

Soeprobo, Tara Bakti (2004), 'Indonesia Country Report', paper presented at the Workshop on International Migration and Labour Market in Asia, Japan Institute for Labour Policy and Training, Tokyo, February 5–6.

Soudi, Khalid and Abelkader Teto (2004), 'A Comparative Analysis of Different Sources of Remittances', in *Arab Migration in a Globalized World*, Geneva: International Organization for Migration.

Stahl, Charles and Fred Arnold (1986), 'Overseas Workers' Remittances in Asian Development', *International Migration Review*, **20** (4), 899–925.

Stahl, Charles and Ansanul Habib (1989), 'The Impact of Overseas' Workers' Remittances on Indigenous Industries: Evidence from Bangladesh', *Developing Economies*, **27** (3), 269–85.

Stahl, Charles and Ansanul Habib (1991), 'Emigration and Development in South and Southeast Asia', in Demetrios G. Papademetriou and Philip L. Martin (eds), *The Unsettled Relationship: Labor Migration and Economic Development*, New York: Greenwood Press, pp. 163–79.

Stalker, Peter (2002), 'Migration Trends and Migration Policy in Europe', *International Migration*, **40** (2) Special Issue, 151–79.

Stark, Oded and David Levhari (1982), 'On Migration and Risk in LDCs', *Economic Development and Cultural Change*, **31** (1), 191–6.

Stark, Oded and J. Edward Taylor (1991), 'Migration Incentives, Migration Types: The Role of Relative Deprivation', *The Economic Journal*, **101** (408), 1163–78.

Stark, Oded, J. Edward Taylor and Shlomo Yitzhaki (1986), 'Remittances and Inequality', *Economic Journal*, **96** (383), 722–40.

Stern, Aaron (1998), 'Thailand's Migration Situation and its Relations with APEC Members and Other Countries in Southeast Asia', Bangkok: Asian Research Center for Migration, Chulalongkorn University.

Stilwell, Barbara, Khassoum Diallo, Pascal Zurn, Mario R. Dal Poz, Orvill Adams and James Buchan (2003), 'Developing Evidence-Based Ethical Policies on the Migration of Health Workers: Conceptual and Practical Challenges', *Human Resources for Health*, vol. 1, published online, 28 October 2003, accessed at http://www.pubmedcentral.nih.gov/.

Storesletten, Kjetil (2000), 'Sustaining Fiscal Policy through Immigration', *Journal of Political Economy*, **108** (2), 300–323.

Straubhaar, Thomas (1986a), 'The Causes of International Labor Migrations: A Demand Determined Approach', *International Migration Review*, **20** (4), 835–56.

Straubhaar, Thomas (1986b), 'The Determinants of Workers' Remittances: The Case of Turkey', *Weltwirtschaftliches Archiv*, **122** (4), 728–40.

Straubhaar, Thomas and Martin R. Wolburg (1999), 'Brain Drain and Brain Gain in Europe: An Evaluation of the East-European Migration to Germany', *Jahrbücher für Nationalökonomie und Statistik*, **218** (5–6), 574–604.

Suro, Roberto, Sergio Bendixen, B. Lindsay Lowell and Dulce C. Benavides (2002), 'Billions in Motion: Latino Immigrants, Remittances and Banking', a report produced in cooperation between the Pew Hispanic Center and the Multilateral Investment Fund, Washington DC.

Swamy, Gurushri (1981), 'International Migrant Workers' Remittances: Issues and Prospects', World Bank Staff Working Paper No. 481, Washington DC: World Bank.

Tan, Edita A. (1993), 'Labor Emigration and the Accumulation and Transfer of Human Capital', *Asian and Pacific Migration Journal*, **2** (3), 303–28.

Tan, Edita A. and Dante B. Canlas (1989), 'Migrants' Saving Remittance and Labour Supply Behaviour: The Philippines Case', in Rashid Amjad (ed.), *To the Gulf and Back: Studies on the Economic Impact of Asian Labour Migration*, New Delhi: ILO–ARTEP, pp. 223–54.

Taylor, J. Edward (1987), 'Undocumented Mexico–US Migration and the Returns to Households in Rural Mexico', *American Journal of Agricultural Economics*, **69** (3), 626–38.

Taylor, J. Edward (1992), 'Remittances and Inequality Reconsidered: Direct, Indirect, and Intertemporal Effects', *Journal of Policy Modeling*, **14** (2), 187–208.

Taylor, J. Edward (1999), 'The New Economics of Labor Migration and the Role of Remittances', *International Migration*, **37** (1), 63–86.

Taylor, J. Edward (2000), 'Do Government Programs Crowd-in Remittances?' at www.thedialogue.org/publications.

Taylor, J. Edward and T.J. Wyatt (1996), 'The Shadow Value of Migrant

Remittances, Income and Inequality in a Household-farm Economy', *Journal of Development Studies*, **32**, 899–912.

Tingsabadh, Charit (1989), 'Maximizing Development Benefits from Labour Migration: Thailand', in Rashid Amjad (ed.), *To the Gulf and Back: Studies on the Economic Impact of Asian Labour Migration*, New Delhi: ILO–ARTEP, pp. 303–42.

Trefler, Daniel (1995), 'The Case of the Missing Trade and Other Mysteries', *American Economic Review*, **85** (5), 1029–46.

Tsay, Ching-lung (2003), 'Taiwan: Significance, Characteristics and Policies on Skilled Migration', in Robyn Iredale, Fei Guo and Santi Rozario (eds), *Return Migration in the Asia Pacific*, Cheltenham, UK and Northampton, USA: Edward Elgar, pp. 112–35.

Ulack, Richard (1986), 'Ties to Origin, Remittances, and Mobility: Evidence from Rural and Urban Areas in the Philippines', *Journal of Developing Areas*, **20** (3), 339–56.

United Kingdom Government (2002), 'Secure Borders, Safe Haven: Integration with Diversity in Modern Britain', White Paper Presented to Parliament by the Secretary of State for the Home Department, London: Stationery Office, February.

United Kingdom Government (2004), 'Migration and Development: How to Make Migration Work for Poverty Reduction', Volume 1, House of Commons International Development Committee, London: Stationery Office, July.

United Nations (2002a), *International Migration Report 2002*, New York: Department of Economic and Social Affairs, Population Division, UN, ST/ESA/SER.A/220.

United Nations (2002b), *International Migration from Countries with Economies in Transition: 1980–1999*, New York: Department of Economic and Social Affairs, Population Division, UN, ESA/P/WP.176.

United Nations (2002c), *World Population Prospects: The 2000 Revision. Volume III: Analytical Report*, New York: Department of Economic and Social Affairs, Population Division, UN.

United Nations (2003), *Levels and Trends of International Migration to Selected Countries in Asia*, New York: Department of Economic and Social Affairs, Population Division, UN, ST/ESA/SER.A/218.

United Nations (2004), 'Report of the Consultative Meeting on Migration and Mobility and How This Movement Affects Women', New York: Department of Economic and Social Affairs, Division for the Advancement of Women, UN, CM/MMW/2003/REPORT.

United Nations Development Program (2002), *Human Development Report*, New York: Oxford University Press.

United Nations Educational, Scientific and Cultural Organization (1992), *Statistical Yearbook*, Paris: UNESCO

United Nations Educational, Scientific and Cultural Organization (1998), *Statistical Yearbook*, Paris: UNESCO

United Nations Educational, Scientific and Cultural Organization (1999), *Statistical Yearbook*, Paris: UNESCO

United Nations High Commissioner for Refugees (2001), *Statistical Yearbook 2001*, Geneva: UNHCR.

United Nations High Commissioner for Refugees (2002), 'Refugees by Numbers', at www.unhcr.ch.

United States Census Bureau (2001), *Profile of the Foreign-Born Population in the United States: 2000*, Washington DC: US Department of Commerce, December.

United States Census Bureau (2002a), *Coming to America: A Profile of the Nation's Foreign Born (2000 Update)*, Washington DC: US Department of Commerce, February.

United States Census Bureau (2002b), *A Profile of the Nation's Foreign-Born Population from Asia (2000 Update)*, Washington DC: US Department of Commerce, February.

United States Immigration and Naturalization Service (2002), *Estimates of the Unauthorized Immigrant Population Residing in the United States: 1990 to 2000*, Washington DC: Office of Policy and Planning.

United States National Science Foundation (2001), 'Human Resource Contributions to US Science and Engineering from China', Issue Brief, Washington DC: NSF Division of Science Resources Studies, January 12.

Van Hear, Nicholas (1998), *New Diasporas: The Mass Exodus, Dispersal and Regrouping of Migrant Communities*, Seattle: University of Washington Press.

Van Hear, Nicholas (2003), 'Refugee Diasporas, Remittances, Development, and Conflict', *Migration Information Source*, San Diego: Migration Policy Institute, June.

Van Selm, Joanne (2002), 'The High Level Working Group: Can Foreign Policy, Development Policy and Asylum and Immigration Policy Really be Mixed?', paper presented at the Conference on Poverty, International Migration and Asylum, Helsinki, September 27–28.

Van Wijnbergen, Sweder J.G. (1986), 'Macroeconomic Aspects of the Effectiveness of Foreign Aid: On the Two-Gap Model, Home Goods Disequilibrium and Real Exchange Rate Misalignment', *Journal of International Economics*, **21** (1–2), 123–36.

Venables, Anthony J. (1999), 'Trade Liberalization and Factor Mobility: An Overview', in Riccardo Faini, Jaime de Melo and Klaus F. Zimmermann (eds), *Migration: The Controversies and the Evidence*, Cambridge: Cambridge University Press.

Vernon, Raymond (1966), 'International Investment and International Trade in the Product Cycle', *Quarterly Journal of Economics*, **80** (2), 190–207.

Vertovec, Steven (2002), 'Transnational Networks and Skilled Labour Migration', Oxford, ESRC Transnational Communities Programme Working Paper WPTC-20-02.

Villegas, Bernardo M. 'Implications of AFTA on Philippine Labor Export' (1993), *Asian and Pacific Migration Journal*, **2** (3), 285–301.

Vogler, Michael and Ralph Rotte (2000), 'The Effects of Development on Migration: Theoretical Issue and New Empirical Evidence', *Journal of Population Economics*, **13** (3), 485–508.

Wadensjö, Eskil (2000), 'Immigration, the Labour Market, and Public Finances in Denmark', *Swedish Economic Policy Review*, **7** (2), 59–83.

Wahba, Jackline (1996), 'Remittances in the Middle East: A Review', paper presented at the Conference on Labor Markets and Human Resource Development, Kuwait, September 16–18.

Wahba, Sadek (1991), 'What Determines Workers' Remittances?', *Finance and Development*, **28** (4), 41–4.

Walmsley, Terri Louise and L. Alan Winters (2003), 'Relaxing the Restrictions on the Temporary Movements of Natural Persons: A Simulation Analysis', Discussion Paper No. 3719, London: Centre for Economic Policy Research.

Weidenbaum, Murray and Samuel Hughes (1996), *The Bamboo Network: How Expatriate Chinese Entrepreneurs are Creating a New Economic Superpower in Asia*, New York: Martin Kessler Books.

Weiner, Myron (ed.) (1993), *International Migration and Security*, Boulder: Westview Press.

Werner, Heinz (2000), 'From Guests to Permanent Stayers? The German Guest Worker Program', Nürnberg: Institute for Employment Research of the Federal Employment Services.

Wickramasekera, Piyasiri (2002), 'Asian Labour Migration: Issues and Challenges in an Era of Globalization', International Migration Papers, No. 57, Geneva: International Labour Office.

Widgren, Jonas and Philip Martin (2002), 'Managing Migration: The Role of Economic Instruments', *International Migration*, **40** (2), Special Issue, 213–29.

Williamson, John (1990), 'What Washington Means by Policy Reform', in John Williamson (ed.), *Latin American Adjustment: How Much Has Happened?*, Washington DC: Institute for International Economics, pp. 5–20.

Woodruff, Christopher and Rene Zenteno (2001), 'Remittances and Microenterprises in Mexico', at www2–irps.ucsd.edu/faculty/cwoodruff.

World Bank (2000a), *Higher Education in Developing Countries: Peril and Promise*, Report of the Task Force on Higher Education and Society, Washington DC, World Bank.

World Bank (2000b), *Albania Interim Poverty Reduction Strategy Paper*, Washington DC: World Bank.

World Bank (2002), *World Development Report*, New York: Oxford University Press.

World Bank (2003a), 'A Proposed Framework to Analyze Informal Funds Transfer Systems: Section II', draft presented at the International Conference on Migrant Remittances: Development Impact, Opportunities for the Financial Sector and Future Prospects, London, October 9–10.

World Bank (2003b), 'Morocco: Economic Monitoring – Fall Update', Rabat: World Bank, September.

World Bank (2003c), *Global Development Finance: Striving for Stability in Develpment Finance*, Washington DC: World Bank, p. 200.

Yang, Dean (2004), 'International Migration, Human Capital, and Entrepreneurship: Evidence from Philippine Migrants' Exchange Rate Shocks', *Gerald R. Ford School of Public Policy Working Paper Series 02-011*, University of Michigan, Ann Arbor.

Yoo, Kil-Sang and Soo-Bong Uh (2002), 'South Korea', in *Migration and the Labour Market in Asia: Recent Trends and Policies*, Paris: Organization for Economic Development and Cooperation.

Yoon, Bang-Soon L. (1992), 'Reverse Brain Drain in South Korea: State-led Model', *Studies in Comparative International Development*, **27** (1), 4–26.

Young, Alwyn (1995), 'The Tyranny of Numbers: Confronting the Statistical Realities of the East Asia Growth Experience', *Quarterly Journal of Economics*, **110** (3), 641–80.

Zachariah, K.C., E.T. Matthews and S. Irudaya Rajan (1999), 'Impact of Migration on Kerala's Economy and Society', Working Paper No. 297, Trivandrum: Centre for Development Studies.

Zachariah, K.C., P.R. Gopinathan Nair and S. Irudaya Rajan (2001), 'Return Emigrants in Kerala: Rehabilitation Problems and Development Potential', Working Paper No. 319, Trivandrum: Centre for Development Studies.

Zachariah, K.C., B.A. Prakash and S. Irudaya Rajan (2002), 'Gulf Migration Study: Employment, Wages and Working Conditions of Kerala Emigrants in the United Arab Emirates', Working Paper No. 326, Trivandrum: Centre for Development Studies.

Zarate, German A. (2002), 'The Hidden Benefits of Remittances to Mexico', draft, State University of New York at Cortland, February.

Ziderman, Adrian and Douglas Albrecht (1995), *Financing Universities in Developing Countries*, Washington DC: Falmer Press.

Zimmermann, Klaus F. (1995), 'European Migration: Push and Pull', *Proceedings of the World Bank Annual Conference on Development Economics 1994*, Washington DC: World Bank.

Zlotnik, Hania (2003), 'The Global Dimensions of Female Migration', *Migration Information Source*, San Diego: Migration Policy Institute, March.

Zolberg, Aristide (1989), 'The Next Waves: Migration Theory for a Changing

World', *International Migration Review*, **23** (3), 403–30.

Zweig, David (1997), 'To Return or Not to Return? Politics vs. Economics in China's Brain Drain', *Studies in Comparative International Development*, **32** (1), 92–125.

Index